Pluto Press Workers'

Jack Eaton and Colin Gill

The Trade Union Directory

A Guide to all TUC Unions

Second Edition

Pluto Press

First published in 1981 by Pluto Press Limited
The Works, 105a Torriano Avenue, London NW5 2RX
Second edition published in 1983

Copyright © 1981, 1983 Jack Eaton and Colin Gill

British Library Cataloguing in Publication Data
Eaton, Jack
    The trade union directory.—2nd ed.
    1. Trade-unions—Great Britain—Directories
    I. Title   II. Gill Colin
    331.88'025'41   HD6663

ISBN 0–86104–395–2

Cover designed by Colin Bailey

Computerset by Promenade Graphics Limited
23A Lansdown Industrial Estate, Cheltenham
Printed in Great Britain by Photobooks (Bristol) Limited
Barton Manor, St Philips, Bristol
Bound by W. H. Ware & Son Limited
Tweed Road, Clevedon, Avon

Contents

Trade Union Abbreviations

ABS Broadcasting Staffs, Association of
ACTT Cinematograph, Television and Allied Technicians, Association of
AMU Metalworkers' Union, Associated
APEX Professional, Executive, Clerical and Computer Staff, Association of
ASBSBSW Boilermakers, Shipwrights, Blacksmiths and Structural Workers, Amalgamated Society of
ASLEF Locomotive Engineers and Firemen, Associated Society of
ASTMS Scientific, Technical and Managerial Staffs, Association of
AUEW Engineering Workers, Amalgamated Union of
AUEW/TASS AUEW, Technical Administrative and Supervisory Section
AUT University Teachers, Association of

BACM Colliery Management, British Association of
BALPA British Airline Pilots' Association
BIFU Banking, Insurance and Finance Union
BRTTS British Roll Turners' Trade Society

CATU Ceramic and Allied Trades Union
CMA Communication Managers' Association
COHSE Health Service Employees, Confederation of
COPOU Council of Post Office Unions
CPSA Civil and Public Services' Association
CSEU Confederation of Shipbuilding and Engineering Unions
CSMTS Card Setting Machine Tenters' Society
CSU Civil Service Union

EETPU Electrical, Electronic, Telecommunication and Plumbing Union
EIS Educational Institute of Scotland
EMA Engineers' and Managers' Association

FBU Fire Brigades' Union
FTAT Furniture, Timber and Allied Trades Union

GFTU General Federation of Trade Unions
GLCSA Greater London Council Staff Association
GMBATU General Municipal, Boilermakers' and Allied Trades' Union
GMWU General and Municipal Workers' Union
GUALO General Union of Associations of Loom Overlookers

HVA Health Visitors' Association

ICFTU International Confederation of Free Trade Unions
IPCS Institution of Professional Civil Servants
IRSF Inland Revenue Staff Federation
ISTC Iron and Steel Trades Confederation

MNAOA Merchant Navy and Air Line Officers' Association
MU Musicians' Union

NACO Co-operative Officials, National Association of
NACODS Colliery Overmen, Deputies and Shotfirers, National Association of

NALGO National and Local Government Officers' Association
NALHM Licensed House Managers, National Association of
NATSOPA Printers, Graphical and Media Personnel, National Society of Operative
NAS/UWT Schoolmasters and Union of Women Teachers, National Association of
NATFHE Teachers in Further and Higher Education, National Association of
NATTKE Theatrical, Television and Kine Employees, National Association of
NGA (1982) Graphical Association, National (1982)
NSBGW National Society of Brushmakers and General Workers
NSMM Metal Mechanics, National Society of
NUAAW Agricultural and Allied Workers, National Union of
NUB Blastfurnacemen, Ore Miners, Coke Workers and Kindred Trades, National Union of
NUDBTW Dyers, Bleachers and Textile Workers, National Union of
NUFLAT Footwear, Leather and Allied Trades, National Union of
NUGSAT Gold, Silver and Allied Trades, National Union of
NUHKW Hosiery and Knitwear Workers, National Union of
NUIW Insurance Workers, National Union of
NUJ Journalists, National Union of
NULMW National Union of Lock and Metal Workers
NUM Mineworkers, National Union of
NUPE Public Employees, National Union of
NUR Railwaymen, National Union of
NUS Seamen, National Union of
NUSMCHDE Sheet Metal Workers, Coppersmiths, Heating and Domestic Engineers, National Union of
NUT Teachers, National Union of
NUTGW Tailors and Garment Workers, National Union of

POEU Post Office Engineering Union

REOU Radio and Electronic Officers' Union

SCPS Civil and Public Servants, Society of
SLADE Lithographic Artists, Designers, Engravers and Process Workers, Society of
SOGAT 82 Graphical and Allied Trades, Society of
SPOE Post Office Executive, Society of
SSPS Sheffield Sawmakers' Protection Society
SUPLO Power Loom Overlookers, Scottish Union of

TASS See AUEW/TASS
TGWU Transport and General Workers' Union
TSSA Transport Salaried Staffs' Association
TURU Trade Union Research Unit

UCATT Construction, Allied Trades and Technicians, Union of
UCW Communication Workers, Union of
URTU Transport Union, United Road
USDAW Shop, Distributive and Allied Workers, Union of

YAPLO Yorkshire Association of Power Loom Overlookers

A Note on Non-sexist Language

A few terms in this book will seem unfamiliar to some readers. In support of union efforts to equalise the standing of their women members with that of the men, we have de-gendered words where possible. In the same spirit, we have not used Mr, Ms, Miss or Mrs before people's names.

We have preferred firefighter to fireman, chairperson to chairman or chairwoman, drafter to draughtsman, coalminer to coalman, supervisor to foreman or forewoman, synthetic to man-made, staffing to manpower, J. D. Smith to Mr or Ms Smith etc.

We feel that it is important that the people who put out fires, chair committees, draw plans, dig coal should be known by what they do rather than by a gender category.

Preface to the Second Edition

The compilation of the *Trade Union Directory* originally took us over three years to complete. We sought to produce a 'number guide' to all TUC-affiliated unions so that trade-union members, shop stewards, branch officers and office representation might have a primer providing at least basic information about other unions apart from their own.

We were very gratified by the response to the first edition, published in November 1981, and the helpful criticism we received from many sources. We decided that a revised and updated edition should be prepared as soon as possible.

This edition contains information on all TUC-affiliated unions up to the time of the 1982 Trades Union Congress. We have continually revised each entry to maintain its accuracy and ensure its contemporary relevance, but it is inevitable that a little of the material will be out of date by the time we go to press, despite the valiant efforts of the publishers to bring out the book quickly.

In a few instances we have made a small reference to significant trade-union developments which took place between the completion date and galley-proof stage. Thus we have mentioned the resignation of Sidney Weighell as general secretary of the National Union of Railwaymen and the impending merger between the Boilermakers and the General and Municipal Workers' Union, announced in November 1982 after a ballot of the members of each union. This was too late for us to present a worthwhile composite impression of the new union, the General Municipal, Boilermakers' and Allied Trades' Union (GMBATU).

Since the first edition of the *Trade Union Directory* appeared, several unions have disappeared as independent bodies. For instance, the National Union of Agricultural and Allied Workers and the National Union of Bleachers, Dyers and Textile Workers have been absorbed into different trade groups of the Transport and General Workers' Union; the National Union of Gold, Silver and Allied Trades is now part of AUEW/TASS; in the printing industry NATSOPA has joined with SOGAT and SLADE with the NGA; the two tiny Felt Hatters' Unions have joined with the National Union of Tailors and Garment Workers. The TGWU amalgamations led to the formation of new trade groups in that union and these trade groups, independent unions until early Summer 1982, were allocated to TUC trade groups eleven (Textiles) and fourteen (Agriculture) for the congress in September.

We have, for the present, maintained the presentation of unions by trade group in the book; it will probably be desirable to alter this in future editions; when the TUC has worked out details for implementing the decision for automatic representation on the General Council of unions with over 100,000 members.

The day of the medium-sized union has certainly not passed and one nagging worry about making a particular membership figure critical is that this in itself could encourage an artificial expansion (or contraction) of some unions to just this size. The whole reform, while confirmed by vote at the 1982 congress, is still in a state of flux; it is under attack by the Transport and General Workers' Union which stands to lose influence, and will inevitably be messy to implement satisfactorily.

Whilst generally keeping to the original format for each entry in the second edition of the book, we have tried to strengthen the material in certain respects. In particular, the issues of internal democracy and the mechanism for existing union influence in Labour Party affairs have been extended, reflecting the public and media interest in the wake of the 1981 Deputy Leadership election within the Labour Party.

This revised edition was written during the summer and autumn of 1982, following publication of the first edition in November 1981.

We are, once again, particularly grateful to the many officers and administrative staff of the trade unions we consulted for all their helpful assistance and support. In some cases we were only able to obtain the information needed from reliable contacts with particular unions rather than from official sources. The book would have lacked a great deal of important material were it not for their help.

In particular, we should like to thank Richard Kuper and Fay Rudd for all the hard work they put in on our behalf, particularly in providing the necessary administrative support when it was most needed; Wendy Davies for taking on the burden of typing up the new materials; and Fanny Campbell for organising the transformation of our manuscript into book form in so short a time.

Finally, we would like to express sincere thanks to both our families. They showed understanding and forbearance in circumstances which other families would have found intolerable.

Jack Eaton
Colin Gill
November 1982

Trades Union Congress

Congress House
Great Russell Street
London WC1B 3LS
01–636 4030

Origins

The TUC came into being in 1868, when the Manchester and Salford Trades Council convened the first of a series of annual meetings of trade unionists at the Mechanics' Institute, David Street, Manchester.[1] The meeting was held for four days from 2 to 6 June 1868, and was attended by 34 delegates representing, it was claimed, 118,367 members. There had been earlier attempts to form a national forum for trade unionists, notably the Grand National Consolidated Trade Union of the 1830s and the Association of United Trades for the Protection of Labour of 1845. The early TUC leaders were by no means committed to a revolutionary philosophy. They were cautious, craft-oriented, and concerned to secure acceptance of trade unionism within a liberal capitalist society whose fundamental values they did not challenge. Indeed, prominent trade union leaders identified themselves with the Liberals, and there were even secret deals with Liberal Party politicians and employers. As Vic Allen noted: 'They accepted their conventions and, with undying gratitude, their patronage, and they sought and accepted responsible, respectable advice. The willingness to accept advice was a willingness to conform.'[2] The early years of the TUC were characterised by the perceived need to secure favourable legislation on trade union affairs.

The growth of 'new unionism' amongst unskilled workers in the 1880s and 1890s led to a wave of new affiliations to the TUC, and these newly affiliated unions brought with them more aggressive socialist-based policies which were shared by many younger craft unionists. Despite the resistance of the older generation of TUC leaders, changes were forced upon them. In 1899 the General Federation of Trade Unions was established by Congress in order to provide a much more co-ordinated approach to industrial action, and in its early days it assumed a greater importance than the TUC itself. However, only a minority of unions joined it, and in time it deteriorated into no more than a defensive mutual insurance for unions — particularly the smaller ones. The GFTU still exists today, and its principal function is to provide research and educational facilities for its affiliates and make representations to government departments on matters of importance to its collection of smaller trade unions (see **General Federation of Trade Unions** under **Trade Union Federations**).

In 1900 the Labour Representation Committee was also set up, which converted itself into the Labour Party in 1906. The creation of this separate political wing of the trade union movement meant that the TUC itself was not involved in direct parliamentary lobbying. The activities of the TUC and the Labour Party were co-ordinated by a joint board, consisting of representatives of the parliamentary committee (set up in 1871 to effect the political lobbying of the TUC), the GFTU and the Labour Representation Committee.

In 1920 the TUC underwent a major structural reform following the experiences of the railway strike the previous year. The parliamentary committee was replaced by a General Council elected from affiliated unions which were divided into 17 trade groups, with an additional group for women's representation. The General Council was seen as a co-ordinating centre for the whole trade union movement, providing a more dynamic means of pursuing trade union objectives generally. It consisted of 32 members, with nominations for election to represent each trade group on the General Council confined to unions within each group, but voting for seats to be taken by the whole affiliated membership. The powers of the General Council were further extended in 1924 and 1928, since when there have been few constitutional changes in Congress organisation. These powers are defined mainly in Rules 11, 12 and 13.

Relations with Affiliated Unions

Rule 11 pledges affiliated unions to keep the General Council informed of any major disputes in which they may become engaged, either with employers or amongst themselves. If a peaceful settlement appears likely the General Council cannot intervene, unless requested to do so, but in the event of a major breakdown in negotiations it may give advice to the unions involved. If the advice is accepted and a strike or lock-out results then the General Council 'shall forthwith take steps to organise on behalf of the organisation or organisations concerned all such moral and material support as the circumstances of the dispute may appear to justify.'[3] Thus the TUC has the powers of coordination but it does not threaten the autonomy of its affiliated unions. The contradictory nature of Rule 11 was exposed during the 1926 General Strike, the first and only occasion when the powers of the TUC to lead industrial action on behalf of the whole trade union movement were tested. While the General Council was able to conduct the General Strike, it had no power to effect an agreement to end the miners' dispute, which was the reason for sympathetic action. In 1971 the TUC came close to sanctioning strike action against the Industrial Relations Bill, and came within a few days of a general stoppage over the case of the imprisoned dock workers in 1972. It is difficult to imagine circumstances that would place the TUC in a position to call a general strike short of, perhaps, a fascist take-over of power in Britain.

Rule 12 gives the General Council its main powers to deal with inter-union disputes by insisting on the submission of all such conflicts to the TUC disputes committee, holding in reserve the threat of suspension or disaffiliation to secure respect for its recommendations. Rule 12 was adopted in 1924 together with a number of 'main principles' governing 'trade union practice' in order to avoid inter-union competition for members; these were extended and improved at the 1939 Bridlington Congress. The 'Bridlington Principles' urge affiliated unions to agree on spheres of influence, recognition of cards, conditions of transfer etc.; to find out whether applicants for membership are, or have been, members of another union, and not to accept them if they are in arrears, 'under discipline' or involved in a dispute; and to refrain from recruiting among a grade of workers in an establishment where another union already organises or has negotiating rights for a majority of them. The disputes committee initially acts in a conciliatory capacity, but if it is unable to effect an agreement it will make an award. Over the years it has built up a body of 'case law' which tends to strongly favour the status quo. Significantly, the disputes committee will not arbitrate in cases where the unions represented on the trade union side of a joint negotiating body are unwilling to accept a further union's claim for representation.

Rule 13 empowers the General Council to investigate the conduct of any affiliated organisation if it is considered 'that the activities of such organisation may be detrimental to the interests of the trade union movement or contrary to the declared principles or declared policy of the Congress,'[4] and, if necessary, to suspend its membership until the matter has been fully considered at the next Congress. The final sanction of expulsion is reserved for Congress itself. This power was used to expel the Electrical Trades Union in 1961 after the serious malpractices of the union's communist leadership had been exposed and condemned by the courts, and also in 1972 against a number of unions who failed to deregister in accordance with Congress policy towards the Industrial Relations Act.

The power is rarely used and the dilemma of the TUC is easily appreciated. The main strength of the TUC lies in its representative character and the loss of one or more of the major unions could seriously jeopardise this. The loss of this representative character is one of the most persuasive arguments used by those unions opposed to the principle of automatic representation (given sufficient membership) to the General Council of the TUC.

Relations with Government

The authority of the TUC has never depended on its limited formal powers. Its moral authority derives from its representative character, strengthened over the years by the cautious development of an agreed basis for common action. Although the powers of the General Council have undoubtedly increased as time has gone by, they have done so not because any affiliated union has been prepared to yield up any part of its autonomy, but because successive governments have themselves increased their participation in economic affairs and thus have shifted the emphasis from industrial to political action by involving the TUC in economic decision-making. The TUC provides a useful central body through which any proposed legislation or administrative action can be undertaken by the government of the day, although since the election of Margaret Thatcher's government in 1979 the TUC is much less involved in consultation.

The TUC's involvement with government really developed during the second world war (shortly after the start of the war, the Prime Minister directed all government departments to consult with the TUC before taking any action on matters likely to affect workers' interests) and was reinforced by the appointment of Ernest Bevin as Minister of Labour and National Service in 1940. In subsequent years the complex structure of councils, boards and committees which was created to advise the government on industrial policy was mainly of a tripartite character, with the TUC treated as an equal partner with the central employers' organisations.

The most important body on which the TUC is represented in the National Economic Development Council, which ostensibly deals with long-term planning objectives but in reality is a mere sounding board for government policies. The TUC has accused the Treasury of rigging its forecasting model to accord with market ideology and assumptions about 'confidential effects' and to obscure the effectiveness of alternative economic strategies. The NEDC has in membership government ministers, representatives of the CBI, heads of nationalised industries and six senior members of the TUC General Council. It is chaired by either the Chancellor of the Exchequer or the Prime Minister and is backed by a servicing group of civil servants. In 1976, the NEDC machinery was developed further by the setting up of 37 sector working parties to cover various branches of the economy. Whilst these SWPs were originally seen as a means of implementing the Labour government's so-called 'industrial strategy', in practice they lack any authority to control the activities of major multinational corporations within their ambit, and at company level there was a total failure to implement the practice of planning agreements as envisaged by the 1975 Industry Act.

Having long since lost faith in sector working parties, the trade unions have, during the period of the Thatcher government, begun to doubt the value of continued participation in the NEDC. By 1982 this amounted to very much less than consultation. Opinions were divided among the general secretaries of major unions who form the TUC economic committee. Moss Evans, TGWU General Secretary, noting the abrasive and hostile tone of Norman Tebbit, the Secretary of State for Employment, believed that this indicated the futility of continued participation in the NEDC (see also **AUEW/TASS**). However, David Basnett of the GMWU argued that the hostility of Mr Tebbit was a reason to hold onto the NEDC. The 1982 Congress voted against withdrawal from the NEDC.

Relations with government have certainly soured, and this is another facet of disturbance of the cosy consensus that dominated economic policy until 1979, unpalatable to many and untoward for those on the left who conveniently caricatured the TUC as inexorably involved in the corporatism of modern Britain. However, the TUC continues to nominate one third or more of the representatives on any quasi-governmental agencies (quangos) such as ACAS, the Manpower Services Commission, the Health and Safety Commission, the Equal Opportunities Commission and the Commission for Racial Equality.

In addition to this, the TUC also nominates representatives to various judicial bodies which have developed for industrial relations purposes. It nominates representatives for the Employment Appeal Tribunal and fills places on the Central Arbitration Committee, and there are 700 TUC nominees on industrial tribunals throughout the country. TUC representatives appear on royal commissions and the TUC also submits evidence to a number of committees of inquiry on diverse subjects — broadcasting, the National Health Service, metrication, the legal profession, education and the press, for example.

Congress

It is important to recognise that the TUC is primarily a policy-making rather than an executive body, and that it is a federal body which enables affiliated unions to develop common policies, to regulate inter-union relations, and to benefit from a number of advisory and other services the TUC provides. Its affiliated unions negotiate terms and conditions of work for around 70 per cent of the total working population: less than half a million trade unionists remain outside the TUC. In 1982 there were 108 unions affiliated, representing a total affiliated membership of 11,005,984. In recent years unions with an avowedly middle-class professional approach to trade unionism have decided to affiliate, notably the National Union of Teachers, National and Local Government Officers' Association, the Association of University Teachers, the Association of First Division Civil Servants, and the Hospital Consultants and Specialists' Association.

Congress itself consists of around 1,200 delegates and meets annually on the first Monday in September for five days, invariably at either Brighton or Blackpool. Its functions are to consider the work of the General Council over the previous 12 months, to discuss and take decisions on motions submitted by affiliated unions, and to elect the General Council for the following year. The proceedings of Congress have frequently been criticised for being little more than a television showpiece with the general secretaries of the major unions tending to dominate the proceedings. Both criticisms are valid, and yet all attempts at reform have been opposed by the General Council. It is extremely rare for General Council policies to be overturned by Congress; the last occasions on which this happened were on the issue of deregistration under the Industrial Relations Act in 1971, and in 1982 when the General Council wished to postpone the issue of automatic representation and Congress voted by a narrow majority to implement this reform.

The General Council

The governing body of the TUC between annual Congresses is the 44 member General Council, which has existed in its present form since 1921. It is elected annually by the block votes of unions at Congress. The General Council is the authentic voice of the TUC, charged with pursuing the aims of Congress, encouraging common action between its affiliated unions, giving assistance with organisation, managing and investing TUC funds and adjusting differences between its member unions. It may wish to consult more widely by calling a special congress, but this rarely happens.

For the time being, all affiliated unions are grouped into 18 trade groups roughly delineating an industry or sector, and each trade group is allocated a certain number of seats on the General Council. Only unions within each trade group may nominate candidates for seats within the group, but if there is a contested election all the affiliated unions are entitled to vote. Once elected to the General Council, a person is representative of a trade group, not a particular trade union. Successful nominees sit on the General Council in their own individual capacity, free to take decisions independently of their own union's policy. Thus the General Council is a body of individuals unrestrained by mandates from their own rank-and-file members. There are five additional seats for women workers. Table 1 shows that some unions' general secretaries are guaranteed seats on the General Council. Indeed, it would be unthinkable for the general secretaries of unions like the TGWU, NALGO, GMWU and ASTMS, and the president and general secretary of the AUEW (Engineering Section) not to be on the General Council.

At the 1981 Congress a motion advocating radical re-structuring of the TUC, to provide for a system which would give automatic representation on the General Council to all unions with more than 100,000 members, was passed with a small majority of 1.3 million votes. The decision was immediately seen as a victory for the right, largely because it would bring on to the General Council representatives from medium-sized unions — like the POEU, craft printers, and bank staffs — which are right-led. The left-led unions — such as TGWU — solidly opposed the plan. However, it would be simplistic to see the debate, which was often esoteric and bitter, as merely a political issue. Whilst such a system of automatic representation according to size of union would tend to favour the white-collar unions at the expense of the industrial unions, and the rightwing at the expense of the left, other factors are important.

First, automaticity would be formally more democratic and might enhance the representative character of the General Council. Second, some small unions still possess bargaining power (ASLEF and the NUS, for example) and third, mere General Council re-structuring would have little effect unless the TUC itself could regain the influence it had before the election of the Tories in 1979 (see **The TUC and the Illusion of Power** below). In any case, whatever system of representation were adopted, it is probably true to say that the problem of achieving both an arithmetically accurate and technically acceptable balance is insoluble, especially at a time when dramatic changes in numbers are taking place between groups. With the decline in the old, established traditional industries, such as coalmining, shipbuilding, textiles and iron and steel, coupled with changes in occupational structure of the labour force in favour of white-collar workers at the expense of manual workers, an acceptable balance is difficult to achieve when the question of the effects of new technology on jobs is taken into account.

Despite a plea from Len Murray for more time for the General Council to consider the issue, the 1982 TUC Congress voted by a narrow majority to go ahead and reform the composition of the General Council. A vote amending the original composite motion and pushing through proposals for automatic representation on the General Council for smaller unions from 1983 onwards was passed by 5.63 million to 5.37 million, a majority of 466,000.

Under the plan, drawn up by the General Council on instructions from the 1981 Congress, seats would be given automatically to all unions with 100,000 members or more. The scheme would allow the smaller unions to decide for themselves on their remaining representatives, thereby ending the trade group system which allowed for the whole Congress to vote for General Council members. The plan provides for an increase in the size of the General Council from 44 (in 1982) to 55 (including the general secretary). The 25 unions which in 1982 had more than 100,000 members would automatically qualify for 37 seats within the total. A further 11 seats would be given to smaller unions, to be elected from among their own numbers, and a further six would go specifically to women, to be elected by the entire Congress.

Consequently, this *Trade Union Directory* appears in the form of trade groups for the last time. Looking through the trade groups and their constituent unions it is difficult not to agree that they had become an archaic, inappropriate and unwieldy method of determining the composition of the General Council, inadequately representing technical, clerical and professional workers, and open to criticism about patronage by the block votes of the large unions. In any case, the trade group arrangement reflected the idea of a gradual transition towards industrial unionism, always an ideal type and hopelessly static in the face of technological change and multinational capital.

The General Council of the TUC had been criticised as a self-perpetuating oligarchy, and the chances of a newcomer upsetting the General Council, with its inbuilt conservatism and bureaucratic form of organisation, were remote. It is divided into a number of sub-committees, with a ranking order of priority, and filled with members largely in order of seniority. The Council in full session largely carries out its business by receiving reports from its sub-committees.

The TUC has formed industrial committees on which non-General-Council representatives sit alongside General Council members. At present there are nine industry committees: construction, fuel and power, health services, hotel and catering, local government, printing, steel, textile clothing and footwear, and transport. The printing committee has already successfully effected a merger between the printing unions, and the steel committee has already bargained directly with the British Steel Corporation, while the Health Services committee maintained a commanding influence over the conduct of the 1982 pay dispute, sometimes to the chagrin of the constituent unions. There is clearly a great deal of scope for such industry committees to formulate common policies between unions in a particular industry, to deal with inter-union problems, and to present a united front to the government on matters of importance in particular industries.

The way the TUC operates has frequently been compared to that of a local authority, conducting its business through standing committees. These committees are wide ranging in character and include finance and general purposes, international, education, social insurance and industrial welfare, employment policy and organisation, economic, and equal rights. All these committees are staffed by members of the General Council and the incumbents of the chairs of such committees enjoy considerable status. There are also a number of joint committees which include other trade union representatives as well as General Council members, and sometimes third parties. These committees include the Women's Advisory Committee, the Race Relations Advisory Committee, the Trades Councils' Joint Consultative Committee, the National Economic Development Council (see **Relations with Government** above), the Standing Advisory Committee to the TUC Centenary Institute of Occupational Health, and the TUC-Labour Party Liaison Committee. All TUC committees are serviced by the TUC 'civil service', a group of research workers who develop considerable expertise in their own particular fields, and many of whom are university graduates.

A great deal of the work of TUC committees involves correspondence and meetings with government departments and ministers and much effort was expended in lobbying Whitehall, especially before 1979. Since then, the influence of the TUC *vis-à-vis* government has waned dramatically.

Regional Machinery

The TUC is a highly centralised organisation in that its regional organisation has always been sparse and under-serviced. In 1973 the TUC reorganised its regional machinery into eight regional TUC councils, on which full-time officials from various trade unions sit, alongside representatives of the county associations of trades councils, of which there were 54 in 1978 (see **Trades Councils** below). The effectiveness of regional TUC councils is largely dependent on the secretaries themselves. For example, Colin Barnett, the Regional TUC Secretary in the North West, is a celebrated publicist of TUC views in that region and is perhaps more widely known in his TUC role than he is as a divisional officer of NUPE. In 1979, the TUC appointed the first of what may be a series of full-time regional

The TUC General Council 1982/83

	Seats	Number of Unions	Delegates	Membership Total	Group Per Seat	Council Members
1. Mining and Quarrying	2	3	58	285,056	142,528	A. Scargill (NUM) M. McGahey (NUM)
2. Railways	2	3	38	250,602	125,301	S. Weighell (NUR) R. Buckton (ASLEF)
3. Transport other than Railways	5	6	103	1,795,360	359,072	A. M. Evans (TGWU) L. Smith (TGWU) W. Greendale (TGWU) D. Gray (TGWU) J. Slater (NUS)
4. Shipbuilding	1	1	11	119,585	119,585	J. G. Murray (GEMBAT)
5. Engineering, Founding and Vehicle Building	4	10	81	1,227,282	306,820	T. Duffy (AUEW) E. Scrivens (AUEW) G. Russell (AEUW) L. G. Guy (NUSMCHDE)
6. Technical Engineering and Scientific	2	4	55	657,690	328,845	K. Gill (AUEW/TASS) C. Jenkins (ASTMS)
7. Electricity	1	1	37	395,000	395,000	F. J. Chapple (EETPU)
8. Iron and Steel and Minor Metal Trades	1	8	28	120,272	120,272	W. Sirs (ISTC)
9. Building, Woodworking and Furnishing	2	3	45	346,709	173,354	G. Lloyd (UCATT) L. Wood (UCATT)
10. Printing and Paper	1	3	80	405,623	405,623	W. H. Keys (SOGAT 82)
11. Textiles	1	12	18	72,763	72,763	E. Haigh (TGWU—Dyers, Bleachers and Textile Workers' Trade Group)
12. Clothing, Leather, Boot and Shoe	1	6	38	195,056	195,056	A. Smith (NUTGW)
13. Glass, Ceramics, Chemicals, Food, Drink, Tobacco, Brushmaking and Distribution	2	9	63	554,407	277,203	C. D. Grieve (TWU) W. Whatley (USDAW)
14. Agriculture	1	1	14	85,000	85,000	J. R. Boddy (TGWU Agricultural Workers' Trade Group)

The TUC General Council 1982/83—continued

	Seats	Number of Unions	Delegates	Membership Group Total	Per Sect.	Council Members
15. Public Employees	5	12	211	2,287,532	457,506	R. Bickerstaffe (NUPE) K. Cameron (FBU) G. Drain (NALGO) F. Jarvis (NUT) E. A. G. Spanswick (COHSE)
16. Civil Servants and Post Office	3	13	144	923,964	307,988	A. M. Christopher (IRSF) J. A. Graham (CPSA) A. D. Tuffin (UCW)
17. Professional, Clerical and Entertainment	2	10	67	418,269	209,134	J. Morton (MU) A. Sapper (ACTT)
18. General Workers	3	1	74	865,814	288,604	F. A. Baker (GMWU) D. Basnett (GMWU) J. F. Eccles (GMWU)

19. Women Workers. There are now five General Council seats for women workers' representatives; any union with women members may nominate for these seats but if there is a contest the whole Congress votes. A vote had to be taken at the 1982 Congress; those elected were: A. Maddocks (NALGO), G. Morgan (AUEW), C. M. Patterson (TGWU), M. Turner (ASTMS) and P. Turner (GMWU).

secretaries when it appointed the Secretary of the Lancashire Federation of Trades Councils, Bob Howard, as regional secretary for the North of England. Since the regional councils were set up in 1974, a trade union official has generally doubled up as part-time secretary, but this role has been growing steadily. Three such regional councils — the North West, Wales, and the South East — now employ research officers. Otherwise, the only full-time TUC staff in the regions are the education officers, who are mainly involved in the provision of TUC-sponsored shop steward training, and who are answerable to Congress House and to a regional educational advisory committee. (See **The TUC and the Slump** below.)

Trades Councils

There are around 440 trades councils in most major cities, towns and districts of the UK. Trades councils meet monthly and consist of representatives of local trade union branches, lodges or chapels. Their function is to assist in improving trade union organisation in their locality and to nominate trade union representatives on a variety of local committees and institutions (e.g. the governing bodies of educational establishments and some local tribunals). Trades councils are deeply embedded in the history of the British trade union movement and provided common links between trade unions long before the TUC itself.

There has always been an uneasy relationship between the TUC and trades councils. On the one hand, the TUC needs them as a means of establishing direct contact with the grassroots of the trade union movement and to ascertain reactions to particular issues. On the other hand, the TUC has frequently found that such contacts provide embarrassing evidence of local dissent and left-wing activity which it sees as a possible threat to its own authority. The conflict is less acute today than it was in the heyday of the trades councils in the nineteenth century and during the 1930s; yet even today they are regarded with some suspicion by the TUC establishment.

Trades councils are not regarded by the trade union movement as independent bodies competent to make local decisions which may conflict with regional or national trade union policy, and trades council representatives remain subject to the rules and policies of the unions that affiliate to them. The TUC encourages its affiliated unions to affiliate to local trades councils and, providing that trades councils adhere to the guidelines laid down by the TUC, they receive modest financial support on a year-by-year basis. Nowadays only about a quarter of all the country's trade union branches actually affiliate to them, and their most important function is to provide a forum for trade union activists in a particular area. (See **The TUC and the Slump** below.)

Women

In 1982 women comprised approximately 28 per cent of the total TUC affiliated membership.[5] Since the second world war women workers have provided the largest recruitment source for trade unions, mainly from the growth in local and national government departments, the National Health Service and office work.[6] At present, the TUC General Council reserves five seats for women workers' representatives (see table above).

Every year the TUC holds a Women's Conference which was set up in 1931 when it was realised that women's special needs were frequently neglected by the trade union movement. The rationale for having a separate conference is that it can act as a forum to debate issues which might otherwise not get an airing in any mixed forum. Resolutions passed at the Women's Conference are passed on to the General Council of the TUC which is under no obligation to take any notice of them, and frequently does not.

The TUC also has a Women's Advisory Committee which consists of 20 members, ten of whom are elected at the TUC Women's Conference, and ten of whom (including the five women on the TUC General Council) are appointed by the General Council.

The supporters of the Women's Conference maintain that it acts as a training ground for women trade unionists and encourages women's solidarity. Opponents say that such a view is merely condescending and a separate conference is a form of 'sexual apartheid'. The emergence of the women's movement, however, has highlighted the need for greater participation and representation of women at all levels of union activity, and the dispute now centres on the best means of achieving this.

It is clear from the union entries in this book that women are grossly under-represented in all aspects of union activity and that they are victims of sexual discrimination at work. The TUC does have a women's officer and is now gradually recognising that women get a raw deal from British trade unions, and that traditional male-dominated attitudes are still rife in many unions.

At the 1979 Trades Union Congress, for example, only three resolutions, out of a total of 113, referred specifically to women. There is mounting evidence that the Equal Pay and Sex Discrimination Acts of 1975 have served to pre-empt any need that might have been felt by trade union negotiators to treat women's equality with more urgency.[7] An equal pay project carried out by the London School of Economics (reported in the *New Statesman* of 31 August 1979) monitored 26 organisations between 1974 and 1977, about what effects the two Acts were having; it showed the remarkable lengths to which employers had gone to minimise their obligations under the Equal Pay Act. There was evidence of employers altering the content of men's and women's jobs to avoid 'like work' comparisons and restricting grading systems to leave women in the lowest grades, as well as altering factors by which jobs were evaluated to favour those done by men, and giving men additional duties to justify restoring differentials. (See also *Feminist Review* 1979, 1.)

The 1980 Women's Conference approved a draft report setting out detailed recommendations for positive discrimination in favour of women in education, training and employment. The theme of the report was that equality cannot be achieved by simply passing laws, and that unions themselves must negotiate positive measures in favour of women, aimed at changing basic patterns of employment. The 1979 Trades Union Congress endorsed a ten-point charter for positive action within trade unions, including such provisions as special seats for women on unions' decision-making bodies and advisory committees at national and local levels to 'ensure that the special interests of women members are protected'.

It is true that the last ten years have seen a blossoming of TUC progressive policies on women, and if all of these policies were acted upon it would revolutionise women's lives. For example, there would be a comprehensive scheme for pre-school child care; improved parental leave; free access to abortion on the NHS; equal opportunities in education, training (including craft apprenticeships) and employment; a recognition that family responsibility should be equally shared; and all legislation, collective bargaining agreements, work practices aimed at enabling this to happen.

As Kate Holman and Anna Coote pointed out in an article in the *New Statesman* of 19 March 1982, the 'problem is, now that the TUC has so many good intentions down on paper, that the gap between theory and practice is wider than ever'. The truth is that unions themselves have not taken much notice of TUC policy and, as Holman and Coote remark: 'More and more male trade unionists have grown accustomed to the language of feminism, and have learnt how to avoid accusations of "chauvinism".'

To be fair, the TUC has scored some important victories for women over the years — defending the 1967 Abortion Act; setting up women-only training courses; and successfully backing campaigns for maternity leave and child benefit.

International

British trade unions maintain formal connections with a variety of international organisations, and the trade union entries in this book show that at least a token stance of 'internationalism' is taken by many British unions.[8] The TUC itself is currently affiliated to three major bodies: the International Confederation of Free Trade Unions (ICFTU); the European Trades Union Confederation (ETUC); and the Trade Union Advisory Committee of the Organisation for Economic Co-operation and Development (TUAC/OECD). The TUC's largest expenditure item is accounted for by its international affiliations — around 30 per cent of the TUC's total expenditure.

The TUC International Committee consists of 17 people and, next to the Finance and General Purposes Committee and the Economic Committee, it is the third most powerful institution in the TUC. It is not particularly accountable and some claim that the links between the TUC's international department and the Foreign Office are stronger than those with the International Department of the Labour Party.

Patrick Wintour claimed in the *New Statesman*[9] that the secretive power of the international department was 'deployed in the service of inertia'. Indeed, in August 1980 the General Council refused to give its wholehearted support to the issue of free trade unionism in Poland, following the outbreak of strikes at Gdansk.

Another example quoted by Patrick Wintour:

> In 1975, for example, a major campaign, with strong ICFTU backing, was organised against the treatment of tea workers by British companies operating in Sri Lanka (Ceylon). But the TUC did next to nothing to press the demand that compensation for low wages and maltreatment should be produced by the multi-nationals.

An ICFTU report stressed that:

> The TUC kept wanting more information, even though it was difficult to obtain, even though time was pressing, and even though it was clear to everyone that the workers were in a bad way.

In fact, the ICFTU is not renowned for its radical initiatives. What few initiatives it has made have often been blunted by the TUC, which provides a sixth of the ICFTU's affiliated membership and one third of its income. The TUC makes no attempt to inform British trade unionists about ICFTU's activities, and those who peruse the TUC Annual Report each year, hoping to glean some detail about the way in which TUC money is spent on international matters, will be sadly disappointed. The reports contain nothing more than uninformative waffle, for example:

> The view was expressed that it would not in general be satisfactory to seek earmarked funds for such purposes and that funds from extrabudgetary sources were in fact earmarked, while any reduction of continuing activities would be dependent in practice on the outcome of the discussion of priorities which the Committee had approached earlier without conclusion and were to take up again.

(TUC Annual Report, 1978, p.218)

Committed (by a resolution of the 1981 Congress) to opposition to the European Economic Community, the TUC finds even limited co-operation in the European Trades Union Confederation difficult. Yet unified action is vital if any progress is to be made against unemployment. The TUC itself gives little chance to initiatives taken at a purely national level. Hence some trade union leaders are reluctant to support the campaign for withdrawal from the EEC, believing that membership should be accepted and that it can yield benefits.

The TUC and the Slump

British trade unions are now having to face up to the fact of record postwar levels of unemployment and the continuing 'de-industrialisation' of Britain. This means that British trade unions have already passed their peak membership levels; with the threat of further unemployment being induced by rapid technological change, the question of 'organising the unemployed' has been posed much sooner than might have been anticipated in 1979. The question is gaining greater urgency as the Tories attack the status of the unemployed by eradicating earnings-related benefit and cut the real value of unemployment benefit.

The history of the TUC's attempt to cater for the needs of the unemployed is not a proud one. In the 1930s the TUC was engaged in bitter battles with the communist-led National Union of Unemployed Workers. Recent years have seen ugly scenes outside TUC conferences as the Socialist Workers' Party's 'Right to Work' campaign sought to lobby senior trade union leaders. It is obvious to everyone that unemployment poses the possibility of a cancerous growth of extremist and racist organisations gaining ground amongst young unemployed workers.

During the 1980s slump, attempts by the Labour-controlled Greater London Council and the West Midland County Council to fund local union resource centres were disallowed by the TUC, despite support for the projects from the local trades and regional councils. TUC General Secretary Murray instructed all the TUC's affiliated organisations to reject the resource centres since they would drive a wedge between the unions and their members.

The centres were intended to provide research and assistance for local trade unionists. Most trade union research departments at head office are small and hard-pressed and assist only national officers. The regional councils have little more than part-time secretarial help. Consequently, local trade unionism receives little information on issues such as employment, new technology or multinational companies and there is little assistance with education or with understanding company finance. For the TUC economic review to propose local planning with a large element of local trade union participation without such help is ludicrous.

Of course, the union hierarchies are uneasy about shop stewards' committees gaining direct access to resource centres. Minutes of the TUC Employment, Policy and Organisation Committee delineate some of the TUC leaders' fears:

> The principle of TUC bodies accepting public funds for activities relating to internal trade union

functions; the inevitable pressure that would come on the TUC and unions to sustain the centres should at some stage — as was likely — the GLC grant be cut and the staff threatened with redundancy; doubts about relying on officers of unions and trades councils to direct and control the centre with eight full-time staff and the fact that to give the go-ahead to the London centre would undoubtedly encourage other trade unionists in other cities to seek similar arrangements with local authorities. What could be emerging was a network of well resourced bodies that would develop outside the movement's structure.

The situation could easily arise, for instance, where a union had decided upon a policy in relation to a closure of a plant only to find that it was being opposed in its policy by a resource centre. Alternative trade union structures could begin to emerge which would be open to manipulation and used to drive a wedge between trade unions and their members.

Clearly, the TUC and union leaders fear losing control of local trade unionists. However, the TUC Employment, Policy and Organisation Committee could not be commended for consistency since it also ruled that nothing was to prejudice the conversion, with the aid of a £170,000 annual county council grant, of a large former police headquarters into a trade union resource, unemployment and community centre.

The first centre to open was in Newcastle in 1977 under the auspices of the trades council and from here the TUC took the idea. Among the 150 centres which have been established there is considerable variation between the provision of sympathy and accommodation and the consideration of radical political action and encouraging unemployed people to consider such actions.

The TUC was always determined that control of the centres should remain in the hands of trades councils and regional councils of the TUC. A bulletin was started which collated local information and set out further guidelines for the functions and management of the centres. Issue Number 2 of this bulletin said that all the centres should provide information, counselling, education and representation on behalf of the unemployed. Issue 4 maintained that it was at the discretion of TUC regional councils to decide which groups should belong to the management committees of centres, the one proviso being that trade union and local authority representatives were always to be in the majority.

A TUC Consultative Conference considered setting up a special TUC section for the unemployed but this attracted little support or enthusiasm from constituent unions. The reasons seemed to be that it would duplicate existing trade union services and would necessitate a rise in union dues.

The history of the TUC's relations with unemployed workers seemed to be repeating itself. Issue Number 6 of the bulletin to unemployment centres specifically stated that, 'Trades councils and TUC centres should not have any dealings with bodies describing themselves as unemployed workers' unions.' The TUC strategy for fighting unemployment was in general seen to be pusillanimous, apparently relying on the hope that a Labour government would be elected soon and implement reflationary policies. For all that, the resource centres have continued to increase and apparently fulfil a useful role.

The TUC and the Illusion of Power

Whilst the TUC makes great efforts to publicise the activities of its committees to its affiliated unions by circulars and pamphlets, the main thrust of its efforts is upwards to the corridors of power in Whitehall. Hence the success of its committees is wholly dependent on the response it receives from the government in power. Coates and Topham have rightly observed that:

What the TUC's method has lacked, historically, has been any mobilising drive to enlist the mass support of its affiliated membership behind all this staid committee work; yet the issues it takes up are commonly potentially popular and vital ones for the whole of our society. When the labour movement had its own newspaper in the *Daily Herald* there was at least a possibility of feeding out to the membership the often superbly documented case material which the TUC prepares and which nowadays reaches only the most limited audience, and often the least sympathetic ears.[8]

The TUC entered the 1980s facing the harsh realities of high levels of unemployment, savage public expenditure cuts, decreasing living standards, and a vitriolic attack on trade union rights with harsh anti-union legislation. At the same time, the total TUC-affiliated membership slumped dramatically from an all-time peak of 12,172,508 in 1979 to 11,005,984 at the end of 1981. Its reliance over the years on an increasingly bureaucratic, inward-looking strategy which was wholly committed to the conventional lobbying system was shown to be a failure when the Thatcher administration came to power.

Historically, the power of the TUC has been relatively high during wartime and during periods of full employment and low during periods of high unemployment. The TUC *appeared* to be exercising more power because of its acceptance into the power structure of government, but this was no more than a facade. The harsh economic and political climate, engendered by the pursuit of monetarist policies by a government hostile to the very existence of trade unionism, could not be overcome solely by relying on the involvement of the TUC in the trappings of the decision-making apparatus of government.

As unemployment continues to climb to record levels it is clear that the British trade union movement in the 1980s will face the most momentous crisis in its history. The broad post-war consensus ensuring continuous improvements in living standards, full employment, and increasing trade union participation in the regulation of a liberal social democratic society has been replaced, in the words of Coates and Topham, by

'marked authoritarianism, increasingly obtrusive and arbitrary police powers, surveillance, and frenetic preparations for an impossible war'. As the TUC considers how to implement the principle of automatic representation on its General Council while experiencing a vitriolic attack on trade-union rights from the most hostile government it has ever had to deal with, it might ponder the political impact of the profound economic and structural changes which are occurring.

Unemployment and Loss of Membership

The rapid decline in union membership continued throughout 1981 and 1982. The largest unions with substantial unskilled and 'semi-skilled' membership in manufacturing, construction and engineering were hardest hit.

The Transport and General Workers' Union recorded a fall from over 2 million members at the end of 1979 to 1.7 million at the end of 1981. The AUEW (Engineering Section) fell by 80,000 to just over one million in the first six months of 1981. GMWU membership fell, but less rapidly after the appointment of a national recruitment officer and then actually increased as a result of amalgamation with the Boilermakers' Society and reconstitution into the General Municipal, Boilermakers' and Allied Trades' Union.

National Union of Public Employees membership actually grew and hoisted this union above the 700,000 mark for the first time. Similar small rises were achieved by the Confederation of Health Service Employees and by the National and Local Government Officers' Association.

White-collar unions in the private sector have fared less well with ASTMS, for many years the 'growth stock' in the TUC, suffering losses of some 65,000 members. APEX was badly hit by the concentration of a large part of its membership in the badly depressed engineering industry and fell by 18,000. The union has established a head office team to explore potential areas of recruitment such as electronics industries and the building societies in the hope of maintaining membership levels.

Unions that give unemployment pay have held membership for longer, but at considerable cost. SOGAT had to raise subscriptions to help cover unemployment payments of about £40,000 a month.

Further Reference

1. The best work on the history of the TUC is V.L. Allen, *The Sociology of Industrial Relations*, Longmans 1971.
2. V.L. Allen, p.153.
3. TUC Rules and Standing Orders, Rule 11 para (d).
4. TUC Rules and Standing Orders, Rule 13 para (a).
5. TUC, 1982. (But note these figures are those *reported* to the TUC; many unions do not break up their membership totals between males and females.)
6. For a discussion of the role of British trade unions in catering for the needs of women, see the paperback by Lindsay Mackie and Polly Pattullo, *Women at Work*, Tavistock 1977. Perhaps the most detailed publication in this area is by Judith Hunt and Shelley Adams, 'Women, work and trade union organisation', WEA, *Studies for Trade Unionists*, vol. 6, no. 21, March 1980. See also Anna Coote and Beatrix Campbell, *Sweet Freedom*, Picador 1982.
7. See the articles by Anna Coote, *New Statesman*, 31 August 1979 and 21 March 1980.
8. Ken Coates and Tony Topham, *Trade Unions in Britain*, Spokesman 1980.
9. Patrick Wintour, *New Statesman*, 2 March 1979.

Scottish TUC

Head Office

Middleton House
16 Woodlands Terrace
Glasgow G3 6DF
041-332 4946

Principal Officer

General Secretary — J. Milne

General

The Scottish TUC was established in 1897. Trade unions with membership in Scotland usually affiliate to the TUC and the Scottish TUC. The Congress is held annually in April and elects a General Council of 21. Affiliated unions are grouped into 11 trade sections:

Section 1 — Fuel and power
Section 2 — Transport and docks
Section 3 — Shipbuilding; engineering, foundries, iron and steel, vehicles and minor metal trades
Section 4 — Building, woodworkers and furnishing
Section 5 — Printing and paper
Section 6 — Clothing, boot and shoe, leather, textiles and ceramics
Section 7 — Food, drink, tobacco and distribution
Section 8 — Non-manual workers
Section 9 — Civil and public servants
Section 10 — Local government employees
Section 11 — Trades councils

In its function as co-ordinating body for the trade unions in Scotland, the Congress has campaigned about regional economic policy and is represented on many committees which are appointed by the Scottish Office. It is also concerned with education, health, housing and other social provisions, significant aspects of which are covered by separate Scottish legislation.

The General Council appoints an economic committee; a general purposes committee (which considers health, housing, political issues and relations between unions) and an education committee.

Delegates to the 1982 STUC emphatically restated their opposition to all forms of incomes policy.

Welsh TUC

Cyngor Undebau Llafur Cymru

Head Office

1 Cathedral Road
Cardiff CF1 9SD
0222-394521

Principal Officer

> *Secretary* — G. Wright

General

The Welsh TUC may be regarded as part of the TUC's regional structure but it is more than that, having rather more autonomy than the eight regional councils in England and having been fashioned into a viable body under the energetic leadership of George Wright, Welsh Regional Secretary of the TGWU, on the office and administrative facilities of which it is largely dependent.

The Welsh TUC co-ordinates trade union action in Wales on matters of specific interest to Wales. It holds an annual conference in late April or early May and has its own General Council.

It has not so far shown itself to be capable of mounting effective action to counter the run-down of the steel and coal industries of South Wales. In January 1981, a delegation from the Welsh TUC visited Mondragon and some of the associated workers' co-operatives in the Basque provinces of Spain. A great deal of work has been put into trying to isolate the most appropriate features of the 'Mondragon model' and to incorporate them in an alternative industrial strategy for Wales.

At the 1981 Welsh TUC Conference a 'Social Plan' recommending that an incomes policy should be part of a social contract with any future Labour government was thrown out amid angry scenes. Hence the Welsh TUC General Council has come out against incomes policy but in support of the 'principle of a minimum wage and a maximum salary'.

Summary of Statistics—Trade Unions

		GROSS INCOME		
	Number of Members	From Members	From Investments	Total Income
	(1)	(b) £000s (2)	(c) £000s (3)	(d) £000s (4)
Unions each with 100,000 members or more:				
Transport and General Workers' Union	1,886,971	26,634	2,736	29,447
Amalgamated Union of Engineering Workers	—	—	—	30
Constructional Section	34,653	770	102	897
Engineering Section	1,166,512	16,401	1,211	17,713
Foundry Section	50,111	764	74	847
Technical Administrative and Supervisory Section	191,562	3,567	172	3,755
National Union of General and Municipal Workers	915,654	15,840	1,869	18,315
National and Local Government Officers' Association	782,343	14,915	526	18,303
National Union of Public Employees	699,156	9,886	864	10,816
Association of Scientific Technical and Managerial Staffs	491,000	8,480	165	8,653
Union of Shop Distributive and Allied Workers	450,287	5,973	553	6,783
Electrical Electronic Telecommunication and Plumbing Union	438,669	6,523	619	7,319
National Union of Mineworkers (h)	369,499	11,466	2,337	14,262
Union of Construction Allied Trades and Technicians	312,000	4,433	232	4,727
National Union of Teachers	272,902	3,343	664	4,116
Confederation of Health Service Employees	216,482	3,166	165	3,403
Civil and Public Services Association	216,415	6,070	386	6,556
Union of Communication Workers	202,993	5,369	238	5,677
Society of Graphical and Allied Trades 1975	199,877	4,050	228	4,973
Royal College of Nursing of the United Kingdom	181,111	2,163	—	2,163
National Union of Railwaymen	167,198	4,407	2,219	6,636
National Association of Schoolmasters and Union of Women Teachers	156,167	1,909	172	2,152
Banking Insurance and Finance Union	141,042	2,155	51	2,220
Association of Professional Executive Clerical and Computer Staff (APEX)	140,292	2,625	330	3,244
Post Office Engineering Union	130,976	3,945	53	4,084
Amalgamated Society of Boilermakers Shipwrights Blacksmiths and Structural Workers	124,068	1,937	347	2,456
National Graphical Association	116,438	3,921	860	4,860
Society of Civil and Public Servants	108,841	3,188	227	3,480
Iron and Steel Trades Confederation	103,865	1,432	919	2,360
Total of above unions with 100,000 members or more	10,267,084	175,332	18,319	200,247
Total of 364 other listed unions with less than 100,000 members	2,357,369	51,728	7,566	66,383
Total of listed unions	12,624,453	227,060	25,885	266,630
Trades Union Congress	—	3,074	248	3,335
Total of 44 other unlisted unions which have submitted returns	11,902	585	47	692
TOTAL for all unions for 1980	**12,636,355**	**230,719**	**26,180**	**270,657**
TOTAL for all unions for 1979	13,212,354	198,025	22,661	234,643

Notes

(a) The gross assets figures take no account of liabilities. The net worth of unions is indicated in column 11.

(b) By far the largest part of the income from members is derived from regular contributions but a very small part (probably less than 1 per cent) is derived from such items as sale of diaries.

(c) Investment income is net of certain items such as outgoings on property held as an investment but for most unions tax paid on investment income has not been deducted.

(d) Total income and total expenditure include all items which increased or decreased a union's total funds during the year and are not confined to normal revenue income and expenditure. Tax recoveries and provisions no longer required are therefore included in total income.

(e) For most unions the figure for total benefits to members comprises sums, such as sickness benefit and dispute benefit, paid direct to individual members; for some unions however expenditure on more general items of benefit, for instance, group insurance policies or convalescent homes, is included.

GROSS EXPENDITURE (columns 5–9) — **TOTAL FUNDS** (columns 10–11) — **GROSS ASSETS (a)** (columns 12–15)

Unemployment Benefit £000s (5)	Dispute Benefit £000s (6)	Total Benefits to Members (e) £000s (7)	Administration Expenses and Other Outgoings £000s (8)	Total Expenditure (d) £000s (9)	Beginning of the Year £000s (10)	End of the Year £000s (11)	Fixed Assets £000s (12)	Investments £000s (13)	Other Assets £000s (14)	Total Assets £000s (15)
	1.511	4.881	22.072	28.533	37.748	38.662	18.145	19.637	2.697	40.479
—	—		26	26	5	9	(g)	—	28	28
—	19	138	766	934	1.159	1.122	356	704	65	1.125
203	2.311	6.574	9.462	17.082	19.360	19.991	6.513	11.092	3.261	20.866
(g)	81	234	678	951	772	668	99	568	130	797
—	190	316	2.953	3.414	3.120	3.461	1.655	1.336	860	3.851
—	553	2.734	13.801	17.338	20.895	21.872	7.794	2.306	11.832	21.932
—	87	488	9.323	16.704	10.489	12.088	6.487	6.320	2.198	15.005
—	53	768	7.254	8.650	(f) 12.115	14.281	3.535	9.041	2.571	15.147
—	237	261	6.730	8.214	(f) 3.595	4.034	4.920	76	2.568	7.564
13	2	264	5.601	6.217	5.805	6.371	620	3.426	2.333	6.379
8	631	1.345	5.179	6.877	8.062	8.504	2.794	5.310	653	8.757
—	—	1.327	9.579	11.329	(f) 21.925	24.858	1.739	15.878	8.762	26.379
15	110	757	3.880	4.843	2.702	2.586	1.294	1.396	117	2.807
—	296	409	3.288	4.285	7.051	6.882	826	5.749	565	7.140
—	—	160	2.700	3.155	2.756	3.004	1.096	1.904	205	3.205
—	233	547	3.768	5.294	5.582	6.844	3.921	2.275	761	6.957
—	—	388	4.475	5.306	5.045	5.416	1.264	3.026	1.126	5.416
99	30	617	3.944	4.672	4.144	4.445	2.280	1.314	1.041	4.635
(g)	1	25	2.138	2.163			—	—	1.407	1.407
—	—	1.293	3.604	5.113	18.115	19.638	3.598	15.658	830	20.086
—	100	330	1.634	2.013	1.806	1.945	477	338	1.316	2.131
—	—	9	1.761	1.830	706	1.096	293	241	594	1.128
—	39	45	2.232	2.592	3.850	4.502	818	2.939	1.059	4.816
—	—	454	2.794	3.501	2.897	3.480	1.903	440	1.405	3.748
—	232	446	1.820	2.364	3.476	3.568	589	2.640	639	3.868
216	1.345	2.378	2.438	4.969	(f) 11.512	11.403	476	8.976	1.978	11.430
—	17	170	3.345	3.589	3.417	3.308	1.374	1.045	1.220	3.639
(g)	7	715	1.825	4.115	100.623	8.868	563	8.560	560	9.683
554	8.085	28.073	139.070	186.073	228.732	242.906	75.429	132.195	52.781	260.405
2,011	1.041	5.214	53.256	61.757	67.456	72.082	18.502	39.204	26.063	83.769
2,565	9.126	33.287	192.326	247.830	296.188	314.988	93.931	171.399	78.844	344.174
		618	2.185	3.721	939	553	73	677	565	1.315
2	—	21	586	651	452	493	124	201	250	575
2,567	**9.126**	**33.926**	**195.097**	**252.202**	**297.579**	**316.034**	**94.128**	**172.277**	**79.659**	**346.064**
514	12.468	34.088	156.763	212.483	273.068	295.228	76.666	172.563	71.047	320.276

(f) These figures have been adjusted to take account of later information.

(g) Less than £500.

(h) These figures include those of the 29 areas and other constituents of the union which submit separate returns.

(i) It may be difficult to correlate the figures in the table with those in the published accounts of the individual trade unions. This is because there are considerable variations in the ways in which unions present information in their accounts and the method of presentation often differs from that required in the annual return, from which the figures in the table have been abstracted. There are more up-to-date figures in the relevant entry for each union.

Group One Mining and Quarrying

Colliery Management, British Association of
(BACM)

Head Office

BACM House
317 Nottingham Road
Old Basford
Nottingham NG7 7DP
0602-786949/785819

Principal Officer

General Secretary — A. Wilson

Membership (1982)

Male 16,170
Female 600
Total 16,770

Union Journal

National News Letter —
quarterly.

Regional Organising Secretaries

- *Scotland*
  North East
  Steetley Brick Ltd
  Northern Works
  J. D. Meads
  BACM, Room 12, 2nd Floor
  Exchange Buildings
  Quayside
  Newcastle upon Tyne NE1 3BJ
  0632-322704

- *North Yorkshire*
  South Yorkshire
  Barnsley
  Doncaster
  Headquarters North
  Thyssen (GB) Ltd
  D. F. Marsh
  24/26 Market Road
  Doncaster
  0302-49152

- *Headquarters South*
  Associated Heat Services
  Approved Coal Merchants
  Scheme
  Compower Ltd
  National Smokeless Fuels Ltd
  Opencast Executive
  SFAS
  British Mining Consultants Ltd
  E. Pate
  BACM House
  317 Nottingham Road
  Old Basford
  Nottingham NG7 7DP
  0602-785819/786949

- *North Nottinghamshire*
  North Derbyshire
  South Nottinghamshire
  South Midlands
  Staveley Chemicals
  G. Malpass
  BACM House
  317 Nottingham Road
  Old Basford
  Nottingham NG7 7DP
  0602-789590

- *Western*
  South Wales
  Tredomen Engineering
  A. E. Draper
  BACM
  Transport House
  Cathedral Road
  Cardiff CF1 9FD
  0222-35681

General

The British Association of Colliery
Management affiliated to the TUC in
1977, and represents those engaged in
professional, technical, managerial or
staff duties in the mining industry or
associated industries in Great Britain.
It came into existence in 1947, and
since then it has enjoyed good relations with its sister unions in the coal
mining industry (NACODS and the
NUM).

History

As early as December 1945, it was decided to form a management trade union in the mining industry known as the *Yorkshire Association of Colliery Officials and Staff* (YACOS). At the outset it was agreed that this union should cater for all non-industrial staff, from the clerk to the colliery manager, and from the supervisor to the chief engineer. Membership grew rapidly, and when branches had formed outside Yorkshire — in the East Midlands, South Wales and the North of England — it was decided to change the name to the *British Association of Colliery Officials and Staff* (BACOS). Following the nationalisation of the coalmining industry on 1 January 1947, BACM was formed in May 1947, and the BACOS membership transferred to BACM some three months later.

After a ballot of all members, BACM affiliated to the TUC in 1977.

Union Officials

BACM has five full-time organisers, a headquarters office manager, a research officer and clerical staff. BACM has a history of continuity. In the 35 years of its existence it has had only four presidents and the third general secretary was only appointed in 1979.

Coverage

The union caters for the needs of those engaged in the management, scientific development and administration of the mining industry and ancillary and associated undertakings, up to NCB board level. It enjoys good relations with the other two mining unions — NACODS and the NUM — and demarcation problems have not arisen since an agreement was made between the three unions in 1953. BACM has a closed shop agreement with the National Coal Board as well as a comprehensive conciliation agreement for dealing with questions of a national character relating to salaries, conditions of employment, disputes etc. The union is a member of the Coal Industry National Consultative Council and the Coke Oven National Consultative Council.

Organisation

The Annual Delegate Conference is the supreme body of government in the union. It consists of representatives from the 14 BACM branches (nine delegates per branch).

The National Executive Committee carries on the business of the union between conferences, and consists of the national officers (president, two vice-presidents and treasurer); the general secretary; 14 branch delegates (one member from each branch); nine vocational group members, one from each of the nine vocational groups listed below. The NEC appoints the general secretary.

A branch of the union is established in each area of the NCB. Members employed at NCB headquarters (e.g. research establishments etc.) are attached to either HQ North or HQ South branches. Other NCB staff, staff employed by independent organisations, are attached to the branch nearest to their place of employment. Where branches cover a large geographical area, sub-branches are formed. Full-time officials service each branch.

To ensure that all sections of management are represented on the National and branch Executive Committees the membership is classified into nine vocational groups as follows:

Mining groups

1. Colliery managers and persons superior to managers
2. Under-managers, deputy managers and assistant managers
3. Other mining officials not in Groups 1 or 2 (mechanisation, safety and training, method study, strata control, ventilation, dust control, planning and opencast officials etc.)

Other vocational groups

4. Mining, electrical, mechanical and civil engineers
5. Mining surveyors (including bona fide apprentices and unqualified surveyors)
6. Administrative staff, industrial relations, purchasing and stores, marketing officials
7. Specialist sections including architectural, coal preparation,

estates, rescue, engineering drafters and tracers, and nurses

8. Scientific, geological, coke oven, chemicals and by-product officials

9. Finance and computer officials

Women

BACM has a small number of women members. There are no women on the National Executive Committee although there is some female representation on branch committees.

External Relations

BACM has no political affiliations, but in July 1982 it appointed two 'parliamentary representatives' to represent the interests of the union in parliament. The two MPs appointed hold Yorkshire seats, and were both BACM members and industrial relations officers for the National Coal Board — Geoff Lofthouse, MP for Pontefract and Castleford, and Alan McKay, MP for Penistone.

It has representatives on the Fuel and Power Industries' Committee and the Nationalised Industries' Committee. In Europe, BACM is represented on the ETUC Energy Industries' Committee, and is affiliated to the FICM (Fédération Internationale des Cadres des Mines), which represents management staff in the coalmining industries of Western Europe.

Policy

Although the BACM has only been an affiliate of the TUC for a short time, it successfully moved a motion at the 1978 Congress calling on the government and the TUC to support and pursue policies to enhance career prospects and rewards for professional, managerial and higher skilled workers. Its main policy concerns the maintenance of differentials in the mining industry.

Colliery Overmen, Deputies and Shotfirers, National Association of

(NACODS)

Head Office

2nd Floor
Argyle House
29-31 Euston Road
London NW1 2SP
01-837 0908

Principal Officer

National Secretary—
A. E. Simpson BEM

Membership (1982)

Male 18,575
Female —
Total 18,575

Union Journal

There is no union journal as such, but minutes of each National Executive Committee meeting are circulated monthly down to area and branch level.

General

The union seeks to organise those who have statutory qualifications as a colliery deputy. This embraces under-officials in the coal industry, i.e. 'overmen, deputies and shotfirers' and certain other officials below the grade of under-manager.

The union is divided into area associations with some relevance to the areas of the National Coal Board. Full-time secretaries are allocated to the areas of Cannock Chase, Durham, Midland, Northumberland, North Western, Scotland, South Wales and Yorkshire, and three of these areas have full-time officers in addition to full-time secretaries. Part-time secretaries are allocated to the areas of Cumbria, Kent, Leicestershire and Staffordshire. There is no departmental split at head office.

The membership of the union has fluctuated in line with the fluctuations in workers in the coal industry. In 1965, the union had a membership of 31,471.

Only those with deputy certificates can be members of the union. There are no women members.

History

Before 1910, when NACODS was first established as a national association, the union existed as a federation of autonomous areas under the name of the *General Federation of Firemen's, Examiners' and Deputies' Associations of Great Britain*. Some area associations have been in operation for more than 100 years. The present title was adopted when the coal industry was nationalised in 1947.

Organisation

The governing body of the union is the National Conference, held annually during the last full week in June. The Conference is composed of the officers, members of the National Executive Committee, and not more than ten delegates from each area association. Important decisions (e.g. acceptance or rejection of wage offers) between annual conferences are taken at specially convened one-day conferences.

The National Executive Committee consists of the president, vice-president, treasurer, secretary, and six other members. All members of the NEC, excluding the secretary, are appointed annually by ballot vote at a National Conference, except that no more than one person from any area association can be elected on to the NEC. All full-time officials are elected.

The union Rule Book provides that strikes can only be called as a result of a ballot vote of the membership following a resolution of a National Conference. A two-thirds majority of those voting is required.

Political Affiliation

The union is affiliated to the Labour Party. It affiliates 99.6 per cent of its members.

Mineworkers, National Union of
(NUM)

Head Office
222 Euston Road
London NW1 2BX
01-387 7631/8

Principal Officers
President — Arthur Scargill
Vice-President —
   Mick McGahey
Secretary — Lawrence Daly

Membership (1982)
Male 249,711
Female —
Total 249,711

Union Journal
The Miner — monthly, distributed free to all members. A number of areas also produce their own journals and regular broadsheets, although there are only three journals in existence at the moment: the *Scottish Miner,* the *Yorkshire Miner* and the *Derbyshire Miner.*

NUM Area Secretaries:

● *Cokemen*
H. Close
17 Victoria Road
Barnsley
Yorkshire S70 2BA
0226-83146

● *Cumberland*
H. Hanlon
Miners' Offices
6 Nook Street
Workington
Cumberland CA14 4EG
0900-3238

● *Derbyshire*
P. E. Heathfield
Miners' Offices
Saltersgate
Chesterfield S40 1LG
0246-34135/6

● *Durham*
T. Callan
Miners' Offices
Red Hill
Durham DH1 4BB
0385-43515/7

● *Kent*
J. Collins
Miners' Offices
Waterside House
Cherry Tree Avenue
Dover
Kent CT16 1RW
0304-206661/206271

● *North Western*
S. G. Vincent
Miners' Offices
Bridgeman Place
Bolton
Lancashire BL2 1DL
0204-21680

● *Leicester*
J. Jones
Miners' Offices
Bakewell Street
Coalville
Leicestershire LE6 3BA
0530-32085/31568

● *Midlands*
J. T. Lally
12 Lichfield Road
Stafford ST17 4LB
0785-3358/9

● *Northumberland*
S. Scott
Burt Hall
Northumberland Road
Newcastle-upon-Tyne NE1 0LD
0632-27351/2

● *North Wales*
E. McKay
Miners' Offices
Bradley Road
Wrexham
North Wales
0978-265638

● *Nottingham*
J. Whelan
Miners' Offices
Berry Hill Lane
Mansfield
Nottinghamshire NG10 4JU
0623-26094/5

● *Scotland*
E. Clarke
5 Hillside Crescent
Edinburgh EH7 5DZ
031-556-2323/7

● *South Derbyshire*
K. Toon
Miners' Offices
Alexandra Road
Swadlincote
Burton-on-Trent DE11 9AZ
0283-221200

● *South Wales*
G. Rees
AEU Building
Sardis Road
Pontypridd
Glamorgan CF37 1DU
0443-404092/5

● *Yorkshire*
O. Briscoe
Miners' Offices
Barnsley
Yorkshire S70 2LS
0226-84006/9

● Group No. 1
Group Secretary — T. E. Bartle

● *Durham Colliery*
Mechanics Association
T. E. Bartle
26 The Avenue
Durham DH1 4ED
0385-61375/6

● *Northumberland Mechanics*
G. Whitfield
56 William Street
Blyth
Northumberland NE24 2HR
06706-2279

● *Durham County Enginemen*
G. A. Crooks
17 Hallgarth Street
Durham DH1 3AT
0385-64828

● Group No. 2 —
Group Secretary — F. Gormill

● *Scottish Enginemen*
F. Gormill
209 St Vincent Street
Glasgow G2 5QQ
041-221-0700/9

● *COSA*
C. T. Bell
14a Bond Street
Wakefield
Yorkshire
0924-63228

● *Power Group*
J. R. Ottey
4 Broad Street
Hanley
Stoke-on-Trent ST1 4HL
0782-262759

General

The NUM organises clerical and manual staff in or around the coalmining industry, together with those employed in ancillary undertakings. The total membership of the union has declined in line with the contraction in the coal industry. Up to 1958 the number of men employed in coalmining fluctuated around the 700,000 level, but then started on a decline which continued until 1970-71, when it settled at 287,200 for the annual average. The union is federally organised with a number of constituent associations or areas which are the result of the amalgamation of the separate district associations to form the National Union of Mineworkers in 1945. The two top national officers, the president and secretary, are elected by the whole membership, and then occupy their posts until retirement as do most area officials. The National Executive Committee comprises elected representatives from each of the constituent associations or areas, and is currently inequitably constituted in relation to the wide variations in membership from area to area. Recent rundowns in the steel industry and the threat of pit closures have served to create a new mood of militant leadership. Joe Gormley was succeeded by Arthur Scargill as president of the NUM as from 5 April 1982. Scargill was elected with a landslide majority, capturing 138,803 out of 197,299 votes, and routing his moderate challengers, Trevor Bell, secretary of the white-collar COSA, Ray Chadburn, Notts area president, and Bernard Donaghy, North Western area president.

History

Coalmining is commonly regarded as the child of the Industrial Revolution of the last 200 years. In fact the Romans made some use of outcrop coal, and the continuous records of the industry stretch back over the last seven centuries. There was a rapid expansion in coal production from the time of Elizabeth I onwards.

Coalmining tended to develop in areas isolated from the large towns, where most other industries were located, and miners were socially isolated from the mainstream of early industrial society. To this isolation was usually added a cleavage between masters and men which was sharper than in other industries. The working of coal was closely bound up with ownership of land so that the relationship between owners and men resembled that of lord and serf. (In Scotland, miners were serfs until 1799. In the English coalfields serfdom had largely been replaced by long engagements — e.g. the yearly bond — by 1700.)

The feudal division was soon overlaid by a capitalist one. The possibilities of miners setting up as independent masters were remote because of the cost of sinking a new colliery, unlike the case in some other industries. Isolation and class division, together with a highly co-operative pattern of work and life, developed in the mining community a strong sense of solidarity and inter-dependence. For a long time, however, the miners were too depressed a group of workers for this solidarity to find expression in trade union organisation. Miners were the first group of workers, outside the ranks of the skilled craftsworkers, to attempt trade union action.

Widespread strikes in Northumberland and Durham in 1740, 1765 and 1810 suggest the existence at those dates of some temporary form of trade union organisation. The repeal of the Combination Acts in 1824 was followed a few years later by the formation of some local unions of miners, of which the best known and successful was that led by Thomas Hepburn on the Tyne.

Local efforts at organisation were followed by the creation at Wakefield in 1824 of the first national union, *The Miners' Association of Great Britain and Ireland*. Greatly weakened by the long strike of 1844 in Durham, it failed to survive the economic crisis of 1847-48. Despite efforts to re-build the association, trade unionism in the coalfields was almost non-existent by 1855.

Revival stemmed from the agitation of Alexander Macdonald for the redress of miners' grievances by legal action, e.g. the right to appoint checkweighers, improved safety laws, shorter working days, employers' liability for accidents, and reform of master and servant law. Some local associations were formed (e.g. in South Yorkshire) in 1858, and in 1863 the *Miners' National Union* was launched at a conference in Leeds.

Macdonald's union did not favour strike action, although it encouraged the development of collective bargaining, The more militant districts, led by Lancashire, formed the rival *Amalgamated Association of Miners* in 1869.

During the boom of 1871-73 miners' wages were relatively high, and the inter-union rivalry had little effect as collective bargaining gradually developed. Macdonald and Thomas Burt, both miners, became the first trade unionists to be elected as MPs. In the trade depression of 1875-79 wages were cut substantially, and the Amalgamated Association was wound up. The National Union had survived as an effective organisation only in Northumberland and Durham, and collective bargaining was only retained by the acceptance of sliding scale agreements whereby wages followed coal prices rapidly downwards.

In many districts, the men resorted to a policy of ca'canny in an attempt to halt the fall in prices. Yorkshire adopted such a policy in 1881, accompanied by opposition to the sliding scale and demands for an increase in wages. Lancashire, the Midlands and Scotland started a new federation along similar lines, In 1888 a conference of the new sliding scale areas set up the *Miners' Federation of Great Britain* with a policy of a living wage, irrespective of prices, and a legal eight-hour day. Northumberland and Durham remained in the National Union in opposition to the legal eight-hour day. When the eight-hour bill finally became law in 1908, they too adhered to the federation.

By 1914 a demand for the nationalisation of the mines was being made by the federation, and this policy was put before the Sankey Commission in 1919.

Half the members of the commission and the chairperson reported in its favour, but the government took no action. After 1920 the coal industry suffered stationary or declining demand and falling prices, and a series of wage cuts were put into operation by the coal owners. This brought a period of embittered industrial relations culminating in the Great Lockout and General Strike of 1926. In the 1930s there were no national stoppages, but unemployment was high, the workforce continued to fall and output did not regain its former levels. Despite the recommendations of several commissions and inquiries little was done in the way of re-organisation or of new developments.

The industrial defeats of the 1920s and the obvious disadvantages of the disunity between districts produced a demand for re-organisation by 1927, and discussion went on during the 1930s.

The government took control of the mines in 1942, and on 1 January 1947, the industry passed into public ownership.

The *Miners' Federation of Great Britain* had been composed of about 40 separate unions, and the federation had already prepared for the advent of nationalisation by altering its constitution in 1945 to become the *National Union of Mineworkers*, following the Nottingham Conference in 1944.

Union Officials

Unlike the AUEW (Engineering Section) which has three levels of nationally elected full-time officers, the NUM has only a single level of such officers. Moreover, the miners' officials, once elected, are permanent, subject only to the rules which impose an age limit at 65 years for retirement. The full-time positions of president and secretary in the NUM have generally been regarded as of equal importance in status and power, although the president is probably more powerful in practice. The president of the NUM presides at meetings of Conference and the National Executive Committee, performs duties 'entrusted to him' by the NEC and sees 'that the business of the union is conducted in a proper manner and according to the rules, and that in the conduct of affairs of the union the rules are duly and properly carried out'.

The secretary also acts as treasurer and conducts the correspondence 'for and on behalf of the union and the National Executive Committee and keeps records of their proceedings'.

The division of power between a right-wing president and a left-wing secretary has been a tradition of more than 20 years' standing in the NUM. Since 1946 the president of the NUM seems to have had the edge in power over the secretary, but it is nevertheless important to note that successive presidents, along with the majority of the National Executive, have been orthodox Labour Party supporters, while three general secretaries have been either officially members of the Communist Party or (as in the case of the present secretary, Lawrence Daly) left-Labour ex-Communist. It is remarkable how the NUM has managed consistently to produce a political 'balance' between the two top posts.

The former president, Joe Gormley, was elected in 1971 when his only competitor was Mick McGahey, who was on the executive committee of the British Communist Party. Gormley was elected by 117,663 votes to 92,883. In 1968, Gormley had stood for election as general secretary when his opponent was Lawrence Daly, and lost. He was then the secretary of the newly named North Western Area of the NUM and a member of the Labour Party's National Executive. In 1971 his only opponent in the presidential election was Mick McGahey, who had won the presidency of the Scottish Area less than a year before by 13,149 votes to 8,499. Gormley was succeeded by Arthur Scargill, who was elected with a landslide majority. Scargill captured 138,803 votes out of 197,299 votes cast.

The current secretary, Lawrence Daly, was an active Communist until 1956, when he broke with the Communist Party because of its acceptance without serious challenge of the 20th Congress of the Soviet Communist Party in its denunciation of Stalin.

He then set up an organisation called the Fife Socialist League, and became a county councillor in Fife in 1958, with a sweeping victory over both the Labour and Communist opponents. In 1964, the Fife Socialist League was dissolved and Daly joined the Labour Party — although he retained his sympathies with the New Left movement. In 1965 he was elected general secretary of the Scot-

tish Area, to become the first non-Communist to hold that office in almost 20 years. A few months after his election he was successful in gaining one of the two Scottish seats on the National Executive of the NUM — after complaints of voting irregularities. The first results had indicated that Daly was the loser to two Communists, but Daly's complaints were upheld by the Scottish executive committee and both he and Alex Moffatt (the Communist president of the Scottish NUM) were declared elected. Daly's post on the National Executive Committee was to his considerable advantage in the 1968 election, when he beat Joe Gormley by just 10,000 votes.

The NUM rules do not assign the vice-president (currently Mick McGahey) any regular powers or duties. McGahey was elected vice-president at the 1973 Conference by 155 votes to 126. (NUM rules provide for the election of the vice-president by Conference and not by the membership as a whole.) McGahey had already reached the age (55) which ruled him out of the presidential election; thus his main electoral role was one of 'kingmaker' for Arthur Scargill.

The NUM uses the single transferable vote system in electing the two top union officials. Voters mark their preferences 1,2,3 etc. and the candidates with the least first preferences are eliminated, in turn, until one candidate has an absolute majority of the remaining active ballots. There are non-transferable votes when voters who support minor candidates fail to rank all the candidates. Full-time area officials are elected under similar voting systems with the count being conducted by an outside impartial agency (usually the Electoral Reform Society) with voting being conducted at the mines. Turnout is high, around 70 per cent.

Area Officials

The NUM is a federal union consisting of 14 geographical areas (see list of area secretaries above); a number of industrial or occupational 'areas'; the Cokemen; the white-collar COSA; two artificial groupings of certain local craftsworkers' associations for purposes of representation at national level; and a number of groups of workers who, by special agreement, maintain a dual affiliation with both the NUM and one or two other national unions (e.g. a group of Yorkshire surface workers who belong to the GMWU). Several of the areas were themselves federations almost to the date of the formation of the NUM in 1945.

Depending on the size of the area, the status hierarchy in the areas largely mirrors that of the national union. There are full-time presidents and secretaries of equal status, and beneath them a number of full-time permanent agents who are elected by referendum in districts within the areas. It is common for the agents to compete against each other when top area posts become vacant. Very small areas may have only one full-time official. The contenders for the lowest level of full-time area vacancies are in some cases the rank-and-file executive councillors, especially when both types of officers are elected on the same ward basis within the area. However, in other areas part-time presidents have been in a position to compete in area-wide elections for the lowest full-time post.

Coverage

The NUM is generally regarded as an approximation to an 'industrial' union, in the sense that it includes the overwhelming majority of manual workers (both surface and underground) in a single industry (coal mining and the production of coke) and is limited to that industry. The white-collar workers in COSA (Colliery Officials and Staffs' Association) were affiliated after the formation of the NUM. COSA still competes with APEX for membership. The other major unions in the industry are the BACM (around 16,000 members) and NACODS (around 19,000 members) although the NUM does include quite a few shotfirers in its ranks. The NUM negotiates directly with the NCB and there is provision for arbitration at both area and national level, as well as pithead conciliation machinery.

Organisation

The supreme powers of authority and government in the NUM are vested in the Annual Conference, which is held in the first week of July. A Special Conference can be called at any time by the National Executive Committee. Annual Conference consists of delegates from each of the constituent areas on the basis that 'each area is entitled to elect two delegates for the first 5,000 members (or fractional part thereof) and one further delegate for each additional 2,500 members (or fractional part thereof) except that in the case of an area comprising constituent associations in different counties, such area shall be entitled to elect at least one delegate from each constituent association within the area' (NUM Rule 24). In effect, what this means is that the NUM Conference is almost exactly divided between left coalfields — Yorkshire, Scotland, South Wales, Derbyshire and Kent, who muster around 129 votes — and the right-wing areas — Nottinghamshire, Durham, Northumberland, Lancashire, the Midlands, cokemen, various craft groups and COSA. This right-wing coalition, despite the fact that it represents fewer actual miners, can usually muster around 136 votes. It needs only one coalfield or craft group to switch sides and the left can win the vote. Conference also has the power to alter the NUM Rules, but in order to do so a two-thirds majority of delegates voting is required. The main rule-change which would considerably alter the political nature of the union would be to amend the rules to provide for a more equitable representation of areas on the National Executive, but an attempt by the Yorkshire area in 1979 to do this was rejected.

At the 1982 Annual Conference, the delegates voted to empower the Executive to 'bring about amalgamation of existing constituent associations consistent with modern and efficient structure and organisation in the coalfields'. This was the first step towards the creation of a new 'model' union which would firmly bear the stamp of its new president, Arthur Scargill. The move would be a far-reaching one, and was designed to

bring the old, local associations —
like the Durham and Northumberland
Mechanics and the Scottish Enginemen together with the white-collar
section, COSA, and the Power Group
— into a full merger with NUM areas.
Such a move would also threaten the
autonomy of these groups and would
tend to centralise power, thus tipping
the balance towards the left-led NUM
areas.

In 1971 Conference voted to change
the majority required in a secret ballot to call a strike from 66 per cent to
55, thus paving the way for the first
national stoppage since 1926. Essentially, the NUM is still a federal body
like its predecessor, the MFGB, and
many elderly office incumbents are reluctant to risk their permanent jobs in
the left's push for democracy.

The National Executive Committee
of the NUM consists of the president,
vice-president and secretary as ex-
officio members together with a number of representative members from
the constituent areas. At present it is
26-strong and is constituted as follows:

President
Arthur Scargill
222 Euston Road
London NW1 2BX

Vice-President
Mick McGahey
5 Hillside Crescent
Edinburgh EH7 5DZ

Secretary
Lawrence Daly
222 Euston Road
London NW1 2BX

Cokemen
H. Close
5 Victoria Road
Barnsley, Yorks S70 2BA

Cumberland
H. Hanlon
Miners' Offices
6 Nook Street
Workington
Cumberland CA14 4EG

Derbyshire
P. E. Heathfield
Miners' Offices
Saltersgate
Chesterfield
Derbyshire S40 1LG

Durham
T. Callan
Miners' Offices
Red Hill
Durham DJ1 4BB

Kent
W. Chambers
42 High Street
St Lawrence
Ramsgate, Kent

North Western
Sid Vincent
Miners' Offices
Bridgeman Place
Bolton, Lancs BL2 1DL

Leicester
J. Jones
Miners' Offices
Bakewell Street
Coalville
Leicestershire LE6 3BA

Midlands
R. W. Storer
Miners' Offices
17 Bulkington Road
Bedworth
Warwickshire

Northumberland
D. Murphy
Burt Hall
Northumberland Road
Newcastle-on-Tyne NE1 8LD

North Wales
E. McKay
Miners' Offices
Bradley Road
Wrexham

Nottingham
Ray Chadburn
Miners' Offices
Berry Hill Lane
Mansfield
Nottinghamshire NG18 4JU

J. Whelan
Miners' Offices
Berry Hill Lane
Mansfield
Nottinghamshire NG18 4JU

Scotland
E. Clarke
5 Hillside Crescent
Edinburgh EH7 5DZ

South Derbyshire
K. Toon
Miners' Offices
Alexandra Road
Swadlincote
Burton-on-Trent DE11 9AZ

South Wales
G. Rees
AEU Building
Sardis Road
Pontypridd
Glamorgan CF37 1DU

E. Williams
AEU Building
Sardis Road
Pontypridd
Glamorgan CF37 1DU

Yorkshire
O. Briscoe
746 Doncaster Road
Ardsley
Barnsley, Yorks

J. Weaver
8 Grange Road
Moorend, Doncaster

J. Taylor
Miners' Offices
2 Huddersfield Road
Barnsley
Yorkshire S70 2LS

Group No.1
T. E. Bartle
26 The Avenue
Durham DH1 4ED

Group No.2
F. Gormill
209 St. Vincent Street
Glasgow G2 5QQ

COSA
C. T. Bell
14a Bond Street
Wakefield
Yorkshire

Power Group
J. R. Ottey
4 Broad Street
Hanley
Stoke-on-Trent ST1 4HL

In addition two representatives of the NUM-sponsored MPs serve as ex-officio members with no voting powers.

At present, the Yorkshire area, with over 60,000 miners, is entitled to just three seats on the NEC while the practically defunct Cumberland coalfield, with one pit and less than 1,000 men, gets one seat. Other tiny 'rotten borough' coalfields such as North Wales, Leicestershire and South Derbyshire, with just a handful of pits each, also get one seat each, as do the cokemen. The NEC seats are allocated according to a system (NUM Rule 12) which totally fails to take account of the rundown of certain mining areas and the rise of others over the past 50 years. The left-wing areas control only a minority of seats on the NEC but represent by far the majority of miners. Arthur Scargill's attempt to change the rules at the 1979 Conference would have given Yorkshire two more seats on an expanded executive of 27 voting members. The political balance would then be 15-12 to the right — which would allow for an upset if a group of occasional waverers like the Scottish craftsworkers opted to change sides.

The NEC usually meets on the second Thursday in each month, and it is not uncommon for the two rival political groups to plan their tactics beforehand.

The NEC of the union over the years has rarely included many working miners, since the NUM's federal origins guarantee a built-in tendency by most areas to field, at NEC level, their best known professionals.

The NEC in the union has considerable constitutional power. Area officials and area executive committees are responsible to the NEC for membership and financial records, negotiations at district or colliery level, and monthly reports. No area has the power to complete an agreement without the approval of the NEC. Despite this, the NUM is a highly decentralised union and branches and areas have complete and constitutionally guaranteed control of all funds (including sickness and retirement) retained by them. The National Office is dependent on a modest portion of the dues collected locally.

Head office of the NUM is organised into the following departments: administration, research, finance, social insurance, industrial relations, international and safety.

In the near future, the NUM Headquarters will be moved from London to a mining area — possibly Sheffield. Again, this decision is in line with Arthur Scargill's desire to 'remodel' the union so that it brings the leadership closer to the rank and file.

Women

Although the NUM does not report in its affiliated membership returns to the TUC that it has women members, there are, in fact, a very small number of female members who work in canteens, colliery offices, and Area Coal Board offices. The NUM has revised its Rule Book to provide for women membership. Female participation in union activities is almost non-existent.

External Relations

The NUM has extensive international affiliations, in particular with the Miners' International Federation, and the union regularly receives visits from other mining unions abroad. The NUM has taken a special interest in the welfare of Bolivian miners.

The miners have always occupied a special place in the labour movement and although their numbers have declined substantially in recent years (627,298 in 1960) they nevertheless wield a great deal of influence over and above their 240,000 votes at the TUC. At present, the NUM sponsors the following 15 MPs:

Dennis Concannon (Mansfield)
Lawrence Cuncliffe (Leigh)
Alex Eadie (Midlothian)
Ray Ellis (Derbyshire NE)
Alan Fitch (Wigan)
George Grant (Morpeth)
Frank Haynes (Ashfield)
Roy Mason (Barnsley)

Michael McGuire (Ince)
Albert Roberts (Normanton)
Dennis Skinner (Bolsover)
Eric Varley (Chesterfield)
Edwin Wainwright (Dearne Valley)
Michael Welsh (Don Valley)
Alec Woodall (Hemsworth)

In the seven parliaments of the 1918-35 period, miners' MPs accounted for no less than 45 per cent of all trade-union-sponsored MPs, and there were 43 NUM-sponsored MPs in 1923. Although mining areas provide the safest Labour seats in parliament, the steep decline of the mining industry has reduced the number of such bastions. The image of the miners' MP as the typical trade union MP is no longer true.

The job of selecting candidates is left to the areas, and very few guidelines are laid down nationally. The miners rigidly limit their selection of candidates to their own occupational group, i.e. a candidate must be a financial member of one of the NUM constituent associations; have been a mineworker for at least five years; or be a union official or ex-union official.

The pattern of NUM sponsorship has changed substantially over the years. In the past, primary stress was laid on the candidate's social origins, record of union service and local standing. Such candidates typically tended to be from a non-conformist background with only elementary education, were in their late 40s or early 50s, and had entered the mining industry at an early age. Nowadays the NUM is putting forward younger men and appears to have waived its ban on younger NUM officials. The NUM's traditional vitality and high membership participation always ensures that the mining lodges produce a large number of talented candidates.

The union received a great deal of press publicity in 1979-80 when the Barnsley Constituency Labour Party voted to disassociate themselves from 'any MP who does not adhere to the party constitution and annual conference decisions', a clear sign that Roy Mason was very much at odds with party activists — including Arthur Scargill, delegate to the Barnsley GMC from Wooley Colliery Branch of the NUM, his previous workplace.

Roy Mason won the Barnsley nomination in 1953 at the age of 28, when the support of local NUM branches was decisive in securing his nomination against more experienced candidates. Mason has defended the Barnsley seat in eight elections since he was elected MP in 1953. He has been at odds with party activists on a number of issues since he became an MP, particularly on German rearmament, the Bomb, Clause 4 and the Common Market. The pro-EEC stance taken by Mason particularly angered the miners (already not entirely pleased at his support for nuclear power when redundancy was rife in the coal industry). In the 1975 Referendum campaign his views were openly of the 'Yes' variety — against NUM policy. His uneasy relationship with his local Party worsened in 1979 when he wrote a letter to the *Star*, the local evening newspaper, which blamed the unions for losing the previous general election. This provoked the miners to organise themselves within the Barnsley CLP, and the chairperson of the Barnsley CLP, Ron Fisher, replied to this by calling some NUM delegates 'political prostitutes'.

During the year 1979-80, a new branch of the local party was established at Scargill's NUM headquarters; miners have been encouraged to join their ward branches; of 190 applications for party membership, 59 came from NUM members and 53 from the Worsborough area of the town where Arthur Scargill lives. The result, in a party with a total strength of 542, was to increase the number of NUM delegates to the GMC from 21 to 62. The 1980 AGM, with a 2:1 majority over Mason's supporters, voted out the chairperson and replaced him with Norman West, a miner and close friend of Arthur Scargill. Likewise, the treasurer and secretary were replaced by left-wingers and Mr Scargill himself and other miners took 10 of the 16 seats allocated to trade unionists. The Yorkshire NUM has thus gained control of Barnsley CLP and has secured a position from which it can dictate the choice of Barnsley's future Labour candidate in any mandatory re-selection process. It is ironic that the NUM was originally instrumental in giving Roy Mason his seat and is now poised to threaten his removal.

Policy

The NUM is unusual in the sense that its Rule Book provides for a direct membership ballot on major policy-making issues. In particular, industrial action can only be pursued following a Conference resolution provided that 55 per cent of those voting vote in favour.

On the whole the policies of the orthodox Labour majority have generally prevailed in the NUM in the post-war years. Major improvements in the working conditions of miners commenced under a Labour government in 1947, after nationalisation and during a coal shortage. As the decline of the coal industry has continued, the main functioning of the union has been to protect miners' interests in the face of increasing mechanisation, pit closures, and the decline of miners' wage levels relative to others.

The 1982 Annual Conference — the first with Arthur Scargill as president of the union — proved to be an historic occasion. Scargill laid down a radical programme for the NUM in his address to Conference. Central to his plan for the future was the insistence that the NUM was entering a new era, a sharp break with the principles and practice of Lord Gormley his predecessor. The new era would be one of resolute resistance to closures, militant wage campaigning, direct accountability of the leadership to the members, demands for massive expansion of coal output, and the primacy of Annual Conference as the policy-making body in the union.

Conference also voted to resurrect unfulfilled resolutions and press them on the NCB once more. Thus a demand for retirement at 55, higher severance payments and other benefits would be added to the negotiating agenda in all future bargaining.

The dominance of the right-wing on the Executive was broken, and the pointers were set for Scargill to begin re-shaping the NUM to reflect a new era of militancy.

The NUM is opposed to the use of

nuclear power in Britain and is against the stationing of cruise nuclear missiles in Britain. Most NUM regions are affiliated to the Anti-Nuclear Campaign.

Recent Events

In January 1972, the Conservative government faced the first national miners' strike since 1926. Coal stocks were high, but concerted picketing at power stations arrested the movement of fuel. Flying pickets were efficiently organised, miners being accommodated and assisted by local trades councils and other sympathisers; Durham miners picked the Didcot Power Station, for instance. Arthur Scargill played a leading role as organiser of an unofficial strike committee at Barnsley. Turbulent scenes preceded the closure of the Saltley Coke Depot at Birmingham. This led to a state of emergency and to three-day working; Lord Wilberforce was appointed to head a Court of Inquiry into the miners' claim. This conceded the claim virtually in full, but the union secured even more in direct negotiations with the Prime Minister before calling off the strike. As is well known, Heath lost the 1974 general election following a further confrontation with the miners.

At the 1980 NUM Conference Mick McGahey, vice-president, was denied a chance of a seat on the TUC General Council by the casting vote of the president, Joe Gormley. This infuriated the left, who had hoped to see Mick McGahey join Arthur Scargill, Yorkshire area president, on the TUC's governing body. Shouts and jeers filled the hall at Eastbourne as delegates complained of electoral irregularities, and alleged that some delegations had broken their area mandate. Joe Gormley refused to allow a card vote and refused to allow his ruling to be challenged. Arthur Scargill had topped the poll with a tie between McGahey and Chadburn for second place.

A confrontation between the South Wales miners and the goverment was narrowly avoided in February 1981 when, following the NCB's announcement of a list of pit closures to conform to government cash limits, decisive strike action in South Wales and the prospect of support from other coalfields induced the government to make more cash available.

In the summer of 1982, hundreds of miners joined hospital picket lines in support of the health workers in their pay dispute.

The Miners' Pay Ballot
Arthur Scargill's plans to revitalise the NUM and develop a new model union with greater accountability to the rank and file suffered a setback when a ballot vote on willingness to take strike action in pursuit of an improved pay offer went against him in November 1982. Scargill proposed a 30 per cent claim, as against the NCB's offer of 9 per cent, and then linked the pay issue with that of pit closures on the ballot paper. The NCB claimed unfair tactics, and launched an intensive campaign in the newspapers, which may have helped sway some votes. Most miners, however, were influenced by the relatively high pay offer and the very high coal stocks held by the NCB in a depressed market.

The vote against action to improve the pay offer was 125,233 to 81,592 — or 61 per cent to 39 per cent. (Kent, South Wales, Yorkshire and Scotland were strong in their support for Scargill; other areas were strongly against him.)

Arthur Scargill brushed aside the defeat as a temporary setback, blaming it on the 'misleading propaganda of the NCB and the filth of Fleet Street'. Even in the face of the electoral defeat, though, he scored some propaganda points by producing a 'hit-list' of 30 loss-making pits, scheduled for closure, leaked to him, he claimed, from NCB headquarters. Three weeks later, the NCB announced that it intended to close 60 collieries over the next eight years, giving 'exhaustion' as the reason.

Further Reference

There is a voluminous literature on industrial relations in coalmining, largely stemming from the unique place the miners occupy in the evolution of the British labour movement. The classic study of the miners is, of course, that by R. Page Arnot, who has produced several volumes of mining histories. Of special note are the following works:

R. P. Arnot, *The Miners: A History of the Miners' Federation of Great Britain, 1889-1910*, Allen & Unwin 1949.

R. P. Arnot, *The Miners: The Years of Struggle*, Allen & Unwin 1953.

R. P. Arnot, *A History of the Scottish Miners from the Earliest Times*, Allen & Unwin 1955.

R. P. Arnot, *The Miners: One Union, One Industry*, Allen & Unwin 1979.

R. P. Arnot, *The Miners in Crisis and War*, Allen & Unwin 1961.

R. P. Arnot, *The South Wales Miners* (2 vols) Allen & Unwin 1967 and 1975.

J. E. Williams, *The Derbyshire Miners*, Allen & Unwin 1962.

J. D. Edelstein and M. Warner, *Comparative Union Democracy*, Allen & Unwin 1975.

J. Hughes and R. Moore (eds.), *A Special Case? Social Justice and the Miners*, Penguin 1972.

M. Jackson, *The Price of Coal*, Croom Helm 1974.

H. Francis and D. Smith, *The Fed: A History of the South Wales Miners in the Twentieth Century*, Lawrence & Wishart 1980.

B. J. McCormick, *Industrial Relations in the Coal Industry*, Macmillan 1979.

W. R. Garside, *The Durham Miners 1919-60*, Allen & Unwin 1971.

M. Pitt, *The World on our Backs*, Lawrence & Wishart 1979.

Andrew Taylor, 'Miners in the eighties: an analysis', *Political Quarterly*, vol. 53, April 1982.

Group Two Railways

Locomotive Engineers and Firemen, Associated Society of
(ASLEF)

Head Office

9 Arkwright Road
Hampstead
London NW3 6AB
01-435 6300/2160
01-794 7220

Principal Officers

General Secretary —
Ray Buckton
Assistant General Secretary —
D. K. Pullen
Organising Secretaries —
A. Atkinson
E. C. Coules
S. J. R. Goff
L. J. Kirk
N. Milligan
W. H. Ronksley
J. Walker

Membership (1982)

Male 26,219
Female 22
Total 26,241

Union Journal and Publications

Locomotive Journal —
monthly.
ASLEF 1880–1892, a centenary
commemorative brochure,
available from ASLEF, £2.
Engines and Men by J. R.
Raynes, a good account of the
1980–1920 period, available
from ASLEF, price £4.
*Flexible Rostering: The Human
Cost,* although not published
by ASLEF itself, has much
current relevance to the union.
(Published by the Working
Environment Research Group,
Bradford University, and
available from the British
Society for Social
Responsibility in Science, 9
Poland Street, London W1.)

General

ASLEF is the smallest of the three rail
unions. It has consistently sought to
preserve its craft traditions and organises staff in the 'line of promotion'
(to footplate) i.e. traction trainees,
drivers' assistants, relief drivers and
drivers. ASLEF has maintained its
credibility by perpetuating the belief
that drivers are an elite amongst railway workers in skill and responsibility
— although it by no means organises
all railway drivers. Its members are
found in British Rail and on London
Transport

The general secretary, Ray Buckton, is on the TUC General Council.

History

ASLEF reached its centenary year in
1980, having started life in February
1880 as a breakaway from the
*Amalgamated Society of Railway Ser-
vants* (later to become the NUR). The
first branches of ASLEF were at
Sheffield, Pontypool, Neath, Liverpool, Leeds, Bradford, Tondu and
Carnforth. The following year
ASLEF registered as a trade union
with its head office in Leeds. By 1900,
membership had reached nearly
10,000. In 1902 the union affiliated to
the Labour Representation Committee.

ASLEF was involved in the first
national rail strike in 1911, which only
lasted for two days but nevertheless
led to recognition by the railway companies. Although further rail union
amalgamations took place subsequent
to the 1911 strike, ASLEF preferred
to retain its autonomy. The long-
standing differences between the

NUR and ASLEF were exacerbated in early 1924. The railway companies had presented proposals to the National Wages Board which embodied a worsening differential between locomotive drivers and other railway grades. ASLEF decided to strike and were out for nine days whilst the NUR instructed its members to work normally. Although ASLEF achieved its objective of retaining its differential, the hostility between the two unions has continued up to the present day. (See **National Union of Railwaymen**.)

Union Officials

All ASLEF full-time officials (i.e. the general secretary, assistant general secretary and the seven organising secretaries) are elected for a five-year period. Only those with at least five years continuous membership of the union are eligible to stand for election.

Coverage

Nearly all ASLEF members are on British Rail or London Transport. They do, however, have 72 members on the new Tyne and Wear Metro. The whole question of the trade union membership and representation of drivers to be employed on the metro was the subject of a hearing of the TUC disputes committee in August 1977 and at a further hearing in September 1977 where the interested parties were ASLEF, NUR and TGWU. The committee in effect allocated the British Railways Board jobs to ASLEF although the award left many outstanding issues to be resolved among the parties themselves.

On British Rail, ASLEF membership consists mainly of staff in the 'line of promotion' (to footplate), i.e. traction trainees, drivers' assistants, relief drivers and drivers. The union does have some members who are ex-drivers, who have perhaps been promoted to supervisors or failed medically and who work as platform or clerical staff. On London Transport, ASLEF members are mainly train drivers and those in that line of promotion. Members in the latter category may be guards or platform staff. ASLEF covers Great Britain but not Northern Ireland.

Organisation

The supreme government of ASLEF is vested in the 46-strong Annual Assembly of Delegates which meets in May or June each year. Delegates are elected by ASLEF members grouped into 46 districts, arranged in such a way as to secure equal representation of the whole membership; three of the delegates must be from London Transport.

In 1982, ASLEF's rules were changed to provide that the two posts of general secretary and assistant general secretary be subject (once the present incumbents have retired) in future to re-election every five years. The changes, which followed the 1981 AAD's decision for the re-election of ASLEF's regional secretaries, was a fillip to the campaign of left-wingers in the union to make full-time officials more accountable to the union membership.

Elections for the ASLEF Executive, for the senior officers, the union's policy-making Annual Assembly of Delegates, the Labour Party Conference and TUC delegations, are all done on the basis of the block vote of branches, or of members paying the political levy, whichever is appropriate. The overall effect of the branch block vote is to give power to the left, which currently holds sway on the Executive.

In addition to the branch block vote, ASLEF's rules provide that individuals who disagree with the candidate selected by the branch can vote individually — though clearly such individual votes count for little against large branch block votes.

The Executive Committee is responsible for the day-to-day management of the union between AADs. It consists of eight members (one from London Transport), elected for a three-year term of office from each of the nine districts of the union. Each district is administered by a District Council.

The union has 237 branches whose sizes range from five members (Pwllheli) to 639 (Stratford). The membership of ASLEF (in January

1982) was distributed as shown in the table below.

Workplace Activity

ASLEF has representation on around 253 joint management-staff local departmental committees (LDCs), with up to four representatives per LDC, depending on the size of the depot. A few LDCs cover more than one depot. Safety representatives appointed under the terms of the Health and Safety at Work Act, 1974, are allocated on a depot basis. There are no LDCs on London Transport.

Women

At January 1982 there were 22 women in ASLEF: seven on London Transport and 15 on British Rail, of whom three were drivers' assistants. London Transport has at least one woman driver and several guard/motorwomen.

External Relations

ASLEF is affiliated to the Labour Party and maintains a Parliamentary Panel, although at present it has no sponsored MPs. Les Huckfield, Labour MP for Nuneaton, nevertheless maintains parliamentary liaison on railway matters. It is also affiliated to the following organisations:

International Transport Federation
Trade Union Reasearch Unit
Scottish Trades Union Congress
Labour Research Department
Committee of Transport Workers in the EEC
Policy Studies Institute
Liberation
Young Railway Workers' Conference
Royal Society for the Prevention of Accidents

National Council for Civil Liberties
Liberation
Anti-Apartheid Movement
British Soviet Friendship Society
Socialist Environmental Resources Association
Chile Solidarity Campaign
British Bulgarian Trade Union Association
National Peace Council
Amnesty International
National Council on Inland Transport
Campaign for Nuclear Disarmament
British Vietnam Association
Haldane Society
Britain and German Democratic Republic Society

The general secretary, Ray Buckton, is a member of the TUC General Council. There was speculation that he would lose his seat on the General Council following the TUC restructuring plans due to be implemented in 1983.

Labour Party Delegation

ASLEF voted for Tony Benn in both ballots at the 1981 Deputy Leadership contest of the Labour Party. Delegates are elected on a branch vote basis (see **Organisation**).

Policy

In its transport policy document *Transport for the Nation*, published in 1976, ASLEF urged the adoption of a national transport policy based on the following principles:

(a) The various modes of transport to complement — 'not compete against' — each other;

(b) The provision of an adequate public transport system accessible to all;

(c) The rationalisation of freight

Region	Adult	Junior	Retired	Total
Eastern	6,943	364	46	7,353
London Midland	6,660	209	47	6,916
Scottish	2,550	79	10	2,639
Southern	3,722	195	—	3,917
Western	3,169	95	32	3,296
LTE	2,010	37	1	2,048
Tyne and Wear	72	—	—	72
Totals	25,126	979	136	26,241

transport so that each mode operates in a way to which it is most suited;

(d) The conservation of resources, particularly energy. Increased use of those transport systems which are most economical in the use of fuel;

(e) The safeguarding of the environment, priority to be given to measures which will reduce the damaging effects of certain transport modes.

ASLEF's opposition to 'flexible rostering' during 1981 and 1982 made the term almost a household word, as a large part of the media engaged in a hostile campaign against the union's opposition.

Recent Events

Relations between the rail unions, particularly between ASLEF and the NUR, have been poor for many years and several disputes between them went to the TUC Disputes Committee for adjudication. During the 1982 rail strikes ASLEF–NUR relations became extremely bitter. Following the alleged 'betrayal' of ASLEF by the Finance and General Purposes Committee of the TUC on 16 July 1982 ('Black Friday' according to ASLEF), the union issued a press statement which concluded: 'The public utterances of the General Secretary of the National Union of Railwaymen have been contrary to every principle of trade unionism. He has by his actions assisted the British Railways Board at every stage.' Prior to this, agreement had been reached between ASLEF and the NUR in 1981 for the setting up of a Federation of Railway Unions (see **National Union of Railwaymen**), but at the time of writing the newly established federation had yet to meet.

ASLEF embarked on a series of one-day strikes in early 1982 over the issue of flexible rostering and whether British Rail had the right to withhold an extra three per cent wage increase — part of the 1981 pay agreement — until ASLEF had conceded flexibility on rosters. The issue was put back to Lord McCarthy, chairperson of the Railway Staff National Tribunal, under the auspices of ACAS for adjudication. In the event, McCarthy judged that ASLEF should accept flexible rosters as part of the introduc-

tion of the 39-hour week, subject to guarantees. In May 1982 ASLEF argued that these guarantees — on the length and unpredictability of rosters, unsocial hours, the right to swap shifts and 'travel to work' times — would make the whole exercise unworkable.

ASLEF's decision to strike in July 1982 was taken on 29 June, after British Rail's decision that new rosters' would be posted at depots from Sunday, 4 July, and anyone refusing to work them would be suspended. A prolonged strike by NUR members (see **National Union of Railwaymen**) would have taken the pressure off ASLEF, but the decision of the NUR Conference to call off their strike over pay and productivity left ASLEF isolated. The ASLEF strike went ahead from 4 July and lasted for two weeks. The strike had to be called off after the TUC Finance and General Purposes Committee (after a marathon meeting involving discussions with ASLEF, the NUR, TSSA, the CSEU, and with representatives of the British Railways Board at ACAS headquarters) agreed on a formula to end the strike which, instead of supporting ASLEF, came to an agreement whereby British Rail would withdraw its intention to give notice of dismissal, and would withdraw its notice to close the railway system on 21 July, provided that ASLEF called off the strike and allowed flexible rostering to go ahead, albeit on a provisional agreement. ASLEF described the decision of the TUC Committee as 'Black Friday' and by any measure it was the greatest humiliation handed out by the TUC to an affiliated union since the TUC refused to support the firefighters' strike in 1977.

The strike left a legacy of bitterness among ASLEF members and will do nothing to improve ASLEF–NUR relations, which represent sectionalism in the British trade union movement at its worst, regardless of the rights and wrongs of the dispute.

Subsequent to the strike, a new draft agreement was drawn up in August 1982 which differed slightly from the McCarthy Railway Staff National Tribunal decision. McCarthy had originally specified that, in flexible rostering, the majority of new shifts or turns should not exceed eight hours. 'Majority' was tightly defined in the agreement as 51 per cent at any depot. The agreement further specified that normally a rostered week would be a maximum of 44 hours over five days though, with local agreement, 52 hours 30 minutes could be worked. Where turns were longer than 8½ hours the figures would be 45 hours and 54 hours respectively. The agreement set up two new joint working parties. One would review the progressive reduction of unsocial hours worked. The other would examine problems of drivers' travel to work — an important point in the ASLEF case. All restored overtime was precluded under the terms of the agreement, though BR went some way towards meeting drivers' fears about exchanging shifts between themselves by stating that 'management will endeavour to assist men who have difficulty in arranging mutual exchanges'. British Rail agreed that any jobs lost through the introduction of such flexible rostering would not lead to compulsory redundancy.

Between May 1980 and June 1982, 17,000 jobs disappeared on British railways. With the Conservative government refusing to provide desperately needed new investment unless British Rail could secure radical changes in working practices, further reductions in membership of both ASLEF and the NUR are likely. The loss of around 3,000 jobs could kill ASLEF's position as a separate union entirely.

Further Reference

N. McKillop, *The Lighted Flame : A History of ASLEF*, Thomas Nelson 1950. This is the official history of ASLEF up to 1949. Whilst it contains a good account of the union's development it suffers from adopting a very uncritical perspective and is extremely biased — especially in describing the NUR–ASLEF disputes.

Railwaymen, National Union of
(NUR)

Head office

Unity House
Euston Road
London NW1 2BL
01-387 4771

Principal Officers

General Secretary—
vacant (see **Recent Events**)
Assistant General Secretaries
— R. J. Tuck
C. Turnock
A. Dodds

Membership (1982)

Male 148,538
Female 8,817
Total 157,355

Union Journal and Publications

Transport Review—
fortnightly. The NUR supplements this with a series of detailed newsletters to particular sections of the membership. The union also has a selection of historical publications: *The Railwaymen, vols 1 and 2, History of the NUR*, the NUR centenary book, *The Railway Servants* and *The NUR 150th Anniversary of Railways.*
People's Road, poems by Joe Smythe, illustrated by Derek Jones: railway poetry by two members of the NUR, specially written for and commissioned by the NUR for the 150th anniversary of the Liverpool and Manchester Railway, 1980. Excellent value at 95p.

General

The NUR is the biggest of the three rail unions and, although its membership has declined substantially in post-war years, it still exerts considerable influence in the trade union movement. The NUR and its precursor, the *Amalgamated Society of Railway Servants*, occupy a special place in the history of British trade unionism, especially in connection with the Taff Vale case and the Osborne judgement, and in having played a prominent role in the events leading to the foundation of the Labour Party. The NUR supports industrial unionism — a continuing difference of principle with the craft union, ASLEF, with which rivalry has persisted, despite some abortive attempts at amalgamation. It is likely to face further membership losses if the labour force on the railways is further cut back in the search for productivity gains, as several economists have recommended and which internal British Rail documents have indicated. The Tory government seems intent on hiving off some of the more profitable areas of British Rail to the private sector but this may not necessarily affect membership.

The former general secretary, Sid Weighell, is a member of the TUC general council.

History

In 1871 a group of railway workers met in Leeds to form the *Amalgamated Society of Railway Servants (ASRS)*. The first general secretary was George Chapman, a mechanic from Woolwich. Within a year of its formation the ASRS had more than 17,000 members.

The period from the early 1880s to 1913 was the significant formative period in the history of railway trade unionism (ASLEF was formed in 1880) and in the trade union and labour movement in Britain as a whole.

The trade union movement suffered two blows from the courts — the Taff Vale case and the Osborne judgement — both involving the ASRS. The Taff Vale case arose from a strike on the Taff Vale railway in South Wales, following the alleged victimisation of a signalman who had led a movement for a pay rise. Although the strike itself lasted only 11 days, the litigation reached the House of Lords where a decision of profound importance was made: that trade union funds were liable for damages inflicted by their officials. The total costs arising from the case, for which the ASRS was made liable,

amounted to no less than £42,000, an enormous sum in those days. Legislation giving trade unions immunity from such actions for damages was passed in the Trade Disputes Act of 1906.

The Osborne case followed an ASRS decision in 1903 to introduce a compulsory political levy of one shilling per member per year to augment Labour Party funds. W. V. Osborne, secretary of the Walthamstow branch of the union and a member of the Liberal Party, decided to bring an action to restrain the union from contributing to the upkeep of the Labour Party — a restraint eventually supported and confirmed by the Court of Appeal. Union leaders reacted angrily and at the 1910 Trades Union Congress a resolution calling for legislation to reverse the Osborne judgement was carried overwhelmingly. It was not until 1913 that a new Trade Union Act provided for this reversal.

The first national rail strike took place in 1911, largely as a result of management's refusal to re-negotiate the terms of arbitration originally agreed in 1907. The strike lasted for just two days. A Royal Commission was set up to examine the operation of the railway conciliation boards and, following its report later in the year, a new scheme was introduced. After many years of insisting on an almost military discipline from their employees, the railway companies conceded recognition of the rail unions, and membership then grew rapidly.

The most important outcome of the 1911 strike was the amalgamation of the ASRS with the *United Pointsmen's and Signalmen's Society* (UPSS), formed in 1880, and the *General Railway Workers' Union* (GRWU), formed in 1890, to form the National Union of Railwaymen on 29 March 1913. The executive committees of these three unions, together with that of ASLEF, had met during and after the strike. At a 'fusion of forces' conference in Manchester in 1911, the main principles of an amalgamation scheme were agreed but ASLEF later withdrew when its executive disagreed with the terms of amalgamation.

At its inception the NUR had nearly 180,000 members, of which 23,158 had belonged to the GRWU and 4,100 to the UPSS. Membership quickly increased to a total of 273,000 by 1914.

After the second world war, the railways declined. Despite nationalisation and attempts to develop a sensible, efficient, integrated transport system, competition from road haulage, buses and — most of all — from private motor vehicles (temporarily advantaged by cheap petrol) cast the railways in a poor light. Employment fell and, with it, NUR membership — from 254,687 in 1965 to 180,000 in 1978. Most of this reduction came with the Beeching cuts which severely mutilated the rail network.

Union Officials

The NUR has 21 full-time officers of whom six are based at head office and the rest distributed throughout the country. For the purpose of organisation, the country is divided into 13 areas and, in addition, one divisional officer has sole responsibility for London Transport staff. All officials of the NUR are elected on a single transferable vote system.

Coverage

The NUR is often described as one of the best examples of an 'industrial' union but this is an oversimplification. The union describes itself as a 'union of railway and ancillary workers of all grades and, historically, the industrial basis of NUR organisation has been affected by the vertically integrated characteristics of the railways before and after nationalisation. The NUR followed the railway companies' moves into bus operation and the diversified activities of British Rail — hotels and catering, docks and harbours (and Sealink ferry services), railway workshops and engineering — all blurring the picture of industrial unionism.

The NUR is in competition with other unions — the TSSA and ASLEF — for recruitment of railway employees. The NUR could be described as more open, in the sense of being willing to take into membership any groups or grades within the railway industry or associated trades and services, such as dock workers and hotel and catering workers. This policy is in sharp contrast to that of ASLEF which retains the traditional exclusivity of a craft union, restricting membership to those grades in the industry who are drivers or 'are in line of promotion to driver'.

In September 1981, with the help of the TUC general secretary, a Federation of Railway Trade Unions was formed to include the NUR and ASLEF. (The TSSA decided not to join the Federation — its main objection being to the last of the federation's eight objectives, which was to work towards the establishment of one union on the railways.) By mid-1982 the Federation was tottering on the brink of collapse, with not one meeting actually taking place. The historic link-up, however loose, between the rival unions was overtaken by the railway strikes of 1982 when relations between ASLEF and the NUR became openly hostile and bitter. The agreement setting up the Federation provided for the NUR to cease recruiting staff on British Rail within the existing line of promotion to train driver and to encourage transfers to ASLEF of staff who, as from 1 September 1981 (the operative date of the Federation), transfer to one of these grades. ASLEF would do the reverse when staff left the footplate line of promotion grades.

An accurate assessment of the coverage of the NUR vis-a-vis ASLEF is extremely difficult. ASLEF claims some 96 per cent of the drivers on the railways as being in membership. In contrast, the NUR has its membership distributed over a very wide range of railway and ancillary grades. It claims 80 per cent of all grades in London Transport and 70 per cent of British Rail workshops staff. It can be estimated that the NUR covers perhaps 50 per cent of salaried staff, National Carriers, Freightliners, docks and harbours, bus drivers and others.

All three rail unions are signatories to a closed shop agreement with British Rail. The NUR is signatory to agreements with:

British Rail (and associated activities)
London Transport

National Freight Corporation
British Transport Docks Board
British Waterways Board
Manchester Ship Canal Company
Ffestiniog Railway
Midland Catering Company
National Bus Company
Forth Ports Authority
Tees and Hartlepools Authority
Port of Tyne Authority
Scottish Transport Group

Organisation

The supreme governing body in the NUR is the two-week Annual General Meeting, commencing on the last Monday in June. There are 77 delegates, one from each divisional area into which the branches are grouped for electoral purposes.

The union's general management is vested in its Executive Committee which consists of 26 lay members elected for a period of three years. The president, general secretary and the three assistant general secretaries also serve on the Executive Committee without the right to vote. The Executive Committee holds mandatory meetings on three fortnights during the year and special meetings take place as necessary in between. In addition, the Executive members are in constant session through subcommittees representing all the various job interests. The Executive Committee, which had its first woman member in 1982, consists of four loco drivers, six traffic representatives, four NCL/Freightliners workers, six railway workshop employees, two permanent way representatives, two from hotels and catering services, two from London Transport and one each from road passenger transport and docks and shipping services.

Sid Weighell made a point of stressing that the NUR is second to none in trade union democracy; an examination of the NUR Rule Book goes a considerable way towards supporting this point of view. The single transferable vote system is used to elect the union's 21 full-time officers, including its general secrtary and assistant general secretary, as well as the Executive Committee and Conference delegates.

The Executive is full-time; the 26 members are elected for three years, with a third of them standing down each year. In 1980, the Executive swung to the left, largely helped by changes in the system of Executive elections agreed in 1978, which removed some of the NUR's 'rotten boroughs'. This new system brought some younger activists onto the Executive and led to an increase of tension between the Executive and Sid Weighell, which manifested itself on several occasions during 1981 and 1982, and was one of the factors which eventually led to Weighell's resignation in October 1982.

In contrast, the NUR Annual Conference is much more moderate in its views. Each of the 77 delegates represents three or four branches, with the larger and more left-dominated branches, such as St. Pancras, Tinsley and Paddington, exercising considerable influence (branch size in the NUR varies from about 100 members to more than 1,000). In many districts of the NUR the branches arrange a rota for attending the Annual Conference. Thus in 1982, 41 were elected as delegates unopposed, and over half were branch officials. While many of them had a great deal of local experience (many were over 50) they tended to defer to the leadership on national issues, and few activists attended the Conference.

The NUR Rule Book also provides for the establishment of district councils covering the country. Their main purpose is to maintain a high standard of organisation throughout the branches in the respective districts. They are consultative bodies and they organise grade committees where delegates from branches discuss problems relating to their own grades.

The total number of NUR branches is 580. The term 'shop steward' is unknown in the NUR but a rough estimate of the number of 'local representatives' is around 3,000.

Women

Women constitute around 5 per cent of the total NUR membership. There is one female representative on the Executive, but no female full-time officials. Women NUR members are generally to be found among hotel staff, carriage cleaners, clerical staff and typists. Recently there has been a tendency for a small number of women to be employed in other grades, such as guards, station staff and even in the footplate line of promotion. The NUR elects delegates to attend the TUC Women's Conference and the Conference of Labour Women every year.

External Relations

The NUR is affiliated to the Labour Party and has a long tradition of parliamentary sponsorship equalled only by the miners' union. Like the miners, the railway workers traditionally exhibit strong solidarity, although events in 1982 during the rail strikes perhaps brought this tradition into question, with ASLEF and the NUR accusing each other of crossing picket lines. Both industries have undergone ruthless rationalisation in the postwar years with a consequent shrinkage in union strength and parliamentary representation. The NUR representatives in the House of Commons tend not to be union officials and in the 1970 parliament all NUR-sponsored MPs were former rank-and-file railway workers who entered parliament at an average age of 48. Recent rule alterations in the NUR now provide for sponsorship of candidates of a wider transport background than railways alone. At the 1980 AGM, the NUR called on the Labour Party to re-introduce its list of proscribed organisations whose political beliefs are incompatible with party membership, (citing particularly the Socialist Workers' Party and the Workers' Revolutionary Party).

At the 1981 Annual Conference, NUR delegates voted in a secret ballot to cast the NUR's block vote in favour of Denis Healey in the Labour Party Deputy Leadership election. Had the decision been made by the NUR Executive, the vote might well have gone for Tony Benn. The union's delegates to the TUC and Labour Party Conferences are elected by branch vote, one from each of the six districts. Policy, however, is laid down by the NEC in accordance with decisions of the Annual General Meeting and Executive Committee.

In his political report to the 1982 Annual General Meeting, Sid Weighell bemoaned the conflicts within the Labour Party: 'Hopes that the vote on the deputy leadership would mean the end of the confrontation within the Party have proved groundless. The struggle continues as bitterly as ever before, and we have paid the price of it in successive by-elections. It will continue because the forces which arrayed themselves behind the Benn candidature, so forcefully opposed by this union, are not interested in compromise. A grouping like the Militant Tendency and other rag tag and bobtail trotskyite groups which have gained influence in recent years are only interested in the Labour Party as a means to an end. Revolution — not reform through the ballot box — is their objective, and the Labour Party is their chosen vehicle.'

The NUR sponsors ten Labour MPs:

L. Spriggs (St. Helens)
G. A. T. Bagier (Sunderland South)
R. H. Lewis (Carlisle)
P. C. Snape (West Bromwich East)
H. Cowans (Newcastle-upon-Tyne Central)
R. Cook (Edinburgh Central)
T. Dalyell (West Lothian)
P. Whitehead (Derby North)
D. Anderson (Swansea East)
D. Dewar (Glasgow Garscadden)

Policy

The NUR advocates the development of an integrated transport system with an expanding role for railways which can be justified economically and environmentally, particularly with electrified railways. The union obviously opposes hiving off any part of railway operations. The railway workers see a parallel with the policies of 1952 when the old British Transport Commission was broken up and the more profitable part of the business — road freight — was restored to private ownership, paving the way for the Beeching cuts.

It continues to be NUR policy to create one union for the railway industry. The NUR's position on incomes policy is best illustrated by an extract of Sid Weighell's speech to the

Sheffield and Chesterfield District Council of the NUR in August 1982: 'We should not be afraid to tell the people we believe in the planned growth of incomes as part of a socialist economic plan for the country's recovery and denounce free collective bargaining as the "philosophy of the pig trough".'

Recent Events

The rail unions are notable for their role in events associated with the Industrial Relations Act of 1971. When the unions imposed a work-to-rule and overtime ban during a pay dispute, the Secretary of State used the emergency procedures available under the Act, applying for a 'cooling off' period (section 138 of the Act). The necessary order for this was granted by the National Industrial Relations Court which deemed the work-to-rule as 'irregular industrial action short of a strike'. After this the Secretary of State applied to the National Industrial Relations Court for a ballot of the union members concerned. This was so ordered and the Commission on Industrial Relations which had become a kind of field officer for the NIRC under the Industrial Relations Act, conducted the ballot. The ballot result showed a substantial majority in all three unions in favour of continued action: clear evidence giving the lie to the still much-canvassed view that secret ballots of union members would restrain militancy. An improved pay offer was needed to resolve the dispute.

Despite such joint action, relations between the NUR and ASLEF have remained cool if not antagonistic. Whether ASLEF members are entitled to a pay differential has remained a bone of contention, and Lord McCarthy's railway pay tribunal has been regularly employed in the search for compromise solutions.

Relations between the NUR and ASLEF worsened considerably on two occasions in 1982. In August 1981, a meeting held under the auspices of ACAS with the three rail unions and BR resulted in a pay and productivity agreement. The productivity understanding committed the parties to complete discussions by given target dates on six issues, including flexible rostering, in exchange for a new pay agreement. Subsequently ASLEF claimed that the 1981 agreement did not require it to discuss any flexibility in work rostering which involved a shift from the guaranteed eight-hour working day established in 1919. After a series of one-day strikes by ASLEF in January 1982, and a Committee of Inquiry chaired by Lord McCarthy, BR responded by modifying the rosters and introducing pilot schemes in different parts of the country. The NUR general secretary appeared to side with BR when he said that if ASLEF never intended to move from the eight-hour day, it should never have signed the original August 1981 agreement.

During 1982, the attitude of BR hardened and the pay and productivity issue surfaced again by the summer. The NUR claimed that it had delivered on all its commitments and that both BR and the government had failed to honour clear promises to use the considerable savings achieved from past productivity measures to improve pay and conditions. The NUR then called a national strike which was abruptly suspended after two days by delegates at the Annual Delegate Meeting, who supported a motion from the platform which asked for the issue to be referred to the Railway Staff National Tribunal. ASLEF called a strike 24 hours later on the issue of flexible rostering, which left it isolated, and after the General Council of the TUC had failed to support ASLEF's case (see **ASLEF**) relations between the NUR and ASLEF were more hostile and bitter than ever before, with both unions measurably weaker.

ASLEF maintains its credibility as a 'craft' union by perpetuating a belief that drivers are an elite among railway workers in respect of skill and responsibility. This belief becomes increasingly difficult to justify; electric and diesel trains and modern signalling are steps toward full automation of the driving function. The mechanisation and simplification of drivers' jobs have affected their status and the drivers' independent line of promotion has all but disappeared. At the same time there has been a drastic decline in the number of footplate workers (total membership of ASLEF declined from 72,000 in 1946 to 27,738 in 1978). In 1976 British Rail employed over 21,000 drivers and 7,000 second drivers but only 13,000 guards. Since work regulations limit what a driver can do without a guard being in attendance, the rationale of a separate footplate workers' grade is increasingly called into question. However, the members of ASLEF still cling to the view that they should have sole negotiating rights for footplate workers and there is strong support for the continued existence of a separate drivers' union, although the NUR has 2,000 drivers in membership.

Both the NUR and ASLEF were facing a series of productivity issues with BR, some of which had already been referred to the Railway Staff National Tribunal at the time of writing. Briefly, there were six main issues involved, all of which threatened jobs among the membership of both unions.

Flexible rostering would affect at least 850 jobs, mainly among ASLEF members but also including NUR guards. The proposals for single staffing of passenger trains, whereby guards would be displaced where newly capitalised technology — electrification, signalling, rolling stock, drivers/signalers communications — allowed for it (e.g. on the Bedford–St. Pancras line) would lead to the immediate threat to 330 NUR jobs. Whilst many guards could be transferred to other guards' jobs, if the principle of dropping guards were to be accepted, over 5,000 guards' jobs would dissappear as sliding-door trains were introduced. The staffing of freight trains, whereby 2,500 NUR jobs would go as guards were removed from freight trains, posed a further threat of job loss; 2,300 ASLEF jobs were in jeopardy as a result of proposals for single-staffing of train engines. The 'trainman concept' whereby rigid lines of demarcation between the NUR and ASLEF would be eliminated over the line of promotion to train driver posed a dangerous threat to the whole notion of ASLEF's belief in its members' skills and responsibilities. According to the 'trainman concept' staff would be able to cross existing union boundaries to rise for instance from station staff to driver. The NUR naturally welcomed this proposal but ASLEF was hostile to the idea. Finally, the proposals for open stations, with ticket staff at stations being replaced by a system of train staff themselves checking tickets and collecting fares had already been agreed by the NUR.

All these proposals for productivity on the railways, together with increasingly hardened attitudes taken by both BR and the government, meant that both main rail unions were facing the greatest test since the Beeching Report.

The Sidney Weighell Affair

At the 1982 Labour Party Conference there was a major row over the NUR's vote for elections to the trade-union section of the Labour Party NEC. The NUR Conference had mandated its delegates to vote for Eric Clarke of the NUM, in line with a long-established tradition that each union would support the other's candidates. It was subsequently discovered that the NUR's vote had in fact gone to Tom Breakell, a right-winger from the EETPU.

Following the publicity about this affair, Weighell surprised his Executive by tendering his resignation before it was able formally to censure him. Soon after announcing his resignation it quickly became clear that if the recalled NUR special conference to consider the McCarthy arbitration award were to ask him to withdraw his resignation, he would be happy to reconsider.

But his faith in the members' judgement was misplaced and his gamble to be returned to office on a wave of membership acclamation failed by 41 votes to 36.

Further Reference

P. S. Bagwell, *The National Union of Railwaymen 1913-1963*, NUR 1963.

P. S. Bagwell, *The Railwaymen*, 2 vols, Allen & Unwin 1963 and 1982.

J. D. M. Bell, *Industrial Unionism: A Critical Analysis*, McNaughton & Gowenlock 1949.

N. McKillop, *The Lighted Flame: A History of ASLEF*, Thomas Nelson 1950.

S. Weighell, 'Rail workshops', *Labour Monthly* 1972.

F. McKenna, *The Railway Workers, 1840-1970*, Faber.

Transport Salaried Staffs' Association

(TSSA)

Head Office

Walkden House
10 Melton Street
London NW1 2EJ
01-387 2101

Principal Officers

General Secretary—
C. A. Lyons
Assistant General Secretaries
— Vacant
N. Hitchin (who also acts as *Deputy General Secretary*)
Finance and Organising Officer
W. I. Etherington
Research Officer—
P. H. Wyatt
Divisional Secretaries—
R. A. Rosser
D. C. Burn
G. D. Orbell
J. Juby
V. N. Birnie
J. L. Richardson
D. D. Lee — (based at York)
C. A. Cullen — (based at Glasgow)
J. D. Casey — (based at Dublin)
President— J. Mills
Treasurer— S. Cohen MP

Membership (1982)

Total 64,361
(The union no longer breaks down its membership between men and women).
These figures reported to the TUC include the 2,402 TSSA members in Ireland. (See **External Relations**.)

Union Journal and Publications

Transport Salaried Staff Journal— monthly,
distributed free to all members. The union publishes an informative booklet, *A Look at Life in the TSSA,* as well as a diary for members.

Divisional Officers

The TSSA divisional officers are nearly all based at HQ in London, although the union maintains three offices in York, Glasgow and Dublin.

● *Eastern Region*
Yorkshire Bank Chambers
46a Coney Street
York Y01 1NG

● *Scotland*
180 Hope Street
Glasgow G2

● *Ireland*
8 Upper O'Connell Street
Dublin 1

General

The TSSA is one of the oldest established white-collar unions in Britain. It organises administrative, professional and technical and supervisory staffs in the transport industry in Great Britain and Ireland, together with associated undertakings. The union caters for such occupations as clerks, typists, drawing technicians, inspectors, station managers, ships' officers, hotel receptionists, chemists, architects, quantity surveyors, computer staff, engineers, and photographers. The TSSA affiliated to the TUC in 1903 and has a long tradition of allying itself with the labour movement. Traditionally the TSSA has been linked entirely with railways, although in recent years, largely as a result of legislation, well over a third of TSSA members are employed outside of British Rail in other transport undertakings.

Tom Jenkins retired as general secretary in 1982, and was succeeded by Bert Lyons, a 52-year-old former railway clerk. Lyons, an assistant general secretary for nine years, polled 36,000 votes — 61 per cent of those cast — in a five-sided contest. The closest runners-up were Derek Lee, a divisional secretary, with 6,700, and Norman Hitchen, an assistant general secretary, with 6,500.

History

The TSSA came into existence in May 1897 at Sheffield under the name of the *Railway Clerks' Association*. Despite the hostility of the railway managements, the RCA managed to maintain its existence and affiliated to the TUC in 1903, by which time it had grown from a membership of 297 in 1897 to 4,034 at the end of 1903.

The RCA faced its first major crisis in 1906 when its general secretary died in tragic circumstances. A young goods agent, A. G. Walkden, accepted the post of general secretary of the RCA at a substantial loss in salary and guided the RCA for the next 30 years. By 1914 the RCA had 233 branches and a total membership of 29,394; up to that time the railway managements refused to recognise or receive representations from the RCA and its only contact with management was through RCA-inspired deputations and round-robins. In 1919, the RCA secured recognition backed by a membership of 84,337 and the threat of strike action. By 1921 national negotiating machinery had been set up.

The inter-war years saw the RCA involved in the amalgamation of the old railway companies, the General Strike in 1926, the election of railway workers to parliament, the establishment of superannuation funds and the foundation of the London Passenger Transport Board. (For greater detail on the history of the railway unions, see **National Union of Railwaymen**.)

An important post-second-world-war event was the transfer of inland transport to state ownership. This was particularly important in road haulage and canals, where independent firms and authorities were welded into nation-wide undertakings, thus providing a reservoir of potential members. In 1951, the RCA changed its name to the Transport Salaried Staffs' Association to reflect its wider membership.

The TSSA has continually widened its membership in the post-war years, largely as a result of transport rationalisation stemming from government legislation, e.g. the 1968 Transport Act, which resulted in the transfer of the railway sundries and frieghtliner business to National Carriers Ltd and Freightliners Ltd. Today, the TSSA has 294 branches and a total membership of over 66,500 (including Irish members) about a quarter of whom are women.

Union Officials

All full-time officials of the TSSA are appointed by the 29-strong Executive Committee. The union employs a divisional secretary for each of the railway regions (the SR divisional secretary also covers BR Shipping and International Services Division and BR Hovercraft); one for BRB HQ, BR Eng. Ltd, NCL; one for London Transport and London Country Bus Services; one for Docks, Hotels, Waterways, BRS and other NFC undertakings; one for travel trade and one for Irish undertakings, including the CIE. All TSSA officials are appointed from within the union.

Coverage

The TSSA represents salaried staff at British Rail and its associated organisations; British Transport Docks; British Waterways; National Freight Company; Freightliners Ltd; British Road Services; Pickfords; London Transport; Manchester Ship Canal and other port authorities; various travel agencies including Thomsons and the Thomas Cook Group Ltd; and transport undertakings in Ireland, including Coras Iompair Eirann (CIE), Ulsterbus, Northern Ireland Railways, and the Londonderry and Lough Swilly Railway.

Organisation

The supreme government of the TSSA is vested in the Annual Delegate Conference, which consists of delegates from branches. Each branch has the right to be represented at Conference by one to three delegates, according to size, and to submit two motions and two amendments for the agenda. Two additional motions and amendments relating to TSSA rules are allowed every fifth year when rule alterations are considered. Conference is held in either May or June each year.

The TSSA branches are grouped

geographically into divisions. At present there are 17 divisions in England and Wales (including a separate division for London Transport), two in Scotland and two in Ireland. Each division is administered by a divisional council which consists of delegates elected by the constituent branches. The delegates in turn elect the council officers and divisional committee. The main function of the divisional council is to oversee the organisation of the TSSA within its constituent branches.

The Executive Committee consists of 21 area representatives elected by ballot of individual members in each divisional council area, plus six sectional representatives who are elected by the whole of the membership by branch ballot. Executive Committee members are elected for a three-year term; they can be re-elected except that they are limited to six years' consecutive service on the Committee. Then they cannot serve again until a further three years have elapsed. The president and treasurer, who are elected annually by branch ballot, are ex-officio members of the EC.

At head office there are departments to look after legal affairs, national insurance and superannuation, research, the *Journal*, organisation, finance and education. TSSA had 294 branches at the end of 1981.

Women

Although women constitute around a quarter of TSSA membership there are no women full-time officers and only two women members of the 29-strong Executive Committee. Women mainly occupy the clerical and typing jobs in transport undertakings.

External Relations

The TSSA has a long tradition of involvement with the labour movement, and it sponsors two Labour MPs: S. Cohen (Leeds South East) and W. H. Johnson (Derby South). A former union-sponsored Labour MP, Tom Bradley (Leicester East) has since defected to the Social Democrats. The TSSA also sponsors MPs in the Dail Eireann (Irish parliament). Over 85 per cent of TSSA's membership contribute to its political fund — a very high proportion given that it is a

white-collar union. The union is affiliated to the Fabian Society, the Association of Friends of Socialist Commentary, United Nations Association and the Socialist Medical Association. The TSSA is also involved in supporting its sister rail and transport unions in Europe in defence of public transport: it is affiliated to the International Transport Workers' Federation, as well as to Transport 2000. The TSSA also has 2,402 Irish members, and the union is affiliated to the Irish Congress of Trade Unions.

The TSSA has not only sponsored younger men for parliament, including even its younger leading officials, but also it has been willing to allow them to combine union and political roles for long periods. For example, Tom Bradley was only 36 and was union treasurer when he entered parliament. He had been a member and former chairperson of the National Executive Committee of the Labour Party before defecting to the Social Democrats.

Labour Party Delegation

The TSSA sent 13 delegates to the Labour Party Conference in October 1981: the general secretary, the president, two members appointed by the Executive Committee, the remainder being elected by branch voting (under a system whereby the whole of each branch's votes are credited to the candidate winning a majority). At the Annual Delegate Conference in May 1981 an emergency motion was carried (including an amendment) which required the delegation to ensure that the Parliamentary Labour Party had a majority voting power in any leadership election. A motion was put forward to support Denis Healey for the Deputy Leadership contest, which was lost, as was a motion to support Tony Benn. The delegation was therefore not mandated by the ADC, and the TSSA Executive Committee subsequently decided that the union's votes should be cast in favour of Denis Healey. The EC had the power to do this under Rule 16 (f).

Policy

The TSSA has actively campaigned for a socialist approach to transport policy both nationally and internationally. It has been heavily involved in advocating that the British rail network should be electrified and extended, and has supported the building of a Rail Channel Tunnel. The ex-general secretary of TSSA, Tom Jenkins, successfully moved the resolution on transport policy for a second successive year at Trades Union Congress 1981. Tom Jenkins also moved motions on transport policy at Labour Party Conferences in 1980 and 1981. The TSSA seconded a motion advocating a reduction in the arms race which was moved by the Inland Revenue Staff Federation in 1978.

Recent Events

The election of the Conservatives in 1979 meant that the TSSA was engaged in opposing cuts in transport services and the hiving-off of profitable state-run concerns to private industry as provided for in the Transport Act, 1980. It was also heavily involved in the rail disputes during 1982 putting much effort into trying to resolve the disputes without recourse to industrial action.

Group Three Transport (other than Railways)

British Airline Pilots' Association
(BALPA)

Head Office

81 New Road
Harlington
Hayes
Middlesex UB3 5BG
01-759 9331/5

Divisional Office

Rooms 29/30
The Beehive
Gatwick Airport
Horley
Surrey

Principal Officers

President — Sir Alexander Glen
General Secretary —
Mark Young

Membership (1982)

Male 4,313
Female 6
Total 4,319

Union Journal

The Log, circulation around 6,000

General

BALPA claims to represent over 90 per cent of all pilots in the UK civil air transport industry. It employs full-time professional staff to run the union. These include, apart from the general secretary, a deputy general secretary, technical secretary, technical assistant, British Airways industrial relations officer, independent pilots industrial relations officer, and a research officer. There is a divisional branch office at Gatwick, which is run by an assistant industrial relations officer for independent pilots. The head office is split into a technical department, British Airways industrial relations department, independent pilots industrial relations department, and administration.

BALPA rules provide that full membership of the union is open to any person actively engaged in British commercial flying who holds a current commercial pilot's licence, a senior commercial pilot's licence, or airline transport pilot's licence or equivalent, provided that he/she does not perform managerial or executive duties with a British Civil Air Transport organisation.

General Secretary Mark Young was a member of the reform group in the ETU which deposed the Communist leadership of that union after the ballot rigging trial (see EETPU). He was later sacked by Frank Chapple and no reason was given for his dismissal.

Organisation

The supreme government of BALPA is vested in a special General Meeting of the whole of the membership specially convened. BALPA organises itself into branches of pilots' local councils at any base where five or more members are employed. A Delegates Conference, representing various sections of the membership, meets each year. The Annual Delegates Conference elects the lay section of the National Executive Council.

The NEC has the power to initiate any kind of industrial action. It may decide to hold a ballot among the members concerned in such industrial action but it is not bound by the ballot result.

History

A pilot's union had been formed as early as 1924, but it only lasted for a short time. BALPA itself came into being in May 1937, following unrest among the pilots of the main government-supported airline — Imperial Airways Ltd. Much of this unrest centred around the use of obsolete aircraft, the lack of new equipment (particularly for de-icing and blind flying) on the Continental routes of Imperial Airways.

An ex-pilot, W. R. D. Perkins, Conservative MP for Stroud, became vice-president of the union in October 1937. As a result of a well received speech in the House of Commons, Robert Perkins was successful in securing the setting up of a Committee of Inquiry into the civil aviation industry.

One of the early problems facing BALPA was the relationship with the professional association for pilots — the Guild of Air Pilots and Air Navigators. As a result of several meetings between the guild and BALPA, an agreement was reached which provided for co-ordination between the two bodies on matters of common interest.

BALPA secured recognition from Imperial Airways in 1938 and affiliated to the TUC in 1943.

External Relations

BALPA is not affiliated to any political party and does not support or sponsor any MPs.

Main Agreement

BALPA has a union membership agreement with British Airways, British Caledonian Airlines and Monarch Airlines. It also has a large membership in most independent airline companies.

Recent Events

BALPA is currently facing the worst recession in the airline industry since the war, with pilot unemployment growing every month. In British Airways alone there were heavy redundancies, with 67 pilots taking early retirement by August 1981.

The collapse of Laker Airways added to the redundancy total. As the chairperson of BALPA noted in the April 1982 issue of *The Log*: 'Sir Freddy Laker has assuredly made a great contribution to folk history; he is also said to have made a great contribution to aviation. Certainly it will never be the same again, although in bankrupting his own business, in failing with such enormous liabilities and in raising the expectations of the general public to an unrealistic and unsustainable level, he might also be said to have brought it into disrepute . . . Finally, amid the talk of the "People's Airline" we return to the former Laker staff. In view of the previous track record I wonder whether "The People's Airline" intends to pay its staff properly and will recognise, consult and negotiate with trade unions; will it grant its "people" the right to help determine the course and future of the organisation in which they too will have a stake?'

Further Reference

Report of a Court of Inquiry under Mr A. J. Scamp into the dispute between the British Airline Pilots' Association and the National Joint Council for Civil Air Transport, cmnd 3428 HMSO October 1967.

A. J. N. Blain, *Pilots and Management: Industrial Relations in the U.K. Airlines*, Allen & Unwin 1972.

Merchant Navy and Airline Officers' Association
(MNAOA)

Head Office

Oceanair House
750-760 High Road
Leytonstone
London E11 3BB
Telephone: 01-989 6677

Principal Officers

General Secretary —
Eric Nevin
Assistant General Secretary —
P. J. Newman
Director of Professional and Welfare Services — D. Seaman
National Secretaries —
W. Wilson
S. Rendell
T. Harding
B. D. Orrell

Membership (1982)

> Male 30,295
> Female 165
> Total 30,460

Union Journal

> *The Telegraph,* approximate circulation 25,000.

General

The association recruits from among all merchant navy officers with the exception of radio officers, and also among flight engineers in civil aviation. The minimum standards of pay and conditions are laid down in the various National Maritime Board agreements to which most UK shipping companies are party.

In addition, company agreements are negotiated with many companies, allowing conditions and pay over and above those obtaining in the National Maritime Board agreements.

History

The MNAOA was formed in 1956 by the amalgamation of the *Navigators and Engineer Officers' Union* (itself formed in 1936) and the *Marine Engineers' Association* which was formed in 1887.

Organisation

The policy-making body is the Biennial General Meeting. However, the absolute control and administration of the affairs and property of the association and the furtherance of objectives authorised by the rules of the association is vested in the Council, except that resolutions carried at a Biennial General Meeting are binding on the Council.

The Council is elected by the membership every four years and is composed of chairperson, vice-chairperson, general secretary, three trustees and 24 other full members, reflecting the different officer sections so as to provide suitable representation for navigating, engineering and electrical engineering officers, officers in civil aviation, officers from the purser's and catering departments, and other particular categories of membership. Council meets at least once every four months.

Council officials are elected by the Council itself which also appoints the full-time officers of the association. The general secretary holds office 'during good behaviour'.

The association has limited branch organisation on account of the world-wide distribution of membership. Instead, a system of liaison officers and correspondents operates. Liaison officers are mainly concentrated in the short sea trades and perform similar functions to those of shore-based shop stewards. Correspondents have a more restricted role in assisting the flow of information between ship and shore.

The nine district offices of the association are distributed around the coast in London, Cardiff, Southampton, Liverpool, Glasgow, South Shields and Hull, Dover and Belfast.

External Relations

The association is avowedly non-political and does not affiliate to any political party.

Policy and Recent Events

In the general recession in world shipping, and company efforts to reduce losses by rationalisation and job cuts on short sea and ferry routes, the MNAOA has been engaged in a series of defensive battles. In 1981 industrial action against the P&O deep-sea cargo fleet was ended following agreement with the company to provide a job security guarantee. The company had planned to sell four refrigeration vessels to a foreign operator and then lease them back. This raised fears among MNAOA members of the ships sailing under flags of convenience and a consequent risk to jobs.

Fiercer confrontations have occurred with the ferry companies. Sealink, the BR subsidiary, obliged to meet stringent cash limits, put in hand economy measures that appeared likely to result in redundancies at Newhaven and Harwich. Crew at Newhaven occupied the Sealink ferry, *Senlac*, for five weeks before the MNAOA secured firm undertakings that the ferry route would be maintained. At Harwich, Sealink planned not only job losses but pay cuts of more than ten per cent. A compromise settlement was reached following a tough stand by the National Union of Seamen.

The union advised its members to protest strenuously about BP's plans to sell more of its fleet. As an official put it: 'Members should ask whether the reward for their role in the South Atlantic is simply praise followed by the dole queue.'

Radio and Electronic Officers' Union
(REOU)

Head Office

4/6 Branfill Road
Upminster
Essex
RM14 2XX
04022-22321

District Office

R. A. White
Assistant to the General
Secretary
REOU
Bridge Chambers
Alfred Gelder Street
Hull HU1 2JQ

Principal Officers

*General Secretary and
Treasurer*
— K. A. Murphy
Assistant General Secretary
— J. Bromley
National Organiser—
P. Curwell

Membership (1982)

Male 3,411
Female 14
Total 3,425

Union Journal

The Signal — circulation
around 4,200.

General

The REOU covers radio officers and radio electronic officers in the British and foreign-flag merchant navies; radio officers and radio operators in the fishing industry; radio officers and radio electronic officers in the off-shore oil industry; shore-based technical personnel dealing with merchant navies, fishing vessels and off-shore oil industry — including technical staff at the head office of the major marine wireless companies, as well as middle management. The union is a party to the National Maritime Board Agreements which are industry wide. All other agreements are on a company or several-companies basis. Only certified radio officers are eligible for full membership of the union.

History

The union was founded in 1912 as the *Association of Wireless Telegraphists*. It amalgamated with the *Cable Telegraphists' Union* in 1921 under the title *Association of Wireless and Cable Telegraphists*. In 1938 it changed its name to *Radio Officers' Union* and in 1967 to its present title.

The commercial use of wireless at sea commenced with the installation of suitable equipment on the German liner Kaiser Wilhelm der Grosse in 1900. The demand for wireless operators was slow moving, and in the first 12 years of the twentieth century British merchant vessels fitted with wireless telegraphy equipment numbered a few hundred. The loss of the *Titanic* and the *Empress of Ireland* gave some impetus and in 1914 the Mercantile Shipping Convention Bill was passed by the House of Commons, making compulsory the carriage of wireless telegraphy equipment on ships carrying 50 or more passengers. Further legislation and the requirements of the first world war led to a trebling of the wireless operators population to 4,500 by 1917.

Many sea-going wireless operators had served ashore as telegraphists prior to going to sea, and had established contact with the Postal Telegraph Clerks' Association. E. R. Tuck, the general secretary of the PTCA, helped to set up the Association of Wireless Telegraphists in 1912. By 1920 the AWT had grown to a membership of 5,108. Despite the fact that the AWT organised over 90 per cent of the wireless operators at sea throughout the first world war, the owners did not formally recognise the union until 1918.

By 1920 an honorary delegate system had been established to maintain contact with a scattered membership and since that year the union journal has published a list of delegates representing the union who are assigned to each ship.

The title of wireless operator has undergone several changes; in 1920 it was changed to wireless officer and this had fairly wide acceptance, but it was not until about 1937 that the present title of radio officer received official approval. In step with the changes in title of the wireless operator, the *Association of Wireless and Cable Telegraphists* became the *Radio Officers' Union* in 1938 and the *Radio and Electronic Officers' Union* in 1967.

The REOU has had several strikes in its history, notably in 1920, 1922 and 1925.

Organisation

The supreme ruling and policy making body of the REOU is the Executive Committee which is elected annually by the membership. It is composed of 15 serving members: 12 from sea-going personnel, two from shore technical personnel, and one from the fishing industry. The Rule Book states that 'no members of the Communist or Fascist parties shall be eligible to be an officer or an honorary delegate of the union'. Industrial action is subject to a ballot of the membership.

All full-time officials in the REOU are appointed.

External Relations

The REOU is entirely non-political. The general secretary is a member of the Transport Industries Committee of the TUC, of NEDO's Marine Electronics Task Force, of the Joint IMCO/ILO Committee on Training, of the MN Pensions Administration, of the MN Training Board, of TEC's Committee of Maritime Studies including the Working Party on Marine Radio, the Home Office Maritime Radio Technical Committee and the PMG Advisory Committee — a small selection from some of the national and international committees on which he represents the REOU.

The union is affiliated to the International Federation of Radio Officers, the International Transport Workers' Federation and the Committee of Transport Workers' Unions in the European Community.

Through the ITF, the general secretary and the national organiser act as ICFTU observers on the Inter-Governmental Maritime Consultative Organisation's committees and subcommittees.

Recent Events

Perhaps the most significant development that currently affects the union stems from the introduction of the microprocessor, which could, foreseeably, lead to the eventual automation of communications, engine-room operation — and even navigation.

Seamen, National Union of
(NUS)

Head Office

Maritime House
Old Town
Clapham
London SW4 0JP
01-622 5581

Principal Officers

General Secretary— J. Slater
Assistant General Secretary/ Treasurer— S. McCluskie
National Secretary—
R. L. Spruhan
Assistant National Secretaries
R. Wilkins
A. McGregor
R. Fleming
Education Officer—
D. Wedlake
Special Services Officer—
J. Kinahan
Information Officer— J. Jump
Research Officer— P. Heaton

Membership (1982)

Male 33,832
Female 1,106
Total 34,938

Union Journal

The Seaman— monthly, circulation around 15,000.

Union Officials

There is no organisational level in the NUS between branch and head office, but branch officials are located at offices (around 20) throughout major ports in the UK and abroad.

General

The National Union of Seamen is one of Britain's long-established unions, although of late it has witnessed a decline in membership due to changes in ship technology and the decline in the UK shipping industry generally. It is the sole organisation representing UK ratings employed in the British shipping industry. Around 80 per cent of its members are employed in the deep sea sector with the remaining members employed in the home trade sector.

The General Secretary, Jim Slater, is a member of the TUC General Council, and the Assistant General Secretary/Treasurer, Sam McCluskie, is a member of the National Executive Committee of the Labour Party.

History

Seafarers were among the first of Britain's workers to recognise the value and importance of trade unionism and, around the beginning of the nineteenth century, sailor's friendly societies were set up in several ports, particularly along the north-east coast. The first national organisation of which there appears to be any record seems to have been formed before the middle of the nineteenth century, noted by the Webbs in their standard work on British trade unionism. The organisation was only a loose federation of practically autonomous port unions, the most prominent of which was the *North of England Sailors and Seagoing Firemen's Friendly Association*, formed at Sunderland in 1879, and known generally as the *Sunderland Seamen's Union*.

Among the members of this association was a deckhand named James Havelock Wilson. In 1887, Wilson set up the *National Amalgamated Sailors and Firemen's Union of Great Britain and Ireland*. The new union, with 500 members, made its first appearance at the TUC in 1888. By the following year, membership had increased dramatically to 65,000, with branches in nearly 60 ports. As a response to the growing influence of the union, the owners set up the Shipping Federation in 1890. In 1893, after a bitter strike at Hull which spread to national level, the National Amalgamated Union went into voluntary liquidation following a costly libel suit. Wilson, by then the MP for Middlesbrough, set up a new union, this time being named the *National Sailors' and Firemen's Union*. The newly-formed union agitated for legislative reform, and by 1910 improvements in the Merchant Shipping Acts had been secured together with the extension of the Workmen's Compensation Acts to seafarers.

The union put forward its claim for the establishment of a National Wages Board in 1911, as part of a charter for seafarers formulated simultaneously in seven maritime countries by the International Committee of Seafarers' Unions. Following rejection, the seafarers' unions in five countries declared a strike, which was supported by the dockers and road transport workers. The principal storm centres of the strike were in the Bristol Channel and in Liverpool. Despite a long and bitter struggle in which police harassment and the use of blacklegs was rife, the union secured informal recognition, although they did not achieve their aim of the establishment of a national negotiating wage board.

With the outbreak of the first world war, the union turned its attentions to securing provision for members and their families who were victims of enemy action at sea. In 1916, following disruptions caused by seafarers going on strike, the government issued an invitation to the union and the Shipping Federation to discuss the possiblity of a national wage, the supply of seafarers, and the regulation of the employment of 'Chinese and other natives'. Following a series of meetings, the National Maritime Board was established to jointly regulate the supply of seafarers and to regulate terms and conditions for various categories of seafarers.

In the early 1920s there was a recrudescence of strike activity. Firstly, there was a severe depression following hard on a freight boom, and falling money wages caused unrest. Secondly, there was bitter inter-union and intra-union strife, for reasons only partly economic.

Unofficial strikes became a major phenomenon in the shipping industry; their most prominent aspect was protest against the leadership of the NUS. At that time, the top priority of Wilson was harmony with the ship owners in order to maintain the National Maritime Board and the closed shop for seafarers, to which end he sacrificed all else. That the unofficial rank-and-file action was not more frequent or widespread is attributable to the necessity of being in favour with the union in order to get a berth. As Henry Pelling observed in *The History of British Trade Unionism*, the NUS in Wilson's final years 'seemed to have become little more than a "company union" '. The NUS was the only TUC-affiliated union to oppose the General Strike in 1926, and funded a right-wing miners' breakaway union (the Miners' Industrial (Non-Political) Union). The NUS was expelled from the TUC in 1928. Following Wilson's death in the spring of 1929, the NUS was re-admitted into TUC membership later in the year.

Havelock Wilson was replaced by W. R. Spence, and relations with other unions and the rank-and-file of the NUS improved. Between 1929 and 1932 the total of world tonnage laid up as a result of the great depression increased fourfold. In 1930, Spence reported to the union that 20,000 seafarers were out of work and six million tons of shipping were lying idle in world ports. When business recovered, Spence pursued an energetic policy which, with the forceful support of Ernest Bevin, secured substantial gains without strike action being taken.

An important development in 1937 was the establishment of a system of joint supply of labour, operated by the NMB in conjunction with the Board of Trade. Considerable progress was also made towards the raising of standards of crew accommodation. Comfort was made a specific require-ment for the first time, and sleeping quarters, mess rooms, hospital arrangements, improved lighting, heating, ventilation, and proper provision for recreation were all embodied in new regulations emanating from the Board of Trade.

During the second world war, the merchant navy suffered heavy losses particularly with the increased use of U-boats. The NUS claim that their losses of life (30,000 men) represented a higher proportion of casualties than that in the armed forces. A number of substantial improvements were made by the NUS during wartime, particularly with the establishment of the merchant navy pool, which facilitated continuous employment for seafarers.

In 1955 the NUS was involved in a nine-week strike which, although confined to two ports and liner shipping, was to resuscitate rank-and-file grievances over the Merchant Shipping Acts, discipline, pay, accommodation, and the lack of union representation on board. Common to all these complaints was a fierce resentment directed against the union leadership for the distance between national and local officials on the one hand and the rank and file on the other, for undemocratic methods, and for complacency and half-heartedness in pursuing union claims.

It was immediately after the 1960 unofficial strike that the National Seamen's Reform Movement came into being. This was formed as a 'ginger' movement, concerned not with replacing the NUS but with changing its policy and direction to one of greater militancy and increased democratic control.

The 1966 seafarers' strike was a milestone in the history of the union. Not only was it directed at the shipowners, but also it took place at a time when the Labour government was attempting to operate a strict incomes policy. Bill Hogarth, the general secretary of the union, centred the NUS claim on a reduction of hours from 56 to 40 a week and a £60 per month wage for seafarers. The strike lasted for 47 days and was concluded with much dissension among union members. During the strike Harold Wilson made his famous statement in the House of Commons about a 'tightly-knit group of politically motivated men' who were out to 'take-over' the NUS leadership for the Communist Party. (One of the men named by Wilson, Jim Slater, is now the general secretary.) However, the Pearson Court of Inquiry set the tone for further changes in the working conditions of seafarers.

Union Officials

The rules of the NUS provide that applicants for union office must have had five years' sea service, and must not have reached the age of 45 years, except in 'special and extraordinary circumstances'. Union officials are appointed by the general secretary and are subject to confirmation by the Executive Council. Since the NUS secured a closed shop agreement with the General Council of British Shipping in 1974, union officials have had more time to devote to the servicing of the membership.

Coverage

The closed shop agreement covers all ratings who are registered under the Merchant Navy Establishment Scheme. Ratings are covered by the National Maritime Board annual agreement, which lays down minimum terms and conditions, supplemented in some cases by company agreements which may exceed NMB rates in a number of areas particularly after the 1981 strikes, during which some companies split away from the General Council of British Shipping.

Subsequent to this, 13 companies, employing a fifth of the shipping industry's workforce of 60,000, approached the unions to discuss breaking away from national pay talks, a move supported by the GCBS. It is possible that within three or four years the industry may have a split bargaining system, with some companies remaining in national negotiations, while others bargain at company or sectoral level.

Organisation

Head office is split into four departments: research and publicity, legal, finance and benefits.

The supreme ruling body of the union is the Biennial General Meeting, to which delegates are elected in proportion to the size of branch. Branches with 100-1,500 members are entitled to send one delegate, 1,501-2,500 two, 2,501-3,500 three delegates, with an extra delegate for each additional 1,000 members thereafter.

The Executive Council is elected every three years by ballot of the whole membership; as from 1981 it comprises 13 members and acts as the negotiating body of the union in a National Maritime Board context. Assistant national secretaries are appointed by the Executive Council. The positions of general secretary, assistant general secretary/treasurer and national secretary, are elected by ballot of the whole membership.

Workplace Activity

The unofficial strike of 1960 and the 1966 strike have resulted in the concept of 'shop steward at sea' in the form of 'shipboard liaison representatives'. The NUS Rule Book provides that such liaison representatives cannot sanction the withdrawal of labour or other forms of industrial action without the consent of an executive officer (i.e. the general secretary, assistant general secretary/treasurer or national secretary). The 1982 Biennial General Meeting agreed to set up shipboard branches in a radical extension of its shore-based organisation. The aim of this was to attempt to cure the union's long-standing problem of apathy among members — 75 per cent of whom are at sea at any given time. Only executive officers have the authority to sanction a withdrawal of labour from any ship while it is safely berthed in the UK. In any dispute likely to affect the majority of the membership, the Executive Council is obliged to take a vote of all members at home, able and willing to vote, before a strike can be called. In the 1981 pay dispute this procedure was avoided by recourse to selective strikes. The union has a ballot procedure on the annual wage negotiations.

Women

Around four per cent of NUS membership consists of women. Nearly all of these are employed as stewards and catering staff on ferries, passenger ships, and North Sea oil rigs.

External Relations

The NUS is affiliated to the Labour Party. There is one sponsored Labour MP, John Prescott, whose constituency is Hull East. The general secretary, Jim Slater, is a member of the General Council of the TUC, and Sam McCluskie is a member of the NEC of the Labour Party.

Labour Party Delegation

At the 1981 Labour Party Conference, the NUS cast its votes for John Silkin in the first ballot of the Deputy Leadership contest, and switched its votes to Tony Benn in the second ballot. The delegation consists of the general secretary, assistant general secretary, and four other EC members. The supreme decision-making body in the NUS is the Biennial General Meeting, which met in 1980 (before the issue of the Labour Party Deputy Leadership came to the fore), and in 1982 (when the matter was not discussed). Without such guiding authority, therefore, the EC were empowered to take whatever decision they chose (under Rules 6.17 and 6.18 of the NUS Rule Book). There were, however, 'soundings' taken of branch opinions before the delegation attended the Labour Party Conference.

Recent Events

The NUS has consistently campaigned, in pursuance of the International Transport Workers' Federation (ITF) to which it is affiliated, against the flying of 'flags of convenience' by shipping companies, on the grounds that such companies use flags of convenience as a means of staffing ships with cheap labour.

One hundred and forty years of disciplinary rules have recently been overturned with the inclusion of a clause which does away with the right of the master to fine seafarers. This is provided for in the 1978 Merchant Shipping Act. Shore-based tribunals,

made up of equal numbers of employer and union representatives, deal with cases of misconduct. The union is also a signatory party to the new Code of Conduct for seafarers which became operative on 1 January 1979. The International Transport Workers Federation (ITF) won an important legal victory in 1980 in its campaign to drive from the seas ships flying 'flags of convenience'. The Court of Appeal decided that any dispute arising from actions taken by the ITF to further that 'ultimate objective' was a trade dispute and covered by the immunities from court action afforded by the 1974 Trade Union and Labour Relations Act. However, subsequent Conservative anti-union legislation would make such industrial action liable in tort.

Following the election of Jim Slater as general secretary in 1974 the union's attitude has toughened on the question of low-paid Asian seafarers employed on British ships. The union has belatedly adopted the policy of wage equality for non-domiciled seafarers — a gross injustice for over 300 years. Government proposals to retain wage inequality in the 1976 Race Relations Bill were resisted. Following a government-sponsored inquiry, the principle of wage equality was accepted by the shipowners.

In 1980, Biennial General Meeting delegates voted 40-24 to reject a Liverpool motion which sought to open merger talks with the TGWU. This was in accord with decisions taken at previous conferences. A motion at the 1982 BGM on similar lines was remitted to the EC.

The NUS has recently begun a recruiting campaign aimed at British divers working in the North Sea, and has achieved a high level of unionisation.

In January 1981 a tortuous pay dispute rapidly developed into a trial of strength between the union and the General Council of British Shipping. The employers finally offered 9.4 per cent on basic pay but the union held out for time-and-a-half for overtime rather than time-and-a-quarter. The employers' unity buckled under worldwide strike action and selective 24-hour strikes in the UK which were able to deploy strategic groups such as ferry crews who had less to gain from the dispute. Conciliation failed and, as the union's position hardened, companies such as Canadian Pacific, Townsend Thoresen and Fyffes split away from the GCBS and came to terms. After five weeks of action it was agreed to refer the claim for time-and-a-half to arbitration. The subsequent award introduced time-and-a-half for all overtime hours except the first two worked on weekdays.

In the summer of 1982, the NUS was engaged in a bitter dispute with Sealink over management's plans to cut costs on the Harwich–Hoek van Holland ferry route; 3,500 members took part in a day-long national strike in support of the Harwich seafarers, and the dispute was eventually settled with the help of ACAS conciliators.

The legislation on closed shops drawn up by the Conservatives in 1982 opened up the possibility of compensation claims by seafarers who left the NUS and were subsequently dismissed. Despite pleas by the General Council of British Shipping and the shipowners themselves, the government refused to amend its legislation.

Further Reference

J. Havelock Wilson, *My Stormy Voyage through Life*, vol.1 (vol.2 not published) Cooperative Press 1925.

Basil Mogeridge, 'Militancy and inter-union rivalries in British shipping, 1911-1929', *International Review of Social Science*, vol.6, no.3, 1961.

S. G. Sturmey, *British Shipping and World Competition*, University of London, The Athlone Press, 1962.

J. Hemingway, *Conflict and Democracy*, chapter 4, Oxford: Clarendon Press, 1978. An account of the conflict between the National Seamen's Reform Movement and the leadership of the NUS from 1960-74.

J. McConville, *The Shipping Industry in the UK*, International Institute for Labour Studies.

Tony Wailey, 'The Seamen's strike, Liverpool 1966', *History Workshop*, May 1978.

J. Kitchen, *The Employment of Merchant Seamen*, Croom Helm, 1980. Comprehensive, but expensive at £60.

Transport and General Workers' Union
(TGWU)

Head Office

Transport House
Smith Square
Westminster
London SW1P 3JB
01-828 7788

Principal Officers

General Secretary —
Moss Evans
Deputy General Secretary —
A. Kitson

Executive Officers

Executive Officer —
L. Smith

National Officers

Financial Secretary —
H. Timpson
National Organiser — R. Todd

Vehicle Building and Automotive
National Secretary —
G. Hawley
National Officer — E. Bone

Power and Engineering
National Secretary —
T. Crispin
National Officer — F. J. Howell

Chemical, Rubber Manufacturing and Oil Refining
National Secretary — J. Miller

Docks and Waterways
National Secretary —
J. Connolly

Commercial Services
National Secretary —
J. Ashwell
National Officer — G. Oram

Passenger Services
National Secretary —
W. Morris

Public Services
National Secretary —
M. B. Martin

General Workers
National Secretary — P. Evans

Building, Construction and Civil
Engineering and Building Crafts
  National Secretary—
    G. P. Henderson

Liaison National Officer
  (above two trade groups)
    B. Cox

Food, Drink and Tobacco
  National Secretary—
    R. Harrison

Administrative, Clerical, Technical
and Supervisory
  National Secretary—
    A. C. Sullivan
  National Officer— T. Lyle

Dyers, Bleachers and Textile
Workers' National Trade Group
  National Secretary—
    E. Haigh

Agricultural and Allied Workers'
National Trade Group
  National Secretary—
    J. R. Boddy

Administration
  S. R. Forty

Legal
  A. C. Blyghton

Education and Research
  National Secretary— R. Scott
    F. Cosgrove (Director of
    Education)

Women
  C. M. Patterson

Civil Air Transport
  J. Collier (Section Secretary)

Membership (1982) (does not
  include new trade groups)

  Male 1,438,445
  Female 257,373
  Total 1,695,818

Union Journal and Publications

  TGWU Record— A monthly
  tabloid newspaper sent to
  branches for distribution by
  shop stewards and branches
  (free to members), edited by
  C. Kaufman.
  Highway—Formerly the paper
  of the Scottish Commercial
  Motormen's Union,
  amalgamated with the TGWU
  in 1971.

The Landworker — formerly
the paper of the NUAAW. This
paper led a vigorous campaign
against the use of the
herbicide 2, 4, 5–T.
Educational booklets,
including: *Tackling Tebbit*— a
shop steward's guide to the
1982 Employment Act.
Research Bulletin— published
monthly. Contains information
about retail price index,
average earnings index, basic
weekly wage index,
unemployment, industrial
production. Supplied to the
union's full-time officers.

Education

An entirely new home-study
course — 'Your Union at Work'
— was devised in 1979 and
replaced the 'Union in Action'
course. A large scale
programme of shop steward
training, supported by
full-time staff in all regions, is
now involving 15,000 stewards
per year. Residential courses
for branch officers are held at
Cirencester and the union's
Eastbourne Centre. The union
provides bursaries for
members pursuing full-time
study at Ruskin College, the
London School of Economics,
Coleg Harlech, Northern College and New Battle Abbey.

Regional Secretaries

● *Region 1 (London and Home
  Counties)*
  S. Staden
  Woodberry
  18 Green Lanes
  London N4 2HB

● *Region 2 (Southern)*
  J. Ashman
  65/75 London Road
  Southampton
  S09 5HH

● *Region 3 (South West)*
  R. H. Nethercott
  Transport House
  Victoria Street
  Bristol BS1 6AY

● *Region 4 (Wales)*
  G. Wright
  1 Cathedral Road
  Cardiff
  CF1 9SD

● *Region 5 (Midlands)*
  B. Mathers
  9-17 Victoria Street
  West Bromwich
  B70 8HX

● *Region 6 (North West)*
  W. Heywood
  Transport House
  1 The Crescent
  Salford M5 4PR

● *Region 7 (Scotland)*
  H. Wyper
  24 Park Circus
  Glasgow
  G3 6AR

● *Region 8 (Northern)*
  J. Mills
  Transport House
  Barrack Road
  Newcastle-on-Tyne NE4 6DP

● *Region 9 (Yorkshire)*
  M. Davey
  22 Blenheim Terrace
  Leeds
  LS2 9HF

● *Region 10 (Humber and East Coast)*
  M. Snow
  Bevin House
  George Street
  Hull HU1 3DB

● *Region 11 (Ireland)*
  J. Freeman
  Transport House
  102 High Street
  Belfast BT1 2DL

General

The TGWU is by far the largest union in Britain. It is a multi-industrial union, open to all types of workers, but approximating to an industrial union in sectors such as oil refining, flour milling and the docks, although in each case it has to share the field with other unions. It is almost the only union for road transport drivers across the whole range of industries; about 20,000 are, however, members of the United Road Transport Union. The TGWU is also characteristically 'general' in having membership among production workers in most manufacturing industries, while also often having membership among clerical and administrative staff in some of those industries. In recent years it has recruited among such diverse groups of employees as garage mechanics, stable lads and girls, bookmakers and hotel staffs.

The union has strongly promoted plant and workplace bargaining by shop stewards and is consequently party to many plant agreements, in addition to the many company and national (industry-wide) agreements to which it is signatory.

History

In March 1920 the *Dock, Wharf, Riverside and General Workers' Union*, whose main source of membership was London, took the initiative in organising a discussion with the shipping staffs on the need for amalgamation. Unity of purpose was achieved and organisational details were elaborated. These were preliminaries. The first real step towards the creation of the TGWU came when a delegation from the other main dockers' union, the *National Union of Dock, Riverside and General Workers*, based in Liverpool and led by James Sexton, agreed to join forces in forming a new union.

There was now an excellent chance of carrying other smaller unions with them. So it was agreed to appoint Ernest Bevin of the DWRGWU as provisional secretary and Harry Gosling (a member of neither union but president of the Transport Workers' Federation) as provisional chairperson of an amalgamation committee which then decided on a list of other unions, all connected with the docks industry, whom they would invite to their next meeting.

There were 59 delegates present, representing 13 unions, when the conference re-amalgamation opened at Anderton's Hotel on Fleet Street on 18 August 1920. From the London area: *National Union of Dock, Wharves and Shipping Staffs* (6,500 members), *Amalgamated Stevedores Labour Protection League* (5,500 members), *South Side Labour Protection League* (2,500 members), *National Union of Ships' Clerks and Grain*

Weighers (East Ham Union) (732 members), *Amalgamated Society of Watermen, Lightermen and Bargemen* (Harry Gosling's union) (7,000 members), *Dock, Wharf, Riverside and General Workers' Union* (Tillet and Bevin) (120,000 members).

From Cardiff came delegates from the *Cardiff Coal Trimmers* (1,600 members) and from Swansea delegates from the *National Amalgamated Labourers' Union*. Glasgow was represented by delegates from the *Scottish Union of Dockers* (11,000), Liverpool by Sexton's union and by the *Liverpool Clerks and Mersey Watermen* and Newcastle by the *North of England Trimmers' and Teamers' Association*.

There had been many such proposed amalgamation schemes previously among these unions but all had foundered. Now Bevin played a master stroke by putting forward proposals on the organisation of the new union which enabled amalgamation to occur and provided a lasting constitutional framework. It was necessary to leave each sectional industrial group — the dockers, road transport, clerical staff, — the autonomy to deal with their own affairs but it was also necessary to prevent autonomy undermining unity which was, after all, the point of amalgamation. Indeed, the Webbs had suggested, in their classic work, *Industrial Democracy*, that it was virtually impossible to combine workers of different occupations in a stable amalgamation. For example, dockers would be certain to argue that they alone should determine issues affecting their own trade, without interference from carters or clerks. This difficulty was met by the creation of trade groups in which members in similar trades and occupations would be grouped together. However, as a check on sectionalism, it was proposed to set up a territorial grouping of members on a geographical basis. Like a hoop around a barrel, there would be a national executive representative of both national trade groups and geographical areas which would have control over finances, strike action and general policy.

At a further meeting it was decided to invite the road transport unions into the amalgamation and their leaders were pleased to accept, their members having just suffered wage cuts as a result of the slump.

In the subsequent ballot of the members of the various unions on the amalgamation, only three unions voted against or failed to obtain enough votes to satisfy legal requirements — the London stevedores, the Scottish dockers and the Cardiff coal trimmers. On 1 January 1922 the *Transport and General Workers' Union* came into legal existence with Ernest Bevin as general secretary. It initially consisted of 300,000 members, most of them dockworkers, transport workers on trams or buses or lorry and cart drivers. The original trade groups in 1922 were docks, waterways, administrative, clerical and supervisory, road transport-passenger, road transport-commercial, general workers. That it was an amalgamation which had penetration into these areas suggests potential expansion but at its outset the TGWU was primarily a dockers' union with the general workers' section as a relatively minor residual grouping. In fact, there was nothing certain about the growth pattern of the TGWU for it was born into the slump and in six of its first ten years, including the first two, it lost members. In 1923 it faced internal revolt in the unofficial strike against wage cuts of London dockers. The unofficial committee was supported by the *Amalgamated Stevedores Labour Protection League* which had stayed outside the TGWU amalgamation and now encouraged disaffected TGWU members to join it. The attempt to organise a larger breakaway was not a success and the strike collapsed. The feud between the TGWU and the stevedores, however, continued, flaring up again in the 1950s dock strikes.

Further rank-and-file opposition in the docks trade group came from the Glasgow dockers who had been belatedly taken into the TGWU, under protest, as part of the Scottish Union of Dock Labourers. From 1929 they set up an Anti-Registration League (registration of dockworkers was a prerequisite for the effective decasualisation of dockwork) and then seceded to form the autonomous Scottish TGWU.

The second most important area of TGWU membership after the docks was road passenger transport, and among the most militant industrial groups in the country during the 1930s was the London bus section of the TGWU. The industry was still profitable, as yet facing negligible competition from private cars, and the workers suffered little from the effects of the slump, average earnings remaining comparatively high. They were a compact body of employees, displaying strong solidarity and possessing a tradition of industrial democracy. They had been a difficult group to integrate into the TGWU amalgamation. Being dissatisfied with the national passenger transport trade group, they pressed for and were conceded a greater measure of self-determination through an elected Central London Area Bus Committee which enjoyed the functions of a national trade group committee with its own full-time officer and the right of direct access to the Executive Council. A rank-and-file movement took control of the Central Bus Committee and, although ultimately outmanoeuvred by Bevin, agitated strongly and caused him a great deal of trouble. At the 1937 Biennial Delegate Conference the Executive Council submitted recommendations based on an enquiry into activities of members of the Central Bus Section. As a result the rules of the union were amended to strengthen the right of expulsion. A section of the rank-and-file movement carried out a threat to form a breakaway union and established the National Passenger Workers' Union in 1938. This breakaway survived another eight years but had no success in shifting the loyalty of most London bus workers away from the TGWU, largely because the TGWU achieved an agreement with London Transport which conferred exclusive bargaining rights and a closed shop.

The TGWU quite rapidly became less of a union of transport workers and more of a general workers' union. In 1929 it amalgamated with the *Workers' Union*, thereby gaining membership of some 100,000 workers in a variety of trades, particularly engineering, doubling the size of the existing general workers' trade group and extending its industrial coverage; this amalgamation was also the origin of the TGWU's membership in agriculture. Previously, in 1926, the power workers' trade group had been established following amalgamation with the *National Union of Enginemen, Firemen, Motormen and Mechanics*. A further territorial region was established following the accession of the *North Wales Quarrymen's Union* into the TGWU (although it retained some autonomy and separate affiliation to the TUC). Another early amalgamation was with the London-based *United Order of General Labourers*.

In the 1920 amalgamation scheme provision had been made for five trade groups and for subsections for numerically important trades within three of the groups. The docks' group had a subsection for coal shipping; the general workers' group had one for metal and chemical trades; and the road transport group had subsections for the passenger and commercial transport workers. As groups expanded it was the union policy to subdivide them into trade union sections as a step toward group status. In 1922, for instance, road transport-passenger and road transport-commercial became full trade groups. A group was able to have its own trade machinery and specialist officers at all levels. The general workers' trade group was used as a residual category and a step towards the formation of new national trade groups, first for metals, engineering and chemicals and then for building in 1938, following amalgamation with the *'Altogether' Builders' and Labourers' Society*. Workers in agriculture, the fishing industry, government and public services and flour-milling had their own sections.

Sections had only a specialist national official and a national trade committee and at other levels had to use composite trade group officials. The right to establish trade groups rested with the Biennial Delegate Conference and each time it met there were a number of claimants to trade group status but very few were conceded.

There were only three years between 1922 and 1940 during which an amalgamation did not take place. (See **Appendix**.) Just prior to the General Strike, negotiations were being held to bring together the TGWU, the National Union of General and Municipal Workers, the Electrical Trades Union and six smaller unions. Negotiations lapsed because of the General Strike and were never properly renewed. In the 1930s the TGWU withdrew its claim to organise the nursing profession and the catering industry, leaving these fields of recruitment to other unions. Bevin had also meticulously steered it away from extending its interests to seafarers when pressed to form an alternative to Havelock Wilson's National Union of Seamen, which had become a company union working hand-in-glove with the employers in the Shipping Federation. Instead Bevin established a close working relationship with Spence, the new general secretary who took over when Wilson died in 1929. This is not to say that the TGWU leadership was averse to widening its spheres of influence. For example, to the indignation of an outraged Jockey Club, it did take up membership of stable lads and girls after an enthusiastic meeting at Newmarket.

Although the TGWU had always had a nucleus of membership in the road haulage industry among its carter members, it proved difficult to extend membership among the multitude of small employing units. However, in 1938 the Road Haulage Wages Act replaced voluntary regulation of wages and conditions by statutory regulation by central and area wages boards. The union had pursued this measure which would not detract from its authority — indeed its effective enforcement depended largely on the vigilance of the union — while it increased union coverage since its jurisdiction extended to C-licence holders operating vehicles for the transport of their own produce.

In 1928 Transport House in Smith Square was opened.

1939-45

The most important change of the war years was that Ernest Bevin became Minister of Labour, Arthur Deakin becoming Acting General Secretary of the union. His rise coincided with the increase in the power and influence of trade unions; they had friends in the government and increased their size and strength as a result of the high level of employment. Membership of the TGWU increased from less than 700,000 in 1939 to over 1.2 million in 1946.

1945 to date

Deakin was elected general secretary in 1945 receiving 58 per cent of the 347,523 votes cast. An important constitutional change was made when the 1945 Biennial Delegate Conference passed a motion barring members of the Communist Party from holding any office in the union, either as lay members or as full-time officials. At present under Schedule 1 (2) of the rules of the TGWU, membership of an organisation which 'in the opinion of the General Executive Council is contrary, detrimental, inconsistent or injurious to the policy and purpose of the union will render the member liable to be declared ineligible to hold any office within the Union either as a lay-member or as a permanent or full-time officer, or such other penalties as in the opinion of the General Executive Council shall seem just.'

In collective bargaining the most significant reform of the immediate post war years achieved by the union was partial decasualisation of port employment under the National Dock Labour Scheme of 1947, which was really a continuation of various wartime schemes in that it provided for local dock labour boards under joint union-management control and guaranteed pay. Despite this, some said because of it, in their improved social and economic position and with increased bargaining power, the dockers engaged in strike action after the war on an unprecedented scale. The strikes were invariably against union advice and in contravention of agreements and negotiating procedures. Such activity culminated in the decision of a group of Hull dockers to secede from the TGWU and join the London-based National Amalgamated Stevedores and Dockers in 1954. They were followed by some other disgruntled dockers in Birkenhead, Liverpool and Manchester. Since this was an infringement of the Bridlington agreement on inter-union relations, the NASD was suspended from the TUC but when the NASD decided to return the new recruits, many refused to go.

There continued to be demands for separate trade groups from many trades among the TGWU membership but Deakin and the General Executive Council were reluctant to increase the number of trade groups, an excess of which they believed would hamper efficient organisation. However, it was necessary to form a chemical workers' section to meet the challenge of competition for members from the Chemical Workers' Union. This section became a full trade group in 1954.

Deakin died in 1954, being replaced by the former deputy general secretary, Tiffin. Frank Cousins was appointed deputy general secretary under Tiffin and was then elected general secretary by a big majority in 1956 after Tiffin's death.

Cousins had made his reputation in the union as a critic of the centralised type of administration developed by Bevin and continued by Deakin. Well suited to a slowly growing new amalgamation in an economy devastated by slump, these policies were inappropriate to the full employment economy of post-war Britain in which bargaining power at workplace level had increased strongly. Deakin's restricted conception of the role of shop stewards and insistence on the negotiating role of full-time officers were likewise inappropriate. Cousins showed more sympathy and understanding with shop stewards but there was no recasting of union organisation.

When Cousins retired, Jack Jones, who had been vigorously propounding reforms to make TGWU organisation more attuned to the realities of workplace power, was elected to succeed him in 1969. During the 1960s change had been taking place, mainly in acceptance of local and plant bargaining, but it was ad hoc, piecemeal and untidy. Now change towards workplace negotiation by shop stewards and reference back of settlements to members was specifically encouraged and given direction by the general secretary. The decentralisation of collective bargaining levels in the TGWU took five main forms:

(1) Movement from national (usually industry-wide) level negotiations to lower (usually workplace) level bargaining. This was true of the docks, engineering, and of bargaining relationships with large companies which had withdrawn from employers' associations or from industry-level Joint Industrial Councils (JICs) e.g. Dunlop.

(2) Increases in the scope and content of lower level and particularly workplace bargaining such that bargaining at these levels more closely determined actual pay and conditions. The vogue for productivity bargaining greatly accelerated this change.

(3) An increase in lay representation on national, regional and company negotiating bodies where representation of full-time officers was reduced to provide seats for shop stewards who were, in this way and others, brought more fully into the official machinery of government of the TGWU.

(4) Reference back procedures were introduced or extended.

(5) District committees were developed to overcome trade group fragmentation.

Union Officials

To implement these changes, Jack Jones established many more district committees and appointed more district officers throughout the union. They were appointed with the express objective of encouraging workplace organisation and autonomy by assisting shop stewards to negotiate for themselves. One consequence of this change was some decline in the authority of trade group organisation.

There was a quite drastic removal of some of the 'old school' full-time officials who did not accept changes such as reference back to members. For instance, Kealey, the union's negotiator with Fords, resigned under pressure in 1969 after failing to comply fully with a delegate conference decision and was replaced by Moss Evans, while at least one other national trade group secretary decided that resignation was now advisable.

Jones was in favour of co-operation on pay policy with the Labour government, being one of the architects of the 'social contract'. But at his last union conference in 1977 he lost an appeal for another year of co-operation with Labour. The domination of the TGWU by its general secretary has been weakened, as Moss Evans who won the election to replace Jones, has discovered. Recent amalgamations leave the TGWU with about 600 full-time officers.

Amalgamations and Growth in the 1970s, Retreat in the 1980s

The union continued to grow, both through fresh recruitment and through further amalgamations, reaching over 2 million members. Of particular significance was the 1972 merger with the *National Union of Vehicle Builders*, establishing a new vehicle building and automotive trade group in the union and strengthening its power in the motor industry. In chemicals its strength increased through the accession of the *Process and General Workers' Union* and, particularly in the drug and fine chemical section of the industry, the belated amalgamation with the *Chemical Workers' Union*, led by Bob Edwards — like Jack Jones, a Spanish Civil War veteran. Earlier, the mergers with the *National Association of Operative Plasterers* and with the *Scottish Tilers and Cement Workers* had established TGWU more firmly in the building industry. Its strength in transport was extended by the amalgamation with the *Scottish Commercial Motormen's Union* and in the docks the amalgamations with the *Watermen, Lightermen, Tugmen and Bargemen's Union*; the *Scottish TGWU* (mainly Glasgow dockers) and the *Iron, Steel and Wood Barge Builders' and Helpers' Association*. More attention began to be directed towards recruitment and effective representation of clerical and administrative membership, but this continued to be a weak point for the TGWU, despite impressive gains in membership.

In the 1980s the TGWU, in common with smaller unions, was faced with a continual decline in membership in the face of trifling improvement in trade and employment following from the resolute and draconian monetarism of the government's deflationary economic policies. The trade groups worst affected were passenger; commercial services; construction; food, drink and tobacco; chemicals and general workers. Over this period the decline in membership was ten per cent, leaving 1.7 million members.

To this must be added the influx of members from unions that elected to amalgamate with the TGWU in 1982, the *National Union of Agricultural and Allied Workers*, bringing 70,000 members, and the *National Union of Dyers, Bleachers and Textile Workers* of 37,000 members. A further thousand members arrived from the old 'blue' union of dockworkers, the *National Amalgamated Stevedores and Dockers*, historically a tenacious rival of the official TGWU policies in London, Hull, Manchester and Liverpool, but no longer financially viable.

Moreover, the TGWU's financial position is relatively healthy and it reported a surplus of £3.4 million for 1981. This has been achieved by doubling contributions over the two years from 1980 to a minimum level of 50 pence, and by avoiding widespread or prolonged strikes and the necessity to provide strike pay. For instance, the union made no general call for strike action by its members in support of the health service workers in their 1982 pay dispute.

In 1982 the General Executive Council reviewed the possibilities for further amalgamations with a number of small textile unions, the National Union of Sheet Metal Workers (NUSMCHDE) and the National Society of Metal Mechanics (NSMM).

Coverage

The wide membership coverage of the TGWU is well enough reflected in its trade groups to need little further elaboration, which would in any case entail listing a huge array of negotiating bodies at industry-wide or national, company, plant and workplace level.

Organisation

Every member of the union is attached to a branch. It is the policy of the union that each member joins with colleagues to elect a workplace representative, usually although not invariably called a shop steward. While the branch remains an important administrative unit for the union at the grass roots and an important channel of communication, exclusively so for nominations and elections, increasingly its functions and machinery and the work of its officers are supplemented and strengthened by that of workplace representatives and shop stewards.

Large-scale production and the spread of so-called 'scientific management' techniques have combined to increase the responsibilities of shop stewards. Rule 11 of the TGWU Rule Book states:

> For the purpose of representing the membership on matters affecting their employment, a shop steward or equivalent representative shall be elected by the membership in a defined working area or at a branch meeting by a show of hands or ballot as may from time to time be determined.
> Shop stewards shall receive the fullest support and protection from the union, and immediate inquiry shall be undertaken by the appropriate trade group or district committees into every case of dismissal of a shop steward with a view to preventing victimisation, either open or concealed.

Since the changes initiated by Jack Jones the TGWU is often referred to as a shop stewards' union.

Regional and district committees

There are eleven territorial divisions or regions. District committees have been widely established in most regions; some unite branches within a district on a community basis irrespective of industry, and others co-ordinate branches in particular industries such as automotive trades, oil trades, or ACTSS (administrative, clerical, technical and supervisory) membership. The rapid growth of the district committee system reflects the development of plant bargaining, resulting in the negotiation of hundreds of agreements on wages, conditions and procedures. This necessitates co-ordination within each district.

The regional committee is the ruling body for each and is a direct link with the General Executive Council. It consists of representatives elected by or from the district or regional trade group committees or by electoral conference within the region, who hold office for two years. These committees mainly function to supervise and co-ordinate regional union activity. The regions have considerable autonomy since, for administrative convenience, the TGWU likes to keep a substantial proportion of its funds at regional level.

National trade group or section committees

Trades groups and sections	Membership (December 1980)
Vehicle Building and Automotive	168,612
Power and Engineering	241,348
Chemical, Rubber, Manufacturing and Oil Refining Industries	125,060
Docks, Waterways, Fishing and other Maritime Services	44,554
Commercial Services	208,172
Passenger Services	128,794
Public Services (inc. Civil Air Transport Section)	188,788
General Workers (inc. Process Industries)	237,953
Food, Drink and Tobacco Industries (inc. Agriculture)	208,551
Building, Construction and Civil Engineering (and Building Crafts Section incorporating National Association of Operative Plasterers)	350,000
Association of Clerical, Technical and Supervisory Staff	146, 803
Dyers, Bleachers and Textile Workers	37,000
Agricultural and Allied Workers	73,000

Although some 20,000 textile members (formerly in the General Workers' Trade Group) have been combined in the new Dyers, Bleachers and Textile Workers' Trade Group (from NUDBTW), they are still included in the General Workers figures above.

Each trade group has a national committee elected from the regions and members hold office for two years. Each national trade group committee deals with the industrial interests of the group membership and may formulate policy on collective bargaining and develop organisation. It considers reports and resolutions from the regional trade group and district committees.

National trade group conferences of trade delegates may, in certain circumstances, be held to consider issues affecting a particular industry. Such issues cannot be discussed at the Biennial Delegate Conference.

Biennial Delegate Conference

The Biennial Delegate Conference is the supreme policy-making authority within the union. Nominations of delegates are made from the branches but election is by ballot vote of regional trade groups on a membership basis. The general secretary, other executive officers, finance, administrative, national trade group and regional secretaries and up to three representatives of the General Executive Council also attend.

Rules revision conference

The 1949 Biennial Delegate Conference established the rules revision conference as the sole authority in the union to make, amend or revoke the rules or constitution of the union. This body meets only every six years, though special rules conferences can be convened. An interesting feature of this body is that its basis of representation is different from that of the policy-making Conference; the delegates are elected on a territorial basis of approximately 1 to 10,000 members, therefore reducing trade bias in the drawing up of new rules. The idea is that rules are for the whole union and not to benefit any particular sec-

tion of it. Some people have speculated about whether the rules revision conference or the Biennial Delegate Conference which created it is the supreme constitutional authority in the union, but this is rather academic. Within the TGWU there are invariably moves at the time of the rules revision conference to make changes, such as to the election of full-time officials.

The 1980 rules revision conference confirmed that only 'employees' could belong to the union, and that meant people in employment. However, some regional and district officials have recruited unemployed people into membership in defiance of this rule.

General Executive Council

The 40-strong General Executive Council is the governing body of the union between Biennial Delegate Conferences. It is responsible for the general administration and management of the union, subject to the policy laid down by the Biennial Delegate Conference to which it reports.

In the GEC are merged the dual structures of the union, the trade and territorial organisation. The territorial representatives of the GEC are elected by ballot of the membership in the regions concerned. There is at least one representative on the GEC for each national trade group committee. Members of the GEC are all lay members with at least two years of financial membership and they hold office for two years. Meetings are held quarterly, special sessions being convened by the general secretary when necessary.

The TGWU is exceptional in nominating lay GEC members to sit on the TUC General Council.

Finance and general purposes committee

The GEC elects a finance and general purposes committee which meets monthly or as convened by the general secretary. It is concerned with finance, properties and investments of the union; stoppages of work and the authorisation of strike pay; emergency problems and other matters referred to it by the GEC.

Full-time and permanent officers

Once elected (in the case of the general secretary) or appointed, these officers hold office 'during the pleasure of the union' which normally means until retirement age. The general secretary is elected by ballot vote of the members; any member of five years standing membership who is nominated by a branch is eligible to run for office. The general secretary is responsible to the GEC for all aspects of policy and administration and is the voice of the GEC at the Biennial Delegate Conference but also outside the union.

The deputy general secretary shares many of these duties. There are national secretaries and national officers for the individual trade groups and there are also regional and district full-time officers. None of these officers, except the general secretary, is elected. They are all appointed by a sub-committee of the GEC after a rigorous examination of their record, experience and training. National trade group secretaries must present regular reports to the GEC.

Women

Women's membership decreased by 37,733 to 291,801 (12.9 per cent of total membership) in the two years to the beginning of 1981 and decreased further to 257,373 by the time membership figures were reported for the 1982 Trades Union Congress. While union activities among women members have increased, it is recognised within the union that more needs to be done; it was agreed at the 1978 TGWU women's delegate conference that this would become an annual conference.

In September 1980 the TGWU launched a campaign to help its women members, including the establishment of women's regional advisory committees. Only seven of the union's 600 full-time officials are women.

External Relations

The union affiliates 1.25 million of its members to the Labour Party which necessitated affiliation fees amounting to £400,000 in 1980. Alex Kitson continues to represent the TGWU on the National Executive Committee of the Labour Party. The union maintains a parliamentary group of sponsored MPs :

Lewis Carter-Jones (Eccles).
Stan Crowther (Rotherham).
Raymond Fletcher (Ilkeston).
Harry Gourlay (Kirkcaldy).
Harriet Harman (Peckham).
Leslie Huckfield (Nuneaton).
Roy Hughes (Newport).
Neil Kinnock (Bedwellty).
Gregor Mackenzie (Rutherglen).
Hugh McCartney (Central Dunbartonshire).
Kevin McNamara (Hull Central).
David Marshall (Glasgow, Shettleston).
Gordon Oakes (Widnes).
Robert Parry (Liverpool Scotland).
Peter Shore (Stepney and Poplar).
Renee Short (Wolverhampton North East).
John Silkin (Deptford).
Sydney Bidwell (Southall).
Norman Buchan (Renfrewshire West).

John Horam (Gateshead West) was sponsored as a Labour MP until he defected to the Social Democrats in 1981.

The TGWU and the Labour Party

Alex Kitson represents the TGWU on the National Executive Committee of the Labour Party and was elected party chairperson following the 1980 annual conference at which, in addition, Larry Smith was elected to the conference arrangements committee.

One of the most controversial debates at the 1980 Conference was about widening the franchise for the election of the party leader. The TGWU supported the general principle and also voted in favour of three different formulae tabled by the NEC. The formula eventually decided at a special conference ensured that the TGWU block vote (the union affiliates about 1.2 million of its membership to the Labour Party: 8 per cent of the entire electoral college) would be of crucial importance in any Labour Party leadership elections. Its role was soon tested when Benn challenged Healey for the Deputy Leadership — a saga that revealed TGWU internal 'consultative procedures', to determine the destiny of the block vote, as a lamentable and embarrassing shambles.

First the standing orders committee at the 1981 TGWU Biennial Conference was able to outmanoeuvre the left so that the issue was never put to the vote there. It then appeared that the broad left-dominated GEC would be able to successfully recommend to the Labour Party delegation that the block vote be placed for Benn — despite the fact that, on a simple count of branches voting within each region, seven of the ten regions favoured Healey. The Benn supporters countered that the regions voting for Benn (Scotland, the North West and London) were the larger regions which together would comprise a majority of members over the other seven regions. This was soon shown to be palpably false. In fact, in the regions where there was a high poll, Benn fared quite badly, while when Healey polled well, he polled extremely well — but the overwhelming impression was of an incoherent and uncoordinated process of consultation. This adverse impression was worsened by the vicissitudes of the TGWU delegation at Conference, which at first split on the recommendation of the GEC to go for Benn and then finally voted for Silkin, the TGWU-sponsored MP, on the first ballot and for Benn on the second ballot.

Following widespread criticism of the process of consultation and deciding on how to cast the block vote, the GEC decided in March 1982 that the method of recommendation by the Executive to the union's delegation to Conference, which has existed for 60 years, would continue, but that there would be no further attempts at 'soundings' or consultation of the regions.

The TGWU Biennial Conference is becoming a graveyard of any hopes the Labour Party leadership may from time to time entertain of securing agreement with the trade unions about prices and incomes policy. The 1977 Conference voted to dump the social contract and a similar decision was reached overwhelmingly in 1981. Another policy that had been advocated by Jack Jones as general secretary — the extension of industrial democracy — was also thrown out by the 1981 conference, against the advice of the GEC.

The TGWU and the TUC

In contrast with the General and Municipal Workers' Union, the TGWU is not enthusiastic about plans to expand the work of the TUC and reduce the autonomy of individual affiliated unions. This includes tough opposition to plans to alter the composition of the General Council, for instance by automatic representation of unions with more than a stipulated membership.

TGWU criticism of such moves typifies the views of many of the traditional manual workers' trade unions, who are suspicious of TUC efforts to increase central authority at their expense. Faced with declining membership, the TGWU has carefully garnered its funds and is not prepared to underwrite extra TUC services while it can provide them itself more cheaply. This attitude was exemplified by the TGWU's objection on financial grounds to TUC plans to set up a national training centre in London and a newspaper sympathetic to the labour movement. Union policy has also been blunt in urging TUC withdrawal from participation in the NEDC and the sector working parties (see **TUC**).

Recent Events

Apart from developments concerning the Labour Party and the TUC, other recent events of significance are mainly about pay, conditions and collective bargaining, and are most clearly set out by trade group:

Vehicle building and automotive

Shop steward and rank-and-file trade union organisation at BL has been largely subjugated so that attempts to impose more exacting work practices are unrelenting. However, the company had the greatest difficulty in obtaining agreement to a revised bargaining structure early in 1982 because shop stewards were suspicious of management's attitudes and intentions, especially towards the closed shop and union-only sub-contracting in line with the Tebbit legislation.

Power and engineering

This trade group, the membership of which declined by 35,000 during 1980, consists of engineering industry manual workers, British Shipbuilders; British Aluminium; electrical cable-making; light metals; iron and steel; gas and electricity supply.

Chemical, rubber manufacturing and oil refining industries

There has been much speculation about the apparent strategic bargaining power of TGWU oil-tanker drivers, but the militancy of the drivers has not so far matched the windy rhetoric of TGWU leadership in 1981 about their capacity to bring down the Thatcher government. These workers are already relatively well paid and did not seem much interested in a possible confrontation with troops at oil refineries. At an oil industry delegate conference in August 1982 shop stewards voted to attempt to bargain on an industry-wide basis with all oil companies except Mobil.

The combine committee of conveners and senior stewards in the chemical industry is officially encouraged and guided and has continued to function.

National agreements in the rubber manufacturing industry were terminated in December 1977.

Docks, waterways, fishing and other maritime services

The national ports shop stewards' committee expressed concern about proposed alterations in the national and local dock labour boards, under which the 21 local labour boards would be replaced by five regional bodies. However, as employment in the docks has declined, so has the influence of this committee, which is now utterly dependent on official TGWU support. A delegate conference voted by 81 votes to 3 for strike action on the issue in April 1982 but then the strike was suspended on the recommendation of officials.

The annual fishing section conference held in Fleetwood in June 1980 established a working party to examine the serious problems besetting the industry. A comprehensive policy document, *Fishing: The Way Forward*, was produced by Melvin Keenan, the TGWU Fishing Liaison Officer and Norman Godman of Heriot-Watt University.

Road transport (commercial)

The TGWU opposed the recommendation of the Armitage report for the introduction of vehicles with a larger legal capacity.

Following a reassessment of its weakened bargaining power, the union proposed the re-introduction of a substantial element of national negotiations into bargaining arrangements for private road haulage.

Passenger services

TGWU members were involved in protest strikes against cuts in services, job losses and the doubling of fares following the Law Lords' ruling against the GLC's cheap fares policy.

Public services

Civil air transport is a sub-section of this trade group and here the TGWU suffered one of its most humiliating defeats in supporting ramp workers who were locked out by British Airways at Heathrow after refusing to accept revised working practices, and after seven weeks were forced to come to terms.

General workers

The textile workers have now been grouped in the new Dyers, Bleachers and Textile Workers' trade group (Group 11).

Food, drink and tobacco

The agricultural workers have now been allocated to the new Agricultural and Allied Workers' trade group (Group 14).

Building, construction and civil engineering

Rates of pay of opencast coalminers, members of the TGWU, tend to be held back by rates which the Civil Engineering Employers' Federation is prepared to offer to workers in other sectors of the industry. As a result the industry produced a profit of £156 million for the NCB in 1981 and a delegate conference of the TGWU brought threats of withdrawal from the civil engineering working rules agreement under which the industry's negotiations are conducted.

Association of clerical, technical and supervisory staff

The National Union of Cooperative Insurance Society Employees (NUCISE) voted by a 3 to 1 majority to merge with the TGWU by becoming part of a new insurance section of ACTSS.

Further Reference

V. L. Allen, *Trade Union Leadership*, Longmans Green 1957. The most comprehensive study of the TGWU and the problems of amalgamation and integration and of the leadership of Bevin and Deakin between its formation and 1955. We are grateful to Mr Allen, for permission to draw extensively on the book for the historical section.

A. Bullock, *The Life and Times of Ernest Bevin*, Vol. I *Trade Union Leader 1881-1940*, Heinemann 1960. Hardly dispassionate but shows Bevin's vital role in the development of the TGWU.

G. Goodman, *The Awkward Warrior*, Davis-Poynter 1980. A biography of Frank Cousins.

F. E. Gannett and B. F. Catherwood, *Industrial and Labour Relations in Great Britain*, P. King & Son 1939, pp.152-202. A chapter on the Transport and General Workers' Union, written by TGWU staff.

R. Undy, 'The devolution of bargaining levels and responsibilities in the Transport and General Workers' Union 1965-75', *Industrial Relations Journal*, vol.9, no.3.

D. Wilson, *Dockers*, Fontana/Collins 1972.

J. Lovell, *Stevedores and Dockers*, Macmillan 1969.

H. A. Clegg, *Industrial Relations in London Transport*, Blackwell 1950.

Industrial Relations in the Coaching Industry, Advisory Conciliation and Arbitration Service Report no.16, 1978. Interesting case studies of an industry where union organisation is not well developed.

Angela Tuckett, *The Scottish Carter*, Allen & Unwin 1967. A history of the Scottish Commercial Motormen's Union which amalgamated with the TGWU in 1971. Alex Kitson was the general secretary of this union.

R. Hyman, *The Workers' Union*, Clarendon Press 1971. This union amalgamated with the TGWU in 1929, greatly augmenting its scope and membership.

M. Stephens, *Ernest Bevin: Unskilled Labourer and World Statesman*, Transport and General Workers' Union 1981.

APPENDIX
List of Amalgamated Unions

1922

Amalgamated Society of Watermen, Lightermen and Bargemen
Amalgamated Carters, Lorrymen and Motormen's Union
Amalgamated Association of Carters and Motormen
Associated Horsemen's Union
Dock, Wharf, Riverside and General Workers' Union
Labour Protection League
National Amalgamated Labourers' Union
National Union of Docks, Wharves and Shipping Staffs
National Union of Ship's Clerks, Grain Weighers and Coalmeters
National Union of Vehicle Workers
National Amalgamated Coal Workers' Union
National Union of Dock, Riverside and General Workers
National Union of British Fishermen
North of England Trimmers' and Teemers' Association
North of Scotland Horse and Motormen's Association
United Vehicle Workers
Belfast Breadservers' Association
Greenock Sugar Porters' Association

1923

Dundee Jute and Flax Stowers' Association
North Wales Craftsmen and General Workers' Union
North Wales Quarrymen's Union
Scottish Union of Dock Labourers

1924

United Order of General Labourers

1925

Association of Coastwise Masters, Mates and Engineers

1926

Weaver Watermen's Association
Irish Mental Hospital Workers' Union
National Amalgamated Union of Enginemen, Firemen, Motormen, Mechanics and Electrical Workers (formed 1889)

1928

Cumberland Enginemen, Boilermen and Electrical Workers' Union (formed 1890)

1929

Workers' Union (formed 1890)

1930

Belfast Operative Bakers' Union
Northern Ireland Textile Workers' Union
London Co-operative Mutuality Club Collectors' Association

1933

National Union of Co-operative Insurance Society Employees
Portadown Textile Workers' Union
Scottish Farm Servants' Union

1934

'Altogether' Builders' Labourers' and Constructional Workers' Society
Scottish Busmen's Union

1935

National Winding and General Engineers' Society

1936

Electricity Supply Staff Association (Dublin)
Halifax and District Carters' and Motormen's Association

1937

Power Loom Tenters' Trade Union of Ireland

Belfast Journeymen Butchers' Association
Scottish Seafishers' Union

1938

Humber Amalgamated Steam Trawlers' Engineers' and Firemen's Union
Imperial War Graves Commission Staff Association

1939

Port of London Deal Porters' Union
North of England Engineers' and Firemen's Amalgamation

1940

National Glass Workers' Trade Protection Association
Radcliffe and District Enginemen and Boilermen's Provident Society
National Glass Bottle Makers' Society

1942

Liverpool Pilots' Association

1943

Manchester Ship Canal Pilots' Association

1944

Grangemouth Pilots' Association

1945

Leith and Granton Pilots
Dundee Pilots
Methil Pilots

1946

Government Civil Employees' Association

1947

Liverpool and District Carters' and Motormen's Union

1951

Lurgan Hemmers', Veiners' and General Workers' Union
United Cut Nail Makers of Great Britain Protection Society

1961

Scottish Textile Workers' Union

1963

Gibraltar Confederation of Labour and the Gibraltar Apprentices and Ex-Apprentices Union, Gibraltar Labour Trades Union

1965

North of Ireland Operative Butchers' and Allied Workers' Association

1966

United Fishermen's Union

1967

Cardiff, Penarth and Barry Coal Trimmers' Union

1968

Scottish Slaters, Tilers, Roofers and Cement Workers' Society
National Association of Operative Plasters (est. 1860)

1969

Amalgamated Society of Foremen Lightermen of River Thames
Irish Union of Hairdressers and Allied Workers
Port of Liverpool Staff Association
Process and General Workers' Union

1970

Sheffield Amalgamated Union of File Trades

1971

Scottish Commercial Motormen's Union (formed 1898)
Watermen, Lightermen, Tugmen and Bargemen's Union
Chemical Workers' Union

1972

National Union of Vehicle Builders (est. 1884, previously United Kingdom Society of Coach Makers)
Scottish Transport and General Workers' Union (Docks)

1973

Iron, Steel and Wood Barge Builders and Helpers' Association

1974

Union of Bookmakers' Employees
Union of Kodak Workers

1975

File Grinders' Society

1976

Grimsby Steam and Diesel Fishing Vessels Engineers' and Firemen's Union

1978

National Association of Youth Hostel Wardens
Staff Association for Royal Automobile Club Employees

1979

Association of Licensed Aircraft Engineers

1982

National Union of Agricultural and Allied Workers
National Union of Dyers, Bleachers and Textile Workers
National Amalgamated Stevedores and Dockers
National Union of Cooperative Insurance Society Employees

Transport Union, United Road
(URTU)

Head Office

76 High Lane
Chorlton-cum-Hardy
Manchester M21 1FD
061-881 6245/6

Principal Officers

General Secretary—
Jackson Moore MBE
Assistant General Secretary—
A. T. Hughes
President— A. Fallon

Membership (1982)

Male 25,700
Female 700
Total 26,400

Union Journal and Publications:
Wheels — bi-monthly. This union newspaper is distributed widely throughout the road haulage industry.
URTU has also prepared a *Cafe Accommodation Handbook* (216 pages) which is compiled by the membership, giving a lorry driver's guide to overnight accommodation and eating facilities. The handbook also contains useful sections on road traffic and EEC regulations etc.

Divisional Officers

The union is split into three divisions:

● *North West Division*
M. H. Durant
2 St Clements Road
Chorlton-cum-Hardy
Manchester 21

● *Northern Division*
W. French
165 Atlantic Road
Greenhill
Sheffield

● *Central and Southern Division*
A. J. Taysome
117 Sandringham Road
The Lawn
Swindon, Wiltshire

General

URTU organises road haulage drivers, although its Rule Book provides for the organisation of 'their assistants and workers employed in production of products that require transportation'. Its members work in road haulage, international haulage, food and drink industries and for some local authorities. Despite its size the union has shown remarkable resilience in surviving in the face of competition. URTU has no political affiliations and is not represented on the General Council of the TUC. It has a small number of women members.

History

URTU has its origins in the *United Carters' Association* which was formed in 1890. In 1891 this body became the *United Carters' Association of England*. The union changed its name to the *United Carters' and Motormen's Association of England* in 1912, and to the *United Road Transport Workers' Association of England* in 1926. It adopted its present title in 1964.

Union Officials

URTU employs three divisional officers and 13 regional officers, apart from the general secretary and assistant general secretary. (URTU rules provide that the president of the union be paid £50 a year.) All full-time officials, apart from the president and general secretary, are appointed by the Executive Comittee. URTU officers must have had at least 12 months' membership of the union at the time of application, and all have spent a large part of their working life within the road haulage industry. URTU claims that it has more officers per unit of membership than any other trade union. The average number of members serviced by an officer in URTU is 1,800, compared with an overall TUC average of 5-6,000.

Organisation

The supreme policy-making body in URTU is the Triennial Delegate Meeting, which lasts for one day, and consists of the president, general secretary and delegates elected by the membership on the basis of one delegate for every 400 members. The day to day management of the union is carried out by the Executive Committee, which consists of the president, general secretary and not more than three representatives from each division. EC members are elected for a three-year term of office. The EC meets once a month. The union consists of two trade groups, one for road haulage and commercial vehicles, and one for bakery, food and drink. Trade group conferences are held. URTU is also organised into sections, which comprise a number of members employed in each work group, and where possible branches may be set up upon the request of a majority of the sections within a geographical area as defined by the EC.

Workplace Activity

Road haulage drivers spend nearly all

their working time on the road, and so membership participation is low in section meetings and union elections.

Women

URTU has a small number of female members, mainly among shop assistants, and in Wilson's Breweries, Manchester. There are no women full-time officers, and the EC is composed solely of males.

External Relations

URTU is not affiliated to the Labour Party. It is affiliated to the International Union of Food Workers, the European Trade Union Committee for Transport Workers, the International Transport Federation, and the European Trade Union Committees for Food and Allied Workers. The union is also represented on the TUC transport industries committee, the Distributive Industry Training Board, the Food Drink and Tobacco Industry Training Board and the Road Transport Industry Training Board.

Policy

The union has always sought to cultivate the image of being the 'Lorry Drivers' Union' and has guarded its independence jealously over the years. It campaigned vigorously against the Labour government's policy of transferring traffic from road to rail, and has campaigned against the 'rail lobby' (including the rail unions). The union has gradually moved away from its opposition to sleeper cabs.

URTU is opposed to the introduction of a reduction in the working week (down to an eight-hour day in January 1980) emanating from EEC Regulations, and EEC proposals to make it easier to obtain HGV Licences. At the 1979 TDM a motion committing the union to actively opposing any racialist organisation was carried.

Group Four Shipbuilding

General Municipal, Boilermakers' and Allied Trades' Union (GMBATU)

Boilermakers' Section
(formerly Amalgamated Society of Boilermakers, Shipwrights, Blacksmiths and Structural Workers (ASB))

Note: at the time of going to press, amalgamation plans with the GMWU were announced; information that follows refers to the union as at 30 September 1982, just prior to the formation of GMBATU.

Head Office

Lifton House
Eslington Road
Newcastle-on-Tyne NE2 4SB
0632-813205/6

Principal Officers

General Secretary—
J. G. Murray
Assistant General Secretary—
A. Scott

Executive Council

Region No. 1 (Scotland)—
J. G. Murray
Region No. 2 (North West and Northern Ireland)—
J. McFall
Region No. 3 (North East)—
J. P. Hepplewhite
Region No. 4 (Midlands)—
L. Hancock
Region No. 5 (South West England and South Wales)
A. C. Hadden
Region No. 6 (South)—
J. C. Bradley

Membership (1982)

Male 119,485
Female 100
Total 119,585

Union Journal and Publications

Monthly Report to Members. Histories of the constituent craft societies and workshop practice manuals are sold to members from head office.

General

The Boilermakers' Society was created and developed as a craft society and despite organisational change as a result of amalgamations in the 1960s and the exigencies of a more flexible outlook by skilled workers' unions in shipbuilding, it has found it hard to slough off craft traditions. Shipbuilding is no longer the main industry in which members of the society are employed; the development of structural steelwork, welding and flamecutting techniques brought new employment opportunities in the engineering and construction industries. However, the ASB still has more members in shipbuilding than any other union, where it organises a range of crafts, including welders, platers, shipwrights, caulkers, burners, drillers, riveters, loftsmen and riggers.

History

As is obvious enough the society was originally formed by makers of boilers, but skills acquired for the craft of boilermaking later found new outlets in the growing nineteenth-century industries of iron shipbuilding, locomotive building and bridge building. In the second half of the nineteenth century the Boilermakers' Society became a union not only of workers who made boilers but also, and above all, of builders of iron ships.

Histories of the society tend to be dominated by eulogies of Robert Knight who was general secretary for nearly 30 years in the period of the great expansion of British shipbuilding. Knight's control of the society's central administration was highly efficient but authoritarian; he opposed militancy and campaigned against the socialists and the new unionists (from general worker unions) in the TUC. A protracted rank-and-file campaign to loosen Knight's grip on the union culminated in the 1895 decision taken by rank-and-file delegates of the General Council of the society to establish a full-time regionally elected executive council to replace the previously locally elected lay executive council

Although 'holders-up' in the ship-yards were grudgingly admitted into membership, the society was elitist and its members held a narrow and exclusive attitude to semi-skilled and unskilled workers. For instance the society opposed the system of piece-work for platers' helpers and decided that it members would not work with platers' helpers who insisted on the system. The result was that hundreds of helpers had to be dismissed and new labourers recruited — with the assistance of the Boilermakers' Society — to take their places. This dispute of the 1880s caused intense bitterness in Sunderland.

Knight was the prime mover in the formation of the Federation of Engineering and Shipbuilding Unions in 1890.

Coverage

The union's non-manual membership (excluding supervisors and managers) is relatively small. It organises loftsmen who are staff employees and staff in quality control, production and industrial engineering.

Organisation

For electoral purposes the amalgamated society's branches are divided into regions: Scotland, North West of England and Northern Ireland, North East of England, Midlands, South Wales and Southern England. They elect a full-time executive councillor for each region. The branches are further divided into districts in each region for purposes of electing representatives to district committees.

The separate craft societies that came together during the 1960s are now more or less completely integrated for electoral purposes.

There is a Biennial Delegate Conference.

Workplace Activity

In shipbuilding the ASB normally has at least two stewards representing each department or trade group in any one yard, although if a particular group is very numerous there may be three stewards and if a group is relatively small it may be represented by only one steward. A typical set-up might be three stewards representing 250 or so welders and tackers, one steward representing ten boilermakers and, in between, two stewards each for caulker/burners, platers and shipwrights.

The role of ASB stewards in:

a) *Substantive negotiations*
The trend has been away from payment-by-results schemes. Nationalisation of the industry has reduced the importance of negotiations over substantive items (including pay) for most stewards.
b) *Productivity bargaining*
Provisions relating to the relaxation of working practices and flexibility in the use of labour: stewards have *not* generally been involved in such provisions in shipbuilding.
c) *Engagement of labour*
Stewards are frequently consulted about this but it is more widespread in ship repairing than in shipbuilding. Some stewards are also responsible for ensuring that apprentice ratios are observed.
d) *Use of labour*
An important function of many stewards is watching trade frontiers to ensure that they are not infringed by other unions. However, such pressure comes as much from work groups as from shop stewards, even though some stewards are particularly vigilant.

In addition to this, stewards also perform the positive function of resolving demarcation disputes before they reach official procedures.
e) *Overtime working*
Stewards keep rotas to maintain fair distribution of any overtime working.

f) *Consultation*
Safety, health and welfare committees.
g) *Individual and collective grievances*
h) *Maintenance of trade union organisation*

In fact, according to the ASB Rule Book this is their only function because it simply states that 'their duties shall be to examine members' contribution cards, to ensure that they are in compliance before they commence work.'

ASB stewards are normally subject to some form of annual election or confirmation to remain in office. The ASB has a shop stewards' committee in almost every shipyard.

External Relations

The ASB is affiliated to the Labour Party and sponsors John Smith MP (Lanarkshire North), Gerald Kaufman MP (Manchester Ardwick), and Andy McMahon MP (Glasgow Govan).

Policy

There is world-wide excess capacity and over-production in shipbuilding. In these circumstances ASB officials are well aware that rigid adherence to craft status and trade demarcations serves no useful purpose. On the positive side they know that this is the opportunity when they should — belatedly — open their ranks and extend their field of recruitment, but they do not appear to have pursued this policy at all vigorously and have not been very successful in doing so. This may be due to reluctance among members with feelings of craft status to accept members without this status into their ranks. In addition, the general worker unions are now firmly established in shipbuilding and may allege poaching if they have established a sphere of influence among these types of workers in the locality. For example, in a case of alleged poaching of six shipwrights' helpers by the ASB from the GMWU at Swan Hunter, the TUC disputes committee ruled that they be returned to the GMWU.

Demarcation disputes in shipbuilding are nowhere near as numerous as they once were. The ASB tended to be the union most frequently concerned in demarcation disputes. However, the amalgamation with the shipwrights and blacksmiths in 1963 and gradual integration since had been the main reasons for decline in the numbers of demarcation disputes between trades now within the union, especially between shipwrights and platers.

Inside the Confederation of Shipbuilding and Engineering Unions it has been customary for the ASB to take the lead in issues affecting the shipbuilding industry. According to the Commission on Industrial Relations (CIR) report on the shipbuilding industry, this greater sense of commitment to the industry has taken the form of an assertion of paramountcy based on independent action.

The ASB has tended to regard the work of its members in shipbuilding as of greater worth to the industry than the efforts of other groups. Traditionally, the construction of a ship's hull — the main work of the steel trades — can be distinguished from outfitting, and this division is symbolised by launching once steel work is mainly completed and movement to a fitting-out berth. These days technical developments have blurred the line dividing steelwork from outfitting, making it relatively less arduous than the ASB might wish to claim. New methods of construction mean that engine and equipment fitting by fitters, plumbers, pipefitters and others goes on alongside hull construction.

Traditionally, ASB members on jobs such as riveting and welding first opposed and then accepted and controlled piecework systems and in its heyday used piecework to achieve a differential in earnings over other groups, especially outfitters — a differential which they have tried to maintain in the face of changes in techniques and payment systems.

In some yards, such as Cammell Lairds at Birkenhead, a rough parity has been the norm but on the Tyne the ASB has defended the boilermakers' differential. Increasingly during the 1970s other groups of workers began to challenge ASB supremacy, and rivalry between ASB and AUEW or EETPU became a common feature of industrial relations, especially at Swan

Hunters. The differential became a source of dispute and led to strikes and an ACAS inquiry at that shipyard.

Recent Events

Nationalisation of the industry was clearly a precursor to wholesale rationalisation and closure of yards, now further accelerated by the Tory policy of requiring public corporations to pay their own way in the midst of world-wide over-production of ships. At a delegate conference in Tynemouth in August 1979, ASB delegates determined to take action against British shipbuilders' plans to close four yards, making 6,000 workers redundant. The ASB has found it difficult to counter redundancy pay.

The ASB has tried to make its amalgamation a reality, but in practice some work groups even now preserve special, privileged positions and the ASB consequently has a number of internal divisions which impair the strength of its claim that it stands for the interests of all steel workers in shipbuilding. It is widely believed in the ASB that its members' relative position would deteriorate if it went into joint negotiations with other unions. The sense of separate identity is strong; ASB leaders were seeking a merger with the General and Municipal Workers' Union in 1977 but their union conference rejected the proposal. However, financial and organisational pressures on the society pushed it towards a merger and the membership finally voted in favour of amalgamation with the General and Municipal Workers' Union in 1982 by a 2:1 majority.

Concern has been expressed that the ASB has lacked the vigour of other unions, which have expanded membership and encroached on work traditionally regarded as the province of ASB members. One union mentioned in this respect is the AUEW Construction Section, which has allegedly encroached on the work of welders who have been obliged to join it in order to take up certain construction jobs — platers, burners and caulkers.

While some delegates at the 1981 Conference argued that this logically demanded an approach to the AUEW about amalgamation, the Executive defeated moves to commit the ASB in this direction. For the Executive, John Heppelwhite argued that such an amalgamation would mean the loss of the society's National Delegate Conference and its power to make policy, while other delegates believed that unions such as the Construction Engineering Union had been swallowed by the AUEW.

In November 1981 the ASB threatened British Shipbuilders with a reversion to yard-by-yard bargaining, the underlying grievance being deteriorating pay and conditions (with the result that shipbuilding workers had slipped from fourth to twentieth place in earnings among manual workers), but the trigger being 120 compulsory redundancies declared at the Dundee yard of Robb Caledon. Finally a national settlement worth about 7½ per cent was achieved in an atmosphere of acrimony with the British Shipbuilders chairperson.

J. G. Murray won the election to replace Chalmers as general secretary but the result was challenged by Barry Williams, the other candidate, a Communist Party member. Allegations of ballot-rigging on both sides led to legal action in the High Court where counsel for Barry Williams sought an injunction barring Mr Murray from taking office. The long legal wrangle ended with the High Court ordering a new ballot, with Mr Murray standing down as general secretary. A. Scott took the place in the interim.

The result of the second ballot re-run was a victory for J. G. Murray by 2,693 votes to 2,083, but following further protests it was decided that another investigation by the Executive Council was necessary and the ballot result was held over.

Further reference

J. E. Mortimer, *History of the Boilermakers' Society, Vol. I: 1834-1906; Vol. II 1909-39*, George Allen & Unwin 1973.

Shipbuilding and Shiprepairing: 1971, Commission on Industrial Relations Report No. 22, Cmnd. 4756.

For further details of the alleged ballot-rigging see R. Rohrer, *New Statesman*, 6 March 1981.

Group Five Engineering, Founding and Vehicle Building

Domestic Appliance and General Metal Workers, National Union of

Head Office

Imperial Buildings
Rotherham
Yorkshire S60 IPB
0709-2820

Principal Officers

General Secretary—
R. D. Preston
Assistant Secretary—
H. Wright

Membership (1982)

Male 4,600
Female 500
Total 5,100

General

Trades represented among the membership have included and, to a diminishing extent in some cases, continue to include moulders, coremakers, fitters, grinders, glaziers, pattern makers, designers, drafters, brass finishers, filers, fettlers, bronzers, enamellers, blacksmiths, boiler welders. Members are generally employed in the domestic appliance, kitchen range, hot water and fender trades or are moulders, fitters or sheet metal workers.

History

The union was founded as the *National Union of Stove Grate, Fender and General Light Metal Workers* in 1890 after some of the men in the trade had joined the Knights of Labour and the representative of that society had led them in a nine-week strike which finally gained a ten per cent pay increase. By 1934 membership had reached 6,000.

Coverage

The union is a member of the Confederation of Shipbuilding and Engineering Unions and the Joint Committee of Light Metal Trades Unions which has a national agreement with the national metal trades federation.

Organisation

There are some 25 branches mainly in Rotherham and the West Pennines, South West Lancashire, the West Midlands and Derby. The Executive Council is elected biennially, two from each of four districts into which the branches are grouped. When the general secretaryship is vacant all branch secretaries are invited to apply. The Executive then considers all applications and a short list is drawn up which is put to a ballot of the whole membership.

Recent Events

Cumulative closures and redundancies left the union with its lowest membership for 50 years and a substantial deficit of expenditure over income from contributions in 1981.

Engineering Workers, Amalgamated Union of
(AUEW)

Engineering Section

Head Office

110 Peckham Road
London SE15 5EL
01-703 4232

Principal Officers

President— Terry Duffy
General Secretary—
Gavin Laird
Assistant General Secretaries
— R. W. Wright
K. Brett

Executive Councillors

Division No. 1: Final ballot to be held in March 1983, between Jim Airlie and Tom Dougan
Division No. 2: J. G. Russell
Division No. 3: G. Arnold
Division No. 4: K. G. Cure
Division No. 5: E. M. Scrivens
Division No. 6: J. P. Weakley
Division No. 7: J. R. Whyman

National Organisers

J. N. Laffey
J. Byrne
W. E. Timms
J. R. Bradley
H. Hewitt-Dutton
D. J. Graham
E. T. Hepple

Regional Officers

Division No. 1: T. Dougan
Division No. 2: J. Bowers
Division No. 3: H. Wilkinson
Division No. 4: P. Povey
Division No. 5: W. Pritchard
Division No. 6: M. T. Burke
Division No. 7: L. Choulerton

Membership (1982)

Total 1,024,205

(including approximately 150,000 women: membership figures were not broken down between women and men)

Union Journal and Publications

AUEW Journal — monthly) — distributed to branches for distribution to members (usually by shop stewards), circulation 145,000.
For a union of its size, the AUEW does not produce many publications from head office. The most important ones include:
An Introduction to the AUEW (Engineering Section) which was compiled in January 1980, and gives a brief outline of the workings of the union.
Welcome to the AUEW (Engineering Section) — a short booklet given to new members outlining in some detail how the union is governed and how it operates.
Shop Steward's Manual — a 32-page booklet setting out the duties of shop stewards.
Safety Representative's Handbook — a 54-page handbook designed for all safety representatives in each of the four sections of the AUEW — packed with detailed and useful information.
Danger: Your Health at Risk a 56-page booklet setting out hazards at work, incorporating information on recent research on health and safety and general advice on safety monitoring, with sections on: chemicals, dust, eye protection, fire risks, glass fibre, grinding hazards, ionising radiation, machine guarding, noise, oil hazards, personal hygiene, vibration damage, welding dangers, working environment, other hazards.
Your Rights and Opportunities in Industry: Apprentices and All Young People, 29 pages.
The union spent £97,884 on its educational work in 1981, covering weekend schools, residential courses and special schools. Over one quarter of all the TUC's postal course students were members of the AUEW (Engineering Section) and it is anticipated that increasing numbers of members will take TUC correspondence courses. Occasionally the union produces recruitment leaflets, designed for immigrant workers in their native languages.

Regional Offices

● *Division 1*
AUEW House
145/165 West Regent Street
Glasgow, G2 4RZ

● *Division 2*
AUEW Office
46-48 Mount Pleasant
Liverpool L3 5SE

● *Division 3*
AUEW House

Bridge Street
Leeds LS2 7RA

● *Division 4*
4 Holloway Circus
Birmingham 1

● *Division 5*
AUEW House
Furnival Gate
Sheffield S1 3HE

● *Division 6*
8 St Paul's Road
Bristol 8

● *Division 7*
28 Denmark Street
London WC2

The AUEW has 27 divisional organisers; 25 assistant divisional organisers; and 124 district secretaries (of whom 25 are part-time). All of these officers operate at various locations throughout the UK and Irish Republic.

General

The AUEW is the second largest union in Britain and consists of four sections:

AUEW (Engineering Section)
AUEW (Constructional Section)
AUEW (Foundry Section)
AUEW (Technical, Administrative and Supervisory Section, otherwise known as AUEW/TASS)

The union has grown from a number of amalgamations in 1851, 1920, and 1969-70. Each section of the AUEW is treated separately in this book. The relations between sections of the AUEW as a whole are discussed under **Relations between AUEW Sections** below.

History

Trade unionism in the engineering industry can be traced back to the emergence of the industry in its post-industrial-revolution form at the end of the eighteenth and the beginning of the nineteenth century. At first machinery was built mainly by millwrights who often combined the function of engineer, mechanic, drafter/designer, and civil engineer in one person. As industrialisation developed, the skills of the millwrights were at a premium and their wages rose well above the rates for skilled workers. The introduction of self-active tools reduced the power of the millwrights and the development of the factory system led to the trade union organisation becoming established among relatively unskilled engineers. By the time the Combination Acts were repealed in 1824-25 successful friendly societies existed in many of the engineering trades which became increasingly differentiated as the division of labour progressed. Various societies (many of which did not survive) were formed in the years prior to and just following the repeal of the Combination Acts covering smiths, millwrights, iron and brass-founders, mechanics, engineers and machinists. Since these trade protection societies were generally confined to one or two trades within a specific locality and limited membership to those who had served an apprenticeship, funds were too low to permit any continuity. The strongest union to be formed in that period was the *Journeymen Steam Engine and Machine Makers' and Millwrights Friendly Society* (known as the *'Old Mechanics'*) which was founded in 1826 in Manchester by John White, the first secretary. White campaigned enthusiastically in Manchester, Bolton, Stockport and Oldham under very difficult circumstances, frequently having to change his lodgings to evade police detection. By 1838, the *'Old Mechanics'* had nearly 3,000 members. Its nearest rival was the *Steam Engine Makers' Society*, formed in 1824 with only 525 members in 14 branches by 1836.

By 1840 a *United Trades Association* of the 'Five Trades of Mechanism' had been formed in Manchester bringing together millwrights, engineers, iron moulders, smiths and mechanics. Although this body was short lived, the attempts by the employers in the North to introduce the Quittance Paper in 1844 led to the formation of a stronger federation known as the *Mechanics' Protective Society of Great Britain and Ireland*. As Jefferys writes: 'The purpose of this society and its branches was not in any way to rival or compete with the existing trade unions among engineers, but rather to act as a defensive alliance between the different societies, so that if one trade was attacked all the trades in that workshop would strike. The Old Mechanics co-operated in building this society.'

It was clear that further amalgamation in the engineering trades was necessary following a number of strikes and the arrest and trial for conspiracy of the leaders of the Old Mechanics in 1847. In 1850, the executive of the Old Mechanics decided to invite the executive councils of the engineers', smiths', millwrights', moulders' and boilermakers' societies to elect deputations to meet and discuss amalgamation.

The first amalgamation

When the *Amalgamated Society of Engineers, Machinists, Smiths, Millwrights and Patternmakers* was launched in 1851 the membership was only 5,000 — less than half of the component societies and smaller than the Old Mechanics of a year earlier. Vigorous campaigning by the new union, helped by the journal *The Operative*, brought the membership up to nearly 11,000 by the end of the year as reluctant branches and societies joined the amalgamation. At its birth the amalgamated society had one paid official, William Allan, the general secretary, and became generally known as the Amalgamated Society of Engineers. The ASE had from the start a high rate of contributions and a generous scale of benefits. Whilst its district committees were permitted a high degree of autonomy, most of the funds were centralised at its London HQ. The general secretary was supervised by an Executive Council elected from the branches in the metropolitan area. Many of the characteristics of the 'new model' union were borrowed from the Old Mechanics and were later hailed by the Webbs as a landmark in the history of trade unionism. Its high contributions and exclusiveness meant that its model of organisation could only be copied by craft unions.

A few months after the foundation of the ASE, it became involved in a desperate struggle with the employers in Lancashire and London, when the employers locked out their trades people when they refused to accept an increase in the number of unskilled workers in shops. The 1852 lockout over dilution was a defeat for the ASE largely because its trade protection fund rapidly proved unable to support ASE members out of work and also because of the clever way the employers manipulated public opinion in their favour. The employers forced their men to sign the Document and the membership of the union slumped far below the figure of the previous year.

During the 1850s the union gradually recovered, and won recognition from a number of employers. Its unity was fostered because members in Scotland and Lancashire were prepared to submerge their regional loyalties and accept leadership from London. Fortunately for the union, the employers' organisations disintegrated, except for moribund local associations.

Jefferys noted that the attempt to crush the ASE out of existence had ended in a paper victory for the employers but it was their organisation that disappeared while the society gained greater strength than ever. By December 1866, membership of the ASE stood at 33,067 and the union's branches numbered 305.

After 1866, the ASE faced fresh challenges. Whilst the ASE had largely escaped the pitched battles in the early 1860s that characterised other trades, the employers realised that the steadily growing amalgamated unions posed a serious challenge to their authority on the industrial front. Allan patiently attempted to display unionism as respectable and efficient, although the general public was usually ill-informed about the issues behind disputes and too readily blamed the workers. Following the murder of a non-unionist in Sheffield in 1866, the employers seized the initiative to demand an investigation with the aim of indicting trade unionism as a whole. In the same year another blow was struck at trade unionism following the decision of the Lord Chief Justice in *Hornsby v Close*, in which the Boilermakers were suing a branch secretary for withdrawal of funds, that trade unions were in restraint of trade and therefore illegal conspiracies not eligible for registration under the Friendly

Societies Act. Thus trade union funds lay unprotected from the wiles of dishonest members. A Royal Commission was set up in 1867 and the efforts of the ASE were directed towards political and parliamentary action.

Allan played a major part in the proceedings of the Royal Commission, together with Applegarth of the Carpenters. The final Report of the Commission in 1869 did not give the employers any grounds for suppressing trade unions. The 1871 Trade Union Act gave the trade unions protection for their funds and the parliamentary lobbying to repeal the Criminal Law Amendment Act was carried out by the newly-formed TUC, which later acted in concert with the Conference of Amalgamated Trades in which Allan was a powerful influence. Allan died in 1874 and John Burnett, the hero of the rank-and-file Nine Hour Movement, was elected general secretary to succeed him. When Burnett assumed the office the membership of the ASE had reached 43,150.

Burnett's period as general secretary was characterised by the strains on the union's structure and organisation posed by the increasing size and diversity of the industry. Burnett preferred to change neither policy nor methods, and the possible changes that could have been made — widening or restricting membership, centralisation or decentralisation, an aggressive or conciliatory policy towards the employers — largely remained unchanged until the reorganisation of the ASE in 1892. The ASE used its strength skilfully against concerted attacks by the employers and successfully defended the nine-hour day. Periodic fluctuations in wages arising from changes in trade took place, but the district committees managed to achieve substantial increases in wages in the 1880s. By 1891 the ASE membership had reached 71,221 and it had 509 branches. Compared with other unions, which often appeared and lasted for only a short time, the ASE maintained its continuity and stability. Burnett resigned in 1886 to take up a newly created post of Labour Correspondent of the Board of Trade, and was succeeded by Robert Austin.

By 1890 it was clear that the ASE needed a radical reorganisation. Its conservatism in policy, its growing unwieldiness, and the rigidity and exclusiveness of its structure combined to weaken the role it could play in the wider labour movement. The ASE was top-heavy and there were inadequate links between the leadership and the branches, with the general secretary overwhelmed by administrative work. A movement for reform in the ASE grew up around Tom Mann and John Burns, who strongly attacked the conservatism and lack of fight of the old trade unionism. Mann had joined the ASE in 1881 but left in 1887 to act as travelling spokesperson for the Social Democratic Federation. In 1889 he was elected president of the dockers' union following his organisation of the 1889 dock strike. He remained active in the ASE and ran for election as general secretary when Austin died in 1891, being defeated by a narrow margin by John Anderson. The impact of Mann's campaign was reflected in the reforms adopted at the Leeds Delegate Meeting of 1892.

The ASE Rule Book still contained provisions which had been inherited from the Old Mechanics, and sweeping changes were made. The Local Executive Council of London members working at the trade was replaced by an Executive Council of full-time officials elected in eight divisions. Six full-time organising district delegates were to be elected and the central district committees were to be abolished. The number of paid officials thus increased from four (general secretary and assistant general secretaries) to 17. Two new sections of membership were created and membership was widened slightly. A superannuation reserve fund was set up to free the ASE's resources for more militant action. The EC was empowered to consult the membership on raising funds to engage in national politics.

During the 1890s the employers managed to build up an effective organisation and in 1898, after a 30-week lock-out in response to the ASE's demand for a 48-hour week, the notorious 'terms of settlement' were imposed which gave the employers the right to introduce any change in working conditions at the commencement of any dispute (the 'status quo' provisions) in federated firms.

Despite this defeat the ASE continued to grow, largely by skilful use of the central negotiating machinery and guerrilla activity in the districts. At the outbreak of world war one in 1914 the ASE membership stood at 174,253.

The period up to 1914 was marked by growing hostility between the members and the leadership as the resentment about the 'terms of settlement' and the lack of policies to deal with the effects of new technology and new methods of organisation built up. A reform movement under Tom Mann's leadership, together with the increasing influence of shop stewards, emphasised direct industrial action at the expense of parliamentary representation (the EC had been active in the launching of the Labour Representation Committee and the membership had rejected proposals for a political levy on behalf of the Labour Party). At the 1912 delegate meeting the rift between the executive and membership came out into the open. It was decided to reduce the EC to seven members, that an independent chairperson should be elected directly by the membership, that the entire EC should come up for election in 1913, and the ranks of the ASE should be open to unskilled workers. The executive opposed these changes, balloted the membership using a one-sided circular, and received their support. The delegate conference was recalled to invite them to retract their decisions which they refused to do. The Executive Council locked themselves in the new headquarters at Peckham Road and refused admission to the provisional Executive Council newly appointed by the delegates. After an undignified skirmish the old EC was ejected into the street, and after legal proceedings the old executive lost their case, giving way after six months in office to the newly elected Executive Council with J. T. Brownlie as the first independent chairperson.

The first world war and the second amalgamation

During the 1914-18 war wage rates were established at national rather than district level with direct contacts between the executive and the war Cabinet. A notable feature of the war years was the growth in the shop steward movement, with a number of major strikes, particularly on the Clyde. The stewards' power grew rapidly in the struggles to defend workers from the attempts of the government and employers to increase production and minimise wage increases while the cost of living and manufacturers' profits grew rapidly. The links on the shop floor between different unions were strengthened by joint committees and in 1917 the amalgamation committees joined the national shop stewards movement. All this served to emphasise that further amalgamation was both possible and necessary. During 1918, following instructions from the delegate meeting, the executive of the ASE started negotiations which resulted in 17 societies balloting their members on amalgamation in May 1919. The membership of the ASE cast 92 per cent of the votes in favour of amalgamation. Other societies having the requisite percentage of votes and majorities were:

Steam Engine Makers' Society
United Machine Workers' Association
United Kingdom Society of Amalgamated Smiths and Strikers
Associated Brassfounders, Turners, Fitters and Coopersmiths' Society
North of England Brass Turners, Fitters and Finishers' Society

Subsequent voting added three more societies to the number in favour:

East of Scotland Brass Founders' Society
Amalgamated Instrument Makers' Society
Amalgamated Society of General Toolmakers, Engineers and Machinists

Of the societies that voted and failed to obtain a 50 per cent poll the most important were the United Pattern Makers' Association and the Electrical Trades Union. As in 1851 the boilermakers again declined to take part, as did the iron founders. The

Amalgamated Engineering Union came into existence on 1 July 1920 with J. T. Brownlie as president and Tom Mann as general secretary. The AEU rules were based on the old ASE, but they made an important attempt to overcome the long-standing problems of the powers of the executive vis-a-vis the membership. In place of the delegate meeting, a national committee consisting of two representatives of each divisional committee was to meet annually to receive a report from the Executive Council and to give guidance as to future policy. Every fourth year the national committee was empowered to consider suggestions and decide on alterations in the rules. Thus for the first time the union was able to make policy decisions other than by changing the rules. Day to day running of the union was to continue in the hands of the Executive Council but members would have the right of appeal against its decision to a final appeal court of 15 members elected by the divisions. The rights of shop stewards were extended through shop stewards' quarterly meetings to be held in each district and they were given representation on district committees. The amalgamation meant that the total membership of the AEU was over 450,000 members.

The period of optimism which followed the second amalgamation proved to be short lived. The severe depression of 1921-22 enabled the federated employers to turn demands for an overall wage increase into a negotiated reduction of wages. Under threat of national lock-out the AEU suffered its first major defeat, and had to concede most of the gains made during the war. The lock-out lasted for 13 weeks on the issue of enforced overtime, and the AEU had to settle on terms similar to those of 1898. The York Memorandum was reaffirmed with a right to enforce overtime working as an additional prerogative of management.

The 1922 defeat again brought into question the narrow basis of the union's membership. In 1914 skilled workers outnumbered unskilled by three to one; by the early 1920s the ratio was almost one to one as technical change forced the pace of re-

form, especially with the increasing use of mass production techniques. The national committee in 1922 amended the AEU rules slightly to admit more semi-skilled workers and in 1926 the union was opened to un-skilled workers; as a result its membership doubled in the years 1933-39, reaching a total of 390,873 in 1939. The AEU had taken the lead in campaigning, with considerable success in the 1930s, for holidays with pay for its members. It had also gained the right to negotiate for apprentices, and many firms secured the 40-hour week.

During the second world war the AEU became for a time the second largest union in Britain, more than doubling its size from 1939 to 825,000 by 1953, but later falling back with the contraction of the engineering industry in the last phases of the war. A substantial degree of the AEU expansion was among semi-skilled workers in the munitions factories, and in 1942 it was decided to admit women into membership, which resulted in the recruitment of 138,717 in 1943. Another major development in wartime was the growth of a more effective federation in the engineering industry. There had been a partial federation in the industry since 1890; and since 1936 it had been called the *Confederation of Shipbuilding and Engineering Unions* (see **Trade Union Federations**) to which the AEU affiliated in 1946. The war also renewed the efforts of the AEU to secure further amalgamation, and the first fruit of these efforts was the admission of the *Amalgamated Society of Glass Works' Engineers* (1944) and of the *Amalgamated Society of Vehicle Builders, Carpenters and Mechanics* (1945).

Recent amalgamations

Today the union is the second largest in Britain, surpassed only by the TGWU; and it is a product of a number of mergers in the late 1960s and early 1970s. On 1 July 1967 the AEU joined forces with the *Amalgamated Union of Foundry Workers*, a very old union with many organisational similarities to the AEU. The two organisations kept their separate rules even though they were fused together under the name of the *Amalgamated*

Engineering and Foundry Workers' Union (AEF). The Engineering Section also retained its identity, and separate rules, after a further amalgamation with the *Constructional Engineering Union* (CEU) and the *Draughtsmen's and Allied Technicians' Association* (DATA) in 1970. The combined organisation became known as the present AUEW and started its new life with a total membership of 1,297,000. The ultimate aim is a common rule book and policy, but to date the merger has been attended by difficulties in the relationship between the sections (see **Relations between AUEW Sections**).

Union Officials

There has been a full-time president of the union ever since its creation in 1921. The president is the senior officer of the union with responsibility in industrial matters, and is entitled to attend and express her/his views at an Executive Council and may vote only in the event of a tie. The president speaks for the union on all external affairs. Like all elected full-time officials in the AUEW (Engineering) the president faces elections by the whole membership by a system of postal voting every three years initially and then every five years until the age of 60 when, having fought two elections, he/she remains in office until retirement at 65. Apart from acting as the external spokesperson of the union, the president is responsible for matters relating to the TUC, awards of merit in the union, and employers correspondence in conjunction with the general secretary.

The general secretary post in the union has been a full-time post ever since 1851. The incumbent is head of the internal affairs of the union, is responsible for the monthly journal and the general office staff, acts as treasurer and, in conjunction with the president, is responsible for employers' correspondence and opening of new branches. The general secretary may attend meetings of the EC and speak but has no vote. He/she is elected by the entire membership and holds office on a similar basis to the president.

The union has two assistant general secretaries who are elected on a similar basis to the general secretary and president by the entire membership. Duties are split between them. At present K. Brett is responsible for organisation and propaganda, education matters, and car supply; R. W. Wright is responsible for political matters and branch correspondence.

The seven executive councillors are elected by the membership in the respective divisions, are best described as the senior national industrial officers of the union, and are allocated duties among them. Each executive councillor has a personal assistant appointed by the general secretary allocated to her/him; these are considered to be part of the technical staff and are ineligible for full-time officer status. Each EC member is responsible for a particular trade, firm or industry, and works in conjunction wth one of the seven national organisers, who are allocated to a particular EC member, and are elected from the same division. About 95 per cent of their time is spent in their allocated industries.

The seven regional officers operate in the regional offices and are, in effect, used as 'spare limbs', being allocated duties by the particular EC member. They are elected by the membership in their particular division.

At present there are 26 divisional organisers and 23 assistant divisional organisers, although in 1981 one division was split so there were 27 DOs. They are elected by the membership within each division. The lowest level of full-time officials in the status hierarchy is the 124 district secretaries (of whom 25 are part-time) who are located throughout the UK and Eire.

The status hierarchy

The rules provide that candidates for full-time posts in the union must have worked in the trade for 12 months prior to candidacy, or have been unemployed, and have been members for at least seven years. An important aspect of the status hierarchy is that very few of the full-time officials are free for unrestricted assignment; the great majority remain in the regions where they were elected. This means that their local base is preserved, and it eliminates many of the possibilities for either harassment by higher officials or for assignments favourable to the winning of national reputations and higher office. Another effect is that, in theory at least, the general secretary is in a position to favour one of the two assistant general secretaries as her/his eventual replacement, by giving one of them suitable field assignments while keeping the other in her/his office. Moreover, control of the *Journal* enables the general secretary to broadcast her/his own political references and influence impending elections. In the September 1980 *Journal* an editorial began: 'No one who reads this *Journal* . . . can fail to recognise the leadership qualities shown by Terry Duffy and the present Executive Council . . .' Despite the fact that the AUEW (Engineering) still retains many craft features, the skilled membership has been heterogeneous and has constituted a declining proportion of the membership. Nevertheless, it is still true to say that the great majority of activists in the union are of craft origins, as are the full-time union officials.

Recent elections

There have been a number of studies recently analysing the elections in the union for evidence of the effects of organised and ideologically opposed electoral organisations within the union which attempt to secure victory for a candidate favouring their particular political line. The union's electoral rules were changed in 1972 from branch balloting to postal ballots. Under postal ballots the numbers voting rose substantially from the 5-11 per cent range of votes under branch ballots to 20-40 per cent plus of those on the electoral roll of the union. Thus the actual average electorate more than doubled overnight and the polling booth was shifted to the 'privacy of members' own homes'. There is evidence to suggest that the opposition faction within the union, which is frequently narrowly based both geographically and by branch, is unable to wield the same influence under postal balloting as it had exercised in the branch.

The introduction of postal voting has recently tended to favour the so-called 'moderate' or right-wing contenders for office. In 1976, Terry Duffy, the current President, challenged and defeated the incumbent, Bob Wright for a seat on the Executive; and in 1978 Wright, now Assistant General Secretary, was defeated by Duffy in the election for the presidency. The press campaign in favour of Duffy emphasised the fact that he was a 'moderate' and that Wright (an amiable and able negotiator) was an 'extreme left-winger', and the poll was unusually high. Many of Wright's supporters in the union argue that Duffy won on both occasions by votes of members who knew little, if anything, of the respective merits of the two candidates.

Apart from the massive task of mailing out around a million correctly addressed envelopes. there is the strong argument that the press influence the result in a particular direction as they did in the Wright *v* Duffy contests. The TUC education services manual *Democracy at Work* argues that postal votes are less than perfect reflections of union feeling and that 'one answer . . . is to develop the role of workplace-based meetings in union elections . . . Another possibility is to improve the standards of *information* available to voters in union elections.'

Before the introduction of postal voting, the left had been able to win branch ballots by concentrating its efforts on a high turn-out in strategic branches, where the left 'slate' of candidates in factory-based ballots could usually outnumber the often scattered votes at porly attended geographical branches. In fact, the left were probably collecting 'loyalty' votes for good service rather than the electorate voting for the policies of the stewards or candidates. The postal vote system not only destroys the 'loyalty' vote but it also makes it extremely difficult for the left to plan their campaign since they have little idea of where their strength lies.

In order to work effectively, the postal ballot electoral roll must have an accurate list of names and addresses of current members. However, as Patrick Wintour pointed out in an article in the *New Statesman* (7 May

1982): 'About 20 per cent of AUEW members are not on the electoral roll. About 20,000 are on the roll but shouldn't be, and as the industry continues to contract that proportion may rise.' Moreover, the Electoral Reform Society does not count the votes (as it does for many other unions that operate postal ballots), such vote-counts being carried out by the union's own vote-counting department, appointed by the general secretary. The vote-counting takes place over several weeks with two Executive Council members acting as scrutineers till the end.

In May 1982, Gavin Laird, the union's executive member for Scotland and the right-wing candidate, beat Ken Brett, assistant general secretary and a Communist, by 96,186 votes to 95,124 in a 23.7 per cent postal ballot poll. *Two weeks earlier*, the *Daily Mirror* had already published a list of successful candidates. The general secretary acts as returning officer, and the counting is shrouded in secrecy. Remarkably, no candidate or candidates' nominees are allowed to witness the count or enter the Ballots Department. The defeated candidate, Ken Brett, complained that he had already written to Sir John Boyd, the then general secretary, complaining of election irregularities in the conduct of the ballot. Such allegations inevitably fan suspicions about election procedures, especially with such a narrow victory for a major trade union post.

Coverage

There are AUEW members in the great majority of manufacturing establishments in the country, and a detailed coverage of the union is too complex to give here. The main industries where the union is concentrated include engineering, iron and steel, shipbuilding, chemicals, paper and boardmaking, electricity, synthetic fibres, rubber and plastics, road transport, motor vehicles, printing, construction, machine tools, government industrial establishments, local authorities, hospitals, railway workshops, sugar, agricultural machinery, aerospace, co-operative movement, oil refining, flour milling and nuclear power generation.

Organisation

The present constitution of the union is largely inherited from the second amalgamation, and elements of its structure can be traced back as far as the Old Mechanics. Essentially, the union has developed a separation of powers limiting the scope of influence of particular officers. The constitution of the AUEW (Engineering) incorporates a conscious separation of executive, judicial and legislative powers, where a policy-making *national committee* legislates, and an elected *final appeal court* interprets the rules in all contentious disciplinary cases. A separately elected *executive* administers the union's affairs from day to day.

National Committee

The National Committee (NC) used to consist of 52 voting rank-and-file union members indirectly elected by and from the 26 divisional committees (which in turn were elected by the district committees), plus seven participating members elected by the annual women's conference and the same number from the annual youth conference.

In 1980 at the Rules Revision Committee it was decided to increase the size of the National Committee to 91. The number of delegates per division was increased to three (from 27 divisions), and the seven seats reserved for women, elected by the union's women's conference, were given voting rights for the first time. In addition, the seven youth representatives were included without voting rights. One extra representative from the three divisions with the highest membership makes up the number. In 1981, the NC was evenly divided between left and right, but this changed in 1982 when the NC's composition moved to a 56–35 majority for the right.

The National Committee initiates policy, reviews agreements with employers and *instructs* the Executive Council for the following year. It also revises the rules every five years. Of course, with only 91 delegates the body lacks the authority of a major delegate conference as is found in many other British unions. Added to this, the gap between their sessions is too long to allow the NC to hold any careful watching brief over the activities of the completely 'professional' seven-person executive, which inevitably strays into policy making rather than implementing policies made for it. There have been several conflicts between the NC and the Executive Council over the years; from time to time the NCs have attempted to reinforce their admitted constitutional role by approving resolutions which have included provisions for their own recall in the event of something happening or failing to happen. In 1966 a dispute between the two bodies resulted in a final appeal court ruling censuring the Executive for failing to act upon such a recall motion. A notorious example, which illustrates the possible serious loss in NC powers, was the occasion in 1967 when the then right-wing president, Lord Carron, cast the massive Engineers' block vote at the Labour Party and TUC conferences in defiance of the instructions of the NC. This became known as Carron's Law, and ended with Hugh Scanlon's election as president in 1967. All Executive Council minutes are highly confidential (only decisions are reported), and thus the NC is further weakened in its policy-making role.

While it is true to say that the NC has generally been free of domination by national and lower level full-time officials and has sometimes acted as a check on the administration, its real role is in the provision of a forum for debates on 'political' issues. A review of the proceedings of national committees shows a left-right split on such issues as nationalisation without compensation, voluntary incomes policy *v* free collective bargaining, postal ballots, proposed national strikes over wage claims etc. In 1982 there was a 56 to 35 majority for the right on the NC. The real significance in political terms is that the NC decides the allocation of the massive block vote of the Engineers at the TUC and Labour Party conferences. Left-wingers might comment that occasional flouting of NC decisions by the Executive Council is not dissimilar to the disregard for Conference decisions by the Parliamentary Labour Party.

District committees

The independence of the National Committee has to be understood in the light of the high level of autonomy and wide range of functions which is afforded to the districts. Rule 12 provides that district committees negotiate with employers and regulate wages, hours of labour, terms of overtime, piecework, and general conditions affecting the interests of the trades in their respective district. The outcome of such negotiations, including possible district-wide strikes, may be binding on all members in a district. The Executive Council may disapprove district resolutions or refuse to permit a strike ballot, but it is not permitted to complete an agreement unless the terms are first submitted to the district(s) concerned. Any disagreement between the EC and a district committee must be submitted to the NC, which consists of district committee members who have also been elected to the divisional committees and, from there, to the NC itself.

Most district committees gain their prominence from the fact that many shop stewards are represented on them, and the district committees have authority to call factory strikes, subject to EC approval (see **Workplace Relations**). The Rule Book provides that there shall be one shop steward for every 3,000 members on each district committee, and shop stewards are elected every December by a meeting of shop stewards called by the district secretary. There is a triennial referendum for the district president and secretary.

At one time it was true to say that the thrust of the AUEW's strength lay in its shop stewards, who were empowered to negotiate for members on the shop floor, and their work was supplemented by the district committees, which were able to enforce a minimum standard of wages and conditions at all the factories in the district. Recently however, the powers of district committees and shop stewards has been eroded by unemployment, irreversible changes in technology and industrial structure, and in rule changes which have been initiated by the right-wing in the union as a result of the introduction of the postal ballot. District committees will soon no longer be able to prevent the 'check-off' system of deduction of union dues in the wage packet, and the introduction of full-time branch secretaries in some branches all serve to prevent activists from keeping in contact with rank-and-file members.

Divisional committees

Divisional committees are a level higher in the union than district committees, and their main function is to act as a body to oversee the union's organisation in the districts and to provide a link between the districts and the EC and NC. Divisional committees elect three delegates each year to the NC, but in the case of the three divisions with the highest membership, an additional delegate is elected. These elections take place annually, following the annual election of branch officers and delegates in November. Not less than two meetings of the divisional committee take place each year, one preceding and one following NC meetings.

Divisional committees in the AUEW now have newly expanded powers — largely at the expense of district committees. For example, the AUEW decided to set up supervisory branches of its own (which would rival the AUEW/TASS branches and were a direct result of the conflict between TASS and the other three AUEW sections: see below). Such supervisory branches would be able to send delegates directly to the divisional committees, thus side-stepping the district committees.

Moreover, representation on the divisional committees is fraught with anomalies. Smaller districts can have greater representation than those with larger membership because a district with fewer than 1,000 members is entitled to send one delegate, whereas a district with several thousands of members is restricted to sending two delegates.

Internal union advisory committees

The union has a set of advisory committees which are intended to streamline the union's organisation in a number of industries where AUEW (Engineering) interests are strong. Each of these is chaired by an EC member assisted by one of the national organisers. At present the following advisory committees are in operation:

Ministry of Defence Advisory Committee
Iron and Steel Advisory Committee
ICI Advisory Committee
Railway Delegate Conference
UKAEA Delegate Conference

Each of these committees meets once a year around March-April.

Women's annual conference
(See **Women**)

Junior workers' annual conference
The EC is obliged to convene annually a conference of junior workers, of between 26 and 52 delegates. Resolutions approved from such conferences are submitted to the National Committee. The annual youth conference is, in effect, a training ground for future officers; it is thus more important than some writers believe. The annual conference of junior workers now elects seven representatives to attend the National Committee, one from each Executive Council division, but these seven delegates have no voting powers.

Relations between AUEW Sections

The conflict between left and moderate candidates in the AUEW has held up the progress of the four AUEW sections towards an effective merger with a common Rule Book and common policies. At present, each section operates under the constitution it had as an independent union, and is still autonomous. The AUEW federation provides for the president and general secretary of the Engineering Section to be the corresponding officers of the AUEW by rule. The Executive Council of the AUEW consists of: the EC of the Engineering Section; plus two representatives from the Foundry Section, one of whom could be its general secretary; plus, similarly, two representatives from the technicians' section; plus one representative from the Constructional Section when its membership is less than 50,000 or two when this is over 50,000 (in 1980 it was 25,000). There is also representation of the four sections in a combined national conference for the AUEW.

At the 1979 61st National Committee of the Engineering Section there were nine resolutions relating to the amalgamation and not one was carried. The votes were evenly split 26-26 with the president declaring each resolution 'not carried'. The voting pattern reflected the left-right split between the various divisions.

The April 1980 National Committee took a different line, reflecting gains for the right in the composition of the NC itself. It decided to press ahead with a full merger of the AUEW's various sections, to end the present relationship with any section that rejected the terms of the merger, and to insist on postal ballot elections for present and future officials of the resulting merger. This is a demand which the white-collar and supervisory section (TASS) has consistently rejected. Some delegates at the National Committee advised TASS to think again or leave, although TASS cannot be ejected against its will from the present loose amalgamation. The strategy of the AUEW (Engineering Section) leadership — endorsed by 29 votes to 23 — was to pull together the Engineering, Foundry and Constructional sections, and the National Union of Sheet Metal Workers, into a single grouping with around 1.5 million members. The TASS conference the following month reaffirmed its commitment to 'one union for engineering' but delegates stressed that their separate sectional identity must be retained. One of the central issues which has frustrated moves toward completing amalgamation is the position of full-time TASS officials (see **AUEW/TASS**), who are appointed on permanent contracts. The AUEW/ TASS General Secretary, Ken Gill, accused some Engineering Section leaders of developing a theory of amalgamation by domination. He accused the Engineering Section of attempting 'bullying and hectoring' and that these antics were discouraging other unions which might have been attracted to the AUEW.

In late 1980 AUEW/TASS successfully sought a ruling from the certification officer that a proposed merger of the three craft sections of the AUEW could not go ahead unless the rules of a new amalgamated union were settled. The original merger proposals would have left in abeyance the question of the amalgamation rules. The three craft sections (Engineering, Construction and Foundry) decided to contest the TASS injunction in the High Court. In November 1981, the High Court upheld the certification officer's decision to prevent a transfer of engagements between the Engineering, Construction and Foundry sections (excluding TASS) together with the National Union of Sheet Metal Workers, Coppersmiths, Heating and Domestic Engineers (NUSM-CHDE). The AUEW (Engineering Section) were due to appeal against this decision, and a hearing fixed for June 1982 was postponed until the following October. Then NUSMCHDE turned away from the proposed merger, and were having separate talks with TASS, as well as the TGWU. The action of TASS in the High Court was successful (see **AUEW/TASS** for details).

Workplace Relations

In 1980 the Engineering Section of the AUEW, had around 2,600 branches and about 40,000 shop stewards, of whom around 2,000 were women. Engineering shop stewards had achieved a presence for some years before the turn of the century, although the first manifestation of steward organisation did not come until the first world war, when both their numbers and powers expanded substantially, especially in engineering and munitions. The inter-war years, with mass unemployment, saw a marked decline in their numbers and influence, although they achieved a degree of partial recognition in the formal procedures in engineering.

In the later 1930s with the resurgence of demand associated with re-armament, shop stewards again achieved prominence, particularly in aircraft manufacture and munitions. The second world war gave a further boost to steward influence and a degree of organisation was achieved through the system of joint production committees in establishments associated with the war effort. The growth in informal bargaining, largely stemming from successive post-war governments pursuing a policy of full employment in the 1950s and 1960s, gave rise to much public and mass media concern about their identification with the twin problems of wage drift and unofficial strikes (particularly in the engineering industry). The number of AUEW (Engineering Section) stewards has risen from about 23,500 in 1960 to 34,000 in 1973 to around 40,000 in 1980.

In the union, the steward is subject to the formal control of his or her district committee. They are elected on the shopfloor by workers, but they are not mandatory. Each district committee convenes general meetings of its stewards at least quarterly and, as stated already, at one of these meetings the stewards elect one or more representatives to the district committee itself (see also **Women**). It is generally true to say that most of the district committee members elected in the branches are shop stewards in their own right.

It is important to note that there is no formal contact between stewards and branches, and the contact between stewards and district committees is inadequate to integrate the operation of stewards into the life of the union. In most establishments where the union organises it rarely has exclusive bargaining jurisdiction, and thus joint shop stewards committees have developed which have almost become independent bodies in their own right, often engaging in negotiations and policy-making quite outside the structure of the union. The combine committees which grew up in various large corporations (such as Lucas Aerospace, British Leyland, Vickers, Fords, Dunlop-Pirelli) are a reflection of the growing awareness of shopfloor workers that the traditional trade union structures based on geographical divisions and organised on a craft basis are incapable of coping with the new and complex problems of these large monopolies.

The Laurence Scott dispute in 1981 highlighted in a dramatic way the difficulties that can arise between union structure and shop steward organisation. Engineering workers at the Laurence Scott plant in Manchester were dismissed with no warning in early 1981, and had been conducting a fight against closure over several months with a sit-in. This culminated in a dawn raid by a posse of bailiffs to eject them, and a famous management helicopter raid to transfer equipment from the factory. Initially the workers had the backing of the AUEW Executive Council but this was withdrawn after the workers rejected a nationally backed formula to end the dispute in July 1981. The Executive ended the dispute despite the wishes of the Manchester North district committee of the AUEW. It was almost unprecedented in the history of the union for the Executive to overturn a district committee decision. Over 1,000 of the AUEW's 2,600 branches protested to the Executive over this decision.

Despite these protests, the National Committee endorsed the leadership's handling of the affair, and voted 53 to 36 not to re-establish official support.

Following the drastic cutbacks in the British motor industry in Leyland, Ford, Talbot and Vauxhall (GM), shop stewards decided to organise a national conference in 1982 on the future strategy of the motor/truck/vehicle industry, including components, supply and distribution. A circular to district committees from the Executive stated that the conference threatened the 'constitution in terms of District Committees and National Committee', and went on to say: 'we trust you will make it clear to our shop stewards that they should not attend such a conference'.

It is clear that the problem of integrating the shop stewards into the life of the union has not been resolved, that conflicts between stewards and unions like the AUEW are likely to appear in the future, and that recent developments in the field of combine and multi-company stewards' initiatives require a positive response from unions like the AUEW to meet the aspirations of their members on the shopfloor. The trend towards takeovers and mergers, leading to increasing concentration of ownership (in which a hundred companies account for half of the UK's manufacturing output, most of which is in multi-plant, multi-union enterprises), has meant that the growth of combines was inevitable; and this has been reinforced by the increasing involvement of shop stewards in national company-level negotiations.

Women

Women have been admitted into the union since 1942 and enjoy the same benefit rights as their male counterparts. Females constitute a sizeable minority in the union and they are specifically provided for in the Rule Book. There is only one female district secretary who was elected in her own right and around 2,000 women shop stewards. Women shop stewards are represented on district committees on the basis of one shop steward for every 3,000 members of the women's section. There is an annual women's conference consisting of women representatives on district committees of between 26 and 52 delegates. The women's conference elects delegates to attend the National Committee. There were seven such delegates on the 1982 91-person NC, all of whom voted with the right-wing on policy issues.

The vast majority of women in engineering are in the lower grades, and tend to be concentrated in assembly work in the electronics industry, soldering and semi-skilled inspection, all of which are boring, taxing and repetitive. A woman working in a tool room is a rarity.

External Relations

The union is affiliated to the Labour Party and sponsors the following MPs:

Norman Atkinson (Tottenham)
Ron Brown (Edinburgh Leith)
Bernard Conlan (Gateshead East)
Joseph Dean (Leeds West)
K. Eastham (Manchester Blackley)
John Evans (Newton le Willows)
Benjamin Ford (Bradford North)
Edward Garrett (Wallsend)
Robert Hughes (Aberdeen North)
Daniel Jones (Burnley)
William McKelvey (Kilmarnock)
Stan Orme (Salford West)
George Park (Coventry North East)
Ernie Roberts (Hackney North and Stoke Newington)
Jock Stallard (St. Pancras North)
Harold Walker (Doncaster)
David Watkins (Consett)

The number of AUEW members paying into the Political Fund at 31 December 1981 was 813,614. The union's group of sponsored MPs has grown significantly since the war. Until 1945 the engineers had an average four or less MPs in each parliament. In 1959 they still had only eight, but in 1964 the number rose to 18, since when it has declined to its present level of 17. The union's rules (providing one candidate per 30,000 political-levy-paying union members) allow room for further growth. All candidates must have at least seven years' union membership to their credit — a provision which gives a reasonably firm guarantee that most of the union's MPs are former workers with a considerable and shared shop floor experience to their credit.

The union administers its parliamentary selection procedure in a highly centralised and meritocratic way. Nominations are made locally to district level. From there they are passed on to the Executive Council which draws up the final panel from the results of competitive examinations, which are held in Eastbourne. The examinations are quite rigorous. Candidates have to describe in writing a pressing local problem; take part in a debate with one of the union's MPs and submit themselves to a mock press conference. Perhaps the most unnerving part of the examination is a public meeting where the candidate is expected to give a 10 minute speech to the accompaniment of a specially imported group of hecklers (including some from the local Conservative Club and local trades club). From this batch of entries the union seeks to put about 30 on its sponsored list. In financial terms, any constituency that selects one will benefit by around £400 per year. The union's sponsored MPs meet with the union three times a year. The union is also affiliated to the following organisations:

International Metalworkers' Federation
Anti-Apartheid Movement
Chile Solidarity
Socialist Medical Association
Labour Research

Liberation
United Nations Association
Confederation of Shipbuilding
and Engineering Unions

J. G. Russell, E. M. Scrivens and Terry Duffy were members of the General Council of the TUC in 1982/3. Sir John Boyd was a member of the ACAS Council and Terry Duffy is a member of the National Economic Development Council. J. G. Russell was elected to the union section of the Labour Party NEC in 1981.

The union at national level pursued the case of Ben Ford, the AUEW-sponsored MP for Bradford North who failed to gain re-selection in his constituency. The local AUEW district committee had originally asked for his sponsorship to be withdrawn, and eventually Patrick Wall, a Militant Tendency supporter was selected by the Bradford North CLP.

At the 1982 NC, delegates voted on a resolution 'to pursue the re-introduction of the "proscribed list" with a view to uniting the Labour Party members and their supporters and become a strong opposition to the present reactionary Tory government.'

The AUEW supports the Trade Unions for a Labour Victory (TULV), but does not contribute financially.

Policy

The policy-making body of the union is the National Committee, and therefore the political composition and balance of the NC is of crucial importance in the policy-making area. In 1980 right-wing members of the union regained a clear majority on the NC by 28 seats to 24. The 1979 NC was evenly balanced, although the left-wingers managed to win a victory in laying down stiff conditions in the national engineering pay negotiations, a move which helped to produce the series of one-day and two-day strikes (see **Recent Events**).

The newly enlarged NC of 91 delegates is now composed of a 56–35 majority in favour of the right-wing.

The functional policy-making role of the National Committee is now minimal, particularly in the bargaining area, as the NC can play no role in local bargaining. In national bargaining the NC decides the policy of the Engineering Section of the AUEW in advance of the joint national conference of the AUEW's four sections. Moreover, the Engineering Section is a large but not a controlling union in the CSEU, which makes it especially necessary to allow the Engineering Section great latitude. While the NC may make its views known, and possibly veto a negotiated national agreement, its members neither participate in negotiations nor advise on negotiations in progress. Nevertheless, the record shows important NC bargaining decisions: for a national strike in 1968, for a cessation of national bargaining and a struggle at district level in 1972, and for a breaking off of negotiations with the Heath administration in 1973. The trade advisory committees, which are not specified by rule and have no authority, nevertheless play a peripheral role in bargaining.

The main policy-making role (which usually attracts the attention of the mass media) is in the political area — particularly in relation to the exercise of the massive block vote at the TUC and Labour Party Conference. During the period of Lord Carron's right-wing rule there were several occasions when NC decisions were flouted under 'Carron's Law'. In 1965, for example, the NC had passed a motion pledging '100 per cent support for the Labour Government' which Carron used to support the platform on every issue. At the 1966 Labour Party Conference, despite the fact that the union had gone on record against the American intervention in Vietnam and in favour of cuts in military expenditure, Carron kept firm control of the pad upon which the votes of the delegation are recorded and placed the union's block vote in favour of the platform while he was at the conference. However, when he was called away on personal business, he had to pass the pad to the senior EC member, Hugh Scanlon, who polled the delegation and in fact cast the votes the other way on both issues. Scanlon, who succeeded Carron in 1967, claimed that he was elected on two main issues: firstly, that policy decisions of the National

Committee are binding on all members from the president downwards; secondly, the final appeal court is the body to which they can go if they think these decisions are wrong.

The delegation to the Labour Party Conference consists of 26 members elected in the divisions, the seven members of the Executive, and the president and general secretary. At the special Wembley Conference of the Labour Party in January 1981, the AUEW delegation had been mandated not to vote for any motion which did not give the parliamentary party at least 50 per cent of the votes in the new method of electing the Labour Party leader. As a result the delegation did not vote on the successful USDAW resolution giving the unions a 40 per cent share. The right-wing leadership of the union is planning to use its influence to refuse further cash help for the Labour Party, unless the party abandons policies which are out of line with the AUEW's thinking.

Recent Events

The union was involved in a major dispute with the Engineering Employers' Federation in the summer of 1979 over its claim for a £80 per week minimum pay for skilled workers with proportionate increases for other grades, two days extra holiday, and a reduction in the standard working week of one hour in 1979, with a 35-hour week to follow by 1982. The decision to call a series of one- and two-day strikes was made by the National Committee in June 1979, when left-wing members of the NC outvoted their opponents and overturned the recommendations of their national leaders by 27 votes to 25. The dispute turned out to be of major proportions, with the employers federation showing unusual resistance to the claim. When the dispute was settled in early October, the CSEU succeeded in effecting a settlement giving engineering workers a 39-hour week from November 1981, which was hailed 'as the most important trade union breakthrough on working hours in Britain for 15 years'. Both the conduct of the negotiations and the final settlement led to a great deal of critic-

ism within the union, and indirectly led to the scandal which arose over the sacking of two union research workers at Peckham Road, the union's headquarters.

Bob Wright, the present Assistant General Secretary, and the two researchers, Alan Hughes and Trevor Eastwood, met in a pub at lunchtime in October 1979 and were discussing the Executive's much criticised settlement of the national engineering claim. As the *New Statesman* reported on 25 April 1980: 'Wright asked the two researchers to prepare in their own time two short pieces on the subjects discussed, using Wright's material, mainly press cuttings. The pieces were for Wright's personal use . . . Wright felt innocent enough to have the work typed up by one of the office secretaries used most frequently by Sir John Boyd.' On discovering the document, Boyd immediately interviewed Eastwood (without any staff representative present), but in the company of two EC members. After interviewing Hughes the following week, Boyd sacked the two researchers after they had refused to resign. They were given no leave to appeal to the Executive. Sir John Boyd made no attempt to see Eastwood, Hughes and Wright together to establish any facts, but did write to Bob Wright the day before the industrial tribunal hearing at which the two researchers were to have their claim of unfair dismissal dealt with. He warned Wright that his conduct was under discussion and that he was to behave as an officer of the union at the tribunal. The tribunal (in April 1980) found that the dismissals were unfair and awarded compensation to the two researchers amounting to around £1,000 each. Wright was warned as to his future conduct at a later meeting of the Executive.

At considerable cost, the union's leadership decided to take the case to the Employment Appeals Tribunal, lost the case, and ended up having to pay extra compensation. One of the researchers who was an AUEW member took his case to the union's Final Appeal Court where his appeal was upheld. Under Rule 20, clause 5, the AUEW Rule Book provides that: 'It shall be incumbent upon the Executive Council to give immediate effect to the decisions of the Appeal Court.' Despite this ruling both researchers remain scked and the EC has refused to re-instate them.

This case was one of a number that highlighted the conflict between the EC of the union and the Final Appeal Court. The 11-member FAC meets annually to provide interpretation of the AUEW (Enginering Section) complex Rule Book and to hear any members' appeals against EC decisions. In 1981 the FAC decided that the union journal, contrary to rule, carried material supporting Terry Duffy's campaign for presidential re-election. The case was over an appeal made by B.P. Kelly, from Doncaster, one of the candidates standing in the 1981 elections for the union's North-Eastern Divisional Executive seat. It was claimed that Mr Kelly's references in his election address to the case of the sacked research officers were deleted without his consent. An emergency application was made to the FAC in October 1981, on the grounds that the ballot count was already taking place. The court decided that there was a *prima facie* case for an appeal. However, the Executive did not forward the correspondence surrounding the case, which, under rule, is necessary for the appeal to proceed.

The second case concerned Laurence Scott (see **Workplace Relations**). An appeal against the EC's decision to withdraw official recognition of the dispute, including disputes benefit, could not be heard because the relevant correspondence again was not forwarded. The Executive argued that the issue was a matter of policy rather than rules. Rule 20, clause 4 of the Rule Book states: 'Executive Council shall not withhold any correspondence requested by the FAC.'

Despite the introduction of postal voting, the left-wing of the union retained its majority on the Final Appeal Court in 1981. Since then the EC has decided to set up a small working party of two representatives from the EC and three members of the rules revision committee, together with the president and general secretary, 'to examine all aspects of the present difficulties, consult our legal rep-resentatives, and thereafter report back their views to the rules revision committee.' Some members on the left in the union suspect that the FAC will eventually be re-constituted so as to nullify its jurisdiction over the Executive.

Finally, the following extract of correspondence between Jeff Rooker, Labour MP for Birmingham Perry Bar, and Sir John Boyd, former general secretary, when Sir John attacked Rooker for accepting an invitation to speak at Roy Fraser's unofficial craft committee (Jeff Rooker is a member of ASTMS and is nothing to do with the AUEW), tells its own story: 'My Executive Council are deeply concerned that reports have reached us regarding a meeting which you are alleged to have addressed in Birmingham on or about Saturday, 6th October 1979. The meeting we refer to was called in contravention of the rules of our union and its express objective was to attack the constitution of this union. If the report of your attendance is accurate, I would be grateful for your early observation and comments.'

Jeff Rooker replied: 'You appear to convey the impression that I am responsible to yourself or to your executive council. I see it as part of my function as a Labour MP to make myself available, if requested, by any group of workers to discuss the political aspects of current problems in our society. These groups may be assembled by a trade union or trade unions. On the other hand they may be called by shop stewards or shop steward combines on a company or occupational basis.'

Sir John Boyd still pursued the matter further: 'Whether you should assist in the setting up of an organisation whose express intention is to attack our trade union is a matter for you to decide. We must point out that wages and conditions of our members are looked after by our respective district committees under the control of our Executive Council, and we would ask you to refrain from involving yourself in the domestic affairs of this trade union.'

Rooker replied telling him he would attend any meetings he wished, in order to articulate the cause of all workers whether they be skilled, semi-skilled or managerial; 'so I hope you will not continue this banal correspondence.'

Recent elections

Bob Wright, who had already been defeated twice by Terry Duffy for national office, stood against him in the union elections for president in late 1980. Terry Duffy was elected outright in the first ballot. Victory in the first ballot for almost any contested post in the AUEW, let alone the presidency, is rare. In a low 24.7 per cent poll, Duffy secured 126,135 votes (54 per cent of the votes cast), giving him a majority of 19,257 votes over the remainder of the candidates. Bob Wright won only 58,826 (25 per cent) of the votes cast. Duffy will now hold the presidential office until his retirement at 65, in 1987.

In 1982, Gavin Laird, an executive councillor from Scotland, narrowly defeated Ken Brett in the election for general secretary to succeed Sir John Boyd by 96,186 votes to 95,124 on the second ballot. Laird will come up for re-election in 1985, and if he wins then will occupy the post until retirement. The only surprise at this result was that Laird's majority was not larger. Despite the unexpectedly high vote for Brett, it is clear that the left in the AUEW is still very weak, and it has lost control in most of the major decision-making bodies within the union.

Recent Rule Changes

With effect from 1981, the delegations to the TUC and Labour Party Conference were elected by divisional committees, and not by branches. The composition of the final appeal court was also elected by postal ballot and not by branch votes in the regions. Both these changes reinforced the process of increasing centralisation of power in the union.

Women delegates to the NC now have voting rights.

Further Reference

J. B. Jefferys, *The Story of the Engineers*, Lawrence & Wishart 1945. An outstanding history of the union, well worth reading.

J. D. Edelstein and M. Warner, *Comparative Union Democracy*, Halsted 1976, Transaction Books, 1979.

Richard Fletcher, 'Trade Union Democracy: the case of the AUEW Rule Book', in Barratt, Brown and Coates (eds.), *Trade Union Register 3*, Spokesman Books 1973.

K. Coates and T. Topham, *Trade Unions in Britain*, Spokesman Books 1980.

Irving Richter, *Political Purpose in Trade Unions*, Allen & Unwin 1973.

K. Coates (ed.), *The Right to Useful Work*, Spokesman Books 1978. This book gives a good account of the Lucas Combine Committee.

R. Undy, 'The Electoral Influence of the Opposition Party in the AUEW Engineering Section 1960-75', *British Journal of Industrial Relations*, 1979.

New Statesman, 7 May 1982.

Engineering Workers, Amalgamated Union of
(AUEW)

Constructional Section

Head Office

190 Cedar Road
Clapham
London SW4 0PP
01-622 4451

Principal Officers

General Secretary —
J. Baldwin
Assistant General Secretary —
L. Spackman

Divisional Officers

London Division

D. Bond
Apex Building
22 Worple Road
London SW19

H. Barr
25 Essex Road
Dartford
Kent

J. Cook
2nd Floor
13 Unthank Road
Norwich

D. Wheaton
588 Rainham Road South
Dagenham
Essex

Scottish Division

T. Lafferty
59 Dee Street
Aberdeen AB1 2EE

T. Maclean and A. Gray
AUEW House
7 Incle Street
Paisley PA1 1 HZ

R. Sneddon
Trade Union Centre
12-14 Picardy Place
Edinburgh EH1 3JT

North East Division

T. Gaynor and T. Woods
78 Borough Road
Middlesbrough
Teesside TS1 2JM

H. Wainwright
Room 3, Winwaed House
64/66 Crossgates Road
Leeds LS15 7NN

G. Garbett
AUEW House
Furnival Gate
Sheffield S1 3HE

Midlands Division

A. Sparrock
6th Floor, St. Martin's House
Bullring
Birmingham B5 5DT

K. Antell
9 St James's Terrace
Nottingham NG1 6FW

North West Division

W. Charles
43 The Crescent
Salford M5 4PE

S. E. Howard
AUEW House
48 Mount Pleasant
Liverpool

South Wales and South West Division

P. Jones
8 St Paul's Road
Clifton
Bristol BS8 1LU

T. King
Ty Can Olog
25 Victoria Gardens
Neath

Membership (1982)

Male 25,075
Female 25
Total 25,100

Union Journal

The Construction Worker—
quarterly.

General

The Constructional Engineering Union amalgamated with the AUEW to become the Constructional Section of that union in 1971. The AUEW Constructional Section represents workers in the construction industry but primarily workers on large construction sites, such as power stations, and in civil engineering projects and factory and plant construction, particularly for the chemical industry. All grades of workers are recruited, the Construction Section's customary membership being among steel erectors, scaffolders, crane drivers, welders, platers and labourers.

History

Constructional workers were first organised by the *Steel Smelters' Union* around 1913, according to V. L. Allen in *Power in Trade Unions*. Special branches were formed for them in various localities. After the formation of the *British Iron, Steel and Kindred Trades Association* (BISAKTA) in 1917, the creation of a separate union for constructional workers was proposed since they were a group of workers outside the iron and steel industry and more akin to the building industry. In 1924 the *Constructional Engineering Union* became a separate entity, although it remained affiliated to the Iron and Steel Trades Confederation until 1930.

Coverage

The main national agreement to which the AUEW (Constructional Section) is party is the Mechanical Engineering Construction Agreement. The union is seeking to extend this agreement to cover the whole industry and to provide higher basic rates and smaller bonus payments. At present much bargaining is between shop stewards and contractors on site, mainly about bonus payments. There are also comprehensive site agreements such as at Shell Carrington and Stanlow.

Organisation

There are about a hundred branches throughout the country. In addition, all major sites where the AUEW (Constructional Section) has members have shop stewards.

The branches are grouped into seven divisions and from each division an executive councillor is elected (two each for the London and Scottish divisions). Together with the president, this makes an EC of ten. Since 1945 all officials have been elected.

John Baldwin won his General Secretary's post for life in an election contest with Leonard Spackman, the union's assistant general secretary. No doubt he viewed his victory by a margin of more than 1,000 votes, in a 41 per cent poll in February 1981, as endorsement for his actions during the Isle of Grain dispute.

External Relations

The AUEW (Constructional Section) is affiliated to the Labour Party and sponsors James Hamilton MP (Bothwell).

The union is helped by and, in its turn, publicises the work of SPAID, the Society for the Prevention of Asbestosis and Industrial Diseases:

Secretary — Nancy Tait
38 Drapers Road
Enfield
Middlesex EN2 8LU

Policy

The national policy of the AUEW (Constructional Section), as forthrightly enunciated by the general secretary, is to establish a national agreement for construction engineering. The industry is fragmented and disunited with the majority of the workforce casually employed in relatively small jobs and paid little more

than the basic rate. There is great variation in earnings even for similar jobs. Furthermore, the bigger jobs where certain grades can exercise bargaining power produce vastly higher earnings through inflated bonus payments. The aim is to secure higher basic wages throughout the industry, with smaller bonuses, and a fair craft differential.

The Constructional Section is in favour of closer amalgamation within the AUEW and is moving in this direction. (See **AUEW Engineering Section**.)

In an extremely hazardous industry, health and safety issues occupy much trade union time. In the early part of 1980 all workers employed by federated companies in the engineering construction industry were covered for sickness, accident and life insurance, after many years of fighting for such a scheme.

Recent Events

The position with regard to the AUEW amalgamation has grown extremely complex. For instance, the policy of the Constructional Section is to try to break away from the present arrangement, but to do so purely in order to merge fully with the Engineering Section immediately afterwards.

The three manual worker unions in the present federated (rather than amalgamated) arrangement are constitutionally unable to achieve a full amalgamation because of the effective power of veto against amalgamation which can be exercised by AUEW/TASS.

The Constructional Section Executive was mandated by its Conference in 1981 to seek to break up the present AUEW arrangements by legal action, since some believe that otherwise a break would require a nine-tenths majority of the members in favour in a postal ballot — a virtually impossible requirement.

Further Reference

Arthur Pugh, *Men of Steel*, ISTC 1952.

Engineering Workers, Amalgamated Union of
(AUEW)

Foundry Section

Head Office

164 Chorlton Road
Manchester M16 7NU
061-226 1151/2

Principal Officers

General Secretary —
R. Garland OBE
Assistant General Secretary —
N. J. Harris

National Executive Council
Area A — G. Howieson
(Chairperson)
Area B — G. P. Burns (Vice-
Chairperson)
Area C — J. Shaw
Area D — W. Baker
Area E — D. H. Cornwell MBE

Membership (1982)

Male 52,661
Female 2,459
Total 55,120

Union Journal

The Foundry Worker. The
journal used to be published
every month, but the NEC
decided in July 1980 to publish
it every two months.
Moreover, the number of
copies printed has been
reduced.

National Organiser

B. Salt
164 Chorlton Road
Brooke's Bar
Manchester M16 7NU
061-226 1151/2

Divisional Organisers

● *No. 1*
J. Taylor
11 Graham's Road
Falkirk
0324-24459

● *No. 2*
J. Blair
11 Graham's Road
Falkirk
0324–24459

● *No. 3*
J. W. McDonald
AUEW House
2nd Floor
High Street
Gateshead NE8 1JB
0632-770 403

● *No. 4*
L. Crossley
2 Victoria Street
Barnsley
0226-203775

● *No. 5*
K. W. Smith
67 Old Meeting Street
West Bromwich
021-553 3876

● *No. 6 (North)*
D. R. O'Flynn
AUEW House
588 Rainham Road South
Dagenham
Essex RM10 7RA
01-593 4893

● *No. 6 (South)*
W. Chapman
AUEW House
588 Rainham Road South
Dagenham
Essex RM10 7RA
01-593 4893

● *No. 7*
G. Tomlinson
AEU House
43 Crescent
Salford M5 4PE
061-736 2465

● *No. 8*
W. Law
67 Old Meeting Street
West Bromwich
021-553 3876

● *No. 8*
A. J. Harvey
67 Old Meeting Street
West Bromwich
021-553 3876

● *No. 9*
AUEW Office
3rd Floor
1/3 Fitzalan Place
Cardiff CF2 1UN
0222-495760

General

The Foundry Section of the AUEW is now poised to ballot its membership on effecting a transfer of engagements to the Engineering Section of the AUEW, whereby a common policy and Rule Book can be formulated. The Foundry Section is the only union dealing exclusively with foundry workers, particularly in the engineering industry. A major problem facing the union is the decline of the engineering, shipbuilding, and iron and steel industries in Britain which is leading to a gradual decline in membership. The union is governed by an all-powerful elected National Executive Council, whose members face election (as do all full-time officials) every five years.

History

The Foundry Section of the AUEW is one of the trade unions in Britain with the longest continuous existence. Its formation can be traced back to 1809 with the formation of the *Friendly Iron Moulders' Society* which held its first meeting at the Hand and Banner Hotel in Bolton. The years 1809-46 saw the birth of a number of craft unions of skilled iron moulders, mainly in Northern England and Scotland, including the *Scottish Iron Moulders' Union* formed in 1831.

The *Friendly Iron Moulders' Society* became the *Friendly Society of Iron Founders of England, Ireland and Wales* (FSIF) in 1854, having decided against amalgamating with the 'Old Mechanics' (see **AUEW (Engineering Section) — History**). In England, and to a lesser extent in Scotland, the ironmoulders gradually evolved a centralised national organisation. A number of local societies of brass moulders had also come into existence during the period 1820-46, and they too evolved into national federations in the 1850s and 1860s, culminating in the formation of the *National Society of Amalgamated Brassworkers* in 1872.

The organisation of non-moulder grades did not appear until the late 1850s and early 1860s, gradually emerging into national federations, such as the Scottish Iron Dressers

(1856), the English Iron Dressers' Trade Society (1863).

During the period of new unionism, trade union organisation spread to the non-craftworkers employed in foundries. Although the FSIF was willing to take into membership some non-craft members, they were unwilling to sacrifice their craft principles. The years 1889-90 thus saw the birth of a number of unions catering for unskilled or semi-skilled workers including:

Welsh Ironfounders' Union (1889)
Central Iron Moulders' Association (1889)
National Union of Stove Grate Workers (1890)
Amalgamated Society of Plate and Machine Moulders (1890)
London United Brass Founders' Society (1890)
General Iron Fitters' Association (1892)

Foundry labourers became organised too. Such unions of labourers included the National Amalgamated Union of Labour, National Labourers' Union, the Workers' Union which later merged into the TGWU and the GMWU.

In 1920, the *National Union of Foundry Workers* came into being, formed from an amalgamation of FSIF, the Associated Iron Moulders of Scotland (formerly the Scottish Iron Moulders' Union), and Amalgamated Society of Coremakers.

Further amalgamations took place in 1943 and 1946. In 1943 the National Union of Foundry Workers absorbed the Scottish Brassmoulders' Union and the Associated Iron, Steel and Brass Dressers of Scotland. Three years later the *Amalgamated Union of Foundry Workers* was formed by an amalgamation between the NUFW, Ironfounding Workers Association and the United Metal Founders' Society.

On 1 July 1967 the Amalgamated Union of Foundry Workers joined forces with the Amalgamated Engineering Union (AEU). Although fusion took place under the name of the *Amalgamated Engineering and Foundry Workers' Union* (AEF), the two organisations kept their separate rules. In 1970 a further amalgamation took place when DATA and the Constructional Engineering Union were added to form the present day four sections of the AUEW. (See also **AUEW Engineering Section, AUEW/ TASS, AUEW Constructional Section.**)

The foundry workers have a history all of their own. Here, it is possible to do no more than set out a brief summary of the main amalgamations that have taken place in the last 170 years. A detailed and informative history of the foundry workers up to 1959 can be found in Fyrth and Collins (see **Further Reference**).

Union Officials

The Foundry Section of the AUEW has many similarities to the AUEW (Engineering Section) in that all full-time officials are elected for a five-year term by the membership. The union at present has ten divisional organisers (there were 13 in 1980), one national organiser, plus the general secretary and assistant general secretary. It is rare for a sitting incumbent to be dislodged from office once elected.

The Foundry Section does not operate a postal ballot system. All ballot papers are sent to branch secretaries who, together with shop stewards, hand one to each member eligible to vote. Shop stewards and shop committees then scrutinise and count the ballot papers and announce the result to shop members. Each candidate is permitted to put 500 words of printed matter on the ballot paper to advocate his cause. All ballot papers are forwarded to the general secretary by registered post within a certain time limit.

Coverage

The Foundry Section of the AUEW is the only trade union dealing exclusively with foundry workers, particularly in the engineering industry. Other unions such as the TGWU, GMWU, ISTC and the NSMM also organise workers in foundries. Even the NUR has some foundry workers in railway workshops.

The Foundry Section negotiates with the Engineering Employers' Federation as part of the CSEU (which has a separate CSEU Foundry Committee). The union is also part of the

National Craftsmen's Co-ordinating Committee in the iron and steel industry and was involved in the steel strike of early 1980. The union also has a sizeable membership in British Leyland and in government industrial establishments, in shipbuilding, and in the light castings industry. There is a large concentration of foundry membership in the West Midlands area.

Organisation

The Foundry section is governed by a full-time National Executive Council consisting of seven members — five area members elected by the membership in each area, plus the general secretary and assistant general secretary. The NEC is a powerful body being responsible for the direction and control of the administrative and general proceedings of the union. Area members of the NEC are elected for a five-year period, and the general seretary and assistant general secretary are similarly elected by a ballot of the national membership for a five-year period.

The rules provide for the NEC to arrange a national membership ballot on any question (other than matters dealt with by the Annual Delegate Meeting) provided that 40 branches request such a vote (Rule 3 (4)).

Compared with many other trade unions, the NEC is an all-powerful body whose decisions are binding on the whole of the membership. It has power to reorganise the union's branches either by amalgamation, merger or closure; it can suspend any member for failing to abide by an NEC ruling; and it has full powers to order industrial action if it is deemed appropriate. The NEC may also transfer any organiser from one division to another. All full-time officials are directly responsible to the NEC.

The union also has a system of district committees, which serve as a link between the branches in each district and the NEC. District committees consist of delegates elected from branches on the basis of one delegate per 350 members, and are elected for a period of 12 months. District committees meet bi-monthly, on Saturdays. In 1980, the Foundry Section had 14 district committees in operation. The district committees elect the delegates to the National Annual Delegate Meeting on a basis of proportionate representation according to occupation and membership total. At the 1980 Delegate Meeting there were 47 voting delegates.

The ADM meets each April and considers resolutions from branches which must first be discussed and accepted by district committee.

The rules revision conference is held every five years and consists of delegates to the particular year's ADM. The NEC may recall the rules revision conference at any time to consider any business submitted by the NEC.

The ADM also elects seven Foundry Section delegates to the AUEW National Conference from its own number.

An arbitration court is provided for by Rule 38, which gives members the right to appeal against any decision made by the union under rule which affects the member concerned.

Workplace Activity

The Rule Book provides for the election of one or more shop stewards for workplace representation in each shop, as well as for the election of a shop committee. Shop committees monitor the operation of PBR (payment by results) and piece work systems, as well as prices in light castings shops.

External Relations

The union is affiliated to the Labour Party, and voted for Denis Healey in the 1981 Labour Party Deputy Leadership contest. About 70 per cent of members pay the political levy.

The Foundry Section of the AUEW is also affiliated to the following organisations:

Confederation of Shipbuilding and Engineering Unions

International Metalworkers' Federation

Labour Research Department

Policy and Recent Events

The main challenge facing the union at present results from the deepening recession which is affecting the founding industry. Not only is the union faced with the decline of the British engineering and shipbuilding industries, but also with technological unemployment in the founding industry. Apart from a drastic decline in national and international demand for castings, the situation is being accentuated by substitute materials being used, e.g. fabrication, plastics and concrete. In the last 20 years some 700 foundries have closed, and in the last five years output from UK iron foundries and UK steel foundries has dropped by 30 per cent and 33 per cent respectively. Jobs in foundries are continually being de-skilled and the industry is suffering from excess capacity. All these factors are accelerating the decline in membership of the union. In 1958, its total membership stood at 71,854 and it has shrunk to its present level of 55,120. The problem facing the union is that its membership is located in those industries and jobs which suffer most from the process of de-industrialisation in Britain.

In July 1982, a plan to rationalise the UK's general foundry industry — with the loss of up to ten foundries and up to 1,500 jobs — was put to the major company in the founding industry, F. H. Lloyd, by the merchant bankers, Lazard Brothers. It is clear that the union is facing major job losses, despite its achievement in holding up its membership level since 1980.

The Foundry Section was to effect a closer amalgamation with the Engineering Section of the AUEW. In January 1981, the NEC arranged a non-legally-binding 'straw poll' of the membership to ascertain its feelings about amalgamating with the AUEW Engineering and Construction sections. Although the poll was just less than 50 per cent, 12,097 were in favour of the merger and 9,961 against. The amalgamation, however, is still held up and subject to legal action (see **AUEW Engineering Section**) after TASS secured the Certification Officer's declaration that the proposed merger was in breach of the existing rule book. (See **AUEW/TASS** for High Court decision.)

Further Reference

H. J. Fyrth and H. Collins, *The Foundry Workers: A Trade Union History*, AEF 1959.

Metal Mechanics, National Society of
(NSMM)

Head Office

70 Lionel Street
Birmingham B3 1JG
021-236 0726

Principal Officers

General Secretary—
C. P. McCarthy
Assistant General Secretary—
L. Ward

Membership (1982)

Male 33,507
Female 5,950
Total 39,457

Union Journal

Metal Mechanics News—
monthly

Union Offices

● *London*
1 Renmuir Street
London SW17

● *Midlands*
Regent House
26 Queen's Road
Coventry

● *Northern*
15 St John Street
Off Deansgate
Manchester M34 DT

27 Cardigan Chambers
1st Floor
Lord Street
Liverpool

59, 59a and 61 Derby Road
Nottingham

1 Stanley Place
Chester

52 Nether Hall Road
Doncaster

15 Charnwood Street
Derby

48 Tobruk Walk
Portobello
Willenhall
West Midlands

● *Western*
7 King Square
Bristol

General

The NSMM was founded in 1872 originally in the brass industry. Since then it has gradually recruited members in the engineering and metal trades generally, and has extended its influence outside the Midlands to the South East, North and West of England. Its drastic membership loss between 1979 and 1981 of nearly 20 per cent of its membership has led to the union raising its membership subscriptions, although this may not be enough to ensure the long-term survival of the NSMM as a separate body.

It is affiliated to the Labour Party and to the Confederation of Shipbuilding and Engineering Unions.

History

The union was founded in Birmingham in 1872 as the *Amalgamated Society of Brass Workers*. In 1874 the name of the union was changed to the *National Society of Amalgamated Brass Workers* and in 1906, as membership grew outside the brass industry, to the *National Society of Amalgamated Brass Workers and Metal Mechanics*, and again in 1919 to the *National Society of Brass and Metal Mechanics*. The present title was adopted in 1945.

The union now has membership throughout the metal and engineering trades generally, especially in the Midlands and Greater London and has attempted to expand its activities in the West and North. The severe loss of jobs in the West Midlands engineering industry has led to a drastic loss in membership, and the future of the NSMM as a separate entity is very much open to doubt.

Union Officials

The NSMM employs 22 full-time officials (consisting of district secretaries and district organisers) as well as the president, vice-president, general secretary and assistant general secretary. All full-time officers of the union are elected by ballot vote of the membership, and the rules of the NSMM debar any full-time official from serving on the National Executive Council.

Organisation

The supreme body of government in the union is the Annual Conference composed of delegates elected from the branches of the union with the number of delegates dependent on size of branch. The Conference lasts for two days, but every fourth year it lasts for four days as it revises the rules.

The management of the union is carried out by the National Executive Council which is 15 strong at present. The rules provide that there should be two seats allocated to female members of the union. Members of the NEC hold office for five years and are elected on a pro rata basis dependent on branch size. The NEC normally meets bi-monthly.

The NEC apportions the branches of the NSMM into districts. Each district appoints a district council, comprising one delegate from each branch. District councils normally meet six times a year, and have wide powers. They regulate overtime in their area, oversee the union's recruitment and organisation, arrange negotiations with employers and have the power to appoint a sub-committee to deal with matters pertinent to a particular industry. The district councils determine overtime and have the power to grant or refuse permission to work overtime and discipline members who disobey the district council's rulings. Each district council is served by a district secretary and one or more district organisers.

The NSMM has 81 branches, mainly in the Midlands and South East.

Workplace Activity

The NSMM Rule Book provides for the annual election of shop stewards in each workplace. They are responsible to the district committee.

Women

Although women members of the NSMM account for less than 20 per cent of total membership they are guaranteed two seats on the National Executive Council by virtue of the Rule Book.

External Relations and Policy

The NSMM is affiliated to the Labour Party, the Confederation of Shipbuilding and Engineering Union, the Railway Shopmen's Council, the International Metalworkers' Federation, the EEC European Metalworkers' Federation and the WEA Trade Union Committee.

The union is now facing considerable membership loss resulting from 'de-industrialisation', particularly in its heartland of the West Midlands engineering industry. The 1982 Annual Conference of the NSMM voted to increase its membership subscription fees in order to maintain viability, but this is only likely to stave off the inevitable amalgamation that must come in the near future. Delegates voted 'to approach smaller unions to amalgamate with the NSMM' and the future of the union is uncertain.

The NSMM affiliated 16,000 members to the Labour Party in 1981.

Delegates at the 1982 Annual Conference of the NSMM called for a wide range of socialist measures to be pursued by a future Labour government. Motions on women's equality, unilateral nuclear disarmanent and against the Conservative anti-union legislation were also passed.

Metalworkers' Union, Associated
(AMU)

Head Office

92 Deansgate
Manchester M3 2QG
061-834 6891

Principal Officer

General Secretary — E. Tullock

Membership (1982)

Male 4,021
Female 18
Total 4,039

General

The AMU is a small union whose membership is primarily located in the engineering industry; it is an affiliate of the Confederation of Shipbuilding and Engineering Unions. The union has a nine-member Executive Committee, which is elected every four years. The general secretary is elected every four years, but once having satisfactorily served two successive terms is eligible to continue in post until retirement without the need to seek further re-election. The AMU was inaugurated in 1863 as the *Iron, Steel and Metal Dressers' Society*, and is making great efforts to expand, although one questions its long term viability given its present size. The union holds a National Conference every two years, and sends one delegate to the TUC Congress each year. The AMU was opposed to the continuation of the two-day stoppages in the engineering industry during the 1979 industrial action.

Military and Orchestral Musical Instrument Makers' Trade Society

Head Office

47 Mornington Terrace
Regents Park
London NW1

Principal Officer

General Secretary—
J. N. Barker

Membership (1982)

Male 193
Female 47
Total 240

General

Workers employed in the trade of making instruments, parts of other work connected with military bands, and working at established firms of military or orchestral musical instru-ment makers are eligible for membership.

History

The society was founded in 1894. From then until 1945, members had to have apprenticeship papers. However, since between 1939 and 1945 no instruments were made, the society had to repeal this rule of apprenticeship so that demand for instruments could be met.

Organisation

The business of the society is carried out by a management committee called the Executive Council. The general secretary is elected.

Patternmakers and Allied Craftsmen, The Association of

Head Office

15 Cleve Road
West Hampstead
Kilburn
London NW6 1YA
01-624 7085

Principal Officers

General Secretary—
G. Eastwood
Assistant General Secretary—
D. Stoddart

Membership (1982)

Male 8,926
Female 2
Total 8,928

Union Journal and Publications

Patternmaker— monthly report of members.
1872–1972: A Pattern of Progress, a centenary history.

Organisation

The union is organised in five geographical areas, each of which has a full-time organiser:

● *Area No. 1*
A. Dorrens
13 Sandyford Place
Glasgow G3 7NB
041-221-4736

● *Area No. 2*
D. Firth
Croxdale House
Croxdale Terrace
Pelaw
Gateshead
0632-696806, and

247 Keldregate
Deighton
Huddersfield
Yorkshire
0484-37904

● *Area No. 3*
P. Bagnall
Room 3
Savoy Chambers
1 Wellington Street
Stockport
Cheshire
061-480 7557

● *Area No. 4*
H. J. Ashmore
14-16 Bristol Street
Birmingham B5 7AA
021-622 3306

● *Area No. 5*
D. Yearley
Griffon House
1 Cinema Parade
Green Lane
Dagenham
Essex RM18 1AA

These five and the general secretary and assistant general secretary are the only full-time officers. Each branch is affiliated to one of the areas. There is an elected Executive Committee of eight, which includes the general secretary, assistant general secretary and, of course, president.

General

Patternmaking is the trade of making patterns for castings in the engineering industry. The trade has changed drastically in recent years. Many foundries have closed and there have been many changes in production methods with the result that foundries now mainly employ semi-skilled moulders and machine operators. The patternmakers' society, a craft trade union, has been alive to this development and has tried to adapt to technological change rather than fight it. The union accepts that the terms 'wood patternmaker' or 'metal patternmaker' are now obsolete and that

membership is all 'patternmakers'. An important development in the trade are the 'master pattern shops', a specialised section of the industry providing patterns for many large companies.

History

Created as the *United Kingdom of Patternmakers* in Sunderland in 1872, the union soon took in other patternmakers' societies in Leeds, London, Glasgow and Smethwick.

External Relations

The union is affiliated to the Labour Party.

Scalemakers, National Union of

Head Office

4th Floor
Herbert House
71 Cornwall Street
Birmingham B3 2EE
021-236 8998

Principal Officers

General Secretary —
A. F. Smith

Membership (1982)

Male 1,251
Female 49
Total 1,300

General

Membership is composed of weighing and testing machine fitters (electrical, electronic and mechanical), sectional workers, mates and all other workers employed in the weighing, testing and counting machine industries and affiliated trades. Essentially the union is a craft trade union and membership is widely spread throughout the UK.

History

In 1909 the *Amalgamated Society of Scale Beam and Weighing Machine Makers* was formed as a result of a strike at Messrs Hodgson and Stead. The word 'amalgamated' had no real significance but was the fashion in those days and looked important. In 1923 the name was changed to the *Society of Scale Beam and Weighing Machinists*, and in 1930 to the *National Union of Scalemakers*. The change of name in 1923 resulted from a split in the union, London branch separating from the rest following wage reductions and a large defalcation in the funds. The separate parts of the union were brought together by the TUC to make a fresh amalgamation in 1928. In 1930 the union opened its ranks to all workers in the industry, although it remains to this day primarily a craft union.

Organisation

The union is divided into branches and is governed by an Executive Council, comprising a general president, vice-president and general and financial secretary nominated by any branch and elected by ballot of the whole membership, and four members elected by ballot vote of the delegates to Annual Conference in May.

Screw, Nut, Bolt and Rivet Trade Union

Head Office

368 Dudley Road
Birmingham B18 4HH
021-558 9197

Principal Officer

General Secretary—
E. C. Bowcott

Membership (1982)

Male 800
Female 300
Total 1,100

This small union was founded in 1914, and all its members are employed at GKN in Birmingham where it recruits all grades of workers. It has been drastically affected by recent redundancies. It sends one delegate to the Trades Union Congress each year.

Sheet Metal Workers, Coppersmith, Heating and Domestic Engineers National Union of
(NUSMCHDE)

Head Office

75/77 West Heath Road
London NW3
01-455 0053

Principal Officers

General Secretary— L. G. Guy
National Officers—
R. A. Marsh
T. D. Nelson
S. Nugent

Membership (1982)

Total 62,601

Union Journal

The Journal— monthly.

District Offices

● *District No. 1*
66 Berkeley Street
Glasgow C3

● *District No. 2A*
691 Rochdale Road
Harpurhey
Manchester 9

● *District No. 2B*
1st Floor
Paramount Building
14 Fraser Street
Liverpool 38JX

● *District No. 3*
Trades Hall
Saville Mount
Leeds 7

● *District No. 4*
Unity House
134 Bromsgrove Street
Birmingham 5

● *District No. 6*
162 Gloucester Road
Bristol BS7 8NT

● *District No. 7*
Wessex House
520 London Road
Mitcham
Surrey CR4 4YQ

● *District No. 8*
14 Kinnaird Street
Antrim Road
Belfast BT14 6BE

● *District No. 9*
176 New Bridge Street
Newcastle-on-Tyne NE1 2TE

General

The NUSMCHDE is a craft union which seems bound for amalgamation with AUEW (Engineering Section) but for the time being remains independent. While its birth as an organisation is comparatively recent, many of the sections amalgamating into the one union for the craft had been in existence for many years and may be regarded as among the pioneers of trade unionism.

History

Sheet metal workers were originally strongly organised by a number of local societies linked together in two unions, the *National Amalgamation of Tin-Plate Workers* (formed in 1889) and the *General Union of Braziers and Sheet Metal Workers* (formed in 1862). These two unions amalgamated in 1920 to form the *National Union of Sheet Metal Workers and Braziers*. Further amalgamation followed with the coppersmiths, the heating and domestic engineers and latterly, in 1975, with the *Birmingham and Midland Sheet Metal Workers' Society*.

Organisation

The union is organised into branches. In addition, at any factory or site where members are employed, they are to elect a shop steward to collect contributions, convene shop meetings and communicate union business. In districts with a sufficient number of branches, there may be district committees established, if so decided by the National Executive Committee. The NEC consists of district lay representatives, members who have at least seven years' continuous membership, elected by ballot vote of the members in the district, and, in addition, the general secretary.

The National Conference takes place biennially, district committees arranging for the representation of branches within their district.

Full-Time Officers

District secretaries and district officers are elected for a period of four years by ballot vote of the members in the branches of the district. To be eligible for election they must have at least seven years' continuous membership.

The same rules and qualifications apply for the election of general secretary and national officers, except that in these cases the ballot vote is of the whole membership.

Workplace Activity

There is a great deal, and large variations in practice. Certain ground rules are laid down which stress mutuality. Some concern was expressed by one district office in 1980 that the union was insufficiently energetic in recruiting heating and domestic engineering apprentices and that this stemmed from old-fashioned ideas; in some cases, for example, apprentices were refused entry into the union until the age of 20 and in some cases were discouraged from participating in shop or site organisation. It is now union policy to encourage acceptance of open-ended training.

External Relations

The union is affiliated to the Labour Party. Its delegates were mandated to vote for Tony Benn in the Labour Party Deputy Leadership contest. It is affiliated to CND.

Policy and Recent Events

The issue of amalgamation has dominated internal policy debates. A special conference was called in September 1979 to consider the NEC recommendation to accept terms negotiated with the Amalgamated Union of Engineering Workers (Engineering Section) (see **AUEW Engineering Section**).

The general secretary here made the case for amalgamation. Membership turnover had been relatively high for a craft union in that it had needed to recruit at the rate of 16 per cent to grow 2 per cent in 1977-79. More importantly, the union was not recruiting skilled workers, although some apprentices were being recruited. The union was not, however, amalgamating because of financial worries, rather because the time was right and the terms were right to move towards one union for engineers. They were, however, to remain as a separate section within the AUEW until the membership agreed that this arrangement could end. They would retain their own ballots in this section and are not subject to postal ballots and they retain their own journal.

There was some opposition to the proposed amalgamation at the special conference. Some delegates felt that identity would be lost in the AUEW and felt that better terms would be secured from the EETPU. From the point of view of the heating and domestic section too, amalgamation with the EETPU, some delegates argued, would be more suitable. Chapple apparently bent over backwards, even to the extent of offering to alter the rule banning Communist Party members from office.

Delegates from the Birmingham and Midland Society pointed to the benefits of amalgamating with the TGWU and becoming the 'most powerful skilled negotiating body in the motor industry'.

Finally, these amendments were solidly defeated, the delegates approving the transfer of engagements to the AUEW.

There was then a delay. The officers of the NUSMCHDE wanted to move quickly to a ballot but a meeting with the certification officer revealed a number of snags. One central point was that because the Foundry and Constructional sections of the AUEW had decided to terminate their existing federal amalgamation arrangement with the AUEW and transfer to the AUEW (Engineering Section), there could be consequent

rule alterations and delay in the finalisation of the agreement on which the NUSMCHDE is to ballot.

This point of view was confirmed by events. The certification officer rejected the terms of the transfer of engagements because one of the four sections concerned (TASS) had not accepted them. The AUEW (Engineering Section), supported by the Construction and Foundry Sections, then challenged this decision in the High Court, but it was upheld. (See **AUEW**.)

Further Reference

A. T. Kidd (Assistant General Secretary 1922-41; General Secretary 1941-43), *History of the Tin-Plate Workers and Sheet Metal Workers and Braziers Societies*, 1949.

Shuttlemakers, Society of
(SS)

Head Office

21 Buchan Towers
Manchester Road
Bradford
West Yorkshire

Principal Officers

There are no full-time officers.
President — E. V. Littlewood

Membership (1982)

Total 92

General

The society was formed in 1891. After the second world war, membership increased to 600, about 90 per cent of all shuttlemakers in the country. The introduction of the shuttleless loom and the loss of Indian markets has brought gradual decline in this employment.

Group Six Technical Engineering and Scientific

Engineering Workers, Amalgamated Union of
(AUEW)

Technical, Administrative and Supervisory Section
(TASS)

Head Office

Onslow Hall
Little Green
Richmond
Surrey TW9 1QN
01-948 2271

Principal Officers

General Secretary — Ken Gill
Deputy General Secretary —
Barbara Switzer
Assistant Secretaries —
John Tuchfeld
Jack Carr
John Jones
National organisers —
vacancy (to be filled end of
March 1983)
vacancy (to be filled end of
March 1983)
Chris Darke

Divisional Offices

● *Division 1*
N. J. McIntosh
AUEW-TASS
145 Morrison Street
Edinburgh EH3 8AL
031-229 8713

W. B. Shields
AUEW–TASS
420 Sauchiehall Street
Glasgow G2 3JD
041-332 0247

● *Divisions 2 and 3*
W. B. Shields, T. Foley
AUEW-TASS
420 Sauchiehall Street
Glasgow G2 3JD
041-332 0247

● *Division 4*
B. Graham
AUEW-TASS
26-34 Antrim Rd
Belfast BT15 2AA
0232-746189

B. Anderson
AUEW-TASS
5 Lower Mount Street
Dublin 2
0001-765379

● *Divisions 5 and 6*
J. Simmons, A. Scott
AUEW-TASS
34 Claypath
Durham DH1 1TU
0385-44888

● *Divisions 7, 8 and 10*
J. Fairley, A. Matson
J. Rice, C. Lomas
R. Henshaw
AUEW-TASS
St. James House
Pendleton Way
Salford M6 5JA
061-737 6051

● *Divisions 9 and 11*
W. Sales, R. Tucker
L. Formby
AUEW-TASS
74 Lumley Street
Hightown
Castleford
West Yorkshire
0977-550884

● *Divisions 12, 15 and 16*
M. Sourani, A. Bashforth
R. Parsons, J. Rowan
G. Hope
AUEW-TASS
6-8 Holloway Circus
Queensway
Birmingham B1 1BT
021-632 4551

● *Divisions 13 and 14*
V. Gapper, F. Hyde
AUEW-TASS
71 Vaughan Way
Leicester LE1 4SG
0533-27177

● *Divisions 17 and 19*
  D. Yeomans, D. Perkins
  AUEW-TASS
  Print House
  65 Baldwin Street
  Bristol BS1 1QZ
  0272-299456

● *Division 18*
  K. W. E. Lane
  AUEW-TASS
  'South Coast'
  19 Brunswick Place
  Southampton S01 2AQ
  0703-30779

● *Division 20*
  R. Longworth
  AUEW-TASS
  Sardis Road
  Pontypridd CF37 1DU
  0443-406311

● *Division 21*
  D. Blockley
  AUEW-TASS
  140 St Helens Street
  Ipswich IP4 2LE
  0473-212136

● *Divisions 22, 23 and 24*
  B. King
  J. Thomas, R. Elliott
  AUEW-TASS
  25 Highfield Road
  Bushey WB2 2HD
  0923-49044

● *Divisions 25 and 26*
  L. Brooke, C. Darke
  S. Martin, B. Sanderson
  AUEW-TASS
  Onslow Hall
  Little Green
  Richmond
  Surrey TW9 1QN
  01-948 0094

Membership (1982)

  Male 162,423
  Female 23,267
  Total 185,690

Union journal and publications

  TASS News and Journal —
  monthly.
  TASS has also produced a
  booklet entitled *Women's
  Rights: And What We Are
  Doing to Get Them* (36 pages),
  which sets out the legal rights
  relating to women at work and

TASS policy in this area.
The union has also produced
three booklets setting out
TASS policy in particular areas
that concern the union (see
Policy):
Engineering Our Future, a
12-page pamphlet setting out
TASS policy in reaction to the
Finniston Report on the
Engineering Profession.
Import Controls Now!, a
28-page booklet arguing the
case for import controls and
the 'alternative economic
strategy'.
*New Technology: A Guide for
Negotiators* (28 pages), a
booklet outlining the effects of
new technology on
employment and setting out
guidelines on negotiating
'technology agreements'.
There are also guidelines on
the optimum use of Visual
Display Units, and a glossary
of computer terms.
In 1979-80 TASS also
produced various forms of
documentation including:
Professional Engineers in
  TASS
Save British Industry
Prospects by Tony Benn
  (Address to 1979
  Conference)
An Outline History of TASS
Health Hazards of VDUs
Negotiations for Equal
  Opportunity in Training
Computer Technology and
  Employment
A New Deal for Office Staff

The union has a national
technical sub-committee
whose main duty it is to
publish technical literature for
TASS members who are
involved in specialist work. A
number of such publications
have appeared recently, such
as *Industrial Conveyors and
Elevators*, which have not only
proved very useful for TASS
members themselves, but also
have served as a recruiting
springboard to attract new
members. The former general
secretary of TASS, George

Doughty, recently wrote a
booklet on *Inventions: How to
Patent Them* which gives
useful advice on gaining the
maximum benefit from
inventions initiated by TASS
members employed in
manufacturing industry.

General

TASS is the white-collar section of the
AUEW, and is one of the four sections created by the amalgamation of
1970 (see **AUEW Engineering Section**). TASS started its life as the
*Association of Engineering and Ship-
building Draughtsmen* and became
known as DATA (*Draughtsmen and
Allied Technicians' Association*) in
1961 to reflect its growing spread of
membership into developing technology in engineering and shipbuilding.
It claims to be the largest white-collar
union in engineering and embraces a
wide range of occupations.

TASS has adopted a left-wing
stance on most issues and this has not
improved its position in what is an
uneasy alliance between the four sections of the AUEW (see **Recent
Events**). It has been in conflict with
other TUC-affiliated unions — in particular the Engineers' and Managers'
Association (EMA) — and has taken
a militant stance against the Tory employment legislation.

The General Secretary, Ken Gill, is
a member of the General Council of
the TUC.

History

The union started its life as the *Association of Engineering and Shipbuilding Draughtsmen*, which was formed
at Clydeside in 1913 largely from
drawing office pesonnel employed at
John Brown's shipyard, Clydebank.
By 1918 membership had risen from a
few hundred to 10,911, and in the
same year it affiliated to the TUC. In
early 1919 it called its first strike at
Holroyd's of Rochdale. By 1920 the
AESD had grown to 11,920 members,
and it adopted a minimum wage policy — below which no AESD member
would accept new employment.

In 1922 the union took into membership members of the *Tracers'
Association* (an all female union) and
the AESD created a special section of
membership for tracers, with provision for representation on the Executive Committee.

In the following year the union
embarked on a series of strikes in
order to gain recognition from employers, the largest strike taking place
at English Electric and lasting for six
weeks. The English Electric dispute
eventually resulted in talks with the
Engineering and Allied Employers'
Federation (the precursor of the Engineering Employers' Federation)
which led to the negotiation of a procedure agreement from March 1924.

Despite the bleak years from the
General Strike until the late 1930s,
membership of the AESD remained
remarkably stable (8,830 in 1927;
13,903 in 1936). During that period
the union pursued a policy of paying
high unemployment benefits to its unemployed members so that they were
not forced to accept low-paid jobs.
This became more important during
the 1950s and 1960s. The upturn in
activity in the engineering industry towards the onset of the second world
war created a favourable climate for
unions such as the AESD, and the
union secured its first national wage
agreement with the Shipbuilding Employers' Federation in 1941 following
pressure being put on the employers
by Ernest Bevin.

In the post-war years the union gradually increased its strength from
38,800 in 1945 to 57,301 in 1958. In
1961 the union changed its name to
the *Draughtsmen and Allied Technicians' Association* (DATA) reflecting
the growing spread of membership
into new and developing technical
areas within the engineering industry.

In 1964, DATA was party to a dispute which created legal history in the
case of *Rookes v Barnard*. Rookes
was employed by BOAC in the drawing office at London airport and he
had fallen out with the AESD (as it
was then called) in 1955. The local
branch of DATA negotiated a 100 per
cent membership arrangement with
BOAC management and Rookes continued to refuse to join the union. The
local branch then wrote to BOAC and
gave notice that they would strike unless Rookes was dismissed. BOAC
then lawfully terminated Rookes's

contract of employment and Rookes subsequently sued the three union officers (Barnard, Fistal and Silverthorne). The House of Lords (overturning an earlier Court of Appeal decision) held that the defendants were guilty of unlawful intimidation because they had threatened to induce a breach of contract and were therefore not protected by Section 3 of the Trade Disputes Act, 1906. This case led to the enactment of the Trade Disputes Act 1965.

On amalgamation with the *Amalgamated Union of Engineering and Foundry Workers* and the *Constructional Engineering Union* in April 1970, DATA became the *Technical and Supervisory Section of the Amalgamated Union of Engineering Workers*. A year later the union's name was changed to the *AUEW (Technical, Administrative and Supervisory Section)*. The amalgamation has been an uneasy one (see **AUEW Engineering Section**) and little progress has so far been made towards the ultimate objective of achieving a common Rule Book and common policy for all four sections of the AUEW.

Union Officials

TASS employs eight officers at headquarters including the general secretary and deputy general secretary. The three assistant secretaries are allocated duties assigned to them by either the general secretary or the Executive Committee.

The three national organisers have responsibility for organisation, central or national negotiations within specific companies, and are allocated duties by the Executive Committee. All full-time officials of TASS are appointed by the Representative Council on the principle of selection. TASS also employs 38 divisional organisers throughout the UK and Republic of Ireland.

The principle of appointing full-time officials for life is one of the central issues which has frustrated moves towards completing amalgamation of all four sections of the AUEW. The AUEW (Engineering Section) insists that full-time officials face regular re-election

Although the May 1980 Representative Council reaffirmed the union's commitment to one union for engineering, delegates stressed that their separate sectional identity must be retained (see **AUEW Engineering Section**).

Coverage

TASS now covers a very wide range of employees, which has considerably broadened its scope from its original base of drawing office personnel and tracers. It now also includes secretaries, clerks, typists, finance and production control staff, sales and service personnel, systems analysts and other computer staff, engineers, supervisors, managers, and testers and inspectors.

Despite its increasing range of occupations, its growth in the 1960s and 1970s has not beeen impressive. In relation both to the increase of white-collar unionisation generally and other white-collar unions (such as ASTMS whose membership in 1971 was 101,346) TASS has not attracted other white-collar groups into its ranks (staff associations etc.) as successfully. The 1980 Representative Council called for a national recruitment campaign in an attempt to reach an eventual membership of 250,000. One of the primary reasons for broadening its recruitment is the threat posed to the design function by the advent of computer-aided design technology.

In recent years TASS has been in conflict with other TUC-affiliated unions, notably the EMA. TASS has consistently opposed the application of the EMA to join the CSEU. The legal action taken by the EMA against the TUC over the GEC/REL award involved TASS in assisting the TUC's solicitors with the preparation of the case. The EEF itself has always opposed any proliferation of unions with whom it negotiates, and has refused recognition to the EMA (see **Engineers' and Managers' Asscociation**).

Organisation

The supreme body of authority in TASS is the Representative Council which has complete control over the policy, the financial affairs and the conduct and management of the union. The annual Representative Council is held in April or May each year, although there is provision for the calling together of special representative councils. There are usually around 100 delegates attending. Each division of TASS has a divisional conference which consists of three representatives from each branch. Divisional conferences elect representatives to the annual Representative Council on the basis of around one delegate per 2,000 members.

The general management of the union is vested in the Executive Committee, which consists of the president, the vice-president, the national women's sub-commitee representative or deputy, and a number of lay delegates elected from the regions. The general secretary and deputy general secretary are ex-officio members. At present the EC is 17 strong. Full-time officials are not eligible for nomination to the EC. Election of EC members is conducted on a branch voting basis, with each branch determining its preference and having one vote per branch, taken at a divisional council meeting.

The Executive Council is also responsible for setting up a national women's sub-committee (see **Women**) which consists of one woman representative from each of the union's 26 divisions.

Divisional councils meet monthly and consist of one representative from each branch within the division, and have a general overseeing role into the union's organisation. Divisional councils have authority to declare industrial action official.

The union has a system of appeals machinery, and the appeal court consists of seven members (elected at each Representative Council conference), together with one other trade unionist, a lawyer, and the general secretary (or deputy) without vote.

Workplace Activity

TASS has around 320 geographical branches, and also attempts to cater, for membership issues particularly, to multi-plant companies by setting up a loose informal system of 'combines' of TASS members. Although 'combines'

are not provided for in the Rule Book, their main role is to ensure lay involvement in increasingly centralised company bargaining in the large engineering and allied corporations in which TASS membership is concentrated. The Executive Committee has a continually updated designated list of such 'combines' of TASS members (e.g. British Shipbuilders, BL Cars, GEC, and British Aerospace). Many TASS shop stewards develop good working relations with stewards and activists from other AUEW sections and operate a system of mutual assistance whereby each section of the AUEW can benefit from any membership gains. Most workplaces have TASS office committees in operation.

It is important to stress that TASS 'combines' are not true shop-steward combine committees — they consist only of TASS members. In fact, the union hierarchy is lukewarm about TASS stewards being involved with stewards from other unions on decision-making bodies — even with other white-collar unions such as ASTMS at Ford.

Women

Women constitute around 15 per cent of total TASS membership, and the union prides itself on the efforts it makes to cater for their particular interests. The union has a long history of female participation in union affairs stretching back to the absorption of members of the Tracers' Association in 1922. Since then there has always been provision for a female representative from the national women's sub-committee (NWSC) on the Executive Committee.

The NWSC meets six times a year, and besides sending a representative to EC meetings also appoints two representatives to attend Representative Council meetings. The union has been active in publishing a number of booklets on women's rights (see **Union Journal and Publications**) and the booklet *Women's Rights: And What We Are Doing to Get Them* lays particular stress on the way employers discriminate against women in the formulation and implementation of job evaluation schemes.

According to the Donovan Report

(1968), of 17,450 trainees undergoing draughtsman (sic) apprenticeships in 1966 only 2 per cent were women. Moreover, of 9,630 undergoing scientific and technological apprenticeships, 1.1 per cent were women, and of the other 12,150 technicians, 1.3 per cent were women. Later figures (1972) show that women formed 2 per cent of works superintendents and department managers in the engineering and allied industries, and only 1 per cent of scientists and technologists.

There is one female deputy general secretary in the union, but there are no female divisional organisers.

External Relations

TASS is affiliated to the Labour Party and sponsors the following MPs:

Joe Ashton (Bassetlaw)
James Lamond (Oldham East)
Albert Booth (Barrow-in-Furness)
Ernie Ross (Dundee West)

Around 46 per cent of TASS membership pay the political levy to the Labour Party. The union has set up a parliamentary panel which meets regularly. The political sub-committee of the union meets the parliamentary group on a regular basis.

The union has affiliations with the following bodies:

Confederation of Shipbuilding and
    Engineering Unions (CSEU)
European Metal Workers' Federation
International Metal Workers
    Federation
National Council for Civil Liberties
    (NCCL)
National Joint Committee of Working
    Women's Organisations
Labour Research Department
Liberation
Anti-Apartheid Movement
National Peace Council
Workers' Education Council
Chile Solidarity
British Standards Institute
Campaign against the Criminal
    Trespass Law (through the
    AUEW)

Unlike the AUEW as a whole, the AUEW (Engineering Section), TASS has generally taken a left-wing policy line on political matters (see **Policy**).

The General Secretary, Ken Gill, is a member of the TUC General Council.

Policy

The main thrust of TASS policy in recent years has been its advocacy of import controls as a means of halting the catastrophic decline of our manufacturing industry. The TASS booklet *Import Controls Now!* argued that import controls covering a range of key industries were urgently needed to enable manufacturing industry in Britain to modernise and re-equip with new technology. A key proviso of the booklet was the notion that import controls were part of a general strategy including a rise in public expenditure; a relaxation of the monetary squeeze; state intervention and planning to ensure a higher rate of investment in keeping with social priorities; extension of public ownership and the role of the National Enterprise Board; effective control over the activities of multinational companies; and a substantial cut in defence expenditure. The union also advocated a major expansion of industrial democracy to ensure workers' participation in all the decisions on investment and employment that affect their working lives. The union gave a guarded welcome to the recommendations of the Finniston Report (see **Recent Events**).

A similar strand of thinking lay behind the TASS pamphlet *Collapse or Growth? An Alternative to Edwardes* on British Leyland. TASS argued that as a result of under-investment for several years BL was too small and that BL must expand its production and not contract, so that BL as a competitor and a potential partner must aim to match the output and quality of its Western European rivals.

TASS was opposed to the sale by the Tory government of British Aerospace shares to private individuals and institutions. The union argued for the need for an integrated approach towards the development of the aerospace industry; collaboration between the manufacturers of aero engines, air frames and the main commercial purchaser (British Airways) is essential. In addition to this, the union believed in European collaboration to compete on a world scale with the American multi-nationals. The union feared that any dismemberment of the industry could only weaken indigenous capability and reduce British Aerospace to the role of sub-contractor to the American multinational aerospace industry.

The majority of TASS membership is located in industries where vast changes in technology are taking place. In general, TASS welcomes the development of new technology but insists that increases in productivity should be distributed on an equitable basis between management and workers.

On the political front, TASS lent its support to the campaign for democracy and accountability in the Labour Party, and supported all three such proposals at the 1979 Labour Party Conference. One might add that whilst TASS argues for Labour MPS to be subject to re-selection by constituency parties it is unwilling to extend the same principle to its own officials. It campaigned for a public enquiry into the death of Blair Peach (largely through the efforts of Joe Ashton MP); actively supported the Anti-Nazi League and the National Council for Civil Liberties; campaigned against the Corrie Abortion (Amendment) Bill; and generally adopted a Tribunite posture on most political issues.

The left-wing stance of TASS exacerbated the growing rift btween TASS and the other three AUEW sections — in particular the Engineering Section (see **Recent Events**).

At the 1982 TASS annual conference, Ken Gill called for an end to tripartism by advocating the withdrawal of the TUC from the NEDC machinery. He added that Len Murray and other senior TUC General Council members should not have cosy chats with Norman Tebbit, the Employment Secretary 'while he is plotting to destroy everything trade unions stand for'.

Recent Events

The uneasy coalition between the four sections of the AUEW is continually shrouded in uncertainty. The Nation-al Committee of the Engineering Section at its April 1980 meeting decided to press ahead with a full merger of the four sections of the AUEW. It also decided to end the present relationship with any section that rejects the terms of the merger, as well as insisting on postal ballots for present and future officials of the resulting merger (see **AUEW Engineering Section**). The National Committee of the Engineering Section together with the two top officials and the whole of the Executive Council is currently right-wing dominated. The strategy of the Engineering Section is to pull together the Engineering, Foundry, and Constructional Sections, together with other unions, into a single grouping. TASS fears that not only might it lose its identity, but it might be swallowed up into an eventual merger with Frank Chapple's EETPU. TASS successfully obtained a ruling from the certification officer, subsequently upheld in the courts, that the Engineering Section's proposals were in breach of the Rule Book, and thus the amalgamation was delayed. The action of TASS in the High Court was successful. The court held that TASS was entitled to a declaration that an alteration to the Engineering Section rules purporting to enlarge the number of its delegates included in the composition of the National Conference of the union was *ultra vires* the instrument of amalgamation and rules of the AUEW. The indications are that TASS will continue to resist a further amalgamation on the Engineering Section's terms, and it could eventually become isolated. Given such a prospect, it might consider amalgamation with another union which has a strong base in the engineering industry, e.g. the TGWU or ASTMS. TASS is still the largest union embracing white-collar workers in the engineering industry, and it is unlikely to be pushed into an amalgamation except on its own terms. In 1982 the National Union of Gold, Silver and Allied Trades (NUGSAT), a small union organising craft workers in the rare metal trade, transferred its engagements to AUEW/TASS.

The bitter rivalry between TASS and the EMA culminated in the EMA deciding to withdraw its application for membership of the CSEU on the eve of the CSEU's annual meeting in 1980. TASS maintained that the admission of the EMA would have led to the further proliferation of unions in the engineering and shipbuilding industry, and the EMA's chances were finally dashed when the National Committee of the AUEW Engineering Section decided to oppose the EMA's application (see **Engineers' and Managers' Association**).

Ken Gill was replaced as chairperson of the Aerospace Committee of the Confederation of Shipbuilding and Engineering Unions (CSEU) by Jack Whyman, a member of the AUEW (Engineering Section) Executive Council. It had been thought that Gill's position as chairperson was secure under an 'unspoken agreement', but the AUEW used its dominant influence to displace him in what the *Financial Times* described as a 'rightwing coup'.

The union is increasingly striving to cater for the needs of professional engineers amongst its membership. Around 30,000 management and professional staff belong to TASS, and the union has set up separate staff branches and a national management advisory committee to ensure that the needs of professional managers are met at the highest levels in the union, although the establishment of management branches has created some tension amongst certain sections of the TASS membership. Separating 'supervision' from 'craft' has historically been a criticism that TASS has levelled at ASTMS — and yet it is implementing such a policy amongst its own members. Yet it has always been TASS philosophy that engineers and managers are best catered for by incorporating them into the mainstream of the trade union movement. TASS pressure was one factor leading to the setting up of the Finniston Committee.

One of the main recommendations of the Finniston Committee was that a statutory Engineering Authority should be established, funded and accountable to the government, with a wide remit to strengthen the engineering dimension in the economy. The main criticism offered by TASS of the Finniston Report is that only strong collective organisation of professional and technician engineers within independent unions would win the improved salaries and status to reflect the valuable role played by engineers in British industry. Finniston rightly pointed out that in many companies, professional engineers work as technicians and technician engineers perform tasks which would be that of professional engineers in others. In the former situation the high talent of the professional is underemployed, leading to loss of job satisfaction. In the latter, expertise is being under-rewarded. Moreover, Finniston argued that employers should allow engineers to play a vital role in the commercial exploitation of their own technological developments and pay them salaries commensurate with their contribution to the company. TASS believes that although Finniston side-stepped the crucial issue of engineers' salary structure and differentials, it was not afraid to highlight the failure of British industry to invest in research and development, and to innovate and create commercially viable products.

Following the publication of the Finniston Report, the government set up an Engineering Council, which as a body would have a wide brief to improve the industry's standards and reduce duplication and rivalry between engineering institutions. The Engineering Council was expected to take over registration of engineers from the Council of Engineering Institutions by early 1983. At the 1982 Annual Conference of the Confederation of Shipbuilding and Engineering Unions, it was decided to press for representation on the Engineering Council, possibly through direct elections by engineering workers. The CSEU proposal was that the Council should embrace 'engineering technicians' and 'technician engineers' as well as chartered engineers and managers. The AUEW (Engineering Section) and the EETPU organise some 250,000 of these craftworkers. The white-collar unions ASTMS and AUEW/TASS argued strongly against the CSEU proposal, which was narrowly passed on a card vote. Both ASTMS and TASS said that the CSEU motion would exclude them from the Council since it did not mention them and that in any case it was contrary to TUC policy. Both Stan Davison of ASTMS and Ken Gill of TASS had been proposed by the TUC for the Council but were not appointed. Ironically, TASS's main rival, the EMA, had already succeeded in securing the appointment of its General Secretary, John Lyons.

The uncertainty over the direction the AUEW amalgamation will take, the continued contraction of British engineering, the challenge of new technology, and the constant rivalry between TASS and other white-collar organisations (particularly the EMA) all continue to provide a challenge to the TASS section of the AUEW.

Further Reference

J. E. Mortimer, *A History of the Association of Engineering and Shipbuilding Draughtsmen*, AESD, London 1960. The official history of the nion up to 1959 written by the national secretary of the Labour Party.

Hilary Wainwright and Dave Elliott, *The Lucas Plan: A New Trade Unionism in the Making?*, Allison & Busby 1982.

Engineers' and Managers' Association
(EMA)

Head Office

Station House
Fox Lane North
Chertsey
Surrey KT16 9HW
093-28 64131/4

Principal Officers

General Secretary and EPEA General Secretary —
John Lyons
Deputy General Secretary and EPEA Deputy General Secretary —
Simon Petch
ASEE General Secretary —
Denis Sweaney
SAIMA General Secretary —
Adrian Askew
Aerospace Association General Secretary —
Peter Fairley

Membership (1982)

Male 43,539
Female 236
Total 43,775

Union Journal and Publications

Electrical Power Engineer — bimonthly, circulation around 40,000.

In 1976 the EPEA (the founding body of the present EMA) commissioned a special report on the subject: *Some Implications of Radioactive Waste from Nuclear Power Generation in the UK up to the Year 2000*, published in two volumes: £4 for the summary report (Volume 1) and £15 for the technical appendices (Volume 2). After exhaustive examination the report concluded that present techniques of nuclear waste management would suffice until the end of the century, but would need to be further developed to cope with an expanded nuclear programme in the next century.
Pensions for Professional and Managerial Staff — a 70-page booklet giving advice on pensions and related matters of interest, written primarily for professional and allied staff in trade unions.

General

The EMA grew out of the decision of the *Electrical Power Engineers' Association* in 1976 to recruit professional, managerial and allied staffs outside the electricity supply industry — particularly in shipbuilding, engineering, aerospace, oil and other industries. In doing so, it encountered hostility both from the AUEW/TASS and ASTMS. In the past three years it has taken legal action against the TUC and ACAS, and has been involved in a bitter inter-union feud which exacerbated the tensions between statutory recognition procedures and the Bridlington rules operated by the TUC. The General Secretary, John Lyons, is a vociferous advocate of 'professional' trade unionism.

History

The union was formed in January 1913 by a small group of 21 power station engineers and registered later in the same year as the *Association of Electrical Station Engineers*. The name was changed to the *Electrical Power Engineers' Association* in 1918. In 1942 the union affiliated to the TUC. The union was given notice of suspension from membership of the TUC in 1972 for failure to comply with Congress policy of non-registration under the Industrial Relations Act, 1971. The National Executive Committee of the union decided in June 1973 to de-register in line with Congress policy and the notice of suspension was lifted.

In 1976 the Annual Delegate Conference took the decision to recruit in industries outside the electricity supply industry. On January 1977 the *Association of Supervisory and Executive Engineers* (ASEE) amalgamated with the EPEA. The *Engineers' and Managers' Association* was formally created in April 1977, and the EPEA became the largest group within this federal organisation. In December 1977 the *Shipbuilding and Allied Industries Managers' Association* (SAIMA) transferred its engagements and likewise became a constituent group within the EMA. During 1979 the *British Aircraft Corporation Professional Staffs Association* (BAC STAFF) and the *British Aerospace Staff Association* (BASA) both transferred their engagements to the EMA and as from 1 October 1979 they were formed by the EMA into the *Aerospace Association*, an industrial group in its own right within the EMA.

Union Officials

At the end of September 1981 the EMA employed 22 officials, the majority of whom were responsible to a group national executive committee. The EMA's officers consisted of a general secretary, deputy general secretary, a negotiating officer, two research officers and an administration manager. The EPEA officers consisted of a general secretary, deputy general secretary, two national officers, one job evaluation officer, nine area secretaries, an administra-

tion manager (who acts for the EMA) and the editor of the *Electrical Power Engineer* (who is also an officer of the ASEE). SAIMA and the Aerospace Association are served by general secretaries who are assisted by the EMA negotiating officer and the research department and other services as appropriate. The EMA's negotiating officer acts as the secretary to the central group.

Coverage

The EMA seeks to organise technical, scientific and managerial staffs in the electricity supply industry, management staffs in the shipbuilding industry, and engineers and managers in the engineering, oil, aerospace and other industries. The union experienced opposition from other TUC-affiliated unions in its efforts to recruit new members outside the electricity supply industry (see **Recent Events**), and has faced similar opposition in its efforts to become affiliated to the Confederation of Shipbuilding and Engineering Unions.

In March 1982 the EMA reached a joint co-operation agreement with EESA (the white-collar section of the EETPU) covering the organisation of professional, managerial and allied staff in the aerospace, engineering and shipbuilding industries. One specific clause of the agreement was designed to enable EESA to take advantage, through the staff side, of the local machinery for managerial staff negotiation in the shipbuilding industry. Another provided for EESA and the EMA jointly to approach the EEF to seek formal procedural arrangements covering the introduction of collective bargaining for professional and senior managerial and allied staffs.

Organisation

The supreme policy-making body of the EMA is the Biennial Delegate Conference. The union is based on the principle that within the overall responsibilities of the EMA each industrial sector has its own group organisation with full industrial autonomy. Currently the EMA is composed of three industrial groups — the Electrical Power Engineers' Association, the Shipbuilding and Allied Industries

Management Association and the Aerospace Association. It is intending to set up a fourth group to cover staff in the engineering industry. Delegates to the Biennial Delegate Conference are elected from the various groups within the EMA, partly by the group executive committees and partly by the membership at large. The rules also provide for each constituent group to have its own policy-making conference and a national executive committee.

The General Executive Council of the EMA is elected at the Biennial Delegate Conference, and comprises a maximum of 26 members, with seats allocated pro rata to the size of each constituent group. The GEC has the power to appoint all EMA full-time officers.

The rules of the EMA provide that in the event of a dispute calling for strike action a secret ballot shall be taken of those members who may be required to be involved in strike action. If 60 per cent or more of those members balloted are in favour of such action the group national executive committee may act accordingly.

External Relations

The EMA has no political affiliation, but Arthur Palmer (Labour MP, Bristol NE) is retained as a parliamentary adviser. John Lyons, the General Secretary, was a member of the National Enterprise Board until its membership resigned *en bloc* in protest against Sir Keith Joseph's plans on the future role of the NEB. For two years he was also chairperson of the NEDO Sector Working Party on Industrial Trucks. He is currently a member of the Post Office Board and is Secretary of the Employees' National Committee in the Electricity Supply Industry. He represents the EMA on the TUC Fuel and Power Industries Committee and the TUC Nationalised Industries Committee.

The EPEA Conference in April 1980 and the EMA Conference in 1981 took an important step toward becoming directly involved in all major national issues at the TUC. Until then the union was confined to taking a part at the TUC only in issues which directly affected its members' industrial interests. In early 1981 the EMA approached the unions representing professional and managerial staff to try to create 'a new centre of influence' within the TUC. The union has become increasingly concerned at the centralisation tendencies in the TUC General Council, accompanied by pressures on unions to amalgamate along lines decided by the General Council. In July 1982 the EMA, BALPA and BACM set up the Council of Managerial, Professional and Allied Staffs (COMPAS) whose objectives were to create a forum in which politically unaffiliated TUC unions representing primarily professional, managerial and allied staffs can (a) exchange information, (b) consider and, where desirable, agree on a common response to issues that affect or may impinge upon their common interests and (c) develop closer working relations between themselves.

Policy

The policy of the EMA on nuclear power has obviously been influenced by the policy of the EPEA. Members of the EPEA operate and maintain the nuclear power stations and are involved in their design and construction. In addition there are some EMA members concerned with nuclear power in other areas — in shipbuilding, in connection with nuclear submarines, and in the engineering industry and in particular the heavy plant industry. The EMA seconded a motion on nuclear policy at the 1979 Trades Union Congress which was moved by the NUM. Briefly, EMA policy on nuclear power is that it is essential to develop nuclear power, alongside other sources of energy that are economically viable, in the decades ahead, provided that it is safe and socially acceptable. Prior to the NUM reversing its policy on nuclear power the EPEA had a formal agreement with the NUM in favour of the balanced development of coal and nuclear energy. Together with other unions in the electricity supply industry it is making available trade union speakers on the subject of nuclear power to other unions and the community generally.

With the decision of the CEGB to seek permission to build a pressurised water reactor (PWR) at Sizewell the EPEA are preparing a report on the safety implications for staff who would be involved in the commissioning and working on the Sizewell PWR.

On industrial democracy, the EMA was strongly critical of the Bullock Report. It had opposed both its terms of reference and its composition. However, the union strongly supported the Labour government's White Paper on Industrial Democracy, published in 1978, with its concept of 'positive partnership' to be developed wherever possible by agreement, but welcomed as well the statutory fall-back procedures for joint consultation on the strategic policy issues affecting a company or industry. The union put particular emphasis on the need for managerial and professional staff to be fully involved in their own right in industrial democracy procedures via their membership of trade unions. The EMA was not itself in favour of worker representation on boards but 'would not argue against that where it was generally desired by employees in a company or industry'. In those circumstances the union would prefer two-tier board structures.

The EMA played a large part in the setting up of the Finniston Committee of Inquiry into the engineering profession. The EPEA moved a motion at the 1976 Congress which was passed unanimously. Subsequently, the Finniston inquiry was set up by the Secretary of State for Industry in July 1977. Generally speaking, the EMA supports the statutory registration of engineers; the creation of a statutory engineering authority; and a thorough review of the education and training requirements of the engineering profession. The Finniston Report was criticised by John Lyons for failing to give sufficient weight to trade union organisation. The EMA makes much play of the fact that the Council of Engineering Institutions have recommended the EMA as the only TUC-affiliated union appropriate for professional engineers in the private sector. This provides much ammunition for the EMA in its battles for recruitment and recognition with AUEW/ TASS and ASTMS (see **Recent**

Events). The union advocated in January 1981 that the government should set up the Council for Engineering, despite the opposition of the professional engineering institutions. The EMA continues to support the creation of a statutory body rather than the chartered Council of Engineering proposed by the government.

The EMA is opposed in principle to the closed shop. It also believes strongly in its political independence. At the 1980 Trades Union Congress it successfully moved a motion, carried by a card vote of 7,998,000 to 3,328,000, calling on the General Council to take into account the views of the now substantial minority of TUC affiliates that are unaffiliated to any political party.

Recent Events

Since the EMA decided to recruit members outside its traditional homeland of the electrical supply industry, it encountered severe opposition from other unions — particularly ASTMS and AUEW/TASS. It also encountered hostility from within the TUC itself, from the Engineering Employers' Federation and from the Advisory Conciliation and Arbitration Service (ACAS).

The decision to recruit outside the electricity supply industry was taken in April 1976. This was quickly followed by a transfer of engagements from the ASEE in early 1977. Later in 1977 the Shipbuilding and Allied Industries Management Association (SAIMA) amalgamated with the EMA. Early in 1979 two of the staff associations within the nationalised aerospace industry (BAC STAFF and the larger British Aerospace Staff Association) made approaches to the EMA which resulted in a transfer of engagements. The EMA is composed of four main groups with membership figures at December 1978 as follows:

EPEA Group	34,406
SAIMA Group	1,612
Central Group	2,090
ASEE only	6,207

The dispute between the EMA and the TUC arose as a result of a Section 11 recognition reference under the Employment Protection Act, 1975, which the EMA submitted to ACAS covering the recognition of members at GEC Reactor Equipment Ltd, Whetstone (GEC/REL). This followed an adverse reaction from the TUC disputes committee which had ruled that the EPEA members' best interest at GEC/REL would be served by joining AUEW/TASS, and that the EPEA should cease recruitment and should not seek recognition. Members of the EPEA at GEC/REL Whetstone rejected the advice of the award and asked the EPEA to continue to represent them. After some correspondence and a further meeting between the EMA and the TUC General Council, the EMA decided to sue the TUC, arguing that the award was based on factual misinformation and went beyond the Bridlington principles in reaching its conclusions. ACAS then halted its inquiries because the writ against the TUC altered the situation and introduced uncertainty as to the EMA's position within the TUC which would need to be resolved before they could proceed to ascertain the opinions of the workers involved and make a recommendation. This led to the EMA's initiating legal proceedings against ACAS. The dispute with the TUC was eventually settled in December 1979, when the EMA dropped the case on the basis that the EMA would respect the findings of the TUC disputes committee, while the TUC would not suspend the EMA from membership or seek to have it expelled. The court action against ACAS resulted in a finding in favour of ACAS, when the House of Lords reversed an Appeal Court ruling in May 1979 that ACAS must proceed with its inquiries into the EMA recognition claim at GEC/REL.

The EMA received a further setback in that its hopes for joining the Confederation of Shipbuilding and Engineering Unions (CSEU) were dashed when the AUEW (Engineering Section) Executive, which had been supporting the EMA's efforts to join the CSEU, was told by its National Committee in April 1980 that it must stop doing so. The AUEW (Engineering Section) leaders had been supporting the EMA's application in spite of the fact that

AUEW/TASS had been the most vocal and determined opponent. John Lyons had described the activities of AUEW/TASS in June 1979, as 'jackboot trade unionism'.

It is clear that the decision of the EMA to recruit outside electricity supply took it into an area fraught with difficulties and lays it open to hostility from unions like ASTMS and AUEW/TASS — both of whom had established collective bargaining arrangements with the EEF and who were hostile to any interference from a union such as the EMA. The whole issue also highlighted the tensions between statutory recognition procedures — now repealed by the Tories — and the Bridlington rules operated by the TUC.

Scientific, Technical and Managerial Staffs, Association of
(ASTMS)

Head Office

79 Camden Road
London NW1 9ES
01-267 4422

Divisional Offices

● *Aberdeen*
25a Carden Place
Aberdeen AB1 1HZ
0224-29490

● *Belfast*
New Forge Lane
Belfast BT9 5NW
0232-681733/4

● *Birmingham*
22 George Road
Edgbaston
Birmingham B15 1PJ
021-454 6091

● *Bradford*
Textile Hall
Westgate
Bradford
West Yorkshire BD1 2RG
0274-727967

● *Bristol*
1 Henbury Road
Westbury-on-Trym
Bristol BS9 3HH

0272 500824/500774/
500699

● *Coventry*
First Floor
26 Queen's Road
Coventry CV1 3DQ
0203-57425

● *Dublin*
38 Lower Leeson Street
Dublin 2
0001-762306

● *Durham*
Rainton Lodge
West Rainton
Houghton-le-Spring
Tyne and Wear DH4 6NU
0783-846527

● *Glasgow*
1 Woodlands Terrace
Glasgow G3 6DD
041-331 1216

● *Haverhill*
21/25 High Street
Haverhill
Suffolk CB9 8AD
0440-702590

● *Hounslow*
28 Staines Road
Hounslow
Middlesex TW3 3JS
01-570 0334/2100/1617
01-572 3124/0144

● *Kendal*
6A Kirkland
Kendal
Cumbria
0539-25757

● *Knutsford*
Bexton Lane
Knutsford
Cheshire WA16 9DA
0565-4136

● *Leeds*
7 Bank Street
Castleford
Yorkshire WF10 1JP
09775-56351

● *Liverpool*
201 Tower Buildings
Water Street
Liverpool L3 1AB
051-236 9601

● *Manchester*
East Road
Longsight
Manchester M12 5GY
061-225 0501

● *Nottingham*
Swiss Lodge
15 Waverley Street
Nottingham NG7 4EA
0602-781564

● *Oxford*
18 St Clements
Oxford OX4 1AB
0865-442166

● *Queensferry*
Baines House
Glynne Street
Queensferry, Deeside
Clwyd CH5 1TA
0224-821830/9

● *Sheffield*
61 Wolstenholme Road
Sheffield S7 1LE
0742-589433

● *Southampton*
20 Bellevue Road
Southampton SO1 2AY
0703-25446

● *South Wales*
4 St Fagans House
St Fagans Street
Caerphilly
Glamorgan
0222 869219/869210

● *Uttoxeter*
2 The Maltings
High Street
Uttoxeter
Staffordshire
088-934111

● *Whitehall College*
Dane O'Coys Road
Bishop Stortford
Hertfordshire
0279-58111

Principal Officers

General Secretary —
Clive Jenkins
Hon. President — Len Wells
Deputy General Secretary —
Stan Davidson
Prime responsibility for
Electronic and Electrical
Engineering; Food, Drink
and Tobacco; Chemical and
Oil Industries; Universities
and Education; Grant Aided
Bodies
Assistant General Secretaries
General Engineering, Vehicle
Building, Aerospace, Steel,

Glass Industry, Civil Airlines, Asbestos, Construction Industry, Shipbuilding, Ceramics, Footwear and Transport — Bob McCusker
Insurance, Finance and Shipping Industries, Leisure Industry, Textiles, Clothing and Carpet Industries, Union's Legal Department — Muriel Turner
National Officers
Roger Beson
Reg Bird
Terry Comerford
John Langan
Roger Lyons
Russell Miller
Paul Talbot
Tim Webb
Director of Research — Barrie Sherman
National Finance Officer — J. McKie
National Secretary Insurance Section — Peter Kennedy
Journal Editor — Alan Brown
Health and Safety Officer — Sheila McKechnie

Membership (1982)

Total 427,500
Medical Practioners' Section
Total 4,500

Union Journal and Publications

ASTMS Journal — Circulation 450,000 (mailed to each member bi-monthly)
Clive Jenkins and Barrie Sherman, *Computers and the Unions*, Longman (Business Data Processing Series) 1977, £4.95.
Clive Jenkins and Barrie Sherman, *The Collapse of Work*, Eyre Methuen 1979, £3.50.
Clive Jenkins and Barrie Sherman, *White-Collar Unionism: The Rebellious Salariat*, Routledge & Kegan Paul 1979, £3.95.
Clive Jenkins and Barrie Sherman, *Collective Bargaining*, Routledge and Kegan Paul 1977.
Guide to Health and Safety at Work: An ASTMS Policy Document (40 pages). Useful guidelines and advice for ASTMS members to improve health and safety in the workplace.
Technological Change and Collective Bargaining (50 pages). A discussion document outlining the implications for white-collar employment of rapidly changing technology, especially micropocessors.
Carbon Disulphide — An Investigation into Heart Disease at Courtaulds. Health and Safety Policy Document. The Health Hazards of Visual Display Units. The Prevention of Occupational Cancer. The Prevention of Occupational Deafness: Control of Noise at Work. Health and Safety and the Supervisor.
ASTMS has also produced a Health and Safety Office circular entitled *Accidents on Youth Opportunities Programme* which alerts its members to increasing evidence that youngsters on YOP schemes are exposed to health and safety hazards in many workplaces and lack adequate protection.
The NEC of ASTMS also publishes its own *Economic Review* which sets out the union's arguments for an alternative economic strategy (see Policy).
ASTMS also has specialist newspapers for UCTA Insurance, NHS (*Medical World*), and many circulars and newsletters for specialist groups of members.

General

The Association of Scientific, Technical and Managerial Staffs claimed to be both the largest and fastest-growing union of salaried staffs in Europe in the 1970s. With around 430,000 members it now ranks as the second largest white-collar union in Britain and the seventh largest union within the TUC. ASTMS organises across many sectors — in particular among scientific, technical and managerial employees in industry, commerce, education and health. From a membership of 80,000 in 1968, ASTMS grew at the rate of 30,000 monthly, partly due to the appeal of General Secretary Clive Jenkins to groups of employees in areas which had traditionally resisted the penetration of white-collar trade unionism — such as insurance, banking and building societies. At the same time, the union has also amalgamated with other organisations (some of which were previously in direct competition with ASTMS) when these organisations eventually felt that their objectives could be best achieved under the umbrella of ASTMS. Since 1980, ASTMS has experienced a ten per cent loss in membership largely arising from the drastic decline in the manufacturing sector.

Clive Jenkins is a member of the General Council of the TUC, and the union is affiliated to the Labour Party.

History

The origins of ASTMS lie in the history of two unions: the *Association of Supervisory Staffs, Executives and Technicians* (ASSET), and the *Association of Scientific Workers* (AScW) which merged to become ASTMS in 1968.

ASSET started life soon after the first world war as the *National Foremen's Union*, created by supervisors in the railway workshops. There was some diversification and growth but little real progress until the second world war and the achievement of recognition by the Engineering Employer's Federation after a long struggle. The EEF had for years held that supervisors should not be union members, but with help from the TUC, ASSET secured a procedure agreement in 1944. A barrier to the growth of the union was the insistence by the EEF that recognition would only apply where ASSET could secure a majority of a specific grade in a plant; this later became a spur to recognition.

The AScW was also campaigning for recognition by the EEF, and achieved it within months of ASSET's success. From its wartime success until 1969, ASSET's growth was restricted by the Foremen and Staff Mutual Benefit Society, an employer-backed provident society for supervisors, whose rules forbade any members to belong to a trade union. A private bill in parliament promoted by the union secured the abolition of the offending rule, and 50,000 supervisors and other staff were at last free to join a union without sacrificing their provident benefits.

By now the union had become ASTMS following the merger in 1968 between ASSET and AScW. The merger of the unions was accomplished amicably, with the larger union — ASSET — accepting a 50-50 allocation of national executive committee seats between the two unions. Clive Jenkins of ASSET and John Dutton (now retired) of AScW became joint general secretaries of the new union. Its strength at that time was less than 80,000 members: within six years it was to pass the 300,000 mark.

Much of the growth of ASTMS can be attributed to the energy and abilities of Clive Jenkins, who publicised the need for workers in traditionally non- or under-unionised sectors of employment to become union members. His own career contains links with both the founding unions of ASTMS: in 1946 he was a branch secretary and area treasurer of AScW, before becoming a full-time official of ASSET. He was appointed General Secretary of ASSET in 1961 at the age of 35.

As the union grew, attracting members from sectors where staff associations rather than independent unions had been the rule, a number of smaller unions and staff associations were merged with it. One important landmark was the merger with the *Medical Practitioners' Union* (1970).

However, whilst mergers certainly demonstrate a recruitment thrust by the union into the financial and National Health Service sectors, they cannot account for more than a small part of the union's growth. In fact two thirds of ASTMS members today have never belonged to a union or a staff association before.

Union Officials

A rapidly growing union like ASTMS inevitably faced organisational and administrative problems in servicing the membership. Newly recruited members have a high degree of dependence on the services of divisional officers and this problem is accentuated for ASTMS in that, in many companies and workplaces, it is not only weak in total potential membership, but also has to compete with other unions and staff associations. A sub-committee of the NEC, the officer coverage/selection committee, is responsible for recruitment, selection and allocation of ASTMS officers throughout the country. The committee contains the general secretary, deputy and assistant general secretaries, president and vice-president and six others.

ASTMS officers come from a variety of sources, and tend to be young. They include several ex-Ruskin College students, graduate trainees, former officials of other unions, as well as former lay representatives who have undergone the necessary training. The composition of the sub-committee indicates the importance that the union places on the selection and training of its full-time officials.

Coverage

ASTMS is active in every major industry — and in smaller ones as well. The majority of its membership is in the engineering industry, and there are large pockets of members in airways, universities, chemicals, computers, steel, food, footwear, tobacco, and international communications. In the National Health Service the union represents the majority of scientific and technical grades, and has enhanced its representative capacity by bringing within its orbit the *Medical Practitioners' Union, Guild of Hospital Pharmacists, the Union of Speech Therapists*, and the *Health Service Chiropodists' Association*.

These bodies of specialist staff which have been incorporated into ASTMS over the last few years have generally been given special status in the union to provide them with appropriate access to the union's policy-making bodies. The Rule Book of ASTMS specifically provides for the establishment of sectional advisory councils to cover such sections of its membership. Each advisory council has a member of the National Executive Council as chairperson and a full-time official as secretary. Such groups include the MPU section, Prudential Insurance staff, Royal Group, Midland Bank staff, GHP, Pearl Section and several others. ASTMS is a signatory party to the Engineering Procedure Agreement. The union opened Whitehall College, its own educational and training college, in Bishops Stortford in 1975.

The following organisations have become part of ASTMS through mergers and amalgamation since 1970:

Union of Insurance Staffs: 1970

Prudential Clerical Staff Association (District Office) and

Prudential Ladies Staff Welfare Association: 1970

Medical Practitioners' Union: 1970

Royal Group Guild: 1971

Midland Bank Staff Association: 1973

Assurance Representatives' Organisation (Ireland): 1973

Clydesdale Bank Staff Association: 1974

Guild of Hospital Pharmacists: 1974

Pearl Section (NUIW): 1974

Forward Trust Staff Association: 1975

Kodak Senior Staff Association: 1975

London and Manchester Section (NUIW): 1975

Midland Bank Technical Services Staff Association: 1975

Union of Speech Therapists: 1975

Health Service Chiropodists' Association: 1976

United Commercial Travellers' Association: 1976

Liverpool and Victoria Managers' Association: 1976

Group 1 Staff Association (Courtaulds): 1977

Excess Insurance Staff Association: 1977

Managers and Overlookers' Society: 1977

Pearl Federation (NUIW): 1978
Refuge Section (NUIW): 1979
Reckitt and Colman Management Association: 1979
Colonial Mutual Life Assurance Society: 1979
Telephone Contract Officers' Association: 1980 (but see **Recent Events**)

The union also began to recruit members of the clergy from all denominations, and has a national working party in operation to co-ordinate union activities in that sector.

Organisation

The supreme governing body of ASTMS is the Annual Delegate Conference, and the managing authority of the union is vested in the National Executive Council which is elected by the membership. ASTMS is divided into 16 geographical divisional councils, each made up of a number of branches within a division. Each division has full-time divisional officers available for guidance and negotiations. In all, ASTMS employs about 100 full-time officers and trainees in main centres throughout the UK and the Irish Republic, and its head office consists of a well staffed research department, legal department, records, finance and despatch departments.

The National Executive Council consists of 22 members, 16 elected on a divisional vote, four elected on a regional vote, two elected on a national vote, and the president and vice-president, also elected nationally. The general secretary is a non-voting member. All ballots are conducted simultaneously and the term of office of NEC members is two years. All full-time officials are appointed by the NEC through its officer coverage selection sub-committee. The divisional councils consist of one member from each branch of 150 members or under and two from branches with over 150 members.

ASTMS divisional councils meet at least four times a year. Their functions are to strengthen and co-ordinate the activities of the branches in the division, and to act as the medium through which the NEC is kept informed of membership matters. Each divisional council member is elected to serve for one year. There are also special groups and advisory committees catering for the needs of particular sections of the membership.

Workplace Activity

There are around 8,000 group secretaries within ASTMS with around 900 branches. In manufacturing ASTMS groups its branches, which are plant branches where possible, into company councils with company conferences to facilitate contact between the plants and allow workplace representatives to take part in company negotiations. There are a whole series of national advisory committees covering particular companies in engineering.

Women

Between 1968 and 1978 ASTMS achieved the highest rate of increase in women's membership of any trade union (721 per cent, from 9,400 to 77,200) and women constitute around 17 per cent of total ASTMS membership. Although women full-time officials are few in relation to the proportion of women membership, one of the union's two assistant general secretaries is a woman, Muriel Turner, who is also on the TUC General Council. ASTMS has set up a women's national advisory council which meets once a quarter. It consists of a representative from each division, plus representatives from the NEC, and is chaired by a woman member of the NEC, Mel Read. The women's NAC receives regular reports on cases in which union members have been involved under legislation dealing with sex discrimination and equal pay. It makes recommendations to the NEC on motions to be submitted to the Women's TUC. A current issue affecting women ASTMS members is the effect of microprocessors on women's employment — particularly in relation to routine office jobs which are primarily carried out by women. The NAC has also encouraged the development of women's advisory committees at divisional level.

ASTMS provides creche facilities at many of its meetings and conferences.

The union's health and safety officer is Sheila McKechnie.

In 1981, Mel Read and Muriel Turner were both re-elected to the TUC Women's Advisory Committee.

External Relations

A characteristic feature of ASTMS is its parliamentary committee, consisting of members of the Parliamentary Labour Party in both houses of parliament and a co-opted member, all of whom are ASTMS members. The committee meets once a month while parliament is in session, and its principal function is to consider matters referred to it by the NEC. A notable success for ASTMS in parliament was the sponsoring of a bill which resulted in the removal of the anti-union rules of the FSMBS (see **History**).

The committee is comprised as follows:

Chairperson: John Tilley MP
Vice-Chairperson: Jeff Rooker MP
Lord Beswick
Lord Briginshaw
Janie Buchan MEP
D. Davies MP (Llanelli)
Terry Davis MP (Birmingham Stetchford)
D. Ennals MP (Norwich North)
David Enright MEP
M. Flannery MP (Sheffield Hillsborough)
J. Hart MP (Lanark)
R. Hattersley MP (Birmingham Sparkbrook)
Dr Stuart Holland MP (Vauxhall Lambeth)
D. Hoyle MP (Warrington)
Lord Jenkins
R. Kerr MP (Feltham and Heston)
A. Lewis MP (Newham North West)
Dr O. Macdonald MP (Thurrock)
Jim Marshall MP (Leicester South)
M. Meacher MP (Oldham West)
I. Mikardo MP (Bethnal Green and Bow)
Dr Maurice Miller MP (East Kilbride)
Jo Richardson MP (London Barking)
E. Rowlands MP (Merthyr Tydfil)
Lord Sefton
Barry Sherman MP (Huddersfield East)
Dr G. Strang MP (Edinburgh East)
Dr Shirley Summerskill MP (Halifax)
S. Thorne MP (Preston South)
J. Tilley MP (Lambeth Central)
Lord Wells-Pestell
F. Willey MP (Sunderland North)
Sir H. Wilson KG OBE (Huyton)
Sheila Wright MP (Birmingham Handsworth)
Secretary — Clive Jenkins

Membership of the committee is open to all ASTMS members who are members of the Parliamentary Labour Party. In the 1979 general election a number of MPs on the committee lost their seats, including the union's Vice-President, Doug Hoyle (since re-elected in a by-election at Warrington). The committee is frequently joined by other members of the NEC, general secretaries of other trade unions, and people with specialist knowledge of the subject matter under discussion.

During 1981 ASTMS sponsored the following MPs: Terry Davis, Dr Stuart Holland, Doug Hoyle, Russell Kerr, Ian Mikado, Dr Maurice Miller, Jeff Rooker, Dr Gavin Strong, Stan Thorne and Fred Willey.

Clive Jenkins is a member of the General Council of the TUC. The Vice-President of ASTMS, Doug Hoyle, lost his parliamentary seat at Nelson and Colne in the 1979 general election (since re-elected for Warrington), but was re-elected on to the trade union section of the National Executive Committee of the Labour Party with an increased vote in October 1979.

ASTMS is remarkable in that whilst it tends towards the left of the Labour Party, 70 per cent of its membership opts out of paying the political levy. The union voted in favour of all three proposals for constitutional change in the Labour Party at the 1979 Brighton Conference, and Clive Jenkins was subsequently appointed to the committee of inquiry into Labour Party organisation in October 1979.

ASTMS and the Labour Party

Rule 36(o) of the ASTMS Rule Book specifies that the delegation from ASTMS to the Labour Party Conference should consist of divisional representatives elected in the divisions, together with a number of delegates appointed by the NEC. In 1981 there were 16 divisional delegates (elected by divisional councils) and 14 people appointed by the NEC (including the general secretary, two assistant general secretaries, the president and vice-president). They were joined by a delegate from the officers' committee. Rule 36(o) also provides that: 'The Association's vote at the Annual Conference of the Labour Party shall be cast in accordance with the decisions of the delegation and shall be in accordance with Association policy.'

At the 1981 Annual Delegate Conference of ASTMS an emergency motion was passed which committed the union to casting its 147,000 block vote in favour of Tony Benn for Deputy Leader of the Labour Party. Since then, ASTMS, in the face of much criticism about how this decision was reached at, has recommended that on future occasions the ASTMS delegation should first carry out a branch ballot, conducted in the same way and on the same general principles as for ASTMS NEC elections.

Policy

ASTMS has generally followed a policy which can be loosely defined as on the left of the Labour Party. It has consistently set its face against any kind of incomes policy and has also campaigned against British membership of the EEC. One of the features of ASTMS is its establishment of national advisory councils to cover matters of particular interest to certain categories of its membership. It also establishes NEC sub-committees on particular areas of concern, e.g. race relations.

The union refuses to co-operate with non-TUC-affiliated bodies in its dealings with management, and it was particularly vociferous in its criticism of such bodies in its evidence to Lord McCarthy in his inquiry into the National Health Service. At the 1976 Trades Union Congress it moved a motion seeking amendments to employment legislation to prevent non-TUC-affiliated unions from obtaining certification.

In 1982 ASTMS supported:
(a) greater trade union control of WEEP schemes, demanding the elimination of employer abuses of such schemes;
(b) the abolition of all private schooling, and free comprehensive education for all from nursery to university;
(c) limits on overtime, if necessary by legislation;
(d) reiterated its support for free collective bargaining;
(e) withdrawal from the EEC without a referendum;
(f) unilateral nuclear disarmament;
(g) campaigning to reduce the working hours of hospital junior doctors;
(h) implementation of selective import controls, the expansion of domestic demand and the expansion of the public sector.

In the past ASTMS has campaigned for heavier fines for employers who are found to be in breach of health and safety legislation; more factory inspectors and the compulsory introduction of joint safety committees. ASTMS accused the Health and Safety Executive of allowing a British company to cover up a report on workers exposed to 2,4,5–T in June 1980. The union also accused BP Chemicals of suppressing information about the impact of vinyl chloride monomer, a chemical used to make plastic, on its employees' health, in July 1980. ASTMS national officials said that the company had asked the University of Wales to embargo a thesis written by one of BP's medical advisers.

ASTMS published a special report on *Carbon Disulphide: An Investigation into Heart Disease at Courtaulds*, and a document on the health and safety dangers facing YOP scheme youngsters (see **Union Journal and Publications**).

At the 1982 Annual Delegate Conference, ASTMS delegates voted to set up an unemployed section within the union with full access to ASTMS benefits, and also instructed the NEC to formulate a comprehensive policy aimed at shortening the time people spend at work over their lifetimes. Delegates also reiterated their support for the alternative strategy for the economy proposed by the TUC, and their opposition to any kind of incomes policy. The NEC was instructed to prepare a report on the position of women within ASTMS in time for the 1983 ADC.

Recent Events

ASTMS has been particularly active in highlighting the employment implications of the introduction of microprocessing technology. Barrie Sherman, the union's Research Director, as well as co-editing a number of books with Clive Jenkins (see **Union Journal and Publications**), has addressed a number of conferences on this topic. The NEC has been arguing for a totally new approach to employment patterns, believing that a reduction in the length of the working week or optional earlier retirement is unlikely to constitute an adequate response. A motion to this effect was put to the 1978 Trades Union Congress, and the TUC followed this up by producing a booklet, *Employment and Technology*, in July 1979.

The union's recruitment campaign in insurance and banking continues to face intense rivalry both with staff associations and with another TUC-affiliated union, the Banking, Insurance and Finance Union (formerly NUBE). The TUC has indicated its preference for ASTMS to have representational rights in insurance, and for BIFU to have similar rights in banking. Both ASTMS and BIFU continue to recruit members in both sectors and staff associations from both banking and insurance are merging with ASTMS and BIFU with no coherent pattern. For example, despite a clear majority of computer staff voting in favour of ASTMS for recognition purposes in the Nationwide Building Society in August 1980, ACAS decided not to fragment the bargaining arrangements with the society's Staff Association.

In the insurance sector, ASTMS claims to have 75,000 members compared to its main rival, BIFU (see **BIFU**), which has around 25,000. The NUIW (see **NUIW**) by 1982 had been reduced to three sections — Royal London, Prudential and Liverpool Victoria — and represents around 19,000 door-to-door agents. Both BIFU and ASTMS claim to be recruiting members in the insurance sector at the expense of the other, and at the time of writing there were rumours that a number of major mergers of staff associations with ASTMS were about to be effected.

Despite this rivalry, both unions worked together during a dispute at General Accident concerning pay in 1982.

At the 1981 TUC Congress, ASTMS failed in its attempt to seek reference back of a TUC disputes committee award, which found against ASTMS in an inter-union dispute with APEX at General Accident despite having originally supported ASTMS in 1974.

Health and safety has become a prominent issue in ASTMS particularly arising from the tragic death of an ASTMS member, Janet Parker; she worked as a photographer at Birmingham University Medical School and contracted smallpox. ASTMS took the unusual step of publishing the Howie Report, categorising microbiological risks in laboratories. The publication of this report not only put pressure on the DHSS but also led to an assurance from the Health and Safety Executive that the standards proposed in the Howie Report would be universally applied in all laboratories handling viruses and bacteria etc., including industrial research and testing laboratories. A report of a committee of inquiry into the outbreak of smallpox at Birmingham University, chaired by Professor Reginald Shooter published, in July 1980, concluded that the University medical school was the source of the outbreak.

The union has also been active in highlighting the dangers of 'mobile Flixboroughs' following the Bantry Bay disaster. It is ASTMS policy to take the issue of health and safety into the collective bargaining arena and to secure agreements at workplace and company level. The union has provided comprehensive guidelines to this effect in its ASTMS guide to *Health and Safety at Work*. Many ASTMS members have a specialist knowledge of occupational hazards and provide a valuable resource for the union to pursue its campaign. The union has also produced a policy document on the health hazards of

VDUs (Visual Display Units), and has emphasised that no one should work at a computer VDU for more than four hours a day or for more than two hours without a break. ASTMS estimates that within four years more than half its membership will be working at VDUs.

ASTMS threatened to take legal action against Burmah Oil over the company's takeover bid for Croda International unless it consulted the employees concerned. ASTMS was making use of the Transfer of Undertakings (Protection of Employment) Regulations 1981 which were introduced in early 1982 in order to comply with an EEC Directive.

In July 1980, ASTMS came into conflict with the Post Office over recognition of 1,000 Post Office telecommunications salespeople, members of the Telephone Contract Officers' Association, who had earlier voted overwhelmingly to merge with ASTMS. The Post Office refused to recognise ASTMS on the ground that to do so would lead to fragmentation in bargaining procedures at a time when the Post Office was trying to reduce the number of unions with which it negotiated. Recognition was also opposed by the Council of Post Office Unions. The Court of Appeal ruled against ASTMS and subsequently ASTMS were required to transfer their TCOA members to other Post Office unions.

The 1982 Annual Delegate Conference of ASTMS nearly ended a day early in uproar as a row over finances broke out. Delegates almost forced the NEC to resign for 'mishandling a levy of branch funds'. In 1981–82 ASTMS suffered a £906,000 deficit of income against expenditure, compared with a £450,000 surplus the previous year. The union had been hit by falling membership at the same time as it financed the purchase of its impressive new headquarters in Camden Town. The Executive had decided in July 1981 to have a levy on branch funds to cope with the problem, which eventually raised £500,000. It was calculated on estimated branch accounts and left several branches in the red. Despite a formal apology from the Executive, speaker after speaker rose to condemn both this and delays in refunds to overcharged branches. A motion demanding the resignation of the NEC was eventually lost by 2 to 1 after delegates had reflected that the union would have been without an Executive for at least four months at a crucial time for the labour movement.

Group Seven **Electricity**

Electrical, Electronic, Telecommunication and Plumbing Union
(EETPU)

Head Office

Hayes Court
West Common Road
Bromley BR2 7AU
01-462 7755

Principal Officers

General Secretary —
Frank Chapple
General Secretary Designate—
Eric Hammond
Plumbing Section Secretary —
Charlie Lovell

National Officers

Engineering—Roy Sanderson
Power Supply—F. Franks
Telecommunications —
Bob Eadie
*Food, Drink and Tobacco and
Productivity and Technical
Services* — Paddy McMahon
and Dave Rogers
EESA — Tom Rice
NHS — Peter Adams

Membership (1982)

Male 365,000
Female 30,000
Total 395,000

Union Journal and Publications

Contact — monthly.
Justice at Work, a summary of
employment legislation.
Shop Stewards Quarterly,
legal and collective bargaining
information for shop stewards
from the union research
department.
Health and Safety bulletins.

General

The sixth largest union in Britain, the EETPU is, as its name suggests, something of a hybrid. The electricians or ETU was formerly a craft trade union which aimed to control the numbers and supply of skilled electricians by controlling apprenticeship. Historically it possessed a membership pattern which paralleled that of the AEU (engineers). Local societies of plumbers existed before 1800 but it was not until 1865 that a national organisation, the *United Operative Plumbers' Association of Great Britain and Ireland* was formed. The plumbers, organising mainly in construction and shipbuilding, amalgamated with the ETU in 1968.

The largest part of the membership is in what is generally described as the engineering industry, especially electrical engineering where the skilled workers retain their grip over the bargaining units. There is a large membership in electrical contracting (all the manual workers) and the electricity supply industry. Also EETPU members can be found in virtually every industrial grouping among the skilled maintenance workers.

The union has begun to recruit clerical, technical and administrative workers, especially in industries where it has traditionally represented manual workers, and consequently has established EESA (Electrical and Engineering Staff Association) as a separate section. The General Secretary, Frank Chapple, is a member of the TUC General Council.

History

The union was founded in 1889. Older hands among EETPU officials are fond of relating that the ETU would not have come into being as a separate organisation had it not been for the exclusive and rather self-consciously elitist attitude of the Amalgamated Society of Engineers. After repeated attempts to gain admission to the ASE, each of which was rebuffed, the electricians founded their own union. As a gesture of encouragement to the new organisation, the ASE gave a copy of its Rule Book and it was on this that the ETU Rule Book was based; it was already 40 years old!

Between the years 1894 and 1907 no less than three consecutive ETU general secretaries were dismissed for defalcation (and the general secretary of the plumbers was dismissed in 1907 for embezzlement and drunkenness).

By the end of the first world war, developments in industry showed that the ETU's organising principles were obsolete. No changes in union organisation took place. By the end of the second world war, control of the union had largely been won by the Communist Party. In the 1950s and early 1960s a long drawn-out struggle between the communists who were in control and the right wing took place, culminating in a legal battle in the High Court about alleged ballot-rigging. In the case of *Byrne v Foulkes*, the losing candidate in the election for general secretary alleged against 14 defendants a fraudulent conspiracy to rig the ballot. After a complex 42 day trial, the court found the case proven against five of the conspirators. The right wing then took over the leadership.

Union Officials

The new Executive, elected soon after the High Court judgement, rapidly acted to consolidate their newly won power in the union. They sacked the assistant general secretary, McLennan, set aside a number of the previous Executive's rule changes and called a new rules revision conference. In the beginning they did not have things all their own way; proposals to extend the period between Executive elections from two to five years were soundly defeated. The right wing also temporarily withdrew proposals to make membership of the Executive a full-time position, and, instead, launched a campaign with extensive use of the press up to the 1965 rules revision conference where the following changes were carried by a small majority:

(1) a full-time Executive Council to be elected every five years;

(2) abolition of the rank-and-file area committees;

(3) power to the Executive to close branches and amalgamate others under a full-time branch officer;

(4) removal of the right of appeal by branches against Executive Council decisions.

In 1962 a rank-and-file appeals committee had been established by the new Executive but in 1969 the Executive abolished it. Instead, the Executive is now both judge and prosecutor since half the Executive constitutes the disciplinary committee and the other half the appeals court. This move was thrown out by Conference but it was subsequently pushed through by means of a ballot of individual members who were not sufficiently apprised of the counter-arguments. This is yet another example to show that, where unions are concerned, secret ballots may not be as libertarian as is assumed.

The ballot was also used to dispose of the elected trustees. Since 1969 all full-time officers have been appointed by the Executive. Communist Party members are barred from holding office, including even the 'office' of Conference delegate.

Among the many proposals to Conference by the right wing, of the few that were not accepted was the proposal that the general secretary, after a second successful election and having reached 55 years of age, should not have to submit himself to any further election. This was not then carried, but under the union's constitution Chapple now remains in the job until retirement. However, in 1982 he decided to retire early, provided the right candidate was elected. The leadership and rule of the General Secretary was also reinforced when the position of full-time president was abolished by ballot vote.

Coverage

Joint bodies on which the EETPU is represented include the Joint Industry Board in Electrical Contracting; the electricity supply industry NJIC; the National Joint Council for Local Authorities' Services (manual workers).

The union has members in virtually every company and organisation, other than the very smallest, and is consequently party to many company and plant agreements.

Organisation

Executive Council

The full-time body of the union responsible for making and carrying out policy, ratifying agreements and integrating the work of the full-time officials with the national policy of the union, the Executive Council, may also participate in pay negotiations. Meetings take place monthly. All members are elected by secret postal ballot for a period of five years or until reaching 65. Elections are for 12 electrical section members from 12 divisions and three plumbing section members. The authority of the executive councillor in his own division is not a personal one but stems from his membership of the primary continuing authority on all matters of policy and administration affecting the union, the Executive Council. The area officials are responsible to the Executive Council as a body and not to any individual member of the Executive Council. At the 1977 Conference the Executive recommendation that full-time officers should be free to stand for election to the Executive was accepted and since then the influence of full-time officials on the Executive has increased.

Branches

The branch is a basic unit of organisation. In recent years a determined effort has been made to make the specialised or industrial branch the rule rather than the exception. Consequently in large industrial concentrations, numbers of small branches have been amalgamated on an industrial basis and have a full-time branch secretary/treasurer who may also act in local negotiations. When the branch is based on one factory or plant the union's shop stewards will belong to that branch and are presumed to work in close liaison with the branch secretary. In a number of cases electricians' and plumbers' branches in the same geographical area have amalgamated to form one

organisational unit. This policy of branch amalgamations has encountered opposition. At the union's Conference at Brighton in 1979 and against Executive advice, delegates voted in favour of a motion from Cardiff which declared that the 'wholesale policy of closure of branches and the spate of compulsory amalgamations that the Executive Council implemented recently in 1978 were not in the best interests of the members concerned.'

The same Conference also defied the leadership to vote for a second motion affirming that branches should be managed by elected branch officials and that 'where branches are being managed by full-time officers this should be considered a temporary measure until a member is elected to the position.'

Another motion, this one successfully opposed by the Executive, argued that the closure of some plumbers' lodges and the transfer of their members to electrical branches was not in the interest of the union and should be reversed. Billy Williams, a delegate from Cardiff, urged that the Executive give specific reasons why branches were closed.

Frank Chapple's view was that such reforms had been discussed since 1965 and that at the 1973 and 1975 Conferences delegates had accepted that plumbing lodges and electrical branches should be merged where possible. The resolution against branches being managed by full-time officials did not conform with the rules of the union confirmed by the rules revision conference of 1975. Chapple has avowed that union policy is not bound by Conference resolutions. 'Resolutions are resolutions — not the laws of the Medes and Persians' has been his maxim.

For example, at the 1981 Conference the North London branch successfully moved a resolution calling for a halt to the policy of closing union branches, but when that branch took legal action to try to prevent its dissolution, it was argued on behalf of the union that its Biennial Conference was not its governing body. The Executive view is that Conference decisions are noted but need not be enacted.

Industrial conferences

In order to bring members with similar industrial interests together, industrial conferences for specific sectors have become an established feature of EETPU organisation. Representatives meet in four separate ways:

(i) area annual industrial conferences,

(ii) area industrial committees,

(iii) national industrial conferences,

(iv) national industrial committees.

In theory this should mean greater democracy but in practice it has not since the conferences can be ignored. Thus, Colin Barker (*The Power Game*, Pluto Press 1972) tells us that the 1970 conference in electrical contracting was effectively declared null and void by Bro. Hammond of the union Executive who declared in *Contact* that: 'the Executive were not going to pay any attention to resolutions adopted by the industrial conference in the contracting industry.'

Workplace Activity

There are around 9,000 EETPU shop stewards but the shop stewards and rank-and-file movements, although of some potential, are largely subdued at present. The reason is the power of head office and Executive which quickly suppress any growth points in the formal organisation of the union. The attitude of the official leadership to shop stewards has hardly changed since it enunciated its policy to the Donovan Commission in 1966:

> The ETU recognises that the function and activity of the shop steward is necessary as the most direct and positive link with their rank-and-file membership. At the same time it is recognised that the position is not without its dangers to the official structure and could have a disruptive effect on trade union discipline since by its very nature the steward/member relationship cannot be rigidly controlled.

In the ETU it was soon realised that, for union policy to be more effectively carried on the shopfloor, it was necessary for the shop steward to be brought into closer contact with other shop stewards in the district who worked in a similar branch of the industry and also with full-time officials who were responsible for the industry at area and national level. This was necessary so that the shop steward might see how her/his actions fitted into the pattern of union policy.

To achieve this, ETU keeps an up-to-date list of the names and addresses of all its shop stewards. Communications can be sent directly from their head office (*Shop Stewards' Quarterly*, for instance). Information can be requested from the shop steward and in such a case the shop steward will communicate directly to the office concerned.

In fact, every effort is made to ensure that *all* communications inside the union go via head office so that a close check can be kept on what is happening in the branches and workplaces. Other than this effort to integrate shop stewards into the official structure of the union, there is little encouragement to shop steward activism. The EETPU places great emphasis on centralised negotiations with the full-time officials in charge. This is true of electrical contracting and, to a lesser extent, of electricity supply. There is, however, a growing unofficial shop stewards' committee in electricity supply. After the 1979 pay settlement, Mike Ellis, the shop stewards' committee secretary, warned Chapple that 'in future there is no way in which Frank Chapple and company will be allowed to go ahead and do a deal with the board and exclude the shop floor.' In 1982 the unofficial power workers' shop stewards' committee was able to press successfully for a ballot on the Electricity Council pay offer which was rejected by 41,249 to 31,801.

Formally, in the EETPU Rule Book (Rule 17) stewards are under the control of the area full-time official and are obliged to carry out instructions of the Executive Council.

Women

There are women shop stewards and branch secretaries and a few skilled or craft-trained women but no women full-time officers.

External Relations

The EETPU is affiliated to the Labour Party. In addition, after a closely fought tussle, Frank Chapple was elected as a one of the TUC's six representatives on the National Economic Development Council. This post automatically gave him a seat on the TUC-Labour Party liaison committee. He was already a member of the TUC General Council.

The 1981 EETPU Conference passed a resolution expressing alarm at the degree of infiltration of the Labour Party by left-wing groups and calling for tougher action against them by the Party's National Executive Committee. However, Chapple made it clear that the EETPU had no intention of leaving the Labour Party unless, in the opinion of his Executive, the right's position within the party becomes hopeless. He has given two officials virtually full-time political roles, including that of persuading members to affiliate to the general management committees of their local Labour Parties. In addition, he has co-operated with other unions to nurture an informal grouping committed to repealing the electoral college method of electing the Labour Party leaders. John Spellar, successful in the Birmingham Northfield by-election for Labour in 1982, was a top research aide for Frank Chapple.

Sponsored MPs

Thomas Cox (Wandsworth and Tooting)
John Grant (Islington Central)
Walter Harrison (Wakefield)
David Stoddart (Swindon)
John Spellar (Birmingham Northfield)

Policy

The EETPU is the closest British equivalent to the business unionism of the USA. Policy could be described as at once authoritarian and opportunist, dictated from head office. Frank Chapple, General Secretary since 1966 but effectively in sole control since the death of Les Cannon, the last full-time president, has mounted a personal crusade on behalf of the social market economy, so long as the union's members draw their share of the wealth.

In *The Power Game*, Colin Barker states that ETU policy (in the late 1960s and early 1970s) had 'often been one of open collaboration with the employers, as in the case of the notorious agreement that set up the joint industry board in the electrical contracting industry'.

This policy has changed under pressure from shop stewards' organisation. Frank Chapple, the chief negotiator formally and factually for the electricity supply industry, has voiced the constant refrain 'nothing less than the miners' since the middle seventies and to judge by earnings figures he has had his way. In 1980, for instance, he had to take up a serious grievance among manual electricity supply workers. An arbitration award in January gave power engineers rises of 2.4–6.5 per cent which meant final pay increase figures of 25.5–28.5 per cent for managers in the supply industry as a result of the 1979 settlement. Chapple made it clear that he expected the employers to make extra allowance for that change in their offer to the manual workers. Doubtless, the EETPU's new incursion into the white-collar field focusses further attention on the differential.

The manual workers' objection was not just one of a widening differential. The relativity between the manual workers and the engineers, on which the award was based, took no account of the productivity improvements of the manual workers which mainly stemmed from large scale reductions in the workforce, a programme begun with the 'status' productivity agreements with the Electricity Council in 1965.

The events of 1979 in pay negotiations between the Electricity Council and the EETPU had shown that there were strong feelings among the workers. In April the officials agreed to recommend to their members acceptance of a nine per cent pay offer. The power workers' joint shop stewards' committee predicted that the offer would be rejected in a ballot of the 95,000 workers, as indeed it was, by a three to one majority.

The shop stewards called upon the negotiators to give 21 days' notice of industrial action in the absence of an improved offer.

Further negotiations brought an offer of 16 per cent but this was also firmly rejected in a ballot. The union leaders were under pressure to obtain a settlement similar to that made by the Electricity Council and the power engineers and white-collar workers, and the eventual settlement was similar at around 23 per cent.

The same pressures from rank-and-file pay demands built up in 1980. Chapple knows that he has to deliver in cash terms to maintain his power base in the union. In 1970 when trouble flared over a pay claim in electricity supply, charged with the grievances about staff cuts for productivity gains, and a work-to-rule immediately severely disrupted industry, Chapple called the work-to-rule off as 'an act of good faith with the nation' but refused arbitration because 'it would undoubtedly have led to strikes and loss of control over our members in the industry'. Loss of control is the dread fear for Chapple.

So, although the ideal is tightly drawn national industry-wide agreements with scope for local increments controlled by work study, the union has to achieve the 'going rate' of settlement. In local disputes where rank-and-file action has clearly undermined central authority, the usual response is to wash hands of the issue, ignoring it and hoping it will go away, as for instance in the long running battle involving EETPU members led by a Communist shop steward at the Inland Revenue office site at Bootle in 1974 and in the unofficial strike of maintenance workers at the Charing Cross hospital in December 1979.

The officials can outstrip the militancy of others normally considered well to their left when their interests are concerned. In 1973 they backed the electricians' strike which paralysed Chrysler's production and led to threats of withdrawal of investment. Jack Jones of the TGWU and Scanlon of the AUEW urged the electricians to return to work while an independent inquiry was conducted but the EETPU rejected this on the grounds that other unions had forfeited the right to advise as their members had crossed picket lines.

To defend members' jobs in the telecommunications apparatus industry, Chapple is emphatic that if the union does not establish a bridgehead in electronics it will decline. ASTMS and EETPU know that the change from electro-mechanical to electronic technology signifies re-drawing of traditional demarcations; there are few guidelines for this and there has already been inter-union conflict.

Chapple and Cannon were among the faction that ousted the Communists in 1962. Since then Chapple and his colleagues have exhibited almost a paranoia about internal opposition in the union, about the left and about rank-and-file movements of all kinds. This fear may have pushed the union too far in the direction of security and, while it has elections, it is a body for which the phrase 'elective dictatorship' is appropriate.

There is a long running battle between the entrenched right-wing leadership of Chapple and his supporters and the left-wing minority on the Executive Council who gained a toehold in the 1973 elections, only to see their policies and personalities discredited through the official organs of the leadership. In *Contact* Chapple wrote before the 1977 conference:

> Having consistently lost the battle of genuinely held elections, the Communist and Trotskyist-based opposition in the union will attempt to regain control through manipulation and intimidation of the conference.

In fact at the previous rules revision and policy-making conference, delegates were asked to abandon motions put up by branches in favour of a new Rule Book drawn up by the Executive that they had never seen before. Obedient to the platform, they accepted so that the Executive won every point.

The leadership is hyper-sensitive. In 1973 three socialists were elected to the Executive, including Harold Best, executive councillor for the Yorkshire division. Chapple said in *Contact* that their policies were 'as old as the hills or as Marx' and that 'without any doubt they would inexorably return to the corrupt and undemocratic regime of which we rid this union 16 years ago.'

Those concerned to exercise a right of reply to these accusations have claimed that their articles and opinions were not printed in the union journal.

When Best stood in the 1976 election for general secretary against Chapple, Chapple won easily but during the election a ballot inquiry was set up by the Executive Council to investigate allegations of interference by external political bodies. The report of that inquiry finally alleged that Best had broken union rules by canvassing and receiving support from the Communist Party. Best vigorously denied these charges and was legally advised that the ballot inquiry had given him no opportunity to speak in his own defence or to challenge the evidence brought against him.

In June 1979 the Executive again ordered an inquiry into the election of a left-winger onto the Executive Council. Wyn Bevan, works convener at British Steel's Port Talbot works, won the election for the South Wales division councillor. It was not unexpected by the left that the leadership might use the declaration of support for Bevan from the far left candidate, Billy Williams of Cardiff, if the latter were eliminated under the single transferable vote system, as a pretext for refusing to accept the (final) result. Bevan is a militant and led a ten-week strike at Port Talbot in 1977.

It seems unwise to stand on a politically left or nonconformist platform in the EETPU elections. Bevan's election was duly declared invalid by the Executive after its members had taken legal advice, and the election had to be re-run, but Bevan won again and, despite further protests, his election was approved.

The decision to re-run was vehemently opposed by the Cardiff branch of the union which has been engaged in a long running fight with the Executive, having been opposed to its creation by executive fiat in imposing the amalgamation of two previously separate branches. The Executive suspended the branch for being such a political nuisance. Frank Chapple ex-

plained that the branch had been suspended because 'a small group of members monopolise the branch meeting place to express their own extreme political views and their opposition to any decision taken by the Executive.' He further resented the fact that the branch was used to promote and distribute unofficial circulars, presumed to be the *Socialist Worker* newspaper or a rank-and-file publication which has criticised official union policy.

In spite of a resolution calling for it to cease, the policy of administrative closure of branches has continued.

Business union or friendly society?

At present, the EETPU can perhaps best be described by the phrase 'renovated friendly society'. It does possess legacies of the old craft-friendly society approach in its suspicion of broader training programmes for electricians and electronics workers and yet seems willing to sell jobs in response to microprocessor and silicon chip technology, albeit as expensively as possible. The private health scheme for its 50,000 members in the electrical contracting industry which was so bitterly attacked by other TUC-affiliated unions is an example of this friendly society approach, as is the emphasis placed on occupational safety.

In fact the private medical insurance scheme was decisively rejected by delegates at the 1981 Biennial Conference in a resolution condemning government failure to provide adequate funds for the NHS, while encouraging the demand for private facilities, for which trade union support by participation was to be deplored. Although Frank Chapple conceded that that Executive would have difficulties as a result because the vote was strongly in favour, he doubted whether the union's contracting members would want to relinquish the scheme and reiterated that the resolution was not binding on the Executive.

The EETPU is in general opposed to legislative interference in industrial relations. In evidence to the Donovan Commission, the officials argued that legislation was not the way to deal with official or unofficial strikes. In addition, the present leadership must find the closed shop a very useful weapon in consolidating its power. In 1972 disaffected trade unionists at Ferrybridge power station used the clauses in the Industrial Relations Act outlawing closed shops and set up the breakaway *Electricity Supply Union*. This had been set up by Arthur Smith, a former EETPU shop steward who claimed that 'the unions showed how disorganised and uninterested in us they were during the 1970 work to rule. They failed to give us clear-cut instructions about how to operate the work to rule and their attitude was responsible for turning it into an ineffective farce.' The Ferrybridge six, as they were known, lost their jobs through union expulsions, decisions confirmed by the industrial tribunal.

It was in keeping with the general EETPU policy that it strongly opposed board level representation for its members and here at least it advanced a tenable argument voiced by many on the left about participation in management:

> The belief that managers implementing the policies of a board composed of 50 per cent trade union representatives will be more acceptable than the current exercise of the managerial function is a dangerous illusion. It could convey the impression that the management has captured or absorbed the trade unions. In particular situations, the workers who held that view might be driven to set up means of alternate representation at the place of work. In a world where state power and management prerogative have become concentrated, more persuasive and yet more remote from those who are affected by the exercise of those powers, the impression that worker directors represent the absorption of trade unions into this scenario of corporate elitism is even more perilous. (EETPU evidence to the Bullock Committee)

Apart from the internal insecurity of the leadership, there are feelings of external vulnerability from the enormous effects of electronic and technological change. Consequently, the EETPU is intent on broadening its base through mergers. So far it has only managed this in the white-collar area.

In December 1979 the EETPU amalgamated with the *United Kingdom Association of Professional Engineers* (UKAPE). In a ballot 78 per cent of a 60 per cent poll of UKAPE's 4,000 members voted to join the *Electrical and Engineering Staff Association* (EESA), the white-collar section. This adds to the EETPU base among professional engineers. The EETPU's penetration among managerial grades increased when members of SIMA, the *Steel Industry Managers' Association*, voted to transfer their engagements to it in September 1980.

In the battle to recruit managerial and professional employees, EESA has reached a mutual support pact with the EMA, and has set up the umbrella organisation, the Council of Managerial and Professional Staffs. Both actions are largely directed against ASTMS.

Recent Events

Frank Chapple described the TUC Day of Action on 14 May 1980 as both 'unwise and untimely'. During the strikes in Poland in August 1980 Chapple condemned the TUC's lack of positive support for the strikers, and condemned the TUC's proposed visit to Poland on the grounds that it would legitimise the rule of the repressive regime — a view shared by many on the left.

Chapple also incurred disfavour among other union leaders as a result of the EETPU's role in the Isle of Grain dispute. As a result he was voted off the TUC finance and general purposes committee but was re-elected to it in September 1981.

In view of his Trades Union Congress responsibilities and his approaching retirement, the EETPU Executive decided to hold elections for a successor to lead the union in tandem with Chapple until his retirement. In the subsequent ballot, Eric Hammond, Chapple's favoured candidate, was elected.

The EETPU has from time to time

been embarrassed by the activities of its Fleet Street press branch, including the Geraghty affair in 1982 when the branch secretary was fined after members failed to observe an injunction against action in support of NHS employees in their pay dispute.

Further Reference

G. Schaffer, *Light and Liberty: Sixty Years of the Electrical Trades Union* 1949.

Electrical Trades Union: The Official History, 1953.

C. H. Rolph, *All Those in Favour?* — an account of the High Court action against the Electrical Trades Union and its officers, 1962.

Colin Barker, *The Power Game*, Pluto Press 1972.

J. O. French, *Plumbers in Unity: The History of the Plumbing Trades Union 1865-1965*, 1965.

Olga Cannon and J. R. L. Anderson *The Road from Wigan Pier: A Biography of Les Cannon*, Gollancz 1973.

Patrick Wintour, 'How Frank Chapple stays on top', *New Statesman*, 25 July 1980.

Group Eight Iron and Steel and Minor Metal Trades

Blastfurnacemen, Ore Miners, Coke Workers and Kindred Trades, National Union of
(NUB)

Head Office

93 Borough Road West
Middlesbrough
Cleveland
TS1 3AJ
0642-242961

Principal Officers

General Secretary —
N. Leadley
Divisional Officers
B. T. Fisher
J. Perring

Membership (1982)

Male 7,212
Female 33
Total 7,245

Union Journal and Publications

There is no journal, although the union has published a short history of the union written by the former general secretary, Hector Smith, *100 Years Struggle 1878-1978.*

General

The NUB has been in continuous existence since 1878. Although its beginnings have a common root with that of its larger sister union in the iron and steel industry (ISTC) it has steadfastly maintained its independence. It organises workers who are employed at blastfurnaces in England and Wales (not Scotland), as well as coke workers and workers engaged at iron and limestone mines and quarries.

It is a shrinking union and it faces a membership decline of drastic proportions stemming from the run-down of the British Steel Corporation. By early 1981 the union's membership had shrunk as low as 7,000. During the steel strike of early 1980, it worked closely with ISTC, but the 1982 General Council rejected a proposal for a merger with ISTC which would have given NUB members very favourable terms.

History

The history of the NUB is closely linked to that of the Iron and Steel Trades Confederation (see **ISTC**). In close association with the *Friendly Society of Ironfounders* (dating back to 1809) there emerged in the North of England in 1862 another union bearing the title of the *National Association of Malleable Ironworkers.* Within a few years this association extended over England, Wales and Scotland and had a membership of some 6,500. It merged with the *Associated Ironworkers of Great Britain*, founded in South Staffordshire in 1863, and changed its title to the *Associated Iron and Steel Workers of Great Britain.*

For more than a dozen years John Kane was the indisputable head of iron workers' organisation in the country, although by 1871 it was clear that blastfurnace workers were becoming increasingly dissatisfied with Kane's organisation. The blastfurnace workers felt that they had been deserted by other workers in the industry in their struggle to oppose wage reductions from 1871 to 1878.

In 1878 two lively meetings were held in the market place at South Bank, near Middlesbrough, at which the project of forming an independent society for blastfurnace workers was considered. At a later meeting the formation of the *Cleveland Association of Blastfurnacemen* was announced. Those present at the meeting included Edward Trow (who later became secretary of the *Associated Iron and Steel Workers of Great Britain*, which succeeded the *old union* of John Kane), William Snow and Pat Walls. In 1880, William Snow, who had experience in the *Cleveland Ore Miners' Association*, was appointed as agent and organiser. The union, however, was confined to the Cleveland district, and in the consequent development of trade unionism among blastfurnace workers the practice of district organisation was followed, such organisations being formed in Cumberland, the Midlands, South Wales and Monmouthshire. In 1887 the *Cumberland Association of Blastfurnacemen* merged with Cleveland to form the *National Association of Blastfurnacemen*. The NAB held its first conference in 1889 when Pat Walls and William Snow were elected as district secretaries. A national executive committee was also elected, its first business being to organise an attack upon the 84-hour week.

At the 1890 conference, district associations in Cleveland and Durham, Cumberland and Lancashire, North and South Staffordshire, Shropshire and the West Riding were represented. In 1892 the *National Federation of Blastfurnacemen, Ore Miners and Kindred Trades*, being a combination of five district associations, came into existence.

Although the blastfurnace workers' federation attended the 1915 conference of unions in the iron and steel industry, chaired by C. W. Bowerman, and assisted in drawing up the amalgamation scheme, they failed to submit it for ratification to its members. The reason given was that the federation was only a loose federation of district unions and it was thought desirable in the first instance to effect a closer union of its component parts. That step was taken in 1919, and in 1921 the first meeting of the Executive Committee of the *National Union of Blastfurnacemen, Ore Miners, Coke Workers and Kindred Trades* was held. Tom McKenna, who had been president of the federation from 1915, and its secretary since 1917, was elected general secretary. Right up to the present time, blastfurnace workers in England and Wales have remained outside the ISTC.

Union Officials

The NUB has two district secretaries who are appointed by the Executive Committee from nominations drawn up by the lodges (branches) in the respective district. District secretaries are responsible for supervising the effective organisation of the union in the various lodges in each district. They attend all meetings of the Executive Committee as ex-officio members with a right to vote; they also act as secretaries to the respective district delegate board. District secretaries must have been union members and have worked in one of the trades organised by the union for at least five years prior to nomination. All NUB male officials retire at 65 years of age, women at 60.

Coverage

The NUB organises workers in the iron and steel industry who are employed at blastfurnaces in England and Wales (plus Monmouthshire). Scottish blastfurnace workers are organised by ISTC. An agreement exists between ISTC and the NUB fixing a line of demarcation as regards the organisation of coke workers attached to iron and steel works.

Organisation

The supreme body of authority in the union is the General Council, which usually meets in July of each year. Delegates to the General Council are elected by each district delegate board each April, on the basis of one delegate per 500 members, with a minimum of four representatives from each district. The district secretary is automatically included in the district delegation by virtue of office.

The general business of the union is vested in the Executive Committee which consists of representatives from the districts on a pro rata membership basis. District secretaries are included in the representation by virtue of their office. At present the EC is eight strong. The union's district delegate boards meet in April and October of each year and consist of at least one delegate from each lodge in the district, with provision for extra delegates from the larger lodges. The chairperson of each district delegate board is a member of the General Council by virtue of office. The boards are serviced by the district secretaries.

The primary unit of the NUB is the lodge. At present the union has 30 lodges which are located where there are concentrations of union members, i.e. at a particular blastfurnace plant, coke oven plant, or at iron or limestone mines and quarries. Each lodge has a chairperson, delegate and secretary, who are all elected by lodge members for a period of two, three and two years respectively. All lodges are under the control of the EC.

Workplace Organisation

Each of the 30 lodge delegates acts as a works representative (shop steward) at the place of work and is responsible to the district secretary on all matters of importance. Lodge delegates also liaise with the lodge committee and regularly report back to each lodge meeting.

External Relations

The NUB is affiliated to the Labour Party and sponsors one Labour MP, James Tinn (Redcar, Teesside). Around 70 per cent of NUB members pay the political levy. The NUB has three members on the TUC Steel Committee out of 17.

Recent Events

The NUB, even before the recent drastic run-down of the British iron and steel industry, was a shrinking union. Its membership in 1971 was 17,281 and by 1979 it had declined to a membership level of 14,366. It is clear that the closures at Shotton, Corby, and Consett, together with the run-down in the labour force at the other main BSC plants, has had a disastrous effect on the NUB.

During the steel strike of early 1980, an alliance was forged between ISTC and the NUB, whereby the two unions co-operated together very closely during the long negotiations. Despite the fact that the 1981 Annual General Council meeting gave the EC full authority to carry out merger discussions, the 1982 AGC rejected a merger with ISTC, which would have given NUB members very favourable terms. Although the NUB decided to soldier on and retain its independence under its new general secretary, its future as an independent viable union must be seriously open to question. (As this book went to press, merger talks with the ISTC had been resumed.)

Further Reference

Jack Owen, *Ironmen*, (a short history of the union from 1878 to 1953 written by the then general secretary) NUB 1953.

Hector Smith, *100 Years Struggle 1878-1978*, NUB 1978.

See also the **ISTC** entry which gives a guide to some publications on iron and steel trade union organisation, some of which are relevant to the NUB.

Iron and Steel Trades Confederation
(ISTC)

Head Office

Swinton House
324 Gray's Inn Road
London WC1X 8DD
01-837 6691

Principal Officers

General Secretary — W. Sirs
Assistant General Secretary — R. L. Evans
National Staff Officer — H. A. Feather
National Officer — K. Clarke

Membership (1982)
Male 93,357
Female 6,818
Total 100,175

Divisional Offices

● *No. 1 Division*
Scotland
8 Royal Crescent
Glasgow G3 7SL
041-332 8435

● *No. 2 Division*
Northumberland and Durham,
Cumbria and Yorkshire
Drinkwater House
210-212 Marton Road
Middlesbrough
Cleveland TS4 2ET
0642-246040

● *No. 3 Division*
South Yorkshire, North
Lincolnshire and Derbyshire
Edgcumbe House
The Crescent
Doncaster Road
Rotherham
South Yorkshire S65 1NL
0709-61541

● *No. 4 Division*
Stafford, Warwick, Worcester
Shropshire and Northampton
Mere Green Chambers
338 Lichfield Road
Fair Oak
Sutton Coldfield
West Midlands B74 4BH
021-308 7288

● *No. 5 Division*
Gloucestershire, Monmouthshire
and the Dowlais-Merthyr district
of Glamorganshire
34-38 Stow Hill
Newport
Gwent NPT 1JE
0633-212822

● *No. 6 Division*
Glamorganshire and
Carmarthenshire
83 Mansel Street
Swansea SA1 5TY
0792-50151

● *No. 7 Division*
Lancashire, North Wales and
Cheshire
Holly House, Mobberley Road
Knutsford
Cheshire WA16 8HT
0565-51399

Divisions 5 and 6 were scheduled to merge in 1982. They were already administered from the Newport office and it was planned to dispose of both No. 5 and No. 6 offices and open up a new office in Cardiff.

Union Journal

ISTC Banner — circulation around 18,500.

ISTC produced a pamphlet during the 1980 steel strike entitled *Sense or Non-Sense: An Appraisal of the Steel Corporation's Thinking* (15 pages) which sought to destroy the claims made by BSC during the strike. The union also published a 180-page book in July 1980 entitled *New Deal for Steel,* setting out ISTC's alternative strategy for the British Steel Corporation.
Evidence submitted by the Iron and Steel Trades Confederation to the House of Commons Committee on Industry and Trade, April 1981, 8 pages setting out the ISTC case for the steel industry and the BSC Corporate Plan.

General

ISTC is the dominant union within the British iron and steel industry. The industry consists of several important sections which are, in effect, industries in themselves. These include the heavy steel section, concerned with the manufacture of pig iron, ingot production and rolling of heavy products; the sheet industry; the tinplate industry; the tube trade; the Sheffield steel trade; and the foundry industry, petering out until it impinges on the engineering trade.

ISTC organises nearly all production and ancillary workers throughout the industry, except for the blastfurnace workers in England and Wales. The TGWU and GMWU have some degree of membership, principally in the finishing departments of the tinplate and galvanised sheet trade and among artisans and mechanics respectively. The membership of the TGWU and the GMWU is confined mainly to the unskilled grades. ISTC also organises around 2,000 middle managers, and has about 5,000 members in precious and minor metal trades in its non-ferrous section.

There are three distinct iron and steel unions operating in the industry — the confederation (ISTC), the Blastfurnacemen (NUB) and the Amalgamated Society of Wire Drawers and Kindred Workers. The first is industrial in character; the second is equally so in the sense that it does not cater for labour outside the industry; the third limits its activities to the industry but specifically caters for people employed in rod and wire mills on an occupational or craft basis.

ISTC has been very much involved in the rationalisation of the steel industry, which has accelerated rapidly over the past three years, and its membership level faces the threat of a severe decline.

Bill Sirs, the General Secretary, is the chairperson of the TUC Steel Committee and is also a member of the TUC General Council and the TUC Economic Committee.

History

Trade unionism in the iron and steel trades has a very long history and limited space can do only scant justice to its development. In 1863 the *North of England Ironworkers* — the first union in the trade to have a continuous existence — was formed. Up to that time there were a number of ephemeral local organisations which appeared following the repeal of the Combinations Acts in 1825. The North of England Ironworkers assumed a national character four years later to become the *Amalgamated Ironworkers' Association* with John Kane as general secretary. Following a long strike called by the North of England Ironworkers in 1866, the Board of Conciliation and Arbitration for the North of England Iron Trade was established in 1869; it was the forerunner of the various forms of joint machinery of negotiation which became a traditional feature of the greatly extended iron and steel industry.

Following the inventions of Bessemer and Siemens, the newly established steel industry produced the formation of the *British Steel Smelters' Association* in 1886, following a strike in Scotland, with John Hodge as secretary. Within a short time, this union had established branches in England and Wales. Scotland was also the birthplace of the first union covering millworkers in the industry — the *Scottish Millmen's Union*, which later became the *Amalgamated Society of*

Iron and Steel Workers. Whilst this union retained a predominantly Scottish flavour, its organisation was later widened to include blastfurnace workers, malleable ironworkers, and finishing trades such as steel tubes, nuts and bolts etc.

Numerous other unions were formed from different sections of the iron and steel industry from the latter part of the nineteenth century to 1914. Such unions were generally local in character and represented specific occupations.

The duplication of unions in the industry had created a serious obstacle to effective organisation in the years up to 1914, a position accentuated by competition from the general labour unions. The weakness of that position became evident as the war progressed and the government took control of the industry. In 1915, a conference was called, chaired by C. W. Bowerman, then secretary of the TUC, to consider the question of amalgamation. A scheme of confederation was evolved which provided for the establishment of a new union, the *British Iron and Steel and Kindred Trades Association* (termed the Central Association), and in addition another body, the *Iron and Steel Trades Confederation*, the Executive Council of the confederation to consist of representatives pro rata of the executives of the amalgamating unions, including the central association. The confederation was vested with powers of taking over the conduct of negotiations, affiliation to the TUC, legal services, benefit administration and all the officials of the amalgamating unions. The scheme was later put to each union and the following unions put the scheme to their members:

The British Steel Smelters, Mill, Iron and Tinplate Workers   40,000
The Association of Iron and Steel Workers of Great Britain   9,000
The Amalgamated Society of Iron and Steel Workers   10,000
The National Steelworkers' Association Engineering and Labour League   3,000
The Tin and Sheet Millmen's Association   3,000

The blastfurnace workers failed to put the scheme to its members and the present union (see **NUB**) has remained outside the confederation right up to the present day. The Amalgamated Society of Iron and Steel Workers and the Tin and Sheet Millmen's Association failed to carry the scheme, but the other three unions went ahead and the Iron and Steel Trades Confederation came into being in 1917. The confederation scheme proved to be so successful that complete amalgamation took place by 1921.

Union Officials

In 1982 ISTC employed 23 officers in the divisions and four national officers. The 1982 Annual Delegate Conference rejected motions calling for the election of national officials. All ISTC officials must have had at least five years membership of the union and at least two years experience in a branch office. The general pattern is that the branch secretaries tend to be the springboards for the promotion ladder into union office.

Coverage

The steel industry is characterised by a number of trade and conciliation boards covering various sections of the industry. The majority of ISTC members are covered by one of the following negotiating sections:

Heavy Steel Trades — British Steel Corporation

Heavy Steel Trades — Independent Steel Employers' Association (national negotiations ended with this body in 1980)

Sheet Trade Board — British Steel Corporation

Staff Section — British Steel Corporation

Staff Section — Other private companies

Middle Management Section — British Steel Corporation.

Despite the fact that the ISEA and MWB agreements at national level no longer operate, ISTC still holds meetings of branches covered in the past by such agreements.

Agreements negotiated nationally on all boards are:

(i) Recognition (staff and middle management)

(ii) Wages

(iii) Holidays with pay

(iv) Guaranteed week/incomes and security

(v) Union membership

(vi) Redundancy

There is now a common staff/manual pension scheme in operation at BSC.

A characteristic feature of the industry is the provision for joint conciliation and/or arbitration within the negotiating machinery in various sections of the industry.

The TUC Steel Committee was set up after the nationalisation of the steel industry in 1967, and it operates as the national negotiating body for the majority of BSC workers on all matters other than wages. Each agreement drawn up has to be ratified by the executive body of each individual union represented on the committee. The unions represented on the committee are the ISTC, the NUB, TGWU, GMWU, and the craft unions are represented by the National Craftsmen's Co-ordinating Committee (NCCC). The TUC provides administrative support.

Organisation

Members of the ISTC are organised in branches connected with the works in which they are employed. At a small works members may all be organised in one branch, but at large integrated works — in some cases employing several thousand workers — a number of separate branches are formed, each branch usually covering members employed in a specific department or process, or engaged on a particular class of work. Each branch elects annually a president, secretary, works representative and a committee, who are responsible for administering the affairs of the branch. Branches are divided into seven geographical divisions plus a London area, each with a divisional officer (except the London area) whose particular duty it is to look after the interests of the members in the division, and to maintain a good state of organisation. Supervision of the whole of the administration of ISTC is conducted from head office, which has accounts, audit, general secretary's and research departments.

The governing body of the confederation is the Executive Council, which is the supreme decision-making authority in the union. An important constitutional rule-change governing the election of the ISTC Executive Council has been agreed. Representation for electoral purposes on the EC is now to be broken down into three sections: public sector (manual), public sector (staff), and the private sector. In future ISTC will have eight divisions (London area being upgraded) for electoral purposes. This change will mean the erosion of the district trade character of some EC representations and will imply a more direct system of accountability between EC members and those they represent. Each EC member holds office for three years. The Executive Council of ISTC meets quarterly and is responsible for overseeing the running of the confederation, as well as appointing the full-time oficials and divisional officers. The general secretary is selected by the EC from a list of nominations from branches and divisions, and once appointed, holds office until retirement.

Bill Sirs is chairperson of the TUC Steel Committee, which is composed of 6 ISTC, 3 NUB, 4 NCCC, 2 TGWU and 2 GMWU representatives. The Steel Committee is not popular in the ISTC. If Bill Sirs had not secured remission of a motion calling for withdrawal from it at the 1979 Annual Conference it might well have been carried.

At the 1982 ISTC Annual Delegate Conference a motion was passed by 91 to 79 votes calling for future Conferences to become the supreme policy-making body of the union. The Executive would have to come to a decision whether or not to accept this Conference vote. During the debate on the motion, Bill Sirs warned that the change would make the ISTC vulnerable 'to the back room meeting boys of the extreme left who will try to destroy this union'. Those backing the motion claimed it would extend democracy in one of Britain's most centralised unions. Any change would require a ballot of ISTC members.

Workplace Activity

ISTC is a highly centralised union with power concentrated at the top. There are around 700 branches in the union and, although on paper they enjoy some degree of autonomy, in practise they are very much under the control of the organisers, senior organisers, and divisional officers. Where members are unemployed they are still allowed to be accredited delegates from branches. The key office within the branches is that of the branch secretary. The steel strike of early 1980 served to politicise many ISTC members, whose experience of picket lines and lobbying ISTC officials must have reminded them of their inability to influence policy decisions within the union hierarchy.

Women

Women members of ISTC are very much in a minority in a male-dominated union. They tend to be concentrated in three main areas: catering and canteen jobs; clerical and administration occupations; and the technical staff sector. Despite their minority situation there are between 20 and 30 women branch secretaries and there are a small number of delegates to the Annual Delegate Conference. No woman has ever stood for election to the Executive Council. ISTC sends a delegation to the TUC women's conference and a delegate to the Conference of Labour Women.

External Relations

ISTC is affiliated to the Labour Party both at national, and local regional level. In many cases, ISTC branches are affiliated to their own Constituency Labour Party. The union sponsors W. Homewood, MP for Kettering and Corby (a former senior divisional organiser) and Donald Coleman, MP for Neath. ISTC has earned itself a reputation for pursuing a policy on the right of the Labour Party, and was closely linked with the Campaign for a Labour Victory. The union achieved a great deal of publicity in June 1979 when Prince Charles addressed the Annual Delegate Conference.

Bill Sirs, the General Secretary, is a member of the TUC General Council and is also chairperson of the TUC Steel Committee, on which ISTC has six members out of 17. Arthur Bell, former divisional officer; Glasgow, was president of the Scottish TUC in 1977-78. Joe Lewis, ISTC president in 1978, is a member of the Agricultural Wages Board. A. L. Evans, Assistant General Secretary, was elected to the Labour Party NEC in 1981. The union is actively involved in Trade Unions for a Labour Victory and, like other unions, is raising its political levy. ISTC has several members of regional Labour Party executives and a number of union members sit on local councils. It maintains a panel of parliamentary candidates, and this was renewed in 1981.

In early 1982, Bill Sirs wrote in the ISTC journal: 'We cannot write off the SDP, who could well be part of a coalition with Labour if Labour fails to clinch a decisive victory.'

Internationally, the union is affiliated to the International Metalworkers' Federation.

Labour Party Delegation

At one time ISTC used to send seven members of the EC (who were usually newly appointed) and seven rank-and-file delegates (who had been formally elected at branch officers' conferences) to the Labour Party Conference, in addition to the general secretary and assistant general secretary.

The total affiliated membership of ISTC to the Labour Party has since fallen, and branch officers' conferences are no longer held. At present the delegates at the ISTC annual conference select seven lay delegates to attend the Labour Party conference, and the EC appoints five of its own number. The selection of Labour Party delegates is carried out in effect on a rotational basis, depending on which works the particular delegate comes from (each division of ISTC operates its own arrangements). The EC, being the supreme decision-making body in ISTC, takes all decisions on which way the ISTC block vote is cast. In 1981, ISTC cast its block vote on both ballots in the Labour Deputy Leadership contest for Denis Healey.

Policy

ISTC has been closely allied to the right wing of the Labour Party and has consistently supported the notion of a voluntary incomes policy and campaigned to stay in the EEC in the period leading up to the Referendum in 1975. Bill Sirs was a signatory party to the document, '*A Better Way*', and has developed a reputation for being a moderate union leader who holds a tight rein over his union. Members who disobey the rules in ISTC are brought into line very quickly.

The 1981 and 1982 Conferences of ISTC voted for unilateral nuclear disarmament and to withdraw from the EEC, thus breaking past policy.

ISTC may become a victim of TUC structural changes if its declared membership falls below 100,000 and thus prevents it from gaining automatic representation on the TUC General Council.

Recent Events

ISTC was involved in a 13-week-long national steel strike from 2 January until Easter in 1980 — the first national strike that the union had been involved in since 1926. The strike was eventually settled by the Lever Court of Inquiry which recommended a settlement of 15.9 per cent. By all measures, this represented a victory for the British Steel Corporation, and the final settlement failed to make up the wages lost by strikers who were demanding 19.7 per cent.

By any standards the cutbacks in BSC steelmaking were savage, and ISTC faced a dramatic loss of membership.

The MacGregor Corporate Plan for BSC was implemented in 1981–82, and rather more than the planned 20,000+ job reductions was achieved. By 1982, with erosion of jobs continuing, total BSC employment was just over 100,000, which was 60 per cent below the 1970 level. Important BSC closures in 1981 were at Templeborough (Rotherham) and Normanby Park (Scunthorpe). In the private sector Duports went out of business as did most of Hadfields and half of Round Oak. Despite these 1981 job reductions and plant closures, UK steel output in 1981–82 rose 4 million tonnes above the depressed 1980–81 level, and it was expected that

1982–83 would show a further slight increase.

ISTC have argued that BSC is over-optimistic about what they will be able to produce in the few plants they will be left with and also over-optimistic how much steel they can sell both at home and abroad. Such a combination will accelerate the decline of BSC. EEC figures indicate that the UK capacity utilisation rates for steelmaking are the highest among member countries. Academics at Warwick University (Rob Bryer and Terry Brignall), arguing against the closure of Corby, showed that BSC would be unable to meet even present demands if closures took place. BSC has consistently refused to reveal what it considers to be its true realisable capacity for making steel. The danger was that BSC would identify a certain level of demand as being that which it could profitably meet, and then savage its plant configuration into a shape that would correspond. ISTC accused BSC of being obsessed by the 'big is beautiful' idea, under which small plants like Consett and Corby were sacrificed in order to load fully the huge modern plants such as Redcar and Ravenscraig. The result, ISTC argued, would be a nationalised sector too slim to take advantage of any upturn in the market. If BSC was to keep its market share it had to do well in the high volume business of iron and steel coil — precisely the area where BSC was weakest.

The 1980 strike did not help inter-union relations. Members of the GMWU, AUEW, and EETPU were involved in strike-breaking, and the GMWU and the craftworkers' leaders showed a lukewarm attitude to the strike. What could have been a good opportunity to cement inter-union relations in the steel industry was missed. There was much bitterness between ISTC activists and TGWU lorry drivers who continued to defy picket lines in many places. The TGWU itself failed to ensure support from its members in the docks and road haulage in some places, and thus the ineffectiveness of the strike was prolonged.

There were also signs that ISTC members were split between those in the private sector and those employed by BSC. There was little evidence that private sector members were prepared to sacrifice very much in order to help their colleagues at BSC. Despite having the Denning Court of Appeal decision against secondary action overturned by the Law Lords to enable ISTC to call out its members in the private sector, the split remained. Only the NUR of all unions exhibited 100 per cent solidarity behind the strike; Sheerness Steel employees, for instance, defied the Executive and continued working during the strike. Although the leadership of ISTC faced many difficulties both from within its own ranks and from other unions in its conduct of the strike, it is fair to say that the strike was conducted with determination.

After the drastic cutbacks and severe loss in membership from 1980 to 1982, ISTC faces an uncertain future with further redundancies on the horizon, possibly stemming from the 'trade war' in steel between the USA and the EEC. Its past moderation mattered little when it was faced with the reality of industrial action. It emerged from the 1980 strike greatly weakened, with open wounds which will take a long time to heal.

During 1982, ISTC was unable to obtain any national pay increase for its members in BSC, and was similarly unable to prevent the Conservative administration from further steel denationalisation.

ISTC was also involved in the worker-director experiment in BSC having two worker directors on the Main Board of the Corporation. The worker-director experiment started in 1967 with Regional Board representation only. Later on the experiment was extended to provide for Main Board representation. Significantly, up to 1979 two of the six ISTC BSC board members were members of the ISTC Executive! When ISTC tried to exercise its right to replace its Main Board directors in 1981 its move was vetoed by MacGregor. There were amalgamation discussions between the Steel Industry Management Association (SIMA) and ISTC, but these were unsuccessful; this soured relations with the EETPU which also sought amalgamation with SIMA. SIMA eventually merged with the EETPU in late 1980.

SIMA represents parts of middle management in the steel industry and during the steel strike passed a vote of no confidence in the BSC Board. The prospect of a merger between ISTC and the National Union of Blastfurnacemen (NUB) collapsed in mid-1982, following a special NUB conference which considered what were generally recognised as favourable terms for NUB members. (As this book went to press, merger talks with the NUB had been resumed.)

Further Reference

P. Brannen, E. Batstone, D. Fatchett and P. White, *The Worker Directors: A Sociology of Participation*, Hutchinson 1976.

A. Pugh, *Men of Steel*, 1951.

E. Taylor, *The Better Temper*, ISTC 1976.

J. Hodge, *From Workmen's Cottage to Windsor Castle*, 1936.

NEDC, Iron and Steel Sector Working Party Progress Report, 1980.

Christopher Hird and Patrick Wintour, *New Statesman*, 25 January 1980.

Roy Moore and Martin Upham, *New Statesman*, 14 December 1979.

Rob Bryer and Terry Brignall, *New Statesman*, 20 July 1979.

For an excellent account of the events leading up to the 1980 steel strike and a well-argued case for the alternative strategy for BSC proposed by the union, see: Martin Upham, 'British Steel: retrospect and prospect', *Industrial Relations Journal*, July 1980.

See also: Frank Wilkinson, 'Collective Bargaining in the steel industry in the 1920s' in A. Briggs and J. Saville (eds.), *Essays in Labour History*, Croom Helm 1977.

R. Rowthorn and T. Ward, 'How to run a company and run down an economy: the effects of closing down steelmaking at Corby', *Cambridge Journal of Economics*, December 1979.

Roy Moore, *The Case for Corby*, ISTC 1979 (an ISTC document written by Ruskin College's Trade Union Research Unit).

A New Deal for Steel, ISTC, 1980.

R. A. Bryer *et al*, *Accounting for British Steel*, Gower Publishing 1982.

J. Kelly, *Marxism Today*, June 1981.

T. Mainwaring, *Capital and Class*, Summer 1981.

Lock and Metal Workers, National Union of
(NULMW)

Head Office

Bellamy House
Wilkes Street
Willenhall
West Midlands WV13 2BS
0902-66651

Principal Officers

General Secretary—
John Martin, MBE, JP
Assistant General Secretary—
D. R. Thomas
Staff Officer— J. F. Torrington
National Officer— L. Wells

Membership (1982)

Male 3,036
Female 2,073
Total 5,109

General

Formed in 1889, the union has membership throughout the lock industry which is located mainly in the West Midlands and particularly Willenhall. The main negotiating machinery is the Joint Industrial Council for the Lock, Latch and Key Industry.

Most companies have been suffering from declining orders resulting in redundancies or short-time working. In these circumstances the employers' organisation, the British Lock Manufacturers' Association, pressed for removal of the cost-of-living supplement agreement and the NULMW was forced to revert to conventional pay negotiations.

Organisation

The industry is so highly localised that no branch organisation as such is considered necesary. There are shop stewards and an elected lay executive of 18 including the president. There are six women on the Executive Council. The full-time officials of the NULMW also do any necessary work for the surviving members of the *Spring Trapmakers' Society* which is in effect part of the NULMW and has only a nominal existence.

External Relations

No political affiliation but the union is affiliated to the International Metal-workers' Federation.

Roll Turners' Trade Society, British

(BRTTS)

Head Office

21 Chester Road
Redcar
Cleveland TS10 3PU
0642-482799

Principal Officer

General Secretary —
L. B. Trainor

Membership (1982)

Total 420

General

This union was founded in 1898 and has membership in the steel industry in Lancashire, the Midlands and South Wales. The union was involved in unsuccessful merger talks with the AUEW in 1974 and 1977.

Sawmakers' Protection Society, Sheffield

(SSPS)

Head Office

This union does not have a head office as such. All communications relating to the union are sent to the secretary's private address:
27 Main Avenue
Totley
Sheffield S17 4FH
0742-361044

Principal Officers

All officers of the union are part time and hold full-time occupations within the industry.
Honorary President —
C. H. Frost
Secretary — A. Marples
Assistant Secretary —
R. Parkin

Membership (1982)

Male 162
Female 5
Total 167

General

The union organises trades people in the sawmaking and light edge tool industries, such as press operators, hardeners, smithers, brazers, grinders, hand set and sharpeners, machine set and sharpeners. The union is party to the Sheffield Light Trades Agreement.

History

The union was founded in 1911 with 280 members. By 1951 the membership had risen to 500 but since then has declined. There are records held in the Archives of Sheffield City Library which suggest that the union had its origins sometime in the late 1700s.

Organisation

All three officers — president, secretary and assistant secretary — are elected annually at the Annual General Meeting. The small membership of the union does not warrant an annual delegate conference. The Executive Committee is made up of shop stewards, and at present numbers ten in all. Any member who is employed at an establishment at which four or more members are employed is entitled to appoint herself or himself as a shop steward, and if he or she so wishes can take a place on the Executive Committee.

External Relations

The union is affiliated to the Sheffield District Trades Council.

Recent Events

The union admitted its first female member in 1976, in accordance with the Sex Discrimination Act 1975, after carefully avoiding the issue for a long period. The union was one of the first to obtain a certificate of independence from the certification officer.

Further Reference

Archives Department, Sheffield City Library for documents relating to the history of the union.

Spring Trapmakers' Society

This union has no independent existence, being for all practical purposes part of the National Union of Lock and Metal Workers. (See **Lock and Metal Workers, National Union of.**)

Wire Drawers and Kindred Workers, Amalagamated Society of

Head Office

Prospect House
Alma Street
Sheffield S3 8SA
0742-21674

Principal Officers

General Secretary — L. Carr
General Treasurer —
H. F. Storey
National Organiser —
A. M. Ardron
National Organiser —
T. B. Mellors
National Organiser —
E. B. Lynch

Membership (1982)

Male 7,037
Female —
Total 7,037

General

The society seeks to organise employees in the wire and wire rope industries as well as those employed by wire goods manufacturers. The membership of the society is centred mainly in the areas Sheffield, Manchester, Birmingham, Warrington, Halifax, Ambergate, Cardiff, Scotland and the North East. Collective bargaining nationally is conducted in the Wire and Wire Rope Industries JIC on which the society has five representatives, compared to one each for the TGWU and GMWU.

History

The society was founded in 1840, as a craft trade union for wire drawers. An amalgamation with the *Fine Wire drawers* took place in 1910 and in the early 1920s the society changed from being a craft trade union to an industrial union covering employees engaged in the manufacturing and processing of wire, in some cases extending from the manufacture of wire rods to the finished product made from wire.

Organisation

The supreme ruling body of the society is the Executive Council, composed of 15 members elected from the districts and branches of the society. The EC itself elects the president and vice-president. The general secretary of the society is elected by the membership for a term of office laid down by the EC. There is an annual delegate meeting of the society which convenes in June, although it serves only as a forum where issues affecting the society can be ventilated. Only the EC has the authority to declare official industrial action.

External Relations

The society is not affiliated to any political party.

Wool Shear Workers' Trade Union, Sheffield

Head Office

50 Bankfield Road
Malin Bridge
Sheffield S6 4RD

Principal Officer

General Secretary —
J. H. R. Cutler

Membership (1982)
    Male 21
    Female 8
    Total 29

General

This union has the distinction of being the second smallest union within the TUC. The entire membership works at one factory making sheep shears of high craft quality in much the same way since the company was established in 1730. About 170 workers are employed at the firm, and around 155 of them are members of the GMWU with whom the shear workers join in the annual pay negotiations. The wool shear workers formed their union in 1890 and at that time there were workers in other factories, although numbers have never risen above a few hundred. Although the union is shrinking, new members do join from time to time. Subcriptions are 10p a week which is intended to help any member in need. The union does not send a delegate to TUC conferences.

Further Reference

The Guardian 24 August 1979.

Group Nine Building, Woodworking and Furnishing

Asphalt Workers, The Amalgamated Union of

Head Office

Jenkin House
173a Queen's Road
Peckham
London SE15
01-639 1669

Principal Officers

General Secretary —
H. M. Wareham
Assistant General Secretary —
D. McCann
Regional Full-Time Officers —
E. Firth
8 Snowdon Close
Raynville Estate
Leeds 13

S. Fullard
29 Atherton House
Sutton Estate
Benwell
Newcastle upon Tyne

Membership (1982)

Male 2,860
Female —
Total 2,860

Union Journal

No journal as such but a newsletter is sent to members.

General

The union represents mainly workers employed in the production of mastic asphalt and its application in the construction industry. It was formed in 1938 when the London-based *National Asphalt Workers' Union* and the *Northern Asphalt Workers' Union* of Manchester amalgamated. Despite its paucity, membership is widespread, the only main area in which the union does not organise asphalt workers being Liverpool. The union has been severely affected by the slump in the building industry, embattled against the 'lump' (labour only subcontracting). There is a national agreement in force for the trade. Regular delegate conferences are in abeyance at present but this is obviated to some extent by taking the Executive Committee once a year to one of the union's geographical centres outside London, co-opting delegates.

Construction, Allied Trades and Technicians, Union of

(UCATT)

Head Office

UCATT House
177 Abbeville Road
Clapham
London
SW4 9RL
01-622 2362/2442

UCATT Regional Offices

● *Scotland*
6 Fitzroy Place
Glasgow G3 7RL

● *Yorkshire*
Winwaed House
64/66 Cross Gates Road
Leeds 15

● *Midlands*
Gough Street
off Suffolk Street
Birmingham B1 1HN

● *London*
11-13 Essex Road
Dartford
Kent

● *South Western*
217 St Johns Lane
Bedminster
Bristol BS3 5AS

● *Northern Ireland*
79/81 May Street
Belfast BT1 3JL

● *Northern Counties*
Archbold House
Archbold Terrace
Jesmond
Newcastle-on-Tyne 2

● *North Western*
137 Dickenson Road
Rusholme
Manchester M14 2JB

● *Eastern Counties*
UCATT Offices
119 Newmarket Road
Cambridge CB5 8HA

● *Southern Counties*
54 Hemstead Road
Southampton
Hampshire SO1 2DD

● *South Wales*
UCATT House
59/61 Cowbridge Road
Cardiff CF1 9AE

● *Republic of Ireland*
56 Parnell Square West
Dublin 1

Principal Officers

General Secretary —
L. W. Wood
Assistant General Secretary —
J. Hardman
Executive Council —
Danny Crawford
Hugh D'Arcy
Jack Henry
Charles Kelly
Glyn Lloyd
Arthur Utting
Albert Williams

National Officials —
T. Graves
S. G. Reading
D. Sanderson
A. Verdeilles
A. Black

Membership (1982)

Male 273,519
Female 1,732
Total 275,251

Union Journal and Publications

UCATT Viewpoint — monthly.
UCATT has also published a
10-page booklet entitled
*Building Britain's Future: The
UCATT View* which sets out
the UCATT arguments against
'CABIN' (the building
employers' campaign against
building nationalisation) and
also puts arguments forward
defending effectiveness of
direct labour departments of
local authorities. Other recent
booklets include: *Contribution
Cuts Hit Everyone* and *Defend
Direct Labour.* The union also
issues a quarterly *Shop
Stewards' and Officials'
Bulletin* and a full-time
officers' *Newsbrief* every two
weeks.
UCATT also issues a shop
steward's handbook, health
and safety literature, and an
advice sheet to members on
the handling of asbestos.

General

UCATT is now the ninth largest union within the TUC and has members
in shipbuilding and repair, steel, engineering, furniture making, local authorities and the National Health Service. The main concentration of
UCATT's membership, however, is
in the private sector of the building
industry — approximately 70 per cent
of its membership. Within the building industry, UCATT seeks to organise all types of workers, i.e. woodworkers, bricklayers, painters,
labourers etc. Membership of the union increased from 260,490 in 1971 to
347,777 in 1980, but has since declined rapidly, as the recession has hit

the construction industry, to its present level of around 275,000. Recruitment and maintenance of membership levels is particularly difficult in the building industry, largely because of the cyclical nature of employment, the continued prevalence of the practice of labour-only sub-contracting (the 'lump'), and the inevitable mobility of labour from site to site following work completion. This difficulty is compounded by the fact that the building industry attracts and moulds workers who seek high earnings, yet who are highly individualistic, independent, 'hard' and who are highly conscious of craft differences. UCATT therefore has to employ a considerable number of organisers throughout the country in order to maintain organisational effectiveness. One indication of such a need is the fact that in 1973 UCATT recruited 40,000 members and lost 53,000. There were around 140 such organisers in 1978 located in the UK and the Republic of Ireland. Major concentrations of the membership are located in the North, London and the Midlands.

History

The first recorded attempts to combine, following the collapse of the medieval guild system, resulted in 1800 in the *Friendly Society of Carpenters and Joiners* at the Running Horse, London. Few records remain of unionism throughout the period of the Combination Acts, but it is certainly true that this period heralded the birth of the unions of bricklayers and masons.

Following the repeal of the Combination Acts in 1824, there occurred a sudden expansion of union activity which was thwarted by the ensuing depression in 1825, except for the carpenters' union. The *Operative Stonemasons' Society* was created in 1831 and became one of the strongest unions in the country.

The *Operative Stonemasons' Society*, along with Robert Owen, supplied the inspiration for the Great Operative Builders' Union, the first attempt at a general union for all building trade workers. This federal body, despite its large size for the time (40,000

members) did not survive for long. At its birth in 1832 hopes were high, but by 1834 the 'Document' had effectively killed off the union, along with its contemporary, the GNCTU. The Operative Stonemasons' Society managed to continue, however, and won considerable victories against the 'Document' by 1846.

Up to 1860 only the masons had managed to retain an effective organisation. After the 'Great Lock-out' of 1859 and 1860 trade unionism flourished once more, with significant victories against the 'Document'. The *Amalgamated Society of Carpenters and Joiners* was founded with Robert Applegarth becoming its secretary in 1862; the *Operative Bricklayers' Society* came under the direction of Edwin Coulson and the London painters formed the *Amalgamated Association of Operative Painters*.

The Trade Union Act 1871 served to provide a more congenial climate for trade unionism, and the building unions slowly prospered and increased in membership.

After the boom of the 1890s, the old unionism of the building trades workers came under severe pressure, only punctuated by the first world war. Between the wars, the building trade unions federated among themselves. The masons joined with builders to become the *Amalgamated Union of Building Trade Workers*, and the two existing unions of carpenters and joiners became the *Amalgamated Society of Woodworkers*. The painters and decorators also reforged old alliances at this time.

Since 1945, the benefits of rationalisation and co-operation have become increasingly evident within the building trades, although the division between craft and non-craft traditions in the union still surfaces occasionally, and the eventual formation of UCATT largely came about because in the 1950s and 1960s all three major unions — woodworkers, painters and bricklayers — had been finding it difficult to stem a decline in membership. The numbers of workers unionised in building and civil engineering declined as a proportion of the labour force from 45 per cent in 1948 to around 30 per cent in the late 1960s. Financial difficulties, coupled with the growing practice of labour-only sub-contracting, fostered an alliance between the Amalgamated Society of Woodworkers' craftsworkers and the painters and bricklayers, albeit as junior partners working under ASW rules. George Smith, who was elected general secretary of the ASW in 1959, was instrumental in using the ASW as a centrepiece for mergers and forging a new union with a regional structure and centralised administration. On 1 January 1970, the *Amalgamated Society of Painters and Decorators* (ASPD) and the *Association of Building Technicians* (ABT) transferred their engagements to the ASW, and in December of that year the *Amalgamated Union of Building Trade Workers* (AUBTW) also agreed to transfer its engagements. UCATT therefore came into existence on 1 July 1971 with 262,600 members.

Sir George Smith's tragic death in late 1978 led to the election of Les Wood, the assistant general secretary, as the new General Secretary of UCATT.

Union Officials

Despite their relatively large number (140 regional organisers in 1978) UCATT officials have to spend a great deal of their time servicing the existing membership rather than recruiting new members. This dependence of the membership on the services of officials is reinforced by the hostility of many building employers to active trade unionists. The building industry is characterised by a large number of very small employers, many of whom operate blacklists of militant trade unionists, and allegations of site stewards that the Economic League supplies employers with photographs of 'militants' are common. The job of the official is made no easier because not only do they face the active hostility to trade unionism by employers, but also they have to battle against individualistic attitudes and the long traditions of self-employment among workers in the building industry. Generally speaking, there are two generations of UCATT officials: the older ex-ASW officers who are declining gradually in

numbers, and a growing number of UCATT ex-activists who tend to be in the 35-45 age group. All union officers are elected (see **Organisation**).

Coverage

UCATT is represented on the National Joint Council for the Building Industry and on the Civil Engineering Construction Conciliation Board. It is also party to a large number of agreements in the building industry, furniture making, exhibition industry, timber container industry etc. UCATT also represents members employed in the public sector, particularly by local authorities and the National Health Services, and is party to various agreements covering these workers.

In 1981 there were moves towards the creation of a new structure to oversee industrial relations in the construction industry, together with a pioneering national agreement drawing in previously separate bargaining arrangements. The formation of a national joint council with equal employee and employer representation and with a high level of full-time staff was seen as a means of bringing 'order' into its often chaotic bargaining procedures and wage levels. The new NJC would negotiate the hourly rate and the bonus rates, while site joint councils would monitor performance at individual locations on the basis of these agreed levels — a similar procedure to that operated in the electrical contracting industry. Such a proposal would tend to limit the activities of shop stewards at the more militant sites.

Organisation

The present organisation within UCATT is a product of major changes in the first five years subsequent to the formation under its present title in 1970. In its early years UCATT operated largely under ASW rules, but it was generally accepted that major rule changes would be made in 1975 by the rules revision committee. Further organisational changes were made at the union's sexennial meeting of the rules revision committee in 1982 (see below).

Traditionally, the ASW had been

an exclusive craft union with an elitist style of leadership. As technological change reduced the number of craft woodworkers and brought into the ASW a growing number of less skilled members, financial and constitutional changes were brought in by the leadership which served to further enhance the remoteness of the union from its members. The leadership of the newly created UCATT set about organising the union into 12 regions, administered by 12 regional secretaries appointed by the Executive Council. The Executive Council also exercised control over the number of organisers in each region. These regional organisers were elected by the membership in each region for a period of five years and, if they were subsequently re-elected, they were confirmed in office until retirement. The district management committees, which met monthly, were replaced by regional councils of elected lay members which met every six months. The annual delegate conference was replaced by biennial conferences at national level and alternating biennial conferences at regional level. These measures served to strengthen the control of the union by the Executive Council at the expense of the activists. George Smith's programme of rationalisation and centralised administration was carried out at the same time. While such changes gave UCATT financial viability it also emphasised the remoteness of head office from union members, the seeming irrelevance of national negotiations, and a feeling amongst many members that the union was becoming undemocratic and unresponsive to the membership. The Building Workers' Charter Group was set up in April 1970 as a means of democratising the union, largely as a response to the recent reforms by activists.

The Building Workers' Charter Group organised ad hoc joint branch committees in large towns, often organised with the assistance of regional organisers. At the 1974 national delegate conference the leadership was defeated on its policy on wages, the Shrewsbury pickets and union structure. The pressure brought on to the national negotiations was so intense in 1972 that the wage demands of the charter group culminated in the longest national building strike since 1924, which depended for its success on flying pickets and ad hoc site action committees. The subsequent rules revision in 1975 resulted in a number of reforms which gave the site activists some satisfaction — such as the election of officials at all levels; larger regional councils with more frequent meetings; a form of district organisation within regions, based on shop stewards and branches; and the concession that regional committees could declare strikes official, subject to Executive Council approval.

The present organisation of UCATT is based on the decisions of the 32-strong rules revision committee which met in 1982. This latest updating of the UCATT rules after a period of six years marked the final stage in a gradual process which saw the union move away from its inherited structure based on the separate trades of woodworking, bricklaying, and painting and decorating. The main effects of the new rules will be to reduce the present executive from seven to five with these members being elected on a purely regional basis, rather than the former method of a regional-trade basis; to cut down the size of regional councils and introduce regionally based special consultative committees covering the various main agreements negotiated by the union.

Interestingly, the rules revision committee rejected a suggestion that there should be secret ballots for all elected posts, and also turned down a suggestion that all officials should stand for re-election every three years instead of five as at present.

The reduction in the EC strengh in UCATT will be achieved by natural wastage as executive councillors retire from 1982 onwards. As of 1982, UCATT was split into 12 regions, and the Executive was to decide how these regions should be further divided to create five electoral divisions for the Executive Council.

The switch to regional representation on the Executive was also extended to the general council of the union. As of 1982, this comprised five woodworkers, three painters, and three bricklayers or labourers. The general council was extended from 11 to 12 members — one for each region. At regional level, the regional councils of up to 25 members were cut back to 5–9 members each, with the savings achieved here allowing the introduction of regional industrial advisory councils. The industrial advisory councils would be comprised of lay members and would cover the main areas of activity within the region. Thus all regions would probably have what would effectively be Joint Board agreement councils. London and Birmingham, in particular, would be likely to have exhibition industry councils, and the Northern region would probably have a shipbuilding council. Other councils might cover local authorities, water services etc.

The aim of this next structure was to give quicker, more effective, and more direct consultation with the membership. It could also speed decision-making in the course of pay negotiations or on the question of industrial action.

Other changes introduced as part of the new rules revision were separate disciplinary procedures for members and officials, and equality for women was written into the Rule Book.

UCATT's policy-making body is the Biennial National Delegate Conference, with the union's policy between conferences being administered by the Executive Council and the general secretary. The general council (now regionalised, see above) is elected for a five-year period and carries out a general overseeing role over the affairs of the union, including the hearing of appeals, examining the accounts of the Executive Council and acting as trustees. The general council also has the power to relieve the Executive Council of its duties in extreme circumstances, subject to ratification from the membership.

UCATT is divided into geographical regions which are administered from a regional office and staffed by elected regional officials. Each region has a regional council which is elected by the membership in that area on a three-year basis. Regional secretaries and other full-time regional officials are elected to serve for a five-year period. Each region must set up a shop steward organisation, to facilitate communication in the mainte-

nance of union activity throughout the region, and which is under jurisdiction of the regional council. UCATT's rules also provide for the establishment of strike committees in the event of an industrial dispute in a particular locality.

There was some speculation amongst industrial correspondents about what effect the new rule changes would have on the political complexion of the union. A great deal depends, of course, on future elections as present members of the Executive Council retire. For the time being, however, UCATT will follow a fairly left-wing policy at least until 1984.

The union's head office is organised into research, finance, branch administration, legal, print, computers, purchasing, stores and despatch departments.

Workplace Activity

Workplace organisation in building is particularly difficult. As each stage in construction is complete the worker knows that he or she will soon have to seek work elsewhere. The image of the tough, individualistic, independent worker is largely correct and in such an environment any kind of workplace organisation is extremely difficult to achieve. Younger workers particularly tend to change jobs frequently, the jobs done by many UCATT members are not in large work units, and the union appears remote from workers. In such circumstances, where a site does become fully organised, particularly on the long-life sites, the stewards tend to be very politically aware as they tend to be the people who are prepared to put their heads on the chopping block in an uncertain industry. Workers who have both an ideology of struggle and organising skills are inevitably in the forefront of site organisation and provide the leftist opposition to what they see as domination of the site activists by the union leadership. The reality of workplace organisation difficulties were summarised by one worker who said, 'When one job finishes you have to start all over again to organise. I haven't been on a site yet where you didn't have to battle.' The leftism of the active building worker arises from insecurity and constant battles to organise.

Perhaps the greatest enemy of workplace organisation is the 'lump' which UCATT sees as making trade unionism almost seem irrelevant. There was a three-pronged drive by the big building employers, the building unions and the government in 1978 to get rid of it. The long term aim is the complete decasualisation of the building industry, although such long established practices, based on the 'lump', have almost assumed a momentum of their own; and such practices will be difficult to eradicate. For example, tax exemption certificates which effectively avoid the 30 per cent deduction of 'lump' earnings at source are regularly traded and exchanged.

Whilst workplace organisation is largely non-existent on many building sites, there are islands of union power at the points of production — usually in cities such as London, Manchester, Birmingham and Liverpool on large scale sites. The proportion of UCATT's membership on 'check-off' reached 41 per cent in 1976.

Women

There are only about 1,750 women members of UCATT; most of these are employed in woodworking establishments. There are a few women craftsworker members who have successfully surmounted the sex barrier into the industry.

UCATT set up a Women's Working Party in January 1982 as a result of the union's NDC. The aims of the Working Party are: to investigate current training opportunities for women in construction and to make appropriate recommendations; and to consider ways and means of encouraging women members to participate in the affiars of UCATT.

External Relations

UCATT is affiliated to the Labour Party, and sponsors two Labour MPs, T. Urwin (Houghton-le-Spring) and Eric Heffer (Liverpool Walton); Glyn Lloyd and Les Wood are both members of the TUC General Council.

Charlie Kelly was elected in 1980 to the Labour Party NEC.

Labour Party Delegation

The UCATT Rule Book (Rule 4) provides that the union shall be represented at the Labour Party Conference 'by the EC and five general council members. In addition there shall be proportional representation based upon the number of regions and determined by the EC in accordance with membership fluctuations.' The additional delegates are elected by branches in the respective regions.

In the 1981 Labour Party Deputy Leadership election, the UCATT delegation voted by 14–12 to cast its vote for Tony Benn — who is a regular speaker at UCATT Conferences. The UCATT EC according to rule 'shall be responsible for submitting resolutions to the TUC and the Labour Party'. As was the case at the 1981 Labour Party Conference, 'in cases where policy has not been decided by the NDC the union delegation shall consider such resolutions and the majority decision shall be binding on all delegates.'

Policy

UCATT is firmly committed to the decasualisation of the building and construction industry and is particularly concerned that there should be a compulsory register of employers and employees to allow for the establishment of bodies which bring stability of workload and greater public accountability. The union also calls for the Construction Industry Manpower Board to be put on a statutory footing. UCATT has also called for measures to educate the public in the advantages of local authority direct works and in particular for legislation to enable direct works departments to compete on equal footing with other private contractors for public contracts. The union has also campaigned vigorously against the practice of labour-only sub-contracting (the 'lump') and has urged that measures should be taken to reduce the high level of accidents in the construction industry — including stricter penalties for employers guilty of health and safety neglect. The construction industry is notorious for its high accident rate (see Health and Safety Executive: *Report on the Construction Industry*, published in 1978).

It is UCATT policy to stop cuts in construction and begin a massive housing/repair programme, and improve the facilities for training. Both these policy items were submitted to the 1982 TUC Congress.

At the 1982 Biennial National Delegate Conference UCATT firmly rejected any move towards the reintroduction of incomes policy by any future government — whether Conservative or Labour. The union's EC had urged support for a qualifying amendment allowing incomes policy to be introduced as part of a programme to redistribute 'wealth and power in favour of working people'.

Recent Events

UCATT has been particularly active recently in the health and safety arena (see **Policy.**) as well as in its efforts at countering the 'CABIN' propaganda against building nationalisation.

Further Reference

S. Higginbottom, *Our Society's History*, ASW 1939.

T. J. Connelly, *The Woodworkers, 1860-1960*, ASW 1960.

UCATT: W. S. Hilton, *Foes to Tyranny: A History of the Amalgamated Union of Building Trade Workers*, AUBTW 1963.

W. S. Hilton, *Industrial Relations in Construction*, Pergamon Press 1968.

Joe England, 'How UCATT revised its rules: an anatomy of organisational change', *British Journal of Industrial Relations* 1979.

Terry Austrin, 'The "Lump" in the UK Construction Industry', in Theo Nichols (ed.), *Capital and Labour: A Marxist Primer*, Fontana 1980.

L. Wood, *A Union to Build: The Story of UCATT*, Lawrence & Wishart 1979.

R. Price, *Masters, Unions and Men: Work Control in Building and the Rise of Labour 1830-1914*. Cambridge University Press 1980. An erudite study well worth reading.

John D'Arcy, *Contract Journal*, 17 June 1982.

Furniture, Timber and Allied Trades Union
(FTAT)

Head Office

'Fairfields'
Roe Green
Kingsbury
London NW9 0PT
01-204 0273/4/5

Principal Officers

General Secretary — B. Rubner
Assistant General Secretaries
— E. Goodall
J. Kooyman
F. Davies

Trade Organisers
General Membership Group —
E. Kent
Woodcutting Machinists Group —
D. Maxwell
Bedding Group, Soft Furnishing Group —
C. Christopher
Polishing and Finishing Group (London and South East) —
W. C. Clifton
Funeral Services Operatives Group — D. R. Coates

Membership (1982)

Male 61,138
Female 7,460
Total 68,598

Union Journal and Publications

FTAT Record — monthly tabloid newspaper.
Shop Officers' Handbook and Guide to Factory Organisation — elementary advice and instruction on negotiation and employment law.
Health and Safety Representatives Handbook and Guide — a useful introduction to legislation and hazards.

General

FTAT is a union for furniture workers in wood, metal and plastic; cabinet makers; frameworkers; upholsterers; polishers; wood machinists; mattress makers; carvers and gilders; glass workers; artificial limb makers; plywood workers. It is also for joiners and other building workers, and for floor coverers, shop fitters, funeral service operatives and musical instrument makers. There is a clerical and supervisory section.

History

The union was founded as the *National Amalgamated Furniture Trades Association (NAFTA)* in 1901 from the amalgamation of the *Alliance Cabinetmakers* (founded in 1868) and the *United Operative Cabinet and Chairmakers' Society of Scotland* which was formed in 1875 from a number of local societies. In 1911 the *Amalgamated Society of French Polishers* (formed in 1853) joined with NAFTA.

NAFTA ceased to exist in 1946 when it amalgamated with the *Amalgamated Union of Upholsterers* to form the *National Union of Furniture Trade Operatives*. The Amalgamated Union of Upholsterers had been founded in 1891 from a number of locally based upholstery unions, the oldest of which could be traced back to its origins in meetings in the Upholsterers Arms in Wardour Street in 1812. In 1969 NUFTO effected amalgamation with the *United French Polishers* and in the following year with the *Midland Glass Bevellers*

In 1972 NUFTO amalgamated with the *Amalgamated Society of Woodcutting Machinists* to form the *Furniture, Timber and Allied Trades Union*. The Amalgamated Society of Woodcutting Machinists had been founded in 1866 as the Mill Sawyers' Union of Birmigham and District. It became the *Mill Wood Cutting Machinists and Wood Turners' Society* and finally the *Amalgamated Society of Woodcutting Machinists*, a northern craft society with head office in Manchester. In 1978 the Furniture, Timber and Allied Trades Union amalgamated with the thousand-strong *Funeral Service Operatives' Union*.

Coverage

The union has membership in, and is party to agreements covering, the following industries:

Furniture manufacture
Bedding and mattress
Pianoforte
Flat glass
Imported timber sawmilling and timber containers
Homegrown timber
Fillings
Veneer and plywood
Musical instruments
Funeral services
Municipal passenger transport
Vehicle building
Building and civil engineering
Engineering

Organisation

The union is divided into trade groups and also into districts for electoral and organisational purposes. There are six trade groups: upholstery and soft furnishings, woodcutting machinists, polishing and finishing (London and South East), bedding and spring mattress, funeral service operatives and the supervisory and clerical general members' group. Most have an elected full-time trade organiser.

There are also district organisers. The general officers of the union — the general secretary and treasurer, three assistant general secretaries, the trade organisers and three trustees (not to be full time-office holders) are all elected.

The supreme authority of the union is constitutionally vested in the Biennial Conference or Special Conference of Branch Delegates. There is an elected General Executive Council of 27 members of the union.

Every officer of the union and the General Executive Council are elected by postal ballot from the membership. Any member of the union is free to be nominated for the positions of general secretary and assistant general secretaries, and the whole membership votes in the elections, whereas district organisers and national officials are elected by a fixed electoral region in an area or, in the case of trade organisers, by the members of that particular group.

Workplace Activity

Shop stewards are not mentioned in the union Rule Book but shop steward representation and workplace activity are well developed.

External Relations

FTAT is affiliated to the Labour Party and to CND. In the Deputy Leadership election in the Labour Party, its card vote was placed for Tony Benn.

Policy and Recent Events

Early in 1980 it became clear that trade was declining at an alarming rate, particularly in the furniture and bedding industries. Short-time working was being applied in many factories while redundancies were being declared in others without any attempt at short time. In some cases, shortly after dismissals (ostensibly for reason of redundancy) had taken place, the remaining workforce had been requested to work overtime and, in some isolated cases, this had been accepted.

The General Executive Council therefore issued the following policy statement:

(a) Redundancies should not be accepted lightly. Every avenue should be explored to try to ensure full employment for everyone concerned;

(b) if this is not possible then efforts should be made to secure a short-time working agreement;

(c) if redundancies are inevitable, joint consultations between workers' representatives and management should take place in accordance with the provisions of the National Labour Agreement and the Employment Protection Act;

(d) if redundancies do take place, the remaining workers should not readily work overtime, except and until those who have been sacked are reinstated and only then if overtime is really necessary.

FTAT membership is concentrated in industries that are likely to be particularly affected by microprocessor technology.

In 1979 the FTAT appealed against an industrial tribunal decision that it was guilty of racial discrimination against 17 Asian members and its appeal was vindicated by the Employment Appeal Tribunal. The EAT ruled that there was nothing to indicate that the Asians who did the 'dirty jobs' in the paint spray shop at a furniture factory had been treated less favourably by the FTAT than any other groups of workers and therefore the decision of the industrial tribunal which had criticised the union and employers for 'lack of communication' with the Asians, probably because of language difficulties, was set aside.

Further Reference

Hew F. Read is engaged in writing a history of the furniture trades unions 1902-1972 as a doctoral thesis for the Centre for the Study of Social History at Warwick University.

Group Ten **Printing and Paper**

Graphical and Allied Trades, Society of
(SOGAT 82)

Head Office

SOGAT House
274/288 London Road
Hadleigh
Essex SS7 2DE
0702-553131

Principal Officers

Joint General Secretaries —
  Bill Keys
  Owen O'Brien
General President —
  A. E. Powell
Organising Secretary —
  H. Finlay
General Officers —
  J. Moakes
  E. O'Brien
  J. Pointing
  H. Miles
  J. Selby
  D. Sergeant
  F. Smith
Papermaking Secretary —
  J. O'Leary
Financial Secretary —
  D. Bartlett

Membership (1982)

Male 161,267
Female 75,393
Total 236,660

Union Journal

SOGAT 82 Journal — monthly,
nominal charge.

General

In 1982 the most significant event in printing industry trade unionism for many years was announced. Ballots of members of both SOGAT and the National Society of Operative Printers, Graphical and Media Personnel (NATSOPA) produced majorities in favour of an amalgamation, and a clear programme for bringing the new union into operation was begun. The new union is intended to be a markedly different alliance from that of an earlier merger between the two unions which fell apart in 1970 after four troubled years. This time a new Rule Book was produced and contentious issues brought to the surface for negotiation and resolution.

The new union will have membership among art, technical, administrative, executive, sales, clerical and process workers in the paper, cardboard, newsprint, packaging and printing industries and in newspaper production and distribution. In Fleet Street SOGAT 82 has members among semi-skilled machine room and clerical workers and at the distribution end of the business.

History

SOGAT is the result of a complex series of amalgamations. Probably the main amalgamation ensuring future growth was that of the *Printers' Warehousemen, Paper Mill Workers* and *Vellum and Parchment Makers* to form the *National Union of Printing and Paper Workers* in 1914. However, a more remarkable amalgamation occurred in 1921 when this union merged with the *National Union of Bookbinders and Machine Rulers*. The printing and paper workers' union had started to recruit women who worked as assistants to the skilled bookbinders, since the bookbinders, a craft society kind of union, had made no effort to recruit the women. This had caused intense conflict between the two unions. Remarkably, they were able to resolve it by amalgamation, an amalgamation which produced the trade sectional governing structure of SOGAT. This was necessary to convince the bookbinders that their craft would be effectively safeguarded within the amalgamation.

Until 1966 SOGAT was known as the National Union of Printing, Bookbinding and Paper Workers. In that year an amalgamation was initiated with the National Society of Operative Printers and Assistants. When amalgamation was terminated in 1972, the National Union of Printing, Bookbinding and Paper Workers was reconstructed as the Society of Graphical and Allied Trades. This name continued after amalgamation with the *Scottish Graphical Association* in 1975.

History (NATSOPA)

While craftsworkers in the printing industry were, by the late nineteenth century, well organised into craft societies such as the *London Society of Compositors*, childworkers, women and labourers were mainly unorganised and often worked in deplorable conditions for miserable wages. In fact, the labourers' work was demanding in nerve, strength, skill and experience, while conditions in the underground machine rooms were crowded, dark, noisy and unhealthy. In 1899 the wages paid for 55 hours of such work were 12 to 14 shillings.

At this time many new unions were springing up. A strike occurred among printers' labourers at the firm of Spottiswoodes for a £1 minimum weekly. Labourers in other firms struck for this and many employers began to accede to the demand. The next step was the formation of a *Printers' Labourers' Union* which emulated the older craft societies in printing by basing itself on the chapel system.

The main area of recruitment at first was not the casual 'unskilled' labourers, but the numerous assistants who worked in the pressrooms of printing firms, especially those who worked on the rotary machines used in newspaper printing. These men

were not 'labourers' so that the title of the union was changed to the *Operative Printers' Assistants' Society*. Later, when the society extended its membership and activities beyond London, the word 'National' was added. A very critical change of title was made in 1912, by the insertion of 'and' between the words 'Printers' and 'Assistants', signifying the union's claim to recruit craftsworkers.

NATSOPA frequently came into conflict with the craft unions that were very hostile to what they considered to be territorial encroachments by the new union. These disputes were exacerbated after 1920 when the craft societies decided to open membership to non-craft workers. Nevertheless, NATSOPA continued to grow and reached 18,000 members in 1939.

In 1952 NATSOPA was involved in a notorious strike and dispute with the anti-union firm of D. C. Thomson but it failed to enforce its claim that the firm should reinstate NATSOPA members whom it had sacked.

Organisation

The merger ballot result in NATSOPA was 16,000 for and 13,000 against. The narrowness of this result is alleged to stem from three issues concerning rules that were unpopular with NATSOPA members. The first concerns the election of national officers for life. In NATSOPA national officers had to submit to a ballot every three years. As this rule is also unpopular with a substantial number of members of the previous SOGAT, attempts to amend it can be expected at Biennial Delegate Conference, the first of which is planned for 1984 (there is a proposal to hold a special policy Biennial Delegate Conference in 1983) and at rules revision conferences.

The old SOGAT rule permitting full-time officers to stand for election to the Executive has also been carried into the SOGAT 82 Rule Book. NATSOPA always had a lay Executive and most members would have preferred that to continue. The London clerical branch of NATSOPA has made a policy decision debarring its full-time officers from standing in ballots for Executive positions.

NATSOPA also had a strong tradition of balloting members about rule changes, whereas the SOGAT 82 Rule Book allows rule changes to be made by decision of Conference.

Officers

Bill Key and Owen O'Brien will be Joint General Secretaries of the amalgamated union until retirement or removal from office when there will again be one general secretary. Upon retirement or any other reason for a general officer's leaving, the decision about whether to replace would be taken by the Biennial Delegate Council.

National Executive Council

It was finally agreed that full-time officers of branches should be allowed to stand for election to the NEC. This is to have 36 members with no more than two being elected from any one branch and no more than one member from any particular chapel being eligible for election while another chapel in the same group is unrepresented. The 36 members of the NEC are distributed within the geographical groups of the union according to the size of membership within those areas.

Biennial Delegate Council

Each branch, group or division with a working membership of not less than 100 members is entitled to one delegate; a second delegate is allowed to branches with 700 working members and thereafter there is an additional delegate for each 500 members. This produces a Biennial Delegate Council of about 470 delegates.

Regional structure

These are 11 groups:

Irish
Northern
Yorkshire
North Western
Scottish
Art, Technical, Executive and Sales
East Anglian
Midlands
Home Counties
South West and South Wales
London District

Branches

In amalgamation discussions it was agreed that, as SOGAT already had 46 branches with full-time officers, it would be better to adopt the SOGAT model for branches and to try to create as many branches with full-time officers as possible, the amalgamation of branches to be carried out by April 1983 at the latest. The amalgamation panel agreed that, in reforming branch committees, attention should be paid to ensuring that there is adequate representation from both former societies to cover the necessary skills and industries in any particular branch.

The new rules will permit former NATSOPA branches far greater autonomy than they had previously. An important factor in this will be the increased branch income. Forty per cent of union contributions will be retained at branch level, and branches will be able to raise additional income through a local fund contribution. Therefore the SOGAT financial structure was adopted but with increased local autonomy. For example, in June 1982 the NATSOPA London machine branch members paid £1.39 per week; under the new rules, 56 pence of this would be retained at branch level.

Workplace Activity

Workplace activity is through the chapel as in other print unions. In Fleet Street the chapels are likely to have a number of officials. In the larger chapels there is an F/MOC, a deputy F/MOC, one or more clerks or secretaries, and a chapel or management committee with a chairperson and some half-dozen members. The F/MOC in the machine department is usually non-working and other members of the committee are likely to have jobs which allow them to spend much of their time on chapel business. In smaller chapels the F/MOC usually has to work, fitting in chapel business when necessary. In both large and small chapels the F/MOCs are paid the earnings of their occupation; they may also receive an honorarium and delegation fees from the chapel, together with expenses. F/MOCs in the larger chapels usually have their own office provided by the management. Most chapels have some access to office facilities.

It is frequently the F/MOC who recruits workers through the union office and allocates them to different tasks. It is the F/MOC who draws up overtime and holidays rotas. It is also the M/FOC and chapel committee who are responsible for discipline. In effect, the M/FOC is a manager. The Economist Intelligence Unit report on the newspaper industry noted that 'Newspaper workers often fail to realise that their industry is almost unique in the degree to which control of labour is in the hands of the unions. The fact that quite large numbers of men spend a large proportion of their working lives negotiating, taking part in deputations and meetings among themselves is not thought to be at all unusual.'

This applies to both SOGAT 82 and the NGA.

Formally, the chapels are well integrated into the wider union organisation. They perform the functions of enforcing trade union rules and agreements and carrying out trade union functions in the workplace and of enforcing collective decisions on all matters within the works which are of interest to the members. However, this form understates the considerable autonomy of the chapels. The chapels in Fleet Street are large and may total over 500 members. They are consequently vital in union elections, many full-time officers being elected on the Fleet Street vote. The weakness of management does not help the union head office to establish control. Many full-time officers are wary of opposing chapel policies with which they disagree because experience teaches them that management often backs down and undermines their authority.

Comparisons and comparability claims are often used in workplace bargaining, and the pay structure in Fleet Street, for instance, is notoriously complex. Members often compare themselves with NGA members, arguing that they are treated as 'second-class citizens' and that the distinction between 'craft' and 'non-craft' is outdated. However, they also mount competitive claims based on comparisons with other members in their own union — for example comparisons by RIRMA (revisers, inkers, roller makers and auxilliaries) with the machine department—because superior chapel organisation has often been able to secure relatively high earnings for members in the machine department.

The union, in common with other print unions, exerts job entry controls in Fleet Street. Job entry controls vary somewhat in the case of 'regular' jobs, in production and maintenance departments. Job entry controls in 'casual' jobs are found mainly in the machine publishing departments.

The Rule Book of what was previously SOGAT paid considerable attention to chapels in an effort to integrate them into the formal governing structure of the union. The attention to branches in the new SOGAT 82 Rule Book suggests that these efforts to integrate chapels will be intensified.

External Relations

Bill Keys is a member of the TUC General Council and chairperson of its equal rights and race relations subcommittees. Before the amalgamation with NATSOPA, the old SOGAT delivered its card vote in the Deputy Leadership election in the Labour Party to Tony Benn. SOGAT 82 is affiliated to CND.

Policy

As with the creation of the new NGA, the creation of SOGAT 82 is intended as an intermediate stage towards the objective of one trade union for the printing industry. The impact of technological change in breaking down discrete job skills made amalgamation a more urgent objective.

Recent Events

Before the amalgamation NATSOPA was concerned in a High Court action against Lord Briginshaw who was alleged to have been part of a conspiracy to cheat and defraud NATSOPA while he was general secretary. Lord Briginshaw, general secretary from 1951 until 1975 when he retired and accepted a life peerage, was alleged to have misappropriated £78,000 from the proceeds of sales of union properties, in collusion wth his former personal assistant and administrative officer, Joan Wing, and a former assistant secretary of the union, Arthur Davis. The union's claim was settled privately after three days in court, the defendants agreeing to pay a substantial sum to NATSOPA.

SOGAT delivered a vehement attack on the TUC's continued participation in the National Economic Development Council. At Conference the debate swayed against tripartism and consensus, which was seen to be hollow against the backcloth of more than 3 million unemployed and the Tebbit Employment Act.

Further Reference

C. J. Bundock. *The National Union of Printing, Bookbinding and Paperworkers*, Oxford University Press 1959.

J. Child, *Industrial Relations in the British Printing Industry*, Allen & Unwin 1967.

P. Routledge, 'The dispute at Times Newspapers Limited: a view from inside', *Industrial Relations Journal* 1980.

Abolition and After: The Paper Box Wages Council, Labour Studies Group, Department of Applied Economics, University of Cambridge, for the Department of Employment 1980.

R. Martin, *New Technology and Industrial Relations in Fleet Street*, Oxford University Press 1981.

Graphical Association (1982), National

(NGA 1982)

Head Office

Graphical House
63-67 Bromham Road
Bedford MK40 2AG
0234-51521

Principal Officers

General Secretary —
  J. F. Wade
General President —
  Bryn Griffiths

Joint Assistant General Secretaries —
  John Jackson
  A. D. Dubbins
National Officers —
  G. Colling
  K. Haughton
  J. A. Ibbotson
  R. Tomlins
  A. Pearson
  J. Willats
  G. Jerrom
  B. Philbin
  F. Tanner
  A. Parrish
  L. Pye
  E. Martin

Union Jounal

Print — monthly. Circulation 100,000.

Membership (1982)

Male 130,154
Female 6,172
Total 136,326

General

The vast majority of NGA members have served time in apprenticeship; it is, without any doubt, a craft union. The main occupations of members are compositors, keyboard operators, readers, stereotypers, machine managers (letterpress and litho), press telegraphists, and, following the amalgamation with SLADE, lithographic artists. This amalgamation is a response to the technological changes which are rapidly being brought into the printing industry and which are quite beyond the capacity of traditional craft controls such as were exercised by the NGA and SLADE.

History

The chapel as a unit of print union democracy is of great antiquity. According to J. Moxon's 'Mechanick Exercises' of 1683, 'Every Printing House is, by the custom of time out of mind, called a chapel.' Such chapels of compositors in the printing trade are the origins of the NGA and are of continuing and immense importance in the union. However, most authorities suggest that the chapel was not fully integrated into wider union organisation of compositors until after

1840, since an early difficulty was the lack of some intermediate unit between chapel and trade society. Nevertheless, there is evidence of successful trade unionism in the enforcement of common rules governing piecework and in efforts to control apprenticeships by London compositors by 1785.

Control of apprenticeships necessarily demanded national organisation which is precisely what the trade did not have, being organised into friendly societies on a purely local basis even after the repeal of the Combination Acts in 1825. There was an attempt to set up a *National Typographical Association* in 1845, but it collapsed in 1848.

Regional unions, in any case, became necessary to properly administer the tramping system of countering local unemployment. In 1849 the Provincial Typographical Association was founded, so named because the London Society of Compositors opted out. By 1890 it had dropped the 'Provincial' and became the *Typographical Association* based in Manchester with a membership of 10,000. The membership of the *London Society of Compositors* had also risen — to 9,000 — and that of the *Scottish Typographical Association*, founded in 1853, stood at 3,000.

In the 1890s the trade of the compositor was assailed by technological change as the linotype machine was introduced into Britain. There was not much displacement of skilled workers since the printing industry expanded immensely, but the new machines created new semi-skilled jobs and other unions emerged in competition with the old craft societies which were eventually forced to open their ranks to semi-skilled machine operators.

From then on, there was more talk of amalgamation of the various craft societies, but the main obstacle remained the London-Provincial divide between them. Not until 1955 did any significant amalgamation take place. Then the London Society of Compositors amalgamated with the *Printing Machine Managers' Trade Society* to form the *London Typographical Society*. This amalgamated with the Typographical Association in 1964 to form the NGA. The amalgamation was followed by those with the *Association of Correctors of the Press* and the *National Union of Press Telegraphists* in 1965. In 1967 the *National Society of Electrotypers and Stereotypers* amalgamated with the NGA and in 1968 the *Amalgamated Society of Lithographic Printers and Auxiliaries* also decided to join its ranks. In 1979 the NGA amalgamated with the small *National Union of Wallcoverings, Decorative and Allied Trades*, but a proposed merger with SLADE fell through.

Coverage

The NGA negotiates with the following employers' organisations over the whole range of terms and conditions of employment:

British Printing Industries Federation
Newspaper Publishers' Association
Newspaper Society
Scottish Master Printers' Association
Advertisement Typesetting and Foundry Employers' Federation
Reproduction and Graphics Association
British Tin Box Manufacturers' Federation
British Association of Lithographic and Plate Manufacturers
News Agency Liaison Committee

In addition, a number of organisations and companies reach comprehensive agreements covering terms of employment with the NGA and these supersede those made with the national employers' federations. Chapels enter into house agreements which are complementary and in addition to the national agreements with the employers' organisations.

Organisation

The basis of the NGA's organisation is the chapel and in every chapel there is a father/mother of the chapel who is the NGA representative in the workplace. Each member of the NGA is also a member of a branch of which there are more than 120 throughout the United Kingdom and Ireland, most being covered by full-time branch administration.

The NGA is divided into seven regions: Irish, London, Midland and North Wales, Northern, Scottish, South Eastern, South Western and South Wales, each of which is administered by a full-time regional and assistant regional secretary, together with appropriate office facilities. Each region has a regional council which is elected by the members who, through their branches, also elect the regional secretary.

At national level the officers of the NGA (general secretary, general president, assistant general secretaries, financial secretary and national officers), elected by ballot vote of the whole membership, are accountable to the National Council which is elected from the regions and from the trade group boards. The trade group boards (letterpress, litho and news) are responsible for negotiations concerning all issues falling within the section of the printing industry which they cover. Ultimately, the trade group boards are accountable for their decisions to the National Council.

Every two years there is a National Delegate Meeting of the NGA at which branches are represented on the basis of one delegate for every 300 members in the branch. This delegate meeting is the 'parliament' of the NGA and decisions taken are ostensibly the basis of NGA policy over the next two years.

Workplace Activity

'Chapel Power' is a force to be reckoned with in printing industrial relations, so is there any conflict of interest with the union officials? The chapels are jealous of their autonomy and yet most of the branches in London stipulate that agreements negotiated by the managements and chapels should be ratified by the branch committee; this was most important in allowing the dissemination of details of settlements reached with particular workgroups during the 1978–79 *Times* dispute and thereby aggravating the continuing argument about differentials. The ruling about ratification by branch committees applies in every case to comprehensive agreements. Branch officials are usually actively involved in the final stages of the negotiations and almost invariably their signature will be on the agreement; in some cases the agreement is between the management and the branch. There is little conflict between NGA chapel and union in practice because, for all practical purposes, the chapels in Fleet Street are the branch. Usually fathers/mothers of the chapel (F/MOCs) sit on the branch committee and are influential in deciding policies. Often full-time officers are former F/MOCs from Fleet Street because the size of chapels in Fleet Street gives them numerical advantage in elections. So full-time officials have much in common with chapel officials. Again, the full-time officers may be powerless in the event of a disagreement with chapel policies because an inconsistent management has cut the ground from under their feet.

Meetings of the chapel usually take place quarterly and procedure is extremely formal. It is obligatory for members to attend on penalty of a fine.

External Relations

The NGA is affiliated to the Labour Party.

Policy and Recent Events

The NGA is a traditional craft union and has been fighting a last ditch struggle to retain control of certain vital stages of the production process as computer technology inexorably invades the printing industry. This resistance placed the NGA at the centre of the *Times* dispute between November 1978 and October 1979.

The effect of new technology on traditional demarcation lines has led NGA to reconsider its attitude to amalgamation, and in late 1979 talks were begun with SOGAT. To begin the process of creating one union for the printing industry, SOGAT combined with NATSOPA (see **SOGAT 82**). The NGA leadership maintained progress by negotiating amalgamation with the Society of Lithographic Artists, Designers and Engravers (SLADE). The 25,000 SLADE members approved the amalgamation by a two-to-one majority. In September

1981 NGA members voted by 46,481 to 16,777 in favour. John Jackson, General Secretary of SLADE, became Joint Assistant General Secretary of the NGA for his working life, after which the post will be abolished.

The NGA has also been engaged in formal talks about amalgamation with the National Union of Journalists (NUJ), a move unanimously approved by delegates to the NGA Biennial Delegate Meeting. The leadership had anticipated a more equivocal response from the delegates, but amalgamation of two such different unions will be complicated. (See **National Union of Journalists**.)

Also at the Biennial Meeting the leaders of the NGA were defeated when they attempted to take control of the level of benefit paid by the union to its unemployed members. Under NGA rules, benefits are fixed in direct proportion to members' contribution rates and, in 1982, £31 was by far the largest benefit payment made by any TUC-affiliated union. With more than 5 per cent of the 130,000 members unemployed, the union had paid almost £1 million in the six months to March 1982, while falling contributions had reduced income by £3,647 a week.

The insecurity of NGA members in Fleet Street was reflected in allegations from some delegates at the Biennial Meeting that secret talks about amalgamation had been under way between the electrical trade union's (EETPU) London press branch and the Society of Graphical and Allied Trades (SOGAT 82).

Further Reference

J. Child, *Industrial Relations in the Printing Industry*, Allen & Unwin 1967.

A. E. Musson, *The Typographical Association*, Oxford University Press 1954.

E. Howe and H. E. Waite, *The London Society of Compositors*, Cassell 1948.

A. J. M. Sykes, 'Trade union workshop organisation in the printing industry — the chapel', *Human Relations*, February 1960.

K. Sisson, *Industrial Relations in Fleet Street*, Heinemann 1976.

Paul Routledge, 'The dispute at Times Newspapers Ltd: a view from inside', *Industrial Relations Journal*, 1980.

R. Martin, *New Technology and Industrial Relations in Fleet Street*, Oxford University Press 1981.

Journalists, National Union of

(NUJ)

Head Office

Acorn House
314/320 Gray's Inn Road
London WC1X 8DP
01-278 7916

Principal Officers

General Secretary —
Ken Ashton
Deputy General Secretary —
Jacob Ecclestone
Assistant Secretary —
R. Norris

Membership (1982)

Male 24,199
Female 8,438
Total 32,637

Union Journal and Publications

Journalist — monthly.
The NUJ has been particularly active, as one might expect, in the publication of informative literature for its members. These include:
Making News: some questions on equality for trainee journalists — a lively little leaflet which brings home to new recruits into journalism the pervasiveness of sexist reporting — particularly in local newspapers.
Provision for Parenthood: how does your agreement stand up? — a leaflet from the NUJ Equality Working Party setting out a model agreement for equality between the sexes.
Workplace Nurseries: the why and how — a step-by-step guide on how to set up a

creche in the workplace. 12 pages, 30p.

Images of Women: guidelines for promoting equality through journalism — an NUJ Equality Working Party pamphlet on sexual stereotyping in journalism. 11 pages.

Black and Front: journalists and race reporting — a pamphlet produced by the Race Relations Sub-Committee of the NUJ, sets out the NUJ code of conduct and guidelines on race reporting. 23 pages.

Journalists: repression and truth in Southern Africa — a pamphlet expressing the NUJ's concern about the repression of press freedom and journalists in Southern Africa, the links between British publishing companies and South Africa, the censorship by the South African regime and the need for extreme care in the reporting or subbing of material emerging from South Africa. 20 pages.

Press Freedom: a proud record — a policy pamphlet on the attitude of the NUJ to censorship and the closed shop. 8 pages.

There is a place for you in the NUJ — a recruiting pamphlet explaining the NUJ and its functions. 7 pages.

Your Policy — a comprehensive guide to the NUJ policy decisions on all industrial and ethical issues (closed shop, press freedom, equality, etc).

Taking Liberties — a comprehensive review of civil liberty issues which the union has taken up in recent years, from the ABC Official Secrets Case to the 1982 judgement against former NCCL Legal Officer Harriet Harman (new Labour MP for Peckham) for contempt for providing a journalist with information which had been entered in evidence in court. 50p.

General

The NUJ is the largest organisation of journalists in the world. It is a multimedia organisation, embracing within its ranks members in newspapers, periodicals, book publishing, radio and television broadcasting, public relations and information services, photo-journalism, editorial design and layout, cartoonists and self-employed freelances. A feature of its organisation is its industrial councils, which have wide-ranging powers, particularly in terms of negotiations for each trade section of the union.

It has championed press freedom and individual liberties. With the development of sophisticated microprocessing technology in printing and broadcasting, the union is facing pressure to merge with other unions.

In 1981 the union opened formal negotiations with the NGA leading towards the first formal merger within the industry between a production union and journalists. If successful the merger would provide the first formal link between people working in broadcasting and those in print (see **Recent Events**).

History

The NUJ was founded in 1907, following a formation conference at the Acorn Hotel in Birmingham. Before that time there had been organisations of journalists in the larger cities and towns, and in the London suburbs where local groupings came together to form what was then popularly called 'the national union'. The founding manifesto, 'To the Working Journalist of the United Kingdom', originated in Manchester.

The union affiliated to the TUC in 1921 but disaffiliated in 1923 because the TUC was trying to raise money, by levy, to support the *Daily Herald* — which was the voice not only of the trade union movement at large, but also of the Labour Party and therefore, in the view of the union, politically partisan. The NUJ re-affiliated in 1940, after four intervening negative ballots. The reason for re-affiliation was the increasingly important role of the TUC in war time.

In 1967, the wheel of history in the union's relations with the *Institute of Journalists* turned full circle. The union had started as a breakaway from the Institute. In the intervening years, in 1921 and 1945-48, attempts had been made to bring about a merger. New talks began in 1965, and in 1967 the dual membership 'trial marriage' arrangement came into force. However, in October 1971 a special joint conference of the two organisations foundered upon three issues: the matter of registration or de-registration under the Industrial Relations Act, the matter of a separate Professional Council and Conference to deal with 'non-industrial' questions and the name of any new organisation. There has been no formal or official relationship between the NUJ and IOJ since. In fact there has been much bitterness of late, particularly centred on the role of IOJ members in NUJ disputes.

Union Officials

The NUJ employs 14 full-time officials other than the general secretary and the deputy general secretary. These consist of the assistant secretary, a head office administrator, an education officer, a broadcasting officer, a technology officer, a freelance organiser, four regional organisers (based in Manchester, Dublin, Wishaw and Swansea), a magazine and books organiser, and three national organisers. The general secretary, deputy general secretary and editor of the *Journalist* are elected by the membership and subject to re-election every five years. All other officials are appointed by the National Executive Council.

Coverage

The NUJ is party to agreements in broadcasting (ITV/ITN, independent radio stations, Visnews, Radio Telifis Eirrean, BBC); national newspapers (Newspaper Publishers' Association, Reuters, Press Association and Extel); provincial newspapers (Newspaper Society, Scottish Newspaper Proprietors' Association, Association of Northern Ireland Newspapers); public relations; magazines and books. The union also has a number of freelance agreements.

Organisation

In common with the print unions, the NUJ Rule Book provides for the establishment of chapels wherever there are four or more members in an office or organisation. Each chapel reports to the branch and is obliged to report any dispute in which it is involved to the branch and the NEC. Each chapel elects a father or mother as the chapel's representative on all matters affecting members' conditions of employment, and each chapel meets monthly. The Rule Book provides that a chapel may instruct all its members to attend a mandatory meeting provided that a motion to that effect is carried at a previous meeting of the chapel. Chapels also elect a clerk to keep their records in order.

The chapel is subject to the branch which is almost invariably based on a geographical location. There are around 180 branches scattered throughout the UK, as well as branches in Eire, Brussels, Paris and Geneva. In London and a few other areas, because of the concentration of members belonging to particular trade sectors of journalism, some branches exist exclusively on a sector basis (magazine, agencies, books, freelance etc.).

The union is divided into geographical units called area councils which are a forum for branch representatives on a wider basis. Area councils have several functions and responsibilities, but principally act as a clearing house of regional problems and as an exchange for ideas and problems. They also serve a useful role in disputes and in conciliation where domestic complaints arise.

Another feature of the NUJ's structure is the tier of industrial councils which have wide ranging powers, particularly in negotiating pay and conditions. Industrial councils exist for each section of the union: national newspapers and agencies; provincial newspapers; broadcasting; magazines and books; press relations and information services; and a separate one for Ireland. The members of industrial councils are elected by members in the appropriate industrial sector. They have autonomy to determine their own policy within the confines of union general policy and they can be overruled by the NEC. A minor function of industrial councils is to act as special advisory committees to the NEC. The freelance industrial council appoints from its number a member to serve, with full voting rights, upon each of the other industrial councils, with the exception of the Republic of Ireland.

The supreme administrative body of the NUJ is the National Executive Council (NEC). The NEC is elected annually from the membership of the union, voting on an industrial sector basis for nominees within each sector. It consists of national officers (president, vice-president, general treasurer) and as many others as are elected by the members in industrial sectors on the basis of one NEC member for each 1500 members in the sector. The general secretary and deputy general secretary are members of the NEC and all committees but do not vote. The NEC also elects, from its own number, specialist committees, the principal of which are provided for under rule and are:

General purposes
Finance
Recruitment and organisation
Employment (a function which has been substantially taken over by industrial councils, but still stands without meeting)
Development and public relations
Education
International

The Annual Delegate Meeting decides policy each year. Branches elect delegates in proportion to size (e.g. one delegate for each 50 members). The ADM is usually held in mid-April, and it elects the president, vice-president and general treasurer. Polling is held at ADM for a variety of committees: appeals tribunal; standing orders; equality working party; committee on technology; race relations; and widows and orphans. The ADM also elects the union's delegates to the TUC, the women's TUC and the Congress of the International Federation of Journalists, and a poll is held to set up an emergency commit-

tee of four NEC members and national officers. The emergency committee has powers to deal with matters as if it were the NEC itself.

Women

There are two women on the NEC and there are only two women full-time officials. Despite this, the NUJ stands out among unions for the efforts some of its members have made to further the cause of women's equality in union affairs. The equality working party (EWP) of the union recently conducted a survey on the level of participation by women in the work of the union. The results proved to be alarming. Membership of the 92 branches that returned the questionnaire included 4,963 women and 14,553 men, a male/female ratio of 2.9:1. Yet the male/female ratios for branch officers ranged from 14.3:1 (chairperson) to 2.5:1 (secretary). In other words, the more important the job is, the fewer women who do it — and as usual women are typecast in the demanding but essentially supportive post of secretary.

The survey found no evidence that women are apathetic about the union, since the results suggested that they attend branch and chapel meetings as regularly as men and hold office at chapel level almost as often. The male/female ratio for FOC/MOC is 3.9:1 compared with a 3.3:1 membership ratio. Nevertheless men still run the union.

In 1980 the NEC amended the abortion policy insofar as it included the Republic of Ireland and, following some protests from Irish branches (the 1967 Abortion Act of course, does not apply in the Republic nor in Northern Ireland) an NEC statement exempted Ireland from the campaigns which the union has supported in the UK. This move was overturned at the 1981 Conference. The EWP has contributed to the child care campaign by producing a booklet (see **Union Journal and Publications**) containing a step-by-step guide to setting up a workplace nursery. It is the first such guide to be produced for employees in the private sector, and it is intended for circulation among the other unions as well as the NUJ.

At the 1982 Annual Conference the union agreed to set up an Equality Council to replace the equality working party. This new council will be made up of seven members of industrial councils, all elected by their specific memberships, to monitor equality matters. A further seven members will be elected from branch nominations submitted to the Annual Conference.

External Relations

The NUJ is non-political. It is affiliated to the Federation of Broadcasting Unions and the Confederation of Entertainment Unions. Until 1980 the union was in membership of the Press Council, but withdrew its four members of the Council, having failed to win reforms to make the Council a more representative body.

In recent years the union has taken a greater interest in international affairs. At the 1980 Athens Congress and the 1982 Lugano Congress of the International Federation of Journalists the NUJ delegations were instrumental in moving the IFJ into a stronger posture on issues such as editorial press freedom and the suppression of the free trade union for journalists in Poland. The present president of the IFJ is NUJ General Secretary Ken Ashton. In 1982 the NUJ President, Jonathan Hammond, gave over his office facilities at the union's HQ in London to the Polish Solidarity Trade Union Working Group as an expression of support for the union's policy in defence of free trade unions.

Policy

At the 1978 Trades Union Congress, the NUJ supported successful composited motions for a return to free collective bargaining and opposition to any restrictive form of government incomes policy, for a 35-hour week and a reduction in overtime working and for an end to public expenditure cuts.

The union's motion at the 1978 Congress calling for the withdrawal of charges under the Official Secrets Act against Aubrey, Berry and Campbell and the substitution of the legislation with a Freedom of Information Act

was the subject of penetrating attention (see **Recent Events**). The TUC sought the withdrawal of the motion on the basis that it was *sub judice*. Despite assurances from the union that there would be no breach of *sub judice*, the President, David Basnett, was not prepared to have the motion discussed. It could be taken, but without debate. The NUJ opposed this and walked out of Congress when David Basnett eventually ruled the motion out of order.

The union has its own code of conduct relating to freedom of the press, censorship, race relations reporting, sex equality etc.

At the 1980 and 1981 TUCs the NUJ made considerable impact on the debates covering the media. In 1980 the union successfully moved a motion calling for a 'right of reply' to be given to people who are victims of press and broadcasting bias. In 1981 after a national ballot the union affiliated to the Campaign for Press and Broadcasting Freedom.

The NUJ carried motions at its 1979 Annual Delegate Meeting including:

the need to establish guidelines forbidding editors to undertake work normally done by NUJ members in dispute, and an agreement with other print unions which would make it clear that in event of official NUJ action they will handle only the editor's normal copy and not connive in strike breaking by handling additional material;

supporting the concept of an agreed strategy between the NUJ and other unions over the NUJ pursuance of a 100 per cent post-entry membership policy;

calling for the replacement of S.2. of the Official Secrets Act and its replacement with a law designed to place on public authorities the burden of justifying official secrecy;

condemning advertisements placed by racist regimes or companies based in countries with racist regimes in the mass media;

condemning NALGO for its failure to negotiate a house agreement for NUJ members employed by NALGO.

The NUJ voted to leave the Press Council on the grounds that it 'provides the ideological underpinning for the press as it exists today' and is too weak.

Recent Events

The NUJ has been preoccupied with legal matters recently. The union's journal, the *Journalist*, along with *Peace News* and *The Leveller* were the subject of contempt proceedings brought by the Crown, after these publications named Colonel 'B' as Colonel Hugh A. Johnstone who gave damaging evidence for the Crown at the committal hearing of the Aubrey-Berry-Campbell official secrets case. All three publications were cleared of contempt on appeal to the House of Lords.

The union was successful in eventually winning the *Express Newspapers v MacShane* case on appeal to the House of Lords. The union appealed against a Court of Appeal decision in December 1978 which granted Express Newspapers an injunction requiring the NUJ to lift its instruction to members at the *Daily Express* not to handle PA (Press Association) copy. The Lords held that the blacking was in furtherance of a trade dispute, therefore the union had immunity in law. In December 1978-January 1979, the union was in dispute with Newspaper Society houses, and the NUJ called out its provincial and PA members. About half the PA members kept working and the agency continued to supply news. It was to stop the use of that material that the union issued its blacking instructions to other members not directly affected by the strike. The Lords judgement in the *MacShane* case hardened the attitude of the Tories in their determination to outlaw 'secondary picketing' in their Employment Act.

The NUJ also had to face legal proceedings in which over 100 members from the combined chapel at the *Birmingham Post and Mail* and the smaller chapel at the *Coventry Evening Telegraph* sought to obtain an interlocutory injunction stating that the Newspaper Society and Press Association strikes were called in contravention of Rule 20 (b) and restraining the union from taking disciplinary action against them for failing to obey

the NEC instruction to withdraw their labour. The application was refused by Mr Justice Slade in the Chancery Division of the High Court in February 1979. As a result of the judgement 96 blacklegs were expelled from the union, but some of them decided to appeal to the Court of Appeal. The NUJ subsequently lost the case in the House of Lords on 30 July 1980. As a result the NEC had to report to the 1982 ADM that all those expelled during the dispute were allowed to rejoin — providing they paid back payments in contributions covering the long period of legal wrangling. Few did.

The then editor of the *Journalist*, Ron Knowles, stated in his section of the Annual Report 1979-80 that, 'On the picket lines the law is less civilised; brutal, in fact. The police have been brutal towards individuals on Newspaper Society picket lines and towards the truth in subsequent court appearances . . . there is a growing problem for journalists who come up against the police, and it is not confined to the picket lines. Increasing attempts are being made by the police to limit freedom to do our work.'

The union was also in the public limelight as a result of its dispute with the *Nottingham Evening Post*. The paper sacked 28 of its staff for joining the NUJ provincial journalist's strike in early 1979. The sacked journalists started up a new tabloid, not as a strike paper but as a straightforward paper for general consumption, called the *Nottingham News*. The paper closed in 1982 despite considerable support from individual union members. Although it had managed to establish itself in Nottingham and built up a circulation that might be envied by many other traditional local papers, it was unable to maintain the level of advertising needed to survive. It was a paper people wanted to buy, but big advertisers were less enthusiastic. Although it kept a low profile on many issues, its radical origins and solid support for Labour, in the end, undermined its hopes of long-term success.

For the past 20 years socialist commentators have lamented the disappearance of the *News Chronicle, Daily Herald* and *Reynolds News* as the national and provincial press has been concentrated into fewer and, without exception, politically right-wing hands. In 1980 two-thirds of all the provincial morning, evening and weekly press was owned by just four companies — Westminster Press, Thomson Regional Newspapers, Associated Newspapers and United Newspapers. Discussions about a new Labour daily or about the ideas stemming from the minority report of the 1974-77 Royal Commission on the Press have led to little so far.

Like many of the other printing unions, the NUJ has to face up to new developments in technology in broadcasting and printing. The dispute at the *Times* (see **National Graphical Association**) lasted for 11 months, and developments in computer typesetting systems and word processors are an increasing challenge to all unions in printing and broadcasting. It would seem to be in the NUJ's interest to seriously consider mergers with the NGA, ABS and ACTT if this technological challenge is to be overcome.

The merger talks with the NGA entered their second year in 1982 in a mood of caution. At the Warwick annual conference NUJ delegates expressed concern at the lack of practical support offered by the NGA to union members in dispute at the *Camden Journal*, where a stoppage over closure had been in progress for more than a year. Early in the merger discussions a Letter of Association had been exchanged between the two unions expressing, among other things, a commitment to mutual support in disputes.

The NUJ with its very open structure, annual meetings, and high degree of industrial autonomy for its sections is in stark contrast to the NGA where there is local, geographical autonomy but a rigid centralist structure based on its National Council and biennial conferences.

Both unions in their discussions have been attempting to identify the best parts of their own structures and graft them on to the organisation of a completely new trade union.

By the end of 1982 the evidence was that serious and profound differences in tradition and style were not going to make the progress towards a merger rapid or uneventful. There is increasing pressure — particularly from the broadcasting members of the NUJ — that talks with the ABS might provide a more fruitful path for the NUJ to take in its efforts to implement its policy of one union for the media.

The dominating theme of the NUJ in recent years has been press freedom and individual liberties. It is cheering to know that this union takes this issue seriously: if journalists don't fight for the preservation of individual freedoms, who will?

Further Reference

P. Beharrel and G. Philo, (eds.), *Trade Unions and the Media*, 1977.

F. J. Mansfield, *Gentlemen, the Press: Chronicles of a Crusade*, (official history of the NUJ) W. H. Allen 1943.

C. J. Bundock, *The NUJ: A Jubilee History 1907-57*, Oxford University Press.

New Statesman, 15 June 1979, 2 February 1979, 4 April 1980.

Denis MacShane, *Using the Media*, Pluto Press 1979.

Group Eleven **Textiles**

Beamers, Twisters and Drawers (Hand and Machine), Amalgamated Association of

Head Office

27 Every Street
Nelson
Lancashire BB9 7NE
0282-64181

Principal Officers

General Secretary —
F. Sumner

Membership (1982)

Total 651

General

Formed in 1866 and reconstructed in its present form in 1889 as an amalgamation of semi-autonomous district unions, it organises employees in the weaving of cotton, linen and synthetic fibres.

Card Setting Machine Tenters' Society
(CSMTS)

Head Office

36 Greenton Avenue
Scholes
Cleckheaton
Yorkshire BD19 6DT
0274-670022

Principal Officers

General Secretary —
G. Priestley

Membership (1982)

Total 124

General

The manufacture of card clothing is an ancient craft. However, carding today is done by machines, the card clothing being wrapped around rollers. The clothing itself is made in sheet form or in strips. The organisational base of the CSMTS has been undermined by the growth in the use of metallic carding. This first came into widespread use in the mid-1950s and by the 1970s it had virtually replaced flexible carding in the cotton textile industry, although the woollen industry continues to use flexible card clothing. Metallic wire carding is not made by the CSMTS members, nor has the society recruited those who do make it, since its manufacture has been regarded by card setting machine tenters as an engineering process not comparable with their own craft.

Collective bargaining is conducted at employers' federation level but plant or company issues are discussed at joint committee level. The major employer is the English Card Clothing Company, the product of a merger of 1897.

History

The decision to establish the society was taken in 1872. Between December 1915 and May 1916 it undertook a strike which became extremely bitter in pursuance of a claim for a cost-of-living increase. This was the longest stoppage by any group of workers during the first world war, and the terms of settlement left little room for doubt that it was a defeat for the union. The union recovered from this and from the effects of the slump to a peak membership of 297 in 1952. However, since then technological change has brought a falling demand for the skills of card setting machine tenters and a decline in membership, though in recent years there has been a revival. The demand for card clothing has stabilised and training of apprentices has restarted.

Organisation

There is an Executive Council of two delegates (now both from Cleckheaton branch) with three general officers — the president, the secretary and the treasurer. This meets independently of the one remaining branch and is the main policy-making body. The branch can nevertheless overthrow Executive decisions by claiming a referendum and obtaining 55 per cent of the vote.

The annual general meeting has no formal power as it has developed on an ad hoc basis, but it is a forum for airing grievances and debating policy.

External Relations

The CSMTS is affiliated to the Labour Research Department.

Further Reference

M. D. Speirs, *One Hundred Years of a Small Trade Union*, to which the authors are particularly indebted.

Carpet Trade Union, Northern

Head Office

22 Clare Road
Halifax HX1 2HX
0422-60492

Principal Officers

General Secretary—
L. R. Smith
Area Secretary—
K. Edmondson

Membership (1982)

Male 1,362
Female 300
Total 1,662

General

The union caters for all occupations within the carpet industry from preparation of yarn, design of carpets, the woven and finished product and in some instances the retail and fitting of carpet products. A staff branch section also caters for managerial and supervisory/administrative personnel.

A national joint council negotiates a national minimum level agreement covering shopfloor workers, while company arrangements apply for the staff section.

History

The union was formed in 1892, originally covering Brussels carpet weavers only in the Halifax district. Since that date the union has changed its name on two occasions and finally to its present form in the 1930s. There have been no mergers or amalgamations but a loose affiliation is formed from five unions with interests in the carpet industry:

Scottish Carpet Union
Kidderminster Power Loom Weavers and Textile Workers
National Union of Dyers, Bleachers and Textile Workers (now the TGWU Dyers, Bleachers and Textile Workers' Trade Group)
Northern Carpet Trade Union
General and Municipal Workers' Union

Organisation

The governing structure of the union is: branch level, Executive Committee and an Annual Delegate Meeting comprising representatives from each of the 14 branches, this being the supreme ruling body. The senior officer(s) are elected by ballot by delegates at the ADM or by the Executive Committee between annual meetings. At present there are no other full-time officers apart from the general secretary and area secretary but there are a few full-time convenors and some part-time branch officials.

External Relations

The union has no political fund and members pay no levy.

Recent Events

In recent years strong endeavours have been made to merge with affiliated unions, initially with the *Scottish Carpet Union* and the *Kidderminster*

Power Loom Weavers and Textile Workers. Talks also took place with the NUDBTW (National Union of Dyers, Bleachers and Textile Workers) which subsequently merged with the Transport and General Workers' Union. The union has also discussed the possibility of a merger with the National Union of Hosiery and Knitwear Workers and the General and Municipal Workers' Union. The union has not given any clear indication that there is a general wish to amalgamate or merge at present.

Cloth Pressers' Society

Head Office

34 Southgate
Honley
Huddersfield HD7 2MT
0484-661175

Principal Officers

General Secretary — G. Kaye

Membership (1982)

Total 18

General

The Cloth Pressers' Society has the distinction of being the smallest union affiliated to the TUC (along with the Sheffield Wool Shear Workers' Union). It was founded as the *Huddersfield Cloth Pressers' Society* in 1872, and amalgamated with the *Leeds Society of Cloth Pressers* in 1934. It is the smallest of all the TUC-affiliated unions in the textiles section of the TUC (Group 11), and nearly all its members are based in Huddersfield. It sends one delegate to the Trades Union Congress.

Loom Overlookers, General Union of Associations of
(GUALO)

Principal Officers

General Secretary — H. Brown
President — R. Richardson
Overlookers' Institute
Jude Street
Nelson
Lancashire BB9 7NP

Membership (1982)

Total 1,603

General

This is a union of 14 autonomous associations of loom overlookers, originally formed in 1885.

Pattern Weavers' Society

Head Office

New Field End
Hill Top
Cumberworth
Huddersfield HD8 8YE
0484-892547

Membership (1982)

Total 60

This small textile union was founded in 1930. It does not send a delegate to the Trades Union Congress.

Power Loom Carpet Weavers' and Textile Workers' Union

Union Motto

Guardians of our rights we stand,
Heart with heart, and hand in hand,
We succour brethren in distress,
And help the wronged to get redress.

Head Office

Carpet Weavers' Hall
Callows Lane
Kidderminster
Worcestershire DY10 2JG
0562-3192

Principal Officer

General Secretary —
David T. Carter

Membership (1982)

Male 2,311
Female 1,575
Total 3,886

General

The union caters for all occupations within the carpet and textile industries from raw material preparation to sales and fitting. It also recruits all grades of white-collar workers.

The union is in loose affiliation with the following unions, which have membership in the carpet industry, to form the National Affiliation of Carpet Trade Unions:

TGWU Dyers, Bleachers and Textile Workers' National Trade Group

General and Municipal Workers' Union

Northern Carpet Trade Union

Scottish Carpet Workers' Union

Together they form the union side in the National Joint Council for the Carpet Industry. There is also a Scottish, Northern and Kidderminster Joint Council for negotiations. Outside these two negotiating bodies each union is free to negotiate terms and conditions at company level.

The Power Loom Carpet Weavers' and Textile Workers' Association has membership at Axminster (Devon), Wilton, Romsey, Warwick, Stourport and Aberdare, besides the main Kidderminster membership.

History

This particular union was formed in 1866 although there are sound historical indications of a trade society for carpet weavers existing in Kidderminster in 1817. It is an example of a union whose establishment followed from the formation of a permanent association of employers. The Power Loom Carpet Manufacturers' Association was formed in 1864 and among its aims were: 'The prevention of strikes and disagreements, the control of labour supply, the protection of the trade in matters connected with wages and the employment of work people, as well as the consideration of all subjects directly or indirectly affecting the trade'.

In 1917 the union opened its membership to the textile workers, many of whom were women, who were employed in the industry but who were not carpet weavers. This strengthened the union and increased its flexibility and capacity for change. In recent years adaptability has more than ever been necessary in an industry subject to various technological changes and to changes in the pattern of demand, such that woven carpets face strong competition from tufted carpets.

So far industry and union have adapted well to being furnishers of comfort and colour for the many, rather than providers of luxury for the few. Some decline in employment would, however, seem certain.

Organisation

The union is governed by an Executive Committee of Management consisting of 12 properly qualified members, elected at a general meeting of the membership. The president elected by ballot at a general meeting of which there are two held every year. The general secretary and full-time officials are elected by a ballot of the whole membership. There are delegate meetings held when necessary. Approximately 97 per cent of the membership contribute to the political fund of the union.

Recent Events

There have been discussions with other trade unions in the carpet industry about amalgamation, particularly with the Northern Carpet Trade Union, but so far without conclusion.

Power Loom Overlookers, Scottish Union of
(SUPLO)

Head Office

3 Napier Terrace
Dundee
Tayside
0382-612196

Principal Officer

General Secretary — J. Reilly

Membership (1982)

Total 120

Power Loom Overlookers, Yorkshire Association of
(YAPLO)

Head Office

Textile Hall
Westgate
Bradford BD1 2RG
0274-27966

Principal Officer

General Secretary —
K. Hattersley

Membership (1982)

Total 866

Textile Workers and Kindred Trades, Amalgamated Society of

Head Office

Foxlowe
Market Place
Leek
Staffordshire ST13 6AD
0538-382068

Principal Officers

General Secretary —
Herbert Lisle
Cheshire Area Office —
Cyril Graves
Organisation Official —
Fred Pakeman

Membership (1982)

Male 1,104
Female 2,457
Total 3,561

Union Journal

Textile Voice — a newsletter —
is issued at regular intervals.

General

The union organises various grades of workers in the North Staffordshire textile industry, but amalgamations have also given it membership in silk and cotton textiles as far afield as Dunfermline, Pontypridd and Farnworth. The union is represented on the Narrow Fabrics JIC and on the JIC for the Silk Industry. It also concludes a number of plant and company agreements.

History

The society originated in 1871 in the shape of a union called the *Associated Trimming Weavers' Society of Leek* which was the oldest of the unions that combined to form the Amalgamated Society in 1919. It organised certain groups of workers in the Leek silk industry. In 1872 there was a three-week strike over demands for wage increases of 20 per cent and upwards, and the *Trimming Weavers' Society* and the small trade societies played the main organising role, though the strike was largely unsuccessful.

More unions were formed in the silk industry in the Leek area and in the 1890s there were, for the first time in this industry, attempts to organise women workers in the trade unions.

In 1907 some of the various small trade societies in the Leek silk industry came together in the *Leek Textile Federation.* William Stubbs, secretary of the *Silk Twisters' Amalgamation* and William Bromfield of the Trimming Weavers' Society were nominated for secretary and Bromfield won the vote.

Another great strike took place in the Leek silk industry in 1913, lasting two weeks and involving 4,000 workers. This time the unions, helped by federation, were more united and emerged with most of their claims conceded.

In 1919 most of the Leek textile unions amalgamated to form the present Amalgamated Society of Textile Workers and Kindred Trades. The amalgamation went ahead smoothly, although the silk twisters remained outside it, continuing alone until dissolution in 1939.

In 1918 the Joint Industrial Council for the Silk Industry was set up with the ASTWKT prominent among its constituent trade unions. The JIC acted more as a conciliation and arbitration body than as a negotiating body. This was largely because of fragmentation of bargaining: sections of the North Staffordshire textile industry came into the orbit of the narrow fabrics industry and, later, the hosiery industry JICs. Agreements on questions of actual wages and conditions were made for Leek, in negotiation with the Leek Manufacturers and Dyers' Association, and for Macclesfield, with the Silk Trade Employers' Association. At an early stage the national silk JIC was subdivided and in 1920 a JIC for the Leek textile industries was established. In the early 1950s the Leek silk JIC was revived as the Leek Joint Consultative Committee which emerged from an idea by Herbert Lisle.

In 1951 the society affiliated to the *Weavers' Amalgamation*, again an idea forcefully advocated by Lisle who favoured an industrial union for textiles. However, the affiliation was not a success and it was decided to withdraw on the grounds that affiliation was 'costing too much'.

In 1965 the *National Silk Workers and Textile Traders' Association* of Macclesfield merged with the ASTWKT by transfer of engagements. It had been in existence since 1903 when it was the *Macclesfield Power Loom Silk Weavers and General Silk Workers' Association* which had not joined the federation of 1907. It brought branches elsewhere, the main ones being in Dunfermline and Yarmouth.

Organisation

The society is governed by a Delegate Board, composed of representatives from each branch, which meets annually in May, when it elects an Executive Council. The Delegate Board fixes all officers' salaries and Executive Council fees and determines the membership levy. Between Delegate Board meetings, the business of the society is conducted by the Executive which has power to call special Delegate Board meetings at any time. Any section of workers who have a grievance which may lead to a strike or lock-out are entitled to send five representatives to state their case before the Executive Council.

External Relations

The union is affiliated to the Labour Party.

Recent Events and Current Policy

Herbert Lisle was born in 1907 and is due to retire as soon as a satisfactory successor can be found. The union's financial position is particularly strong and this must necessarily loom large as a consideration in any possible merger proposals.

Further Reference

F. Burchill and J. Sweeney, *The Amalgamated Society of Textile Workers and Kindred Trades — A History of Trade Unionism in the North Staffordshire Textile Industry*, Department of Adult Education, Keele University 1971.

Textile Workers' Union, Amalgamated

Head Office

Textile Union Centre
5 Caton Street
Rochdale OL16 1QJ
0706-59551/58367

Principal Officers

General Secretary—
Jack Brown
Assistant General Secretary—
Raymond W. Hill

Membership (1982)

Male 12,810
Female 10,250
Total 23,060

General

The union embraces workers employed in the cotton and allied fibres spinning and weaving industry with a limited membership in carpet factories and texturising. The union bargains at national industry-wide level with the British Textile Employers' Association.

History

The union was established in 1974 following a merger of the principal unions in the cotton and allied fibres industry. These included the former *Amalgamated Weavers' Association*, the *National Union of Textile and*

Allied Workers, the *Operative Cotton Spinners and Twiners*, the *Amalgamated Textile Warehousemen* and the *Textile Officials' Association*.

Union organisation in cotton textiles traditionally took the form of numerous self-administered, largely autonomous local associations. With few exceptions they were all members of seven federations, known, somewhat misleadingly, as amalgamations, each restricted to a particular occupation or group of occupations at a certain stage in the production process (e.g. the former *National Association of Card, Blowing and Ring Room Operatives*).

At one time, when the cotton textile industry in Britain was prosperous, the trade unions in the industry were a powerful force in the labour movement.

Plans for unity, amalgamations and alliances among the cotton unions often failed, however, as did the plan for a cotton workers' federation (a super-amalgamation of all cotton unions) in 1920. In that year the cotton unions together reached a peak membership of about half a million.

Since then the industry has been in decline, mainly through the rise of foreign textile industries with lower labour costs. The unions participated in various rationalisation schemes and later in modernisation and re-equipment of mills and re-deployment of labour. This could do little to counteract massive redundancies; in 1960 alone 37,000 workers applied for redundancy compensation.

This contraction necessarily meant also a contraction in union membership and the trade unions have been obliged to amalgamate (an authentic amalgamation this time) in order to operate economically.

Organisation

The union is the product of a recent amalgamation and hence retains a distinctly federal type of organisation. It consists of a number of autonomous districts but this number is gradually being reduced and at present stands at 11 districts. There is a Central Executive Council consisting of one representative from each district that pays levies to the Amalgamated Textile Workers' Union for 500 members or more, with an entitlement to a further seat on the executive council for districts with 4,000 members or more. Districts appoint their Central Executive Council representatives.

The Central Executive Council meets monthly and is answerable to the Central Representative Meeting which is convened six times a year. Delegates to the Central Representative Meeting are appointed by districts on the basis of one delegate for every 500 members or part thereof, on whose behalf they pay levies to the ATWU. These delegates are almost exclusively rank-and-file members of the union and at each meeting the Central Executive Council tenders a report of its activities to the delegates for confirmation, reference back or rescinding.

The Central Representative Meeting is the highest authority in the union, together with the Annual General Meeting which establishes policy. All national officers are appointed subject to the confirmation of the Central Representative Meeting, following interviews and, if necessary, examination.

The Central Executive Council is empowered to call strikes but the Central Representative Meeting can reverse any such decisions.

External Relations

The ATWU affiliates to the Labour Party on behalf of all districts and their members on whose behalf political levies are paid by the districts to the ATWU.

Further Reference

H. A. Turner, *Trade Union Growth, Structure and Policy*, Allen & Unwin 1962 (a comparative study of the cotton unions).

Joseph L. White, *The Limits of Trade Union Militancy: The Lancashire Textile Workers 1910-14*, Greenwood Press 1979.

Transport and General Workers' Union (TGWU) Dyers, Bleachers and Textile Workers' National Trade Group

(formerly NUDBTW)

Bradford Office

National House
Sunbridge Road
Bradford
West Yorkshire BD1 2QB
0274-25642

National Trade Group Secretary

E. Haigh

Membership (1982)

Male 23,037
Female 14,115
Total 37,152

General

The former NUDBTW covers all sections of the textile industry and, now combined with the TGWU's previously existing membership in that sector in a new trade group, is almost doubled in membership strength. (Membership figures above are for the former NUDBTW only.)

The two main national agreements are those between the TGWU and the British Textile Employers' Association and the Wool Textile Employers' Council.

Wool textiles, dyeing and finishing, and the carpet industry are in severe decline. The executive of the NUDBTW recommended that members should vote to join the Transport and General Workers' Union, and the ballot result showed 20,210 in favour, 4,749 against.

History

Trade unionism among textile workers can be traced to before the eighteenth century but organisation was small scale and lacked cohesion. The former NUDBTW was shaped mainly by two important amalgamations. In 1922 the *National Union of Textile Workers* was formed by the amalgamation of the *National Society of Dyers and Finishers*, the *General Union of Weavers and Textile Workers*, and the *Yeadon and Guiseley Factory Workers' Union*.

In 1936 the *National Union of Dyers, Bleachers and Textile Workers* was formed by the amalgamation of the National Union of Textile Workers, the *Amalgamated Society of Dyers, Finishers and Kindred Trades* and the *Operative Bleachers, Dyers and Finishers' Association*. The last major strike in which the union was involved in the wool textile industry was in 1930. There have been three official inquiries into wages and working conditions in the industry: the Morris Report of 1925, the MacMillan Report of 1930 and the Ross Report of 1936. The last major strike which affected the union in the textile finishing trade was in 1928.

Organisation

The offices of the new textiles trade group of the TGWU will be at what was the NUDBTW office in Bradford. The TGWU already had members in the textile industry in its general workers trade group; these are now combined in the textiles trade group which is conspicuously small for a TGWU trade group.

Policy and Recent Events

At its last Conference delegates of the National Union of Dyers, Bleachers and Textile Workers decided that only nationalisation could save the British textile industry.

Group Twelve Clothing, Leather and Boot and Shoe

Boot, Shoe and Slipper Operatives, Rossendale Union of

Head Office

7 Tenterfield Street
Waterfoot
Rossendale
Lancashire BB4 7BA
070-62 215657

Principal Officers

General Secretary —
T. Whittaker
Assistant General Secretary —
M. Murray

Membership (1982)

Male 1,668
Female 2,608
Total 4,276

Union Journal

At one time the union did publish a journal called *Unity*, but this has not been published for some years.

General

The Rossendale union covers Rossendale, East Lancashire and the Fylde area, catering for all footwear workers in those areas. Formed in 1895, it has steadfastly retained its independence from its larger sister union, NUFLAT. It has two full-time officials, the general secretary and the assistant general secretary. It is party to an agreement with the Lancashire Footwear Manufacturers' Association. The union is administered from head office.

Organisation

The supreme policy-making body of the union is the General Meeting of all members, which is held in March and September each year. The union is managed by an Executive Committee which is representative of the various departments in the trade, and six areas, i.e. Rossendale, Burnley, Blackburn, Fylde, Chorley and St Helens, and Bury. The Executive Council has the power to appoint the general secretary and all full-time officials, subject to approval by the General Meeting. The union maintains a workplace representative system. The union provides each representative with a well written handbook.

External Relations

The union is affiliated to the Labour Party.

Further Reference

For a more detailed account of the place of Rossendale union in the footwear industry see:
J. F. B. Goodman et al, *Rule-Making and Industrial Peace*, Croom Helm 1977.
Alan Fox, *The History of the National Union of Boot and Shoe Operatives: 1874-1957*, NUBSO 1958.

Footwear, Leather and Allied Trades, National Union of the
(NUFLAT)

Head Office

The Grange
Earls Barton
Northampton NN6 0JH
0604-810326

Principal Officers

General Secretary —
S. F. Clapham
General President —
R. B. Stevenson
Assitant General Officer —
G. G. Stewart

Membership (1982)

Male 24,969
Female 25,103
Total 50,072

Union Journal and Publications

Journal and Report —
bi-monthly with a circulation
of around 5,500. Copies are
given to branches for
distribution on request.

Union Offices

*The Leather Trade Group
National Secretary is based at:*

Leeds Trades Council Club
21 Saville Mount
Leeds
0532-628676

NUFLAT is based on branch
units and is organised for
electoral purposes only into
districts. There is no regional
organisation as such but the
union has 17 offices
throughout the country where
full time branch officers are
located (see **Organisation**).

General

NUFLAT was formed under its present title in 1971 by amalgamation between the *National Union of Boot and
Shoe Operatives*, the *Amalgamated
Society of Leather Workers*, the
*National Union of Leather Workers
and Allied Trades* and the *National
Union of Glovers and Leather Workers*. The union organises the vast
majority of manual workers in the UK
footwear manufacturing industry. It
also organises, to a more limited extent, in footwear repairing and components, and since 1971 in the leather
producing, made-up leather goods,
and gloving trades. Membership in
footwear manufacturing is around 90
per cent of the total labour force, and
in the footwear ancillary trades is
around five per cent of total membership. The membership of NUF-
LAT has declined from 94,000 in
1940, 78,000 in 1960, to its present
level of around 50,000. NUFLAT has
a sphere of influence agreement with
the *Rossendale Union of Boot, Shoe*

and Slipper Operatives — a union
which did not respond to amalgamation proposals. Talks have been held
between NUFLAT and NUHKW about the possibility of further amalgamation in order to face the common
problems, including foreign competition, affecting the industries in which
all three unions organise, although no
progress has been made to date.
Women members now slightly outnumber their male counterparts.

History

The *National Union of Boot and Shoe
Operatives* was formed in 1874, having originally been called the *National
Union. of Operative Riveters and
Finishers*, seceded from the *Amalgamated Cordwainers' Association* in
1873. It was formed primarily to cope
with the problems arising from the
trend from a hand-sewn craft industry
to a machine-made trade, especially
in relation to satisfactory payment
systems. The union was launched in a
period of prosperity and labour shortage, but by 1876 the boot and shoe
trade was moving into the shadows of
unemployment, short time working,
and downward pressure on wage
rates. The early years of the union up
to 1889 were no more than a period of
survival, with the preoccupation of
the union centred on limiting and controlling the downward tendency of
wage rates and coping with the problems of piece work. Until the 1890s,
development was mainly through local joint boards of conciliation and
arbitration. The first National Conference of Conciliation and Arbitration
was held in August 1892 in Leicester
Town Hall; it considerably widened
the range of bargaining to the national
level.

A major clash took place in 1895,
resulting in the Great Lock-out which
lasted for nearly six weeks. The terms
of settlement negotiated between the
union and the Manufacturers' Federation were very favourable to the employers and the scope of collective
bargaining was reduced and managerial prerogative strengthened. The
Great Lock-out considerably weakened the union, and it was not until
1907 that union membership began to
recover from this calamity. Mem-

bership rose sharply, from about 24,000 in December 1906 to over 30,000 in December 1909, and 49,000 by 1914.

The years of the first world war considerably strengthened the union. It increased in membership to 83,000 by 1918 and in May 1919, the first Joint Industrial Council for the boot and shoe industry was established. The optimism within the industry proved to be short lived when the post-war boom collapsed in 1920, and wage reductions took effect in 1921.

The 1920s and early 1930s proved to be a period when the union was engaged in a purely defensive struggle from a position of weakness and dependence as severe slumps began to bite in the industry. Technical change led to a reduction in staffing particularly among male workers. The decline in the number of male operatives was slightly offset by the rise in the number of female operatives, a rise due mainly to a considerable growth of fashion wear and a consequent need for more operatives in the closing departments and shoe rooms, departments exclusively or mainly female preserves. Superimposed on these trends were the heavy cyclical slumps of 1921-23 and 1930-33 which dramatically weakened the union. However, the union policy of moderation in return for employer acceptance of collective bargaining and encouragement of union membership enabled the union to weather the storms of the inter-war years.

The post-war years saw the union assume a role which was greatly influenced by James Crawford, who was elected general president in 1944. Crawford's solution to the problems of the inter-war years was the creation of an efficient and competitive footwear industry, within a healthy national economy. This philosophy was characterised by union co-operation in exchange for job preservation and material well-being. If productivity outstripped demand, the labour force would have to decline and alternative employment be accepted. The union was committed never to return to the inter-war years of having a 'surplus army' of labour attached to the industry. In the event, the labour force in footwear has de-clined sharply, although the Crawford philosophy has not been seriously questioned. The late 1960s and 1970s have witnessed an acceleration of decline within the industry with an increasing incidence of redundancies, closures, short time working, and unemployment. Both the union and the employers have co-operated in lobbying the government to impose import quotas and restrictions to protect the industry from foreign competition, with little success to date.

Union Officials

NUFLAT is based on branch units, with no regional organisation as such (see **Organisation**). The general president and general secretary are the two most senior officers in the union. The assistant general officer 'understudies' both the president and secretary. The national secretary, leather trade group, is the officer with special responsibility for the membership in that particular trade group. The only union officers between the general officers and branch full-time officials (BFTOs) are the national organiser and area officer in the case of the footwear trade group, the former being under the direction of the General Executive Council and footwear trade group executive committee through the general president, and acting as trouble shooters, and the latter being responsible for looking after members in branches which do not have a full-time officer. In the case of the leather trade group, there is a national organiser under the direction of the General Executive Council and the leather trade group executive committee through the national secretary, and there are divisional secretaries who service the membership and organise within the area under their control.

All the officers of the union are elected by a ballot vote of the membership (total membership in the case of national officials and branch membership in the case of BFTOs). The area officer is appointed by the General Executive Council. NUFLAT officers tend to be long serving and all post-war national officers have previously been BFTOs. Branch full-time officers are predominantly male (only three out of 36 are female), middle-aged or older, having spent the majority of their working life in the footwear or leather industries with little experience outside. Nearly all BFTOs have worked within their own branch areas. In the absence of a regional structure, and with the tradition of branch autonomy and separateness in the union, they have played, and continue to play a major role within NUFLAT. Invariably they tend to dominate the two executive committees because they tend to be elected by their branches. Because there is a tradition of a high BFTO member ratio in the union, BFTOs tend to be in close contact with events at the workplace and often are in close touch with senior management in an industry which tends to be geographically concentrated with a predominance of small, family owned firms. In sum, the BFTO is in close contact with the shopfloor and plays a dominant role in branch affairs. As Goodman emphasises, this dominance exercised by the BFTO is 'both conducive to, and reinforced by, both membership apathy and a relatively undeveloped shop steward function'.

Coverage

NUFLAT is a party to the following agreements:

The National Conference Agreement between NUFLAT and the British Footwear Manufacturers' Federation

The Leather Producers' Association

The Industrial Leathers Federation

The United Kingdom Fellmongers' Association

The National Joint Standing Committee for the Gloving Industry

The National Joint Wages Board for the Leather Goods Trades

The NUFLAT Rule Book has long made provision for a secret ballot of members on agreements reached tentatively at the footwear NJC — an example of membership participation which is rare in British trade unions. The footwear trade group membership rejected the negotiated agreement in 1976 and 1978.

Organisation

The supreme authority of NUFLAT is the Biennial Delegate Conference. The union is based on branch units, organised, for electoral purposes only, into districts. The members of branches in each of the 13 districts elect one representative (almost always a BFTO) to serve on the footwear trade group executive committee — nine districts in the case of election to the leather trade group executive committee — for a period of two years, who in turn elect representatives from within those bodies to serve on the General Executive Council, which between Biennial Delegate Conferences is the governing body of the union.

The general president, general secretary and assistant general officer all sit on the footwear trade group executive committee, the national secretary sits on the leather trade group executive committee, and all of these officers sit on the General Executive Council in each instance by virtue of their office. There is a tendency for each electoral district to be dominated in numerical terms by one large branch, and invariably it is one of the BFTOs from that branch who tends to be elected. This means that the General Executive Council is dominated by BFTOs with a low turnover of official positions and a correspondingly high level of experience and length of tenure in office. Attendance at branch meetings is rarely higher than three per cent and thus the picture is one of a small group of enthusiasts under the guiding influence and *de facto* authority of the BFTOs. NUFLAT is therefore characterised by a high degree of centralised authority, which is further reinforced by such factors as the large size of many branches, the dispersion of membership over a large range of small companies, and the quiescent nature of unionism in small, family owned companies.

Workplace Activity

Although NUFLAT has over a thousand union representatives and 50 branches, workplace activity is undeveloped. There are several reasons for this. Firstly, the union's commitment to the high BFTO–member ratio enables the BFTO to be in close touch with events, to be at the workplace very quickly and with a role greatly facilitated by the concentration of small, family owned firms in particular geographical areas. In many cases workplace representatives are in fact called shop 'presidents'. The union representative's role is limited almost invariably to the collection of dues and acting as an information link between the BFTO and her/his members. Membership apathy is high and branch turnout rarely exceeds three per cent.

The predominant payment system in the footwear and leather trades is one of piecework, with a great deal of standardisation and formalisation in payment systems embodied in district bargaining on prices — largely the concern of the BFTO. Workers have an individualistic orientation to work and the management system reinforces the personal relations that develop informally between workers and supervisors. Only in the larger companies will the shop president have much involvement in the settlement of workplace issues.

Women

Women members outnumber their male counterparts in NUFLAT and yet there are only three women BFTOs and one female member of the General Executive Council. Women members tend to be generally apathetic. Moreover, female workers tend to be located in the low paid occupations with the exception of certain highly skilled operations in the 'closing' departments in the footwear industry.

External Relations

NUFLAT is affiliated to the Labour Party, and the rules of the union provide for the sponsoring of one parliamentary agent. Graham Mason unsuccessfully fought Northampton South for Labour, but is currently being sponsored as a parliamentary agent. NUFLAT does not have a representative on the TUC General Council. All three general officers are members of the Economic Development Committee for the Footwear In-

dustry. NUFLAT voted against all three constitutional changes at the Labour Party Conference in October 1979, and voted for Denis Healey in the Labour Party Deputy Leadership election in 1981.

Policy

NUFLAT has consistently campaigned against low cost imports in the footwear and leather industries which it sees as the main reason for the decline in employment in those industries. Most of these imports come from places such as Taiwan, Hong Kong and South Korea. It has also pressed for the retirement age of men to be progressively reduced to the age of 60. NUFLAT moved Composite Motion 12 dealing with government grants and aid and the National Enterprise Board at the 1979 Trades Union Congress.

Recent Events

NUFLAT secured a union membership agreement in its footwear section by national negotiation in 1977, an objective which NUFLAT had sought for many years. As contraction continues to beset the footwear and leather industry, there are continuing discussions taking place with other unions about the possibility of merger, amalgamation or federation, but to date no specific recommendations have been reached. There have recently been heavy redundancies and closures in all sections of the related industries of footwear manufacture, component manufacture, leather producing and made-up leather goods. The union has had to streamline its administrative structure and some reduction of the number of officers has resulted from natural wastage.

Further Reference

J. F. B. Goodman, E. G. A. Armstrong, J. E. Davis and A. Wagner, *Rule Making and Industrial Peace: Industrial Relations in Footwear*, Croom Helm 1977. A well written, comprehensive account of the footwear industry to which the authors are particularly indebted.

Alan Fox, *A History of the National Union of Boot and Shoe Operatives*

1874-1957, 684 pages, Oxford: Basil Blackwell 1958. The official history of the union by a distinguished industrial relations academic.

Hosiery and Knitwear Workers, National Union of
(NUHKW)

Head Office

55 New Walk
Leicester
LE1 7EB
0533-556703

Principal Officers

General President—
D. A. C Lambert
General Secretary—
G. E. Marshall
National Officers—
J. Matlock JP
T. Kirk
J. C. Smith
J. Kelly (CATSA – Staff Section)
M. A. Humphrey

Membership (1982)

Male 15,552
Female 42,759
Total 58,311

Union Journal

The Hosiery and Knitwear Worker— distributed free to members, published four times a year, 15,000 copies printed.

Union Offices

● *Hinckley District*
(Hinckley area of Leicestershire, Staffordshire, Mid-Wales)
9 Clarendon Road
Hinckley

● *Leicester District*
(Area — Leicester, East and South Leicestershire)
14 West Walk
Leicester

● *Mansfield and Sutton District*
(Area — North East Nottinghamshire)
85 Outram Street
Sutton-in-Ashfield

● *North Western District*
(Area – Cheshire, Lancashire, Cumbria, North Wales)
63 Window Lane
Garston
Liverpool 19

● *Southern District*
(Area — South England and South Wales)
5 Parade Court
Bourne End
Buckinghamshire

● *Ilkeston District*
(Area — North West Nottinghamshire, Derbyshire)
2 Mundy Street
Heanor
Derbyshire

● *Loughborough District*
(Area —Loughborough and its environs, part of Derbyshire)
35 Factory Street
Loughborough

● *North Eastern District*
(Area — Yorkshire, Durham, Northumberland)
Circle House, 2nd Floor
Lady Lane
Leeds 2

● *Nottingham District*
(Area — centre of Nottingham and Lincolnshire)
Union House
Church Street
Basford
Nottingham

● *Scotland*
44 Kelvingrove Street
Glasgow
G3 7RZ

General

NUHKW came into being in 1945 following an amalgamation of several small district unions situated in the Midlands. At that time the approximate membership of the union was 22,430, and since then the union has developed into a national organisation of just under 60,000 workers employed in factories throughout Great Britain. The membership of NUHKW is heavily concentrated in the Midlands (Hinckley, Ilkeston, Nottingham, Leicester, Loughborough and Mansfield) and these districts of the union account for around 71 per cent of the total membership. As its name implies, the union organises workers employed in the hosiery and knitwear industry, who are involved in the making-up process for ladies hosiery, underwear, full-fashioned outerwear, cut and sewn outerwear, half hose and socks, as well as warehousing and auxiliary jobs. The union also has a staff section (CATSA) which caters for workers such as supervisors, mechanics, warehouse workers, clerical staff and designers. The possibility of amalgamation with other specialist unions in the clothing, textile and footwear industries is now an item to which NUHKW is giving very serious consideration.

History

Trade unionism within the hosiery and knitwear industry stretches back for just over 200 years, and it has been the subject of numerous studies by two generations of economic historians. Before the introduction of the factory, hosiery workers were usually called framework knitters, and the hosiery industry was still largely a domestic industry in 1850. Garments were made up on a hand-driven stocking frame which stood either in the worker's own home or in a small workshop.

Hosiery trade unionism in its early days was characterised by a sharp distinction between the more highly paid and usually more highly unionised workers in the large towns in the Midlands (Leicester and Nottingham particularly) and the poorly paid, usually non-unionised village workers; a fragmentation into numerous small trade societies; and a strong dependence on economic prosperity. These three characteristics were to survive long after the supersession of the hand frame by the factory system around 1880.

One of the features of the hosiery industry during the 1860s was the emergence of a conciliation board for industry, largely due to the efforts of the Nottingham manufacturer, A. J. Mundella. The board adjudicated on all disputes regarding wages, and consisted of nine hosier representatives and nine workers' representatives, and was chaired by Mundella. In the last quarter of the nineteenth century the board was to become a model for institutionalised conciliation arrangements in many other industries, such as lace making, building trades and coal. However, Vic Allen suggests that it effectively 'disarmed trade unionism at a significant period of its growth'.

The 1914-18 war led to the establishment of strong employers' associations, an improvement in management/union relations, the establishment of national bargaining, and the inception of a Joint Industrial Council following the Whitley Committee's recommendations in 1917.

Before the end of 1920, the postwar boom came to an end, and the hosiery industry was in the depths of a major slump. The inter-war years from 1920 to 1939 were generally a period of high unemployment, falling memberships, dwindling finances, and sagging morale. Although the number of low cost, country factories continued to decline, new hosiery manufacturing regions began to develop in Lancashire and in London and the Home Counties, quite outside the control of the hosiery unions, and usually paying lower wages than in the Midlands.

During the 1920s the possibility of forming a national union was scarcely considered. In 1921 the unions were approached by Andrew Conley, the secretary of the *Tailor and Garment Workers' Union*, with proposals for an amalgamation. This was rejected out of hand. The TUC attempted to promote an amalgamation of the unions in the industry in 1923, again without success.

The first serious attempt to create a national union did not come until 1935, by which time the threat from the new hosiery districts was making the traditional structure of trade unionism appear totally anachronistic. Horace Moulden, general secretary of the *Leicester Union*, believed that the case for a national union was stronger than ever, but despite his close friendship with Jack Brewin of the Ilkeston Union, the talks collapsed in 1937, in the face of determined opposition from the *Hinckley Union*.

With the onset of war, the shortage of labour, the government's decision to control prices and profits in the industry and the importance of trade union co-operation in the war effort meant that the unions were soon to find themselves in a very favourable bargaining position. The unions' most important bargaining achievement in war years came in March 1945, with the signing of the first ever minimum wage agreement for the industry. A second major achievement for the Hosiery Federation was the establishment of a *Scottish Hosiery Union* with a membership of almost 2,500.

The common fear of the recruiting intentions of the TGWU and the GMWU, together with the decision of the Manufacturers' Federation in 1940 to admit firms to its membership without any obligation to observe JIC agreements, served to persuade the unions that the establishment of a national union was essential. The NUHKW came into existence on 1 January 1945, with Clifford Groocock as general secretary.

The first priority of the NUHKW was the need to increase its staffing level and to recruit hosiery workers in the new areas of the industry — in Lancashire, Yorkshire and the Home Counties. The growth of the NUHKW outside the Midlands inevitably brought it into conflict with other unions — particularly the TGWU, GMWU and the National Union of Dyers, Bleachers and Textile Workers. Particularly close relations existed between the NUHKW and the Tailors and Garment Workers' Union.

As the union gradually extended its organisation outside the Midlands, it faced the problem of maintaining its membership by setting up shop committees at the larger factories. The process of establishing an industrial union, representing all hosiery workers in the UK, was still far from completed in 1951.

The post-war years have seen an enormous increase in productivity in the hosiery industry, as a result of the introduction of new machinery, new methods of working and new fibres. While the industry's net output has trebled, the number of production workers employed in the industry has fallen. The industry's total labour force (including white-collar staff employees whose numbers have risen sharply) was in 1974 almost exactly the same size as in 1951. In such circumstances, the union's growth levelled out, and from December 1979 to December 1980, the total workforce in the British hosiery and knitwear industry fell by 12 per cent. Since then a steady stream of further redundancies reduced the union's membership from over 70,000 at the end of 1979 to its level of around 58,000 at the end of 1981. The prospect of continuing foreign competition makes it almost inevitable that in the near future NUHKW will merge with other unions in allied industries.

Union Officials

NUHKW employs three national officers, 12 district secretaries, six assistant district secretaries, and four district officers. The Rule Book of the union provides that fulltime officials must have been members of the union for a continuous period of at least three years and be not less than 21 years of age. Whilst most full-time officials in NUHKW have spent a large part of their working lives within the industry, a recent trend has developed whereby newly appointed, full-time officials tend to be in their early 30s and to have worked outside the industry.

Coverage

Around 70 per cent of the total membership of NUHKW is concentrated within the Midlands, and in many cases covers almost 100 per cent of the manual labour force. The total numbers employed in the hosiery and knitwear industry fell by 13,000 during 1980, with further redundancies taking place each month. Historical reasons account for such a large concentration within the Midlands area, and in some areas of the country the union only exists in small pockets of membership or is non-existent. Around 4,000 workers in the Borders area of Scotland (around Hawick) are members of the GMWU, a union which made a significant recruiting effort in the industry at the end of the second world war. The GMWU have their own separate agreement with the employers.

Organisation

The governing body of the NUHKW is the annual National Conference, which is comprised of all members of district committees plus full-time officers of the union, all of whom have voting rights at Conference.

The National Executive Committee comprises 13 lay members, one nominated from each district, and ten officers, including the general president and general secretary, and meets monthly. The officer members of the National Executive Committee, other than the general president and the general secretary, are elected by National Conference.

The union is divided up into 13 districts, all of which, with the exception of the staff section, are established on a geographical basis. The district committee is elected by the membership in each district and serves for a period of two years, elections being held annually when half the members retire, thus giving a continuity on the committee.

Rule 99 of the NUHKW provides for the establishment of an 'Inner Cabinet' consisting of the general president, general secretary, secretary, vice-president and four lay members. This body has the power under Rule 100 to act on behalf of the NEC between meetings.

Rules revision takes place every five years. The NEC appoints all full-time officials, and the general president and general secretary are appointed by election from nominations submitted by district committee from among existing full-time officials by a vote of delegates to the National Conference.

Workplace Activity

The union has membership in around 700 factories ranging in size from a few employees to large establishments, such as Courtaulds. The hosiery and knitwear industry is characterised by a heavy reliance on piecework, although the union's policy is to replace this method of payment by some form of time work or measured day work. This reliance on piecework gives ample scope for local bargaining, particularly in the larger establishments. In addition to this, the bargaining power of the union has been strengthened by the fact that labour costs in the industry account for only a small proportion of total costs. Wage bargaining is now almost entirely a matter for factory floor agreements, which are negotiated in conjunction with the local union official. Such bargaining is monitored by each of the sectional committees of the union which operate in particular sections of the industry.

Although the Rule Book expressly provides that factory committees 'shall not make, or cause to be made, any new agreements either on working hours, conditions, or wages without the consent of the district officer of the union', in practice this is often done, and factory committees have some degree of autonomy. However, it would be inaccurate to overstate the extent of workplace bargaining within the union. Workplace bargaining depends for its success on the support and activism of rank-and-file workers; as numerous resolutions to Conference calling for 'improved communications' in the union amply demonstrate, an apathetic membership within NUHKW appears to be as much the enemy of greater workplace control in the industry as is the degree of control exercised by the union's leadership.

Women

Women constitute some 73 per cent of NUHKW's membership, and thus the union is predominantly a female union. Despite this there is only one full-time officer, Helen McGrath, who was appointed as a district officer in November 1978. Men tend to dominate the most remunerative jobs in the industry — e.g. the dyeing and finishing trade.

Women usually account for around one-third of the membership of the union's district committees. The union also makes special provision in holding meetings at a time of the day which is most convenient for its women members.

At the 1982 NUHKW National Conference, delegates voted for a survey to be carried out by the NEC on the existence and extent of sexual harassment at work within the industry.

External Relations

Despite the early involvement of the hosiery unions in the TUC and the parliamentary committee in the late nineteenth century, NUHKW has never affiliated to the Labour Party. The Rule Book provides that 'affiliation to other bodies shall be on the direction of the national conference', and in recent years a decision to recommend affiliation has been passed comfortably at several conferences. In 1981, a ballot was held among members of the NUHKW which resulted in 13,414 voting to set up a political fund, with 17,054 votes against. The leadership of the union is strongly in favour of affiliation to the Labour Party and a further ballot will be held at a time which offers a 'more reasonable chance of success'.

Policy

NUHKW has consistently campaigned for the replacement of piecework in the industry by some form of measured day work or time work. It has a tradition of co-operation with the employers which can be traced back to the conciliation board system of the nineteenth century, reinforced during two world wars. In parallel to this NUHKW has also pursued a policy of co-operation with the government in the knitting industry strategy group. Of late, the union has become increasingly critical of the EEC and the decline of the UK textile industry, and its traditions of co-operation with government are under a great deal of strain.

At the 1982 National Conference, NUHKW delegates voted for a motion expressing total opposition to the acceptance by the British government of the US policy on the arms race and called for the closure of all British nuclear bases, a reduction in arms expenditure, the scrapping of the Cruise and Trident programmes, and a reversal of the decision to site the neutron bomb in Europe.

Conference delegates also voted for the introduction of selective import controls, the restoration of exchange controls over the export of capital, and for the setting up of an enquiry into labour conditions and rights of workers 'in free trade or enterprise zones'.

Recent Events

A significant event in recent years has been the Multi-Fibre Agreement under the auspices of GATT regulating the trade in clothing and textiles between the developed and developing countries.

As adverse trade conditions continue, the NUHKW has seen its membership shrink rapidly from over 74,000 to 58,000 at the end of 1981. In recent years the creation of the union's staff section (CATSA) is one way in which NUHKW has been casting its recruitment net more widely. The union has also absorbed a number of very small local unions recently, representing workers either in the finishing trades or in other closely allied industries, the largest of which was the *Nottingham and District Hosiery Finishers' Association* in 1969 with a membership of 3,200.

The industry in which NUHKW operates is now experiencing a gradual blurring of craft distinctions and the recognition of the need to become part of a larger union. However, continuing discussions with unions in the clothing and textile industry have so far come to nothing. Efforts are still being made to agree proposals for amalgamation with the National Union of Tailors and Garment Workers (NUTGW).

The Mansfield Hosiery Mills dispute of 1972 was notorious for the NUHKW's connivance in racial discrimination in employment.

In 1982, David Lambert was elected to succeed Harold Gibson as general president of the union. After four eliminating ballots for the election of general secretary, George Marshall secured 95 votes against his rival Jack Matlock's 93 votes.

Further Reference

Richard Gurnham, *Hosiery Unions 1776-1976*, 197 pages, NUHKW 1976. The official history of the union sympathetically written and particularly illuminating on nineteenth century developments and serving as a useful bibliographical guide for historical sources.

V. L. Allen, 'The Origins of Industrial Conciliation and Arbitration', *International Review of Social History* IX, 1964. A critical view of the union's participation on the conciliation boards in the nineteenth century.

CIR Report No. 76 Mansfield Hosiery Mills Ltd. A report critical of the union's attitude towards immigrant workers.

Tailors and Garment Workers, National Union of
(NUTGW)

Head Office

16 Charles Square
London N1 6HP
01-251 9406

Divisional Offices

● *Eastern and Midlands*
Trade Union Offices
Club Street
Kettering
Northamptonshire
NN16 8RB

● *Ireland*
44 Elmwood Avenue
Belfast BT9 6BB

● *Leeds and Yorkshire*
Circle House
29 Lady Lane
Leeds L52 7LS

● *London and Southern*
45 Axe Street
Barking
Essex IG11 7LX

● *North East*
4 Cloth Market
Newcastle-on-Tyne NE1 1EX

● *North West*
409 Wilmslow Road
Withington
Manchester M20 9NB

● *Scotland*
Albany Chambers
534 Sauchiehall Street
Glasgow G2 3LX

● *Western*
14 North Road
Cardiff CF1 3DY

The union also has 16 area offices within the eight divisions.

Principal Officers

General Secretary —
A. R. Smith
Deputy General Secretary —
Anne Spencer

Membership (1982)

Male 7,825
Female 73,936
Total 81,761

Union Journal and Publications

The Garment Worker — monthly. The NUTGW has also published a pamphlet: *Employment in Clothing: A Struggle for Survival,* 19 pages, which sets out to describe the economic factors that have led to a decline in the clothing industry and the action that has been taken to attempt to stem this decline. The union is currently preparing a pamphlet on the effects on the industry of changes in the law relating to the employment of women in the wake of the Equal Opportunities Commission proposals in that area.

General

The NUTGW is the largest union in the clothing and textile industries, with around 90 per cent of its membership being female. In the three years from May 1979 the clothing industry lost 65,000 jobs in the U.K. The job losses have been concentrated in the larger factories and in tailored outerwear, the areas where the union has the highest level of organisation. Recruitment of members at previously unorganised factories has been insufficient to offset the large membership decline, although the NUTGW has managed to recruit more white-collar workers into its clerical and supervisory section.

A large proportion of the union's membership is employed in wages council sectors. The NUTGW merged with the two small felt hatters' unions (the *Amalgamated Society of Journeymen Felt Hatters and Allied Workers* and the *Amalgamated Felt Hat Trimmers', Woolformers' and Allied Workers' Association*) in October 1982.

History

In the very early days, the tailor made the entire garment with his own hands. In London the best hand-made garments were made by what is known as the retail bespoke or the West End trade. Division of labour in the industry began when work was parcelled out to apprentices. Later, the journeyman who worked at home employed his wife or daughter to help him with the tasks. By the middle of the nineteenth century it was common practice for a journeyman, a wage earner who worked for a master contractor, to employ one or two 'kippers', that is female tailors. The invention of the treadle sewing machine made further inroads in the handicraft trade when it became customary to make parts of the garment by machine.

In the early and middle nineteenth century, Scandinavian and German tailors entered the London clothing industry and brought with them new skills in ladies' tailoring. The middle of the nineteenth century also witnessed the growth of 'sweated labour'. Some of the master tailors set up premises in the East End of London and hired a small number of workers. The wages of the female homeworkers were exceedingly low — and the jobs often performed by dockers' wives. In Leeds, however, there was no cheap inelastic supply of female labour, and thus the self-contained 'factory' was more common. Homework thus multiplied in London, but not in Leeds.

The immigration of Russian and Polish Jews into Britain in the 1880s and 1890s brought innovations into the tailoring industry, which led to homeworkers themselves hiring their family and relatives and setting up shop with further sub-division of tasks to rationalise and increase their production. The 'sub-divisional' system of production became the exclusive province of the Jewish sub-contractor who combined a high degree of division of labour with relatively high wages. At the same time 'sweating' among the East End female homeworkers was so severe that it led to the Trade Board Act of 1909 — the forerunner of the wages council system. The

Trade Board Act was immediately applied to the ready-made and wholesale bespoke tailoring trades. The Act raised the wages of the female workers, but it scarcely affected the Jewish tailors — whose wages were generally above the legal minimum. The Act led to the drawing together of competing unions and to the formation of employers' associations.

Trade union organisation in tailoring had existed long before the Trade Board Act. London journeymen tailors were among the first craftsworkers in Britain to form trade unions. Organisation centred around local trade clubs at public houses. In 1833, the London tailors formed the *First Grand Lodge of Operative Tailors* which joined the *Grand National Consolidated Trade Union* inspired by Robert Owen. After a strike which was a total failure, this organisation was short lived.

In 1866 an amalgamation of many small societies with a membership of about 2,000 formed the *Amalgamated Society of Tailors*. Until world war one, this union confined its activities to recruiting the skilled handicraft tailors, and was conservative and pacific in its policies. Such conservatism led to a breakaway union being formed from its London West End branch in the form of the *London Society of Tailors and Tailoresses*.

The immigrant Jewish tailors from Poland and Russia formed trade unions during the last quarter of the nineteenth century — particularly in London. However, these unions were tiny and fragmented, and lacked any degree of permanence or stability. Anti-alien sentiment in England reached a peak towards the end of the nineteenth century, and this served to unite the Jewish unions. The *United Ladies' Tailors and Mantle Makers' Union* was a result of such unification when it was formed in 1901. This union had a continuous existence until 1939, when it amalgamated with the NUTGW.

The multiplicity and fragmentation of unions within the clothing industry continued until 1916, fuelled as it was by rivalry between Leeds and London, and anti-alien sentiment against the Jewish unions. Finally in 1916, the

Clothing Operatives and the *Amalgamated Jewish Tailors* — both with headquarters in Leeds — merged with the *London Society of Tailors*, the *London and Provincial Cutters* and the *London Tailors', Machinists' and Pressers'* Union. Thus, the *United Garment Workers' Union* was formed, the first clothing union to succeed in uniting the Jewish with the English workers, and cutters with the low paid factory women. In 1920 this amalgamation was followed by the addition of the *Scottish Operative Tailors and Tailoresses* and the industrial union was re-titled the *Tailors' and Garment Workers' Union*.

In 1932 the NUTGW assumed its present title when the *Amalgamated Society of Tailors* merged with the *Tailors and Garment Workers' Union*. The *United Ladies' Tailors and Mantle Makers' Union* merged with the NUTGW in 1939.

Union Officials

The NUTGW employs eight divisional officers and 32 area officers. All full-time officers, with the exception of the general secretary and assistant general secretary who are elected by a ballot of the membership, are appointed by the Executive Board. Divisional officers co-ordinate all the work in their division and are responsible to the Executive Board through the national officer.

Full-time officials in the union tend to have a long background within the clothing industry, with an age range of between 30–45 years of age although recently there has been a tendency for younger, full-time officials to be appointed from outside the union — usually graduates from Ruskin College, Oxford, or from the LSE. The clothing industry is characterised by a low level of workplace bargaining, and thus full-time officials tend to be fully stretched with a high degree of membership dependence on them.

Coverage

A large proportion of the NUTGW membership is employed in the wages council sector. The formation of a clothing manufacturing wages council by the amalgamation of seven wages councils has reduced the number of wages councils on which the NUTGW is represented from 12 to six. A similar amalgamation was due to come into effect in Northern Ireland in 1982. Both these amalgamations were the result of union initiatives.

There has also been an amalgamation of employers' associations recently so that the NUTGW is party to national agreements with only two: the British Clothing Industry Association and the Federation of Merchant Tailors.

The NUTGW is organised into eight divisions, and its membership is less concentrated regionally than associated unions like NUFLAT and NUHKW:

Division	Membership (Dec. 1981)	Per cent of Total
East and Midlands	10,182	12.5
Leeds and Yorkshire	14,178	17.4
London and Southern	4,845	5.9
North West	12,137	14.9
North East	11,147	13.7
Western	7,436	9.1
Scotland	12,621	15.5
Ireland	9,069	11.1
Total	81,625	100.0

Organisation

The supreme policy-making body in the union is the General Conference, which meets every two years. Delegates to the General Conference are elected from the 300 or so branches. The union's general management is vested in the 15-member Executive Board, which was re-constituted from 1 January 1980 to more adequately reflect the changing patterns within the clothing industry. A General Conference was held in 1981. The Executive Board consists of 15 lay members plus the general secretary (in a non-voting capacity). The lay members are elected by a ballot vote of the membership to serve for two years. At the end of this period they are eligible to stand for re-election.

The Executive Board meets at least quarterly and is responsible for the union's finances and property. The EB also appoints full-time officials and has the power to sanction official strikes. Both the general secretary and deputy general secretary are elected by a ballot vote of the whole membership. Jack Macgougan retired as general secretary at the termination of the 1979 General Conference, and his successfor Alec Smith, was elected unopposed. Anne Spencer was successful in a high poll as deputy general secretary, in spite of opposition from three other candidates — including the former national officer. The general secretary of the union also acts as its treasurer.

As with all other full-time officials, the national officer is appointed by the Executive Board, and is responsible for co-ordinating the activities of the union's divisional and area officers.

The NUTGW also has a system of divisional councils, which are comprised of the Executive Board members representing or residing in the division, the full-time officers serving in the division, and a number of rank-and-file representatives.

Workplace Activity

The union has around 2,200 shop stewards and around 300 branches. The clothing industry is characterised by a large number of small establishments which makes trade union organisation very difficult. Almost half the labour force of the clothing industry is employed in plants of under a hundred workers.

In a study by Boraston, Clegg and Rimmer (*Workplace and Union*), it was reported that in one particular district of the NUTGW there were nearly 4,000 members in three branches. Only one of these held meetings and had a branch committee. The work of the other two branches was transacted by the full-time officer who acted as secretary for all three branches, although he was served by a secretarial staff of three who enabled him to give most of his time to plant business.

Only a few large plants have head stewards, and shop stewards within the union tend to be inexperienced with most of their time on union business being devoted to piecework problems. There is a high turnover of stewards, and workplace organisation is characteristically weak, with a high dependence on the full-time officers. The union devotes a considerable amount of its resources to shop steward training, and provides each steward with a handbook giving practical advice on dealing with members' problems.

Women

Women constitute around 90 per cent of the NUTGW membership, the highest proportion of all TUC-affiliated unions with the exception of the Health Visitors' Association. There are only five women full-time officials in the NUTGW out of 40. Moreover, the most highly paid occupations within the clothing industry are largely the preserve of men. These are the cutters, the 'aristocrats' of the industry who negotiate a 'log' or task. The structure of the clothing industry means that chances of promotion are slim for women workers, because there are no posts available for promotion; although some women do become supervisors, they are seldom considered for managerial positions. It is commonly the case that factory grades consist only of machinists and managers, with sometimes a machinist in between.

The areas of the clothing industry where the proportion of women is highest are the manufacture of lingerie, hats, caps, dresses and shirts which are particularly poorly paid. Wage rates in sectors such as outerwear and rainwear, where more men are employed, are significantly higher. (See *Department of Employment Gazette*, October 1973).

Three out of every four delegates to the NUTGW Conference in 1981 were women, and in 1981 elections to the Executive Board the membership elected six women and nine men.

External Relations

The NUTGW is affiliated to the Labour Party, the Irish Congress of Trade Unions (ICTU), the General Federation of Trade Unons (GFTU) and the International Textile, Garment and Leatherworkers' Federation (ITGLWF).

The General Secretary, Alec

Smith, was elected to the TUC General Council to replace Jack Macgougan in September 1979. Alec Smith also chairs the TUC Textile, Clothing and Footwear Industries Committee, which consists of four TUC General Council members and 29 representatives of unions in the cotton and allied textiles, wool textiles, synthetic fibre, clothing, hosiery and knitwear, carpet, dyeing and finishing, and footwear and leather industries. Four other NUTGW officers also sit on the committee. The union also nominates five representatives to serve on the Clothing and Allied Products Industry Training Board.

Policy

The NUTGW ranks tenth of the top 20 trade unions in female membership, and given its high proportion of women members one would expect that women's issues would receive a high degree of priority in its policy. In 1977 the union moved a resolution at the Trades Union Congress calling for amendments to the Equal Pay Act to give effect to the International Labour Organisation formula of equal pay for work of equal value.

The union has also been concerned with the report of the Equal Opportunities Commission which recommended that, with few exceptions, the hours-of-work provisions in the Factories Act should be abolished. The union moved a resolution at the 1979 Trades Union Congress, stating that a first principle concerning the working life of all must be their health, safety and welfare, and called for discussions to be initiated with the Health and Safety Commission with a view to extending the protection afforded at present to women on night work and shiftwork to men and to those other categories of women at present without such protective legislation.

A long term concern of the NUTGW has been the issue of low cost imports into the footwear, leather and allied trades, hosiery and knitwear, and clothing industries. The union has supported motions calling for import controls at the TUC in 1972, 1976 and 1977. It also played an important role in the initiation of the investigation of social and economic conditions in Hong Kong by Professor H. A. Turner, following resolutions by the NUTGW in 1974 and 1977.

The union is attempting to organise homeworkers, many of whom are exploited by unscrupulous employers in the garment industry, but seems powerless to effect any improvement in their conditions.

Recent Events

The primary concern of the NUTGW has been to fight for the retention of a UK clothing industry which is viable and secure. Concerted action by the NUTGW and the trade associations in the clothing industry led to the Labour government taking a firm line within the EEC on the renewal of the GATT Multi-fibre Arrangement. The EEC negotiated a whole series of such agreements and, in the case of the UK, 98 per cent of all low cost textile and clothing imports are now covered by import restraint measures.

More than four jobs in every ten were lost in the UK clothing industry in the 25 years to 1976. The industry, in 1951, employed over half a million workers — 118,000 men and 434,000 women. This represented 7.9 per cent of total employment in manufacturing industry. By 1977 the numbers employed had shrunk to 57,000 men and 256,000 women. In the three years from May 1979 the clothing industry lost a further 65,000 jobs in the UK, mainly in larger factories and in tailored outerwear — areas of high union concentration. The membership decline of the NUTGW accelerated rapidly from 117,362 at the end of 1980 to 81,761 at the end of 1981.

The union is now reaching a point where amalgamation with other unions is increasingly likely. It is possible that the NUTGW may merge with its sister unions NUHKW and NUFLAT, given their common problems of increased foreign competition and a declining workforce, although the NUTGW's affiliation to the Labour Party could prevent the largely apathetic and apolitical female memberships of its two sister unions voting for amalgamation. In 1973 and 1974 talks were held with the *National Union of Dyers, Bleachers and Textile Workers* (NUDBTW) and the *Trans-*

port and General Workers' Union (TGWU) but the amalgamation proposals led nowhere. Talks with the NUDBTW were renewed in 1977 but again broke down, largely over pension fund differences between the two unions. However, the question of amalgamation of some sort is becoming increasingly urgent.

Closed shop agreements were concluded wih 65 different employers up to 1979.

A strike ended in Salford in July 1980 with a victory for 70 women machinists who stopped work to fight for their right to belong to a trade union. The 11-week strike began when the women were sacked by management at Klein Brothers Ltd after joining the NUTGW. Helped by local trade unionists, they organised an effective picket and a boycott of Klein's goods — menswear marketed under the Bendyck label. Despite attempts to break the strike by contracting production out to smaller firms and homeworkers, the management was eventually forced to agree to talks with ACAS. The women returned to work after a guarantee that a ballot on union recognition would be held at the factory.

The largest strike in the history of the union occurred in 1982 when a five month dispute over union recognition at Rulecan Ltd, Runcorn, ended with the company going into liquidation. Fifty union members were sacked for walking out after the company cut wages and withdrew recognition from the union. A feature of the dispute was the company's use of the 1980 Employment Act in threatening and seeking injunctions against NUTGW officers and USDAW members at a

mail order company who had taken sympathetic action.

The union was campaigning in 1982 against worsening conditions in the East End of London. Employers who were being forced by the Inland Revenue to comply with normal employment practice were attempting to impose unsatisfactory terms and conditions. Attempts were made to get workers to sign 'agreements' to be paid on a 'self employed' basis which would have deprived them of all employment rights, including even such basic rights as paid holidays. The campaign produced some success in recruitment, particularly among Turkish workers.

Further Reference

Margaret Stewart and Leslie Hunter, *The Needle Is Threaded*, Heinemann/Newman Nearne 1964. An historical account of unions in the clothing industry.

Shirley W. Lerner, *Breakaway Unions and the Small Trade Union*, Allen & Unwin 1961. A fascinating account of the rivalries of the many unions in the clothing industry leading up to the formation of the NUTGW in 1939.

Boraston, Clegg and Rimmer, *Workplace and Union*, 1975. This book, which is essentially a study of workplace industrial relations in a number of unions, has a small section devoted to the NUTGW.

For a fuller account of the position of women workers in the clothing industry: *Women at Work*, Tavistock 1977, provides an excellent contemporary picture. It also exposes the appalling treatment of women homeworkers in the garment industry by unscrupulous employers.

Group Thirteen **Glass, Ceramics, Chemicals, Food, Drink, Tobacco, Brushmaking and Distribution**

Bakers, Food and Allied Workers' Union

Head Office

Stanborough House
Great North Road
Stanborough
Welwyn Garden City
Hertfordshire AL8 7TA
07072-60150

Principal Officers

General Secretary —
Joe Marino
National President — T. O'Neill

Membership (1982)

Male 22,820
Female 17,740
Total 40,560

Union Journal

The Food Worker, 12 pence.

Regional Officers

● *P. Sagoo*
'Danecourt'
26 Church Hill
Walthamstow
London E17 9RY

● *G. Martin*
Royal Exchange Building
Room 169
Mount Stuart Square
Cardiff

● *J. Bryan*
4th Floor, Room 29
Grenville Buildings
12 Cherry Street
Birmingham B2 5AR

● *A. Sprawson*
86 Deepdale Road
Preston
Lancashire PR1 5AR

● *W. Molloy*
10 Greenside Road
Pudsey
West Yorkshire LS28 8PU

General

The union deals with four national agreements, these being with the Federation of Bakers (covering the bulk of the union's membership), the National Association of Master Bakers (small bakeries) and the Plant Cake agreement and the Co-op agreement. It also has partial responsibility for the National JIC Biscuit Workers agreement. There are also members in the retail bread and flour confectionery trades. Obviously, a major item of plant level negotiation is overtime and shift work.

History

Trade unionism in baking began in 1849 in the house of a Mr Hollingworth in Manchester where operative bakers met for friendly society purposes. There was then no limit to hours worked (a bill to prohibit night work in baking had been thrown out in 1848) and a living-in system existed which meant that workers practically lived on the job. A code of rules of the *Amalgamated Union of Operative Bakers of England* was drawn up in 1861 and in 1864 Thomas Hudson was elected part-time general secretary. In 1883 John Jenkins became general secretary and in the *annus mirabilis* of the new unions, 1889, a bakers' strike took place in London, but with no clear result. A Whitley council called the Joint Council for Bread, Baking and Flour confectionery was set up in 1918 but did not survive long.

Throughout the union's existence it has campaigned against night work in the baking industry. In 1919 the Mackenzie committee of enquiry on night baking reported that it was objectionable on social grounds. W. Banfield who became general secretary in 1915 worked vigorously to abolish night work, especially after being elected to parliament in 1932. In 1938 a private members' bill was successful and its effect was to prohibit night work from 11 p.m. to 5 a.m., but it was conditional on the absence of a trade board for the industry so that the employers countered by setting up a trade board, later superseded by a wages council.

By 1958 various national agreements had effectively limited night working in those parts of the industry that were union organised.

In 1940 the union extended its activities to include biscuit workers and it has since expanded into other areas of food production.

Organisation

For the purpose of government the union is divided into:

(a) an Annual Conference of Delegates elected by the members;

(b) an Executive Council elected at Annual Conference;

(c) five regions;

(d) districts consisting of geographically grouped branches.

Shop stewards are the 'recognised medium intervening with the employer on workshop grievances and on any proposed changes to existing shop practices'. Rule 14.62 also states that 'shop stewards will avail themselves of such opportunities as may be offered by the union to increase their understanding of trade unionism in general and the wages structure and legislation affecting our trade in particular.'

In any district where there are two or more branches, there is a district board, composed of delegates from the branches, which meets quarterly. The appointment of all organising district secretaries is sanctioned by the Executive Council. Those nominated for such jobs by the branches may be required to take a test before proceeding to ballot election by postal vote.

The Executive Council co-ordinates the districts into five regions, each region being administered by a regional board of three members from and elected by each district board within the region. The regional boards also meet quarterly. In each region there is a regional officer appointed by the Executive Council of the union.

Nominations from the branches are taken for vacancies as general secretary and president but the Executive Council still acts as a selection committee and can issue test papers and make a selection of candidates for election. Elections are by ballot postcards issued to every member and then sent to a firm of accountants appointed by the Executive Council.

External Relations

The Bakers' Union is affiliated to CND. In the Labour Party Deputy Leadership election it delivered its card vote for Tony Benn.

Recent Events

In both December 1974 and December 1978 the union took official strike action in support of claims for increases in basic rates of pay. In 1974 the union achieved an award after arbitration which was generally acceptable throughout the industry, but the outcome of the 1978 strike cannot be construed as anything other than a defeat. There was a tactical miscalculation and many bakery workers either did not come out in response to the strike call or began to return to work very soon after going on strike so that, by the end, more than half were ignoring union instructions. This disunity was exploited in sections of the press and radio and television news.

In addition, the Transport and General Workers' Union and the General and Municipal Workers' Union were slow to assist the Baker's Union. They did not 'black' flour mills and hence flour continued to enter the bakeries. The Bakers' Union 'flying pickets' were ineffective.

The structure of the industry is such that it is extremely difficult for the union to mount effective action. The large baking establishments of Allied Bakeries and Rank Hovis McDougal would be easy targets to hit by strike action, but they have automated processes so that managers were able to take over the production lines quite effectively. Another reason that there was no bread shortage for the final consumer was that smaller baking companies (outside the Bakers' Federation) either agreed to pay employees more than the federation offer or could keep going anyway because employees were not unionised.

The economics of the bread producing industry have changed. The supposed economies of large scale automated production have been reduced by increased administrative and transport costs. Furthermore the industry has for some time had considerable excess capacity, thus weakening the position of the union.

At the Annual Conference that followed the six-week strike, delegates voted to hold ballots before national strikes could be called, the main argument being that members who in fact, continued to work and crossed picket lines during the strike would have struck if they had had an opportunity to vote.

In 1979 Sam Maddox died while in office, necessitating an election for general secretary. Following a written test under TUC supervision, the candidates went forward to a secret ballot of the union membership. Joe Marino, a left-wing trade unionist was clearly elected.

Membership fell drastically after the 1978 strike by around 17,000 workers in federation bakeries (all other bakeries were unaffected), and although there was some recovery as a result of vigorous recruitment efforts, it has been difficult to maintain membership in the face of closures and lay-offs.

In one example of a concerted recruitment campaign at the King Henry Pie bakery in Manchester, initial success was followed by redundancies and replacement staff were reluctant to join. In the end a ballot on union recognition conducted by ACAS was lost by 56 to 27.

Further Reference

Bakers' Union: Our history 1849-1977, Bakers, Food and Allied Workers' Union.

Blind and Disabled, National League of

Head Office

2 Tenterden Road
London N17 8BE
01-808 6030

Principal Officer

General Secretary—
M. A. Barrett

Membership (1982)

Total 3,115

Union Journal

The Advocate— quarterly.

General

Founded in 1899 as the National League of the Blind, the league took its present title in 1968. Members are in a variety of trades such as bedding, upholstery, wire, machine knitwear, boxmaking, light engineering, weaving, boot repair, braille printing, telephone operating, basket, brush and matting trades.

Policy

At the 1977 Congress, the League put a motion to remove sex discrimination as applied to Family Income Supplement. Motions on mobility needs of the disabled and disability allowances for severely disabled people were put forward.

Brushmakers and General Workers, National Society of

(NSBGW)

Head Office

20 The Parade
Watford WD1 2AA
0923-21950

Principal Officer

General Secretary—
A. J. Parsons

Membership (1982)
Male 365
Female 360
Total 725

General

The brushmakers' trade union has the distinction of being the oldest trade union with the longest continuous existence in the world. In fact, its origins can be traced back to 1747; and it is known that a Brushmakers' Benevolent Institute was established in 1828 to act for all the local societies of the day, those for which records still exist including Manchester (formed (1747), Bristol (1782), Lyme Regis (1786), Leeds (1791) and London (1806) which acted as the head sociey of the national union. The *National Union of Brushmakers* was formed early in the twentieth century, and the addition of 'General Workers' to the title took place in 1971. The union was one of those expelled from the TUC for failing to comply with TUC policy on non-registration under the Industrial Relations Act 1971. Membership is declining rapidly (from 2,575 in 1971 to its present level of 725).

Further Reference

William Kiddier, *The Old Trade Unions: From Unprinted Records of the Brushmakers*, Allen & Unwin 1931.

Ceramic and Allied Trades Union
(CATU)

Head Office

Hillcrest House
Garth Street
Hanley
Stoke-on-Trent ST1 2AB
0782-24201/2/3

Principal Officers

General Secretary—
  A. W. Clowes
Assistant General Secretary—
  H. Hammersley
Organisers— A. Martin
  J. K. W. Arnold
  G. Bagnall
  C. J. Fawkes

Membership (1982)

Male 15,174
Female 15,000
Total 30,174

General

This union was first founded around 1827 as a craft union of Operative Potters, later becoming the *National Society of Male and Female Pottery Operatives* and in 1919 the *National Society of Pottery Workers*. In 1970 it became the *Ceramic and Allied Trades Union*. At first it organised only pottery workers but later workers in allied trades and throughout the industry were recruited. The union has also begun to recruit white-collar workers. Membership is mainly in the North Staffordshire area. The union was in favour, as official policy, of entry into the EEC. Its officers are influential in the General Federation of Trade Unions.

Recent Events

Britain's pottery industry has been in great difficulties. Because half of the total output is usually exported, the industry suffered from the high exchange rate. The American market which traditionally takes up to 25 per cent of production has dried up and home sales dropped by 30 per cent in 1980. The workers' real wages have consequently suffered.

Further Reference

William H. Warburton, *The History of Trade Union Organisation in the North Staffordshire Potteries*, Allen & Unwin 1931.
Frank Burchill and Richard Ross, *A History of the Potters' Union*, Ceramic and Allied Trades Union 1977.

Co-operative Officials, National Association of
(NACO)

Head Office

Saxone House
56 Market Street
Manchester M1 1PW
061-834-6029/6020

Principal Officers

General Secretary—
  L. W. Ewing
Assistant General Secretary—
  K. Yorath
Assistant Secretary—
  D. Williams

Membership (1982)

Male 5,372
Female 322
Total 5,694

Union Journal

NACO and the Co-operative Press Ltd jointly edit a monthly journal entitled *Co-operative Marketing and Management* which has a section reserved within it for NACO material. It is distributed to all NACO members.

General

NACO caters for all officials and managers employed by the co-operative movement: managerial personnel with retail, wholesale and productive societies, and the Co-operative Insurance Society. The coverage of NACO membership extends into a wide range of industries — particularly in retailing. The membership of NACO has declined in line with the contraction and rationalisation of the co-operative movement generally — from about 8,500 in 1966 — although the merger of the CWS with the Scottish CWS helped to offset this decline. NACO faces some competition from the white-collar section of USDAW (SATA) and ASTMS, although there are strong indications that it is holding its own.

History

NACO was formed in 1971 by an amalgamation of the former *National Union of Co-operative Officials*, *National Co-operative Managers' Association Ltd* and the *Co-operative Secretaries' Association*. The *National Union of Co-operative Officials* was formed in 1917; NACO was one of the first trade unions to organise management at all levels.

Union Officials

The only full-time officials employed by NACO are the principal officers as above.

Organisation

The supreme ruling body in the union is the Annual General Meeting. The national executive of NACO is entitled the General Council, which is comprised of 22 people elected sectionally on a geographical basis by postal ballot. The branches, of which there are 65, are called constituent associations. There are also loose associations of craft managers (e.g. CIS managers, butchery managers, laundry managers etc.) organised nationally within the union to cater for sectional interest groups. There is also an appeals tribunal which serves as the ultimate appeals body to deal with matters relating to expulsion of members, refusal to admit into membership, and actions taken by NACO officials which may be considered to be contrary to the rules of the union. All full-time officials are appointed by the General Council. The Rule Book provides that industrial action can only be taken with the approval of the General Council by a two-thirds majority vote of that body.

Workplace Activity

The 62 constituent associations in NACO comprise 20 district associations consisting of various categories of managers in one area. Nineteen district craft associations, 13 national craft managers' associations, three CWS representatives' associations, three regional CWS associations, and four secretarial associations. Generally speaking, there is little workplace activity amongst the NACO membership.

Women

There are only 322 female members out of a total of 5,694 NACO members, although in 1979-80 the women membership doubled. There are no women on the General Council nor are women's affairs given any separate representation by the union. To a large extent, the small number of women in NACO is a reflection of the fact that few women reach managerial posts in the co-operative movement. Two thirds of NACO women are located in the retail societies, (mainly in drapery, fashions and womenswear) whilst the other third are employed by the CWS.

External Relations

NACO has no formal political affiliation to any party, nor has it any sponsored MPs. However, a number of NACO members are Labour and Co-operative MPs, including Ted Graham, MP for Edmonton. The full-time officials of the Co-operative Party are NACO members. The union is keen to stress its 'non-political' stance, despite its association with the co-operative movement.

Policy

NACO policy is largely centred around its collective bargaining function within the co-operative movement, and it has generally fostered close relations with management.

NACO runs some 15 educational conferences and seminars each year in an attempt to improve the management skills of its members.

Recent Events

There have been several approaches to NACO by both USDAW and ASTMS, with a view to amalgamation, but NACO has seen no overriding advantage in merger.

Licensed House Managers, National Association of
(NALHM)

Head Office

9 Coombe Lane
London SW20 8NE
01-947 3080/5941

Principal Officers

National Secretary —
H. Shindler

Membership (1982)

Male 11,643
Female 6,111
Total 17,754

Union Journal

NALHM News — produced at irregular intervals; 10,000 copies are distributed via branches.

General

The union was formed in 1969, prior to which managers' interests were represented by the managers section of the National Federation of Licensed Victuallers.

The union holds sole bargaining rights for licensed house managers with the major breweries and has several post-entry closed shop agreements.

It is organised into regions and branches. There is a full-time organiser for each region.

There is an Annual Conference in April. A regional committee composed of delegates from branches serves each region and the regional committee appoints its representatives to serve on the National Committee. The Executive and Finance Committee consists of the national officers plus three members elected from the National Committee.

Recent Events

From 1975-77 NALHM was engaged in a long running jurisdictional dispute with the Transport and General Workers' Union over the right to recruit pub managers in the Birmingham area. Trouble chiefly centred around a pub called the Fox and Goose, blacked by brewers' drivers, members of the TGWU, which became known as the 'pub with no beer'. In the end the ruling of the TUC disputes committee under the Bridlington Principles was endorsed by Conference and the TGWU accepted the ruling.

Shop, Distributive and Allied Workers, Union of
(USDAW)

Head Office

'Oakley'
188 Wilmslow Road
Fallowfield
Manchester M14 6LJ
061-224 2804

Principal Officers

General Secretary —
Bill Whatley

Deputy General Secretary —
John Flood
President — S. Tierney
Adminstration Officer —
Geoff Walker
*Central Treasurer and
Executive Officer* —
A. W. Hilton

National Officers

Sid Williams
Les Watson
Garfield Davis
Michael Gordon
G. Martin
Syd Tierney
Terry Sullivan
Bill Connor
Bill Cowan

Membership (1982)

Male 165,970
Female 271,884
Total 437,854

Union Journal

USDAW produces a monthly journal, *Dawn*, with a circulation around 126,000, which is distributed in bulk to the membership via branch secretaries. The union does not publish any specialist pamphlets.

Union Offices

USDAW is divided into eight divisions, and the union employs 125 area organisers spread throughout the divisions in addition to its national and divisional offices. Divisional officers are located at the following USDAW offices:

● *South Wales and Western Division*
W. J. Jones MBE, JP
Caerwys House
1 Windsor Lane
Cardiff CF1 3RN
0222-25626

● *Eastern Division*
T. P. Callinan
'Dilke House'
Malet Street
LondonWC1E 7JA
01-580 8641

● *Midlands Division*
J. Toogood
10 Pershore Street
Birmingham B5 4HT
021-622 2995

● *North Western Division*
J. W. Gardner
145 Edge Lane
Liverpool L7 2PG
051-263 7521

● *Manchester Division*
J. C. Callahan
13 Warwick Road
Old Trafford
Manchester M16 0QX
061-872 3527

● *North Eastern Division*
N. B. Capindale
Concord House
Park Lane
Leeds LS3 1EJ
0532-441881

● *Scottish Division*
Bill Cowan
'Muirfield'
342 Albert Drive
Glasgow G41 5PG
041-427 1121

● *Southern Division*
R. A. Hammond
'Dilke House'
Malet Street
London WC1E 7JA
01-580 8641

There are 25 other USDAW offices throughout the eight divisions.

General

USDAW is the sixth largest union in Britain. It came into being on 1 January 1947, upon the amalgamation of the *National Union of Distributive and Allied Workers* (NUDAW) and the *National Amalgamated Union of Shop Assistants, Warehousemen and Clerks* (NAUSAWC). USDAW membership is distributed approximately as follows: around 140,000 are employed by retail co-operative societies and Co-operative Retail Services (about 31 per cent); 20,000 (just under 5 per cent) are employed by the Co-operative Wholesale Society (CWS); around 120,000 (26 per cent) are employed in private retail distributive trades — including shoeshops, menswear, food stores etc.; approximately 140,000 work in the industrial sector (just over 30 per cent), particularly in chemicals, food manufacturing, milk processing and distribution and transport; and about 25,000 are located in the optical, hairdressing, credit collection and other miscellaneous trades. USDAW has a white-collar section— SATA, the Supervisory, Administrative and Technical Association — with around 12,000 members, as well as an insurance section.

Around 60 per cent of USDAW's membership is female, although there are only three women members on the 16 strong Executive Council, and the union has no female national or divisional officers.

The long serving general secretary, Lord Allen, retired from the union in May 1979 and was replaced by Bill Whatley who succeeded Lord Allen on the TUC General Council from September 1979.

Despite the economic recession during 1980–82, USDAW's membership held up remarkably well at 438,000, a small decline from its level of 470,000 two year's previously.

History

USDAW was formed by the amalgamation of the *National Union of Distributive and Allied Workers* (NUDAW) and the *National Amalgamated Union of Shop Assistants, Warehousemen and Clerks* (NAUSAWC) in 1947. Both these unions grew out of smaller local unions which gradually increased in size and scope and merged with one another. NUDAW and its forerunners concentrated their organisation efforts mainly on workers in co-operative employment. In 1921, following an amalgamation between the *Amalgamated Union of Co-operative Employees* and the *Warehouse and General Workers' Union*, NUDAW came into being with a membership of 105,000. By contrast, NAUSAWC and its forerunners organised the private retailing and wholesaling sector, by the recruitment of shop assistants and, later, warehouse workers and clerks into the union. By 1920, following the absorption of the *National Association of Grocers' Assistants*, the membership had grown to 86,000. Following further amalgamations, NAUSAWC (108,781 members) and

NUDAW (267,497 members) merged together in 1947 to create USDAW.

The latest addition to the union is the Scottish bakers section which was formed from the transfer of engagements of the *Scottish Union of Bakers and Allied Workers* to USDAW in January 1978.

Union Officials

USDAW employs 114 area organisers spread throughout the eight divisions, as well as its nine national officers, eight divisional officers, and eight deputy divisional officers. The union is comparatively well staffed by fulltime officials in relation to its membership size, and it also employs some 124 administrative personnel at its headquarters in Manchester.

There are obvious reasons why USDAW should employ so many staff. Every year the union has to recruit well over 100,000 new members in order to simply maintain its total membership size. For example, in 1981 the union recruited 100,780 new members. With such a high turnover of members, it is important that the administrative machinery of the union is run efficiently. Another reason is that there is a high dependence by the rank-and-file on the services of fulltime officials — particularly area organisers — as workplace bargaining at local level is weak (see **Workplace Activity**).

There is a very strong tradition within USDAW of appointing its officers from inside the union. Nearly all officials have at some time or another been branch secretaries or workplace activists, who are then 'promoted' to the level of area organiser. This career structure serves to act as an impediment to organisational change, with so many interests at stake. The former general secretary, Lord Allen, for example, served as a member of USDAW for 46 years, and had been an USDAW official since 1946. In recent years, however, there has been a slight tendency for area organisers to be appointed from outside the union, either from other unions, or from Ruskin College, Oxford.

USDAW operates an extensive education and training scheme which enables it to produce its own 'home-grown' officials. Priority is given to the training of workplace representatives in schools which are attended by about 900 people each year. Some 1,000 people enrol annually for the union's home study course, and each year preparatory courses are provided for those members who wish to develop the necessary knowledge and skills to occupy full-time positions within the union.

The office of president of USDAW is a lay office, but it can be held by a full-time official. Such an official retains a normal job and carries out the role as president as well. The current president, Syd Tierney, is also a national officer who works under the general secretary. Generally speaking USDAW presidents are either MPs or full-time officers, although the post of president is intended as a lay position. In April 1981 Tierney was re-elected President of USDAW for a third term.

Coverage

Roughly 200,000 of USDAW's membership are employed either by the Co-operative Wholesale Society or by retail co-operative societies. The co-operative sector membership (as a proportion of total membership) is declining rapidly as the union recruits new members in the retail trade outside the co-operative sector. This historical dependence on the co-operative sector accounts for the union's headquarters being sited in Manchester (some 23 per cent of the total membership of the union is located either in the Manchester or North Western divisions).

USDAW covers a wide range of occupations. The majority of members work in retail and wholesale distribution, but considerable numbers are engaged in food manufacturing, chemical processing industries, or service trades such as catering, laundries and hairdressing. The union organises shop managers as well as sales assistants, factory or warehouse supervisors along with operatives, drivers, clerks, insurance salespeople, butchers at abattoirs and milk rounders, in addition to meat packers and dairy process workers.

USDAW is represented on 16 wage councils, often alongside other unions, and thus is responsible for representing pockets of low paid workers in various sectors. USDAW is party to agreements covering various classes of worker in the following trades or industries:

Retail Co-operative Societies
Co-operative Wholesale Society Ltd
Retail distributive trades
Multiple wines and spirits
Multiple tailoring
Mail order
Hairdressing
Credit trade
Retail meat trade
Wholesale meat and kindred trades
Bacon curing industry
Milk industry
Catering
Baking trade
Flour milling
Seed crushing, compound and provender
Aerated waters
Laundry trade
Dental technicians
Gelatine and glue
Soap, candle and edible fats
Glass containers
Road haulage
Co-operative Retail Services Ltd
Co-operative Insurance Society
Multiple footwear
Retail multiple furnishing
Drapery and department stores
Pools industry
Check trade
Retail pharmacy
Multiple meat trade
Hide and skin
Wholesale grocery and provisions
Milk Marketing Board
NAAFI
Biscuit industry
Food manufacturing
Cocoa, chocolate and confectionery
Brewing industry
Opthalmic optical industry
Chemical and allied industries
Surgical dressings
Rubber manufacturing
Boot and shoe repairing

Organisation

The supreme-policy making body of the union is the Annual Delegate

Meeting, which meets for a period of four days usually towards the end of April. The union's general management is vested in the 16 member Executive Council which is elected by branch ballot. Voting papers containing the names of candidates are prepared and issued by the central office of USDAW to all branches. A special branch meeting is then convened to which all branch members are summoned. Only members who attend the branch meeting are entitled to vote. The whole membership figure of the branch is credited to the candidate receiving the most votes. This means, of course, that active members in large branches have more power than those in small branches. Moreover, it is not uncommon in some very large USDAW branches (with, say, a total membership of 5,000) for a vote to take place among the 100 or so members attending to vote, for a small majority in favour of one particular candidate to be translated into an apparent result of 5,000-nil.

Branches

There are more than 1,200 branches of the union throughout the UK. The majority of the union's branches are organised either on a single employer or trade basis. Most branches are either composed of members from the same employer (e.g. Kellogg's Ltd in Manchester) or of members working in one particular trade (e.g. multiple tailoring).

USDAW official handouts stress that, 'the branch structure of USDAW is designed so that members are grouped together where they have similar interests. Only in districts or towns where there are too few members to organise branches in this way are there mixed branches comprising members from a number of trades or employers.'

In fact, USDAW has many branches that cover huge areas and in which members work for many employers. Such branches are not conducive to the development of trade union consciousness or any sense of group identity. In such branches, which are generally described as area or holding branches, it is impossible to have any sense of employer or geographical identity in common, nor is it possible for members to acquaint themselves with other USDAW members in the same town, and it is almost impossible to effect links with trades councils and other bodies.

One example of such a huge area or holding branch is that of Birmingham dry goods. It draws its 1,400 members from an area covering Stafford, Worcester, Coventry and Dudley. Most of its members work in retail trades, e.g. newsagents, furniture, British Home Stores, Sketchley Cleaners, Allied Carpets etc. Within this huge area covered by the Birmingham dry goods branch there are other members of USDAW who are placed in other branches. This kind of branch organisation strengthens the power of the union hierarchy, since members are entirely dependent on the USDAW full-time officials whose deployment is controlled by divisional officers, and not the membership.

There are no rules in the USDAW Rule Book about the frequency of branch meetings, except that the branch must meet to cast its votes in the union elections. In practice, this means that a branch might only meet once a year. All other matters are dealt with by the branch committee (assuming there is one). In union elections, candidates can produce election addresses and send a bulk supply to central office, which then sends *one* copy to each branch.

Divisional councils

Divisional councils are based upon the eight divisions of the union throughout the country. Each divisional council is composed of ten members who are nominated and elected by the branches in each division every two years. Divisional councils meet usually once a month, together with the divisional officer. Divisional councils not only oversee the union's activities within the division but also negotiate local agreements on wages and conditions for members who are not covered by a national agreement.

Executive Council

The Executive Council comprises the union's president, general secretary, and 16 executive councillors (two from each of the eight divisions) who are nominated and elected every two years by branches in their division. Full-time officials of the union are eligible to stand for EC office, although the EC has been traditionally composed of an overwhelming majority of lay members. The Executive Council meets monthly.

Annual Delegate Meeting

Every USDAW branch is entitled to elect at least one delegate to attend and vote at the ADM. Branches with a membership of over 500 are entitled to one further delegate for every additional 500 members. The voting strength of a branch delegate(s) is equal to the total number of members of the branch the delegate represents.

Federations

Federations within USDAW are groupings of union branches in a locality or region. Branches elect representatives to attend federation meetings, which are usually held once a quarter. There are some 33 federations in USDAW, and their function is to stimulate the exchange of views between rank-and-file members and to arrange social and educational activities.

Trade conferences

Trade conferences have been held within USDAW since 1950. They are arranged annually or biennially for each of the trades or industries in which the union has substantial membership and where some form of negotiating machinery exists in which the union plays a substantial part. Each branch with the relevant trade interest elects its delegates to the appropriate national trade conference.

In the case of the retail co-operative trade and the retail private trades, delegates to the national trade conference are elected by specially convened divisional trade conferences.

In recent years the trade machinery has been adapted to provide for occasional conferences of delegates representing the union's membership in some of the large and widely spread

national companies (e.g. John Lewis department stores). Trade conferences are consultative and advisory and their decisions are subject to endorsement by the union's Executive Council.

USDAW also makes special provision for certain sections of membership, particularly 6,500 Co-operative Insurance Society agents, SATA, and the members of the former Scottish Bakers' Union.

Headquarters

To aid the Executive Council and its officers, USDAW headquarters maintain several departments. These are: audit, publicity and public relations, education and training, finance (including records and benefits), legal, organisation and method (including productivity), and research and economics.

The general secretary of USDAW is elected by a national vote of union branches, but once elected remains in office unless the ADM or a special delegate meeting dismisses him/her or calls upon him/her to resign.

Workplace Activity

There are around 20,000 USDAW shop stewards who are elected by workplace groups. USDAW rules provide that shop stewards are responsible at all times to the branch committee and serve for a period of two years. Shop stewards must be 18 years of age or over and have been a member of USDAW for at least 12 months and have attended at least 50 per cent of branch meetings.

Workplace bargaining is not very well developed in the trades or industries in which USDAW is represented, except perhaps in the industrial sectors such as the chemical industry. The lay membership of USDAW is generally disorganised, and has a high degree of dependence on the servicing of full-time officials. Given the fact that there is an annual membership turnover within the union at around 36 per cent, full-time officials are kept busy and workplace activity is minimal compared to other large unions. USDAW has initiated a new form of training for its shop stewards, involving a 'first aid' self-learning kit using video-tape technology. The video-film can be used on colour television sets at home or at work.

Women

USDAW has a high percentage of women members at around 60 per cent. A substantial proportion of women USDAW members work in retailing, which is a sector characterised by high turnover of membership and the employment of casual and seasonal workers. Around 15 per cent of women in USDAW are part-time workers, and whilst a closed shop agreement with co-operative stores exists to preserve union membership, it is doubtful if many women are union activists. There are no female full-time, national or divisional officers, nor are there females on USDAW's parliamentary panel (see **External Relations**).

The Executive Council submitted a document to the 1982 Annual Delegate Meeting entitled 'Women in USDAW'. This document tended to address itself to the problems of women in the trade union movement generally, and said little about USDAW itself. However, the EC committed itself to set up a working party during the following year 'to consider the whole question of equality between men and women in USDAW' and report back to the 1983 ADM. Although nearly two-thirds of USDAW members are women, only two out of 16 are on the EC, 17 out of 76 on divisional councils and nine out of 139 are negotiating officials.

External Relations

USDAW is affiliated to the Labour Party and maintains a parliamentary panel. At present it sponsors two Labour MPs:

T. Torney (Bradford South)
R. Powell (Ogmore)

In the 1979 general election, the union's President, Syd Tierney, lost his parliamentary seat at Birmingham, Yardley.

USDAW's Rule Book lays down a precise set of procedures for parliamentary sponsorship, with the union's branches voting every two years on candidates for the parliamentary panel. Despite the democratic rules governing USDAW sponsorship policy, there has been a strong oligarchic element in the union's selection policy. The necessary first step towards ultimate parliamentary membership has been the gaining of a full-time union post, and the chances of a rank-and-file USDAW member getting on to the panel are virtually nil. USDAW-sponsored MPs tend to be older and tend to come from the upper reaches of the union's hierarchy. This characteristic of USDAW parliamentary sponsorship policy is in keeping with the career structure in USDAW among its full-time officials in the industrial as well as the political field. The union's President, Syd Tierney, for example, was quickly found a full-time job in the union as a national officer following the loss of his seat in May 1979.

The General Secretary of USDAW, Bill Whatley, replaced his predecessor Lord Allen on the TUC General Council from September 1979.

The number of members paying the political levy at the end of 1981 was 404,654 representing 92.4 per cent of the total membership, and political contributions for the year amounted to £207,125. At the 1979 and 1980 Labour Party conferences, USDAW cast its votes against all three proposals for constitutional change — very much in line with its historical tradition of allying itself on the right of the Labour Party.

USDAW contributed £5,000 to the Trade Unions for a Labour Victory Voluntary Levy Fund in 1981, and supported Denis Healey in both ballots in the 1981 Labour Party Deputy Leadership contest. The union's proposition that the Labour Party Leader and Deputy Leader be elected by an electoral college based on 40 per cent of votes going to trade unions, 30 per cent to constituency parties and 30 per cent to MPs was carried at the 1981 Wembley Labour Party Conference.

TUC Delegation

USDAW sends 26 elected delegates to Congress, of whom six are union employees. In addition, the Executive Council can appoint an *unlimited number* of additional delegates, and does appoint a substantial number, normally EC members and central office officials.

Labour Party Conference Delegation

USDAW sends 18 elected delegates to the annual Labour Party Conference, of whom four are union employees. In addition, all USDAW-sponsored MPs (at present two) are added to the delegation, with full voting rights, and the Executive Council can appoint an *unlimited number* of additional delegates. The EC generally appoints a substantial number; normally, the delegation consists of 34 to 36 people (with votes) with only 18 elected.

The USDAW delegations to both the TUC and the Labour Party Conference are bound by rule to follow the decisions of the Annual Delegate Meeting. However, in cases where the mandate is vague or ambiguous, or where a motion has parts which both accord and conflict with the mandate, or where there is no mandate, then the decision is within the discretion of the delegation — and not the Executive Council. The *composition* of USDAW delegations to both wings of the labour movement is therefore an important matter.

The 1982 USDAW ADM gave 'qualified support to the Labour Party inquiry into the Militant Tendency' but stated its unwillingness for the Labour Party to embark on a policy of expulsions. The same motion emphasised the union's support for the full development of Labour Party democracy and 'changes which will help to ensure that the democratically agreed policies decided by Annual Conference will be followed by a future Labour government'.

Policy

USDAW has been instrumental in supporting several resolutions at recent Trades Union Congresses. It has consistently supported motions relating to the problem of the low paid worker, and has called for the implementation of a minimum earnings guarantee. It has also given its support to women's rights in employment. For instance, it proposed a mo-

tion at the 1976 Trades Union Congress requesting the government to amend the Equal Pay Act 1970 to provide for equal pay for work of 'equal value' instead of equal pay for work 'of the same or broadly similar nature'. USDAW was one of the leading supporters amongst unions in supporting the Social Contract between the TUC and the Labour government in 1975. USDAW has always opposed Sunday trading (see **Recent Events**).

At the 1981 TUC Congress USDAW's Executive Council submitted two propositions, one on 'Women's Rights to Full Employment' and the other on 'Industrial Training Boards'. The first proposition was combined with a number of similar propositions covering 'Women's Unemployment' and was adopted by Congress. The second proposition was also combined with a number of similar propositions dealing with 'Industrial Training' and was again adopted by Congress.

At the 1982 ADM, delegates voted for supporting the decision of the 1981 Labour Party Conference calling for unilateral disarmament by Britain and the scrapping of all nuclear weapons and the cancellation of the Trident projects. This decision particularly pleased the broad-left group in USDAW, who, whilst weak in the union as a whole, are nevertheless well organised. The broad left group is by now well established at USDAW ADMs, and although it has been largely unsuccessful in union elections, is nevertheless an important development.

The 1982 ADM also supported the struggle against victimisation and dismissal, organised by the union of black workers at the South African subsidiary of Rowntree-Mackintosh. This campaign was also sponsored by the GMWU, the TGWU and the Anti-Apartheid Movement.

An emergency motion on the Falkland Islands/Malvinas called on the government 'to negotiate an honourable settlement' and 'take no military action to resolve the dispute'.

Recent Events

Despite a notable upsurge in membership in 1979, USDAW, like nearly all other unions, has experienced a decline in membership from 1980 onwards, although its membership loss was not as bad as had been feared.

USDAW faces many new challenges in the 1980s, largely resulting from the changing pattern of retailing. There has been a decrease in the overall total of retail units in Britain, and a tendency for an increase in unit size with the arrival of the supermarket and hypermarket. Moreover, the effects of the microprocessor in retailing, warehousing and distribution will have profound effects on the retail trade and USDAW members in particular.

The recession in the retail trade is a constant source of worry for the union, and the 1982 ADM deplored the decision of Woolworths to sell 25 of its prime sites in major towns and cities.

The union was involved in a dispute with Foyles' Bookshop in London during 1982: 17 of the Foyles' staff were dismissed, allegedly for union activities, and the bookshop was subjected to a well publicised picket by USDAW officials and dismissed staff. The dismissed workers alleged that many graduate staff were taken on for only short periods, were underpaid and were dismissed before they were entitled to job security. Despite the failure of the picketing to force Foyles to recognise the union, an Industrial Tribunal subsequently ruled that USDAW members Siobhan Lanigan and Susan Taylor should be reinstated for a minimum of five months at £80 per week. Subsequently, the Tribunal chairperson agreed to Foyles request to suspend the decision pending a review of the case in August. At the time of writing, the case had still not been settled.

The 1982 ADM voted to set up a working party to consider the implications for USDAW of the various pressures to amend the 1950 Shops Act and introduce Sunday trading. The working party would consider a series of options within six months and arrange for a national ballot of the union's membership before the 1983 ADM.

An attempt by the Liverpool Dry Goods branch at the 1981 ADM sought to make the deputy general secretary post in the union subject to election every four years, instead of being subject to appointment by the Executive Council. The Executive Council had established the position without changing the rules, but the motion was lost by 214,721 votes to 74,564.

Further Reference

Sir William Richardson, *A Union of Many Trades: The History of USDAW*, 400 pages, USDAW 1979. The official history of USDAW.

Tobacco Mechanics' Association

Head Office

42 Tillmouth Avenue
Whitley Bay
Tyne and Wear
0632-480946

Principal Officer

General Secretary—
J. Middleton

Membership (1982)

Total 239

General

This union was formed in 1897 and known until 1975 as the Cigarette Machine Operators' Society. It sends one delegate to the Trades Union Congress.

Tobacco Workers' Union

Head Office

9 Station Parade
High Street
Wanstead
London E11 1QF
01-989 1107

Principal Officers

General Secretary—
C. D. Grieve
Deputy General Secretary—
T. Marsland
Financial Secretary—
J. Garwood
Administrative Officer—
P. Duffy

Membership (1982)

Male 7,357
Female 10,925
Total 18,282

Union Journal and Publications

It is laid down in rule 51 of the TWU that there shall be a union journal published: *The Tobacco Worker* — bi-monthly.

General

Agreements on pay and conditions are negotiated on a national company basis. The major company agreements are with British American Tobacco, Carreras Rothmans, Imperial Tobacco and Gallaher. These companies have diversified into other manufacturing industry, especially food and drink, and in such circumstances the Tobacco Workers' Union is often a minority union among total employees of the company concerned. The tobacco industry's procedure agreement and such agreements as the Equal Opportunities Agreement are negotiated at the national joint negotiating council.

History

The union was founded in 1834 by a group of journeymen tobacco spinners employed in the tobacco trade in London and was entitled the *Friendly Society of Operative Tobacconists*. The first secretary of the union was Robert Stevens. In 1836 membership was extended to tobacco cutters, stovers and driers (again all highly skilled members) and the union's title was changed to *United Tobacconists' Society*.

Membership spread throughout Britain. In 1851 membership was opened to cigarette hand makers. In 1881 the union's title was again changed to the *United Operative Tobacconists throughout the Kingdom*. At the union's conference in 1918 the decision, in principle, was taken to extend membership to all tobacco workers, whether male or female, skilled or unskilled. This conference decision laid the basis for an industrial union and by 1925 it was finally implemented and the union

reorganised. New rules were adopted opening membership to any person employed in the tobacco trade and the union's new objectives included 'to secure the complete organisation of the workers in the tobacco trade'.

The title of *Tobacco Workers' Union* was adopted and Andrew Boyd appointed as first full-time general secretary. In 1946 the *National Cigar and Tobacco Workers' Union* — whose roots go back to 1833 — transferred engagements to the Tobacco Workers' Union.

Organisation

The supreme government of the union is formally the Biennial Conference consisting of delegates elected by the members in the branches who meet to consider the report of the previous two years and to formulate policy. General administration of the union's business and government is by the Executive Council for which each of the five geographical districts of the union elects one delegate for every 3,000 members for a three-year term of office. Day to day administration of union business is by full-time officials who are appointed.

External Relations

The TWU is affiliated to the Labour Party and the Scottish TUC.

Policy and Recent Events

Doug Grieve, the General Secretary, is perhaps best known for opposing the ban on smoking during conference proceedings at the 1979 TUC. More correctly and importantly, the TWU has put forward motions to TUC on such issues as the special branch and special patrol group, pre-school care (1978); adult literacy, recognition by British-owned companies of black trade unions in South Africa (1977); unemployment and the economy, racialism, Argentina, an embargo on arms and investment in South Africa (1976); abortion rights, tax evasion (1975). At the 1982 TWU Conference motions condemning apartheid, supporting Solidarity in Poland and appealing for unilateral nuclear disarmament were carried.

Terry Marsland, the Deputy

General Secretary, was appointed to the EOC (Equal Opportunities Commission) in 1980, following Home Office reconsideration of an earlier veto on the appointment. (It is thought that the reason for the previous veto related to her membership of the Communist Party.)

Group Fourteen **Agriculture**

Transport and General Workers' Union (TGWU) Agricultural and Allied Workers' National Trade Group

(formerly NUAAW)

London Office

Headland House
308 Gray's Inn Road
London WC1X 8DS
01–278 7801

National Trade Group Secretary

Jack Boddy MBE, JP

Membership (1982)
Male 73,000
Female 12,000
Total 85,000

Union Journal and Publications

Landworker — monthly.

General

The NUAAW began life in 1906 as the *Eastern Counties Agricultural Labourers' and Smallholders' Association* and adopted the title National Union of Agricultural and Allied Workers in 1968 in recognition of its extended activities into industries allied to agriculture, including horticulture, forestry, chicken processing, mushroom packing, apple sorting and egg packing.

Declining membership and financial difficulties (there was a loss of £49,489 in 1979 and a further loss of £134,458 in 1980) compelled the union to seek a merger with a more powerful and financially sound trade union. After lengthy negotiations with the Transport and General Workers' Union, the Executive Committee recommended a transfer of engagements to that organisation on the basis that there would be established a separate trade group, the Agricultural and Allied Workers' National Trade Group. A postal ballot of the whole membership on this proposal took place in January 1982 and resulted in 29,787 voting in favour with 4,709 against, 52 per cent of those eligible to do so having voted.

Despite this overwhelming majority the completion of the merger was delayed by complaints of disaffected members to the certification officer. Eventually all of these complaints were found to be groundless and the merger was completed in time for the Biennial Conference which duly became the inaugural annual trade group delegate conference in May 1982.

History

Agricultural workers are, of course, famous in the annals of trade union history generally as a result of the Tolpuddle Martyrs in 1833–34. Six Dorset labourers were sentenced to deportation to Australian penal settlements for seven years, having been found 'guilty' of administering and being bound by secret and unlawful oaths under an act passed in 1797 (see *Sharpen the Sickle!* by Reg Groves for a full account of the Tolpuddle Six).

Agricultural trade unionism developed on a local basis throughout much of the nineteenth century, and many of these local unions were short lived. In 1872 the *National Agricultural Labourers' Union* led by Joseph Arch was formed after a conference of delegates in Leamington Spa. Much of the initiative for organising workers came from the London Trades Council, who attempted to unify the various local independent unions into one body without much success. Although some of these unions united into larger units such as the *Federal Union of Labourers*, there were several unions seeking to represent agricultural workers well into the present century, including the *Workers' Union*.

The NUAAW was founded by George Edwards as the *Eastern Counties Agricultural Labourers' and Smallholders' Association* in 1906. The union grew slowly (unreliable figures quote the membership as 227 in 1906; 4,141 in 1910; 21,045 in 1920; 31,016 in 1930; and 162,533 in 1947). It changed its name to the *National Agricultural Labourers' and Rural Workers' Union* in 1909 and to the *National Union of Agricultural Workers* in 1920.

Organisation

See **Transport and General Workers' Union**. The new trade group will retain its Headland House headquarters, its monthly paper, *Landworker*, its unique legal aid system of 24-hour coverage and its own national committee to reach decisions relating to the agricultural industry. Instead of a Bennial Conference, there will now be an annual delegate trade group conference.

Policy and Recent Events

Delegates at the inaugural trade group conference voted by a large majority to scrap the Agricultural Wages Board and replace it with direct farmer–farmworker negotiations backed by a statutory Joint Industrial Council. The trade group will also continue to campaign against the sale of Forestry Commission land. There was a renewed call for a system of union-appointed safety representatives in agriculture and for tighter control of the use of agricultural chemicals, including the banning of 2,4,5–T.

In what amounted to its final battle as an independent trade union, a thousand NUAAW members struck in February 1982 against Bernard Matthews, a Norfolk turkey processing firm. The union sought a 25 per cent increase on basic pay and increased holiday entitlement. The strike became bitter as work continued in two processing factories and picketing had to be conducted in freezing temperatures. Help poured in from other trade unions, including £1,000 from the National Union of Seamen and a further £1,000 from the East Anglian region of ASTMS. As a result the NUAAW was able to negotiate a moderately successful pay settlement, and keep its closed shop.

Further Reference

Portrait of a Poison by Judith Cook and Chris Kaufman with introduction by Moss Evans, Pluto Press 1982. The story of the farmworkers' union's continuing campaign for a ban on the controversial weedkiller 2,4,5–T.

Reg Groves, *Sharpen the Sickle*, Porcupine Press 1949. History of the NUAAW to 1948.

Group Fifteen **Public Employees**

Educational Institute of Scotland, The
(EIS)

Head Office

46 Moray Place
Edinburgh EH3 6BH
031–225 6244

Principal Officers

General Secretary —
John D. Pollock BSc,FEIS
Deputy Secretary —
Keir Bloomer
Organising Secretary —
Frederick L. Forrester MA
Negotiating Secretary —
Robert Beattie MA, FEIS
Assistant Secretaries —
Arthur Houston MA (Further Education)
Suzanne Kreitman (Solicitor)

Membership (1982)

Male 16,200
Female 30,315
Total 46,515

Union Journal

The Scottish Educational Journal — circulated free to all schools and colleges having members.

General

The EIS has membership among registered teachers in day schools and lecturers in further and higher education. Also in membership are registered teachers in prisons, educational administration, nursery schools, the educational psychologists' service and advisors' service. The further education membership is organised in an autonomous national section which is formally linked with the National Association of Teachers in Further and Higher Education.

History

The union was established in 1847 and is one of the oldest in Britain. At the time illiteracy was widespread in Scotland. Of the inmates of Scottish prisons only one in 15 could read and write. In Paisley over 3,000 children between the ages of three and fifteen were attending no school. In those days the Educational Institute of Scotland was founded. In spite of denominational differences and political prejudices, Scottish teachers, imbued with Christian charity, united to make themselves better teachers. They did not associate merely for mutual benefit, but to proclaim the necessity for education and to establish the value of sound learning. Therefore, in its early years the aims of the institute were to build a programme of educational reform, to provide facilities and to secure tenure and maintain salaries of teachers.

Organisation

The Annual General (delegate) Meeting is the supreme court of the EIS, making and rescinding policy and exercising the right of approval, disapproval or amendment of all decisions taken by subordinate bodies since the last General Meeting. The principal subordinate body is the Council of members elected on the basis of local association constituencies and others representing special interests, which meets four times a year.

The Council has an Executive Committee and a number of other committees including an education committee and a parliamentary committee. All committees submit their minutes to the Council through the Executive Committee which meets monthly. The minutes of Executive and Council meetings and associated reports are submitted to the Annual General Meeting for approval. Of the local associations, only two have full-time secretaries, these being the Glasgow Local Association and the Lanarkshire Local Association.

Recent Events

Within the past few years the EIS affiliated to the TUC and to the Scottish TUC. These events emphasised the institute's commitment to the two main aspects of its work — that of a trade union committed to the welfare of its members and of a professional association dedicated to the 'promotion of sound learning' in Scotland. The membership is aware that the simultaneous pursuit of these aims can lead to a conflict of interests. However, the adverse effects of industrial action by teachers on the standards of the educational service provided in Scotland have been shown to be minimal and the membership of the EIS is as committed as ever to the longer-term aim of the promotion of sound learning.

The institute places great importance on objectivity and analysis. Consequently it has welcomed the recommendation of the 1982 Arbitration Body that comparability should become part of the input to annual salary reviews.

The EIS has proposed a comprehensive education and training system on the Open University model for over 16s. Credits leading to an award would be built up over a number of years of full-time and part-time study. All courses should be open to the unemployed and to all age groups.

The institute feels that the Scottish educational system is sufficiently distinct from that south of the border to need a separate planning and co-ordinating body which would validate and assess all post-compulsory education. The EIS is not opposed to adults being admitted to secondary school classes, provided that staff have agreed. Adults attending secondary school should be eligible for unemployment benefit under the same conditions as adults in colleges of further education.

Fire Brigades Union
(FBU)

Head Office

59 Fulham High Street
London SW6 3JN
01–736 2157

Principal Officers

General Secretary —
Ken Cameron
Assistant General Secretary
Mike Fordham
National Officers —
Ray Martindale
Don Riddell
D. Higgs

Membership (1982)

Male 29,700
Female 300
Total: 30,000

Union Journal and Publications

Firefighter — circulation 12,000.
The union has also produced a pictorial history of the FBU to mark its 50 years of existence from 1918–68: *The Fire Brigades Union: Fifty Years of Service.*

General

The Fire Brigades Union began in London in 1918. It now has in membership over 90 per cent of all uniformed personnel (wholetime, of all ranks) in the 68 local authority fire brigades in the UK. Some brigade officers belong to the *National Association of Fire Officers*, although the FBU is gradually extending its dominance into the brigade officer ranks (see **Recent Events**). The FBU has a left-wing tradition and was recently involved in a national strike during the winter of 1977–78. Ken Cameron, the General Secretary, is a member of the General Council of the TUC. The late Terry Parry was the TUC president from 1979–80.

History

Fire brigade trade unionism began in London. The London firefighters were nearly always on duty; they had two hours leave a week but were otherwise confined to quarters in small fire stations and under strict discipline. Throughout the country in the early 1900s there were fewer than 3,000 full-time professional firefighters; most of the large provincial fire brigades were staffed by the police.

In 1913 some men in the fire brigade joined the *National Union of Corporation Workers* (later NUPE). They formed a branch and fought for recognition for fire brigade trade unionism by London County Council. This was resisted and the conflict led eventually to a ballot on strike action in 1918. Askwith, the government conciliator, was called in and devised a compromise formula whereby a firefighter's 'representative body' (nominally not a union) would be recognised and could be accompanied by a 'spokesman' who did not need to be a member of the London Fire Brigade.

There was already in existence a firefighter's benefit society which in 1918 registered as a friendly society, calling itself the *Fireman's Trade Union*. Without rancour and with full agreement with the National Union of Corporation Workers, the firefighters' branch merged with this new union. One Jim Bradley, a radical member of the National Union of Corporation Workers' Executive, was appointed for representative purposes and, in 1922, became general secretary. The union began to expand outside London but many provincial fire brigades were still police brigades and, although improved pay and duty systems were awarded by the report of the Middlebrook Committee on pay and conditions of professional firefighters, actually obtaining these improvements from local authorities proved to be difficult.

In 1930 the union's name was changed to the *Fire Brigades Union*. During and shortly before the war years local authorities organised the *Auxiliary Fire Service*. Many members of the FBU rejected and resisted this organisation and tried to boycott the AFS, fearing that it would drag down the pay and conditions of service of regular firefighters. When John Horner became general secret-

ary, at 27 years of age, he reversed this policy, forming the AFS section of the union. With nationalisation of the service to form the National Fire Service, the union was able to combine the AFS section and the regular section.

However, in 1947 the fire service was reorganised and decentralised to county council level and this had the effect of somewhat weakening the union. In 1952 the Ross award broke the link between firefighters pay and police pay. While the principle of the 60-hour week and double shifts had been conceded in 1940 by the London County Council, the union was hectically engaged in the early 1950s in defending the newly won two-shift duty system, as some local authorities tried to restore some kind of continuous duty.

Union Officials

The FBU employs only the general secretary, assistant general secretary, and the few national officers as full-time officials — all of them ex-firefighters. Under FBU rules, all national officials are elected for five years by a ballot conducted through the union's branches, with the union's chartered accountants acting as returning officers.

In 1981, the former assistant general secretary, Dick Foggie, was standing for re-election, but for the first time an incumbent FBU official was challenged when Mike Fordham, a national officer, stood against him. Mr Foggie applied and had the election suspended 'pending inquiry, investigation and possible proceedings' after making allegations about an electoral campaign which he said was designed improperly to influence the election against him. A TUC inquiry (costing the union over £14,000) by Lord Wedderburn, Lord McCarthy and George Doughty (former general secretary of DATA) was then set up. The committee in general rejected Mr Foggie's allegations. The election was then re-run with Fordham winning by 13,055 votes to 10,989 for Foggie. The TUC recommended new election guidelines and the establishment of an election appeals committee, which were embodied in an EC recommendation to the 1982 Annual Conference. Delegates at the Conference rejected the recommendations by 25,553 to 12,988 on a card vote, because some members had not had time to consider what changes were necessary in union rules as a result of such a proposal.

Coverage

The FBU has in membership over 90 per cent of all uniformed personnel (wholetime firefighters of all ranks) in the 68 local authority fire brigades of Great Britain and Northern Ireland, and also has some part-time members among its ranks. Some brigade officers belong to the non-TUC-affiliated National Association of Fire Officers. National pay and conditions of firefighters are dealt with by local authorities through the National Joint Council for Local Authority Fire Brigades.

The FBU won a major victory in 1982 about the representation of fire officers on the national negotiation machinery. The FBU had claimed all along that the National Association of Fire Officers were over-represented in relation to their numbers. NAFO refused to participate in a headcount of officers, so the employers were able only to determine the number of officers in FBU membership. The FBU had all along claimed to represent about 50 per cent of the officers. This was confirmed by the headcount, which found that 49.3 per cent of officers were FBU members. When the members of the small Retained Fireman's Union, and those officers not in a union were removed from the total, it was estimated that the FBU had 55 per cent of the total. As a result, the employers revised the representation on the negotiating machinery to reflect this headcount.

Organisation

The supreme government of the union is vested in the Annual Conference, with general administration by the Executive Council. The membership is divided into 14 regions to assist democratic administration. The Executive Council consists of one representative from each region (London has two), and there is one representative from the Officer's National Committee. These representatives are elected every four years and are eligible for re-election.

The general secretary, assistant general secretary and national officers are elected by ballots conducted through the branches with a firm of chartered accountants (named by Annual Conference) acting as returning officers. They hold office for five years and are then eligible for re-election. The president is elected in the same way but must have served at least four years on the Executive Council.

Within each fire authority there is a brigade committee comprised of one delegate from each branch within the brigade's territory. To expedite union business and to strengthen brigade committees within each region there is an elected regional committee; in the case of London and Northern Ireland these committees are one and the same.

The officer's national committee advises the Executive Council on matters affecting the conditions of employment of union members who are of the rank of station officer and above, and on their organisation and recruitment.

The basic unit of organisation is the branch, and these are normally based in individual fire stations.

Workplace Activity

There are around 120 shop stewards based at fire stations throughout the UK. Many of these are brigade secretaries or brigade chairpersons.

Women

Women comprise 10 per cent of FBU membership. Nearly all of them are employed as control room staff at fire stations or brigade headquarters. Not surprisingly, women feature little in the affairs of the FBU; all brigade secretaries are male, although there is one female on the Executive Council. However, there is a section of the union which deals with the interests of control room staff, and women occupy positions as representatives in 10 out of the 14 regions of the union.

External Relations

The FBU is affiliated to the Labour Party, and the General Secretary, Ken Cameron, is a member of the General Council of the TUC.

The FBU is affiliated to a wide range of political and libertarian pressure groups etc. as follows:

Anti-Apartheid Movement
Labour Research Department
Socialist Medical Association
National Council for Civil Liberties
Workers' Educational Association
League for Democracy in Greece
Amnesty International
Public Services International
Federation of British Fire Organisations
National Federation of Professional Workers
Labour Action for Peace
Royal Humane Society
British Pensioners
Pre-Retirement Association
Liberation
National Peace Council
Marx Memorial Library
Haldane Society
Fire Protection Association
British Safety Council
United Nations Association
Fabian Society
Association of Labour Workers
British Council for Peace in Vietnam
Anti-Nazi League
British Standards Institute
Labour Common Market Safeguards Committee
Campaign for Nuclear Disarmament

Labour Party Delegation

At the 1981 Annual Conference, an emergency resolution requiring the FBU to ascertain the wishes of the membership for the Labour Party Deputy Leadership contest 'by a show of hands at branch level of the political levy members, numbers for and against being forwarded to brigade secretaries who will in turn forward Brigade figures to Head Office' was carried, despite opposition from the Executive. As a result, the FBU was committed to supporting Denis Healey for Deputy Leader, although the union leadership were more inclined to support Tony Benn.

Policy

At the 1978 Trades Union Congress the union's motion on the nationalisation of the Fire Service was remitted to the General Council. The motion criticised the division of responsibility for controlling the fire service and providing fire cover, which has existed since 1948 when the wartime nationalised fire service was handed back to individual county boroughs and county councils. The Home Secretary, assisted by professional advisers and the Central Fire Brigades Advisory Council, is responsible for all technical aspects of the service. On the other hand the local authorities, through the National Joint Council for Fire Brigades, are the arbiters on all questions concerning the conditions of service of firefighters, including pay, hours and holidays.

FBU policy has been on the left of the labour movement and it still carries a foreword in its Rule Book stating that the union 'has as its ultimate aim the bringing about of the Socialist system of society'.

At the 1982 FBU Annual Conference motions were carried opposing the Conservative government's anti-trade union legislation; opposing public spending cuts; condemning US policy in El Salvador; calling for a legal restriction on overtime working; and confirming that in future Labour Party Leadership elections the FBU vote would be by show of hands at branch level, with brigade secretaries forwarding the results to head office. The FBU also confirmed its support for unilateral nuclear disarmament.

The FBU is affiliated to the Anti-Nuclear Campaign as the union has a direct interest in emergency preparations and transport of nuclear waste material. The East Anglian Region is also affiliated to the ANC and is actively involved in East Anglian Trade Union Campaign against the pressurised water reactor.

Recent Events

The union was involved in the first national strike in its history from 14 November 1977 until 16 January 1978. The strike ended in an agreement that firefighters' pay should be linked to the average earnings of the upper quartile of male manual workers, this to be phased over two years, 1978–80. The agreement also provided for a reduction in the standard working week from 48 to 42 hours.

Despite an attempt by the government to renege on this agreement in the autumn of 1980 by including the firefighters in the public sector 6 per cent pay ceiling, the agreement for 1980–81 was 'honoured' in two stages after the firefighters began to take industrial action.

The FBU campaigned vigorously against government proposals to require some large fire authorities to reduce establishments — staff and pumps — in order to cut expenditure, culminating in a national rally of protest on 10 October 1979. Around 9,000 firefighters from all over the country marched through the city of Nottingham. The union is particularly concerned at the Greater London Council's discussion paper on the future development of the London Fire Brigade which envisages reducing the fire service cover in the area. The FBU claims that, on some occasions, neighbouring services have had to be called in, denuding their own areas of some fire cover.

At the 1980 Trades Union Congress, the FBU called for a full public inquiry into the government's proposals for changes in fire policy which the FBU claims were designed to support political moves to cut public expenditure, irrespective of the consequences.

Further Reference

Industrial Relations in the London Fire Service. Report of a Committee of Inquiry of the Advisory Conciliation and Arbitration Service 1977.

Committee of Inquiry concerning the Election of Assistant General Secretary, FBU 1981, February 1982.

Greater London Council Staff Association
(GLCSA)

Head Office

150 Waterloo Road
London SE1 8SB
01–633 5927

Principal Officers

Being a regionally based organisation, there are no national officers as such. The corresponding work is undertaken by members of the secretariat, as follows:

Secretary — F. T. Hollocks
Deputy Secretary — A. Capelin
Assistant Secretaries I — P. G. Seares
D. E. Small
Assistant Secretaries II — A. Robertson
J. Caley

Membership (1982)

Male 9,899
Female 6,778
Total 16,677

Union Journal

There is no union journal. However a monthly staff journal, *London Town*, is financed mainly by the GLCSA and supplied free to all members. It is produced by an independent limited company and only the pages headed 'Staff Association News' are directly controlled by the GLCSA.

General

The association, as the majority organisation for Greater London Council/ Inner London Education Authority non-manual staff, is a party to all agreements covering the salaries and conditions of service of such staff. Eight of the ten staff representatives on the Whitley committee are GLCSA representatives.

History

The GLCSA was founded in 1909. Even though its founders hardly thought of it as a trade union until well after 1918, its purpose and significance were realised by senior officials of the GLC and officers were warned by their chiefs that if they were identified with this organised movement among the staff to form a protective association they would endanger their own careers.

In 1910 the association affiliated to NALGO but this did not necessitate any sacrifice of independence since NALGO was at that time a federation of autonomous guilds. However, after a short earlier break (1911–12), the GLCSA withdrew from affiliation in 1916. The connection has never been re-established despite a number of overtures from NALGO.

The GLCSA affiliated to the Federation of Professional, Technical and Clerical Workers in 1918. It achieved an equal pay for women agreement in 1952. In 1956 it affiliated to the TUC.

Coverage

The GLCSA covers several hundred trades including architects, administrators, clerks, doctors, education workers, engineers, lawyers, planners, scientists, schoolkeepers, surveyors, technicians and typists. It is the major organisation on the staff side of the GLC/ILEA Whitley council. It is also represented on the Thames Water Authority regional staff negotiating body and the national negotiating bodies for water service staffs.

Organisation

The government of the association is vested in a General Committee which is elected annually in March or April on the basis of one representative for approximately every 40 members. This General Committee elects an Executive Committee which is responsible for the day to day management of GLCSA business including finances. The General Committee has the power to appoint and dismiss a secretary of the association.

Policy

Majority opinion among members is that their interests are best served by remaining in an organisation separate from NALGO. Their salaries, grading structure and conditions of service are significantly better than those of local government officers outside London. The GLCSA believes that this would be unlikely to continue if the separate negotiating machinery which exists for GLC/ILEA staff were destroyed. Separate negotiating arrangements would be seen as anachronistic in the context of an expanded NALGO and hence amalgamation with that union would lead eventually to pressure for absorption into the national Whitley Council. Moreover, a considerable majority of GLCSA membership are concerned to preserve the party political neutrality of their union.

Health Service Employees, Confederation of
(COHSE)

Head Office

Glen House
High Street
Banstead
Surrey SM7 2LH
073-73 53322

Principal Officers

General Secretary—
Albert Spanswick
Assistant General Secretary—
David Williams
National Officers—
Terry Mallinson
Hector McKenzie
Rose Lambie
Colin O'Kane
Research Assistant—
Chris Oldfield

Membership (1982)

Male 50,427
Female 180,282
Total 230,709

Union Journal and Publications

Health Service— monthly to members, circulation 100,000.
COHSE Union Stewards Handbook— an extremely useful handbook featuring information about COHSE and the NHS; negotiations; disciplinary action and NHS employees and the law and NHS employment.
Stewards Handbook Supplements

Regional Secretaries

● *No. 1. (Northern)*
Andy Vanbeck
Townsville House,
274 Heaton Road,
Newcastle upon Tyne NE6 5ZE

● *No. 2. (Yorkshire and
Humberside)*
Martin Kineavy,
98 Mansfield Road,
Sheffield

● *No. 3. (North Western)*
Eric Cooper
381 Bury New Road,
Prestwich,
Manchester M25 5AW

● *No. 4. (West Midlands)*
Bob Wilshaw,
Dartmouth House,
67 Birmingham Road,
West Bromwich

● *No. 5. (North East Thames and
East Anglia)*
Keith Taylor,
27 Romford Road,
Stratford,
London E15

● *No. 6. (North West Thames and
Oxford)*
Pat McGinley,
112 Greyhound Lane,
Streatham,
London SW16

● *No. 7. (South Western)*
T. Taylor
Silverlea House,
4 Billetfield,
Taunton

● *No. 8. (South East Thames)*
Bob Harmes,
24 Harmer Street,
Gravesend

● *No. 9. (Scotland)*
Keith Hickson,
75–77 Abbeygreen,
Lesmahagow,
Lanarks

● *No. 10. (Wales)*
Ted Davies,
Millbourne Chambers,
High Street,
Merthyr

● *No. 11. (Northern Ireland)*
Bill Jackson,
27 Ulsterville Avenue,
Lisburn Road,
Belfast

● *No. 12. (East Midlands)*
Keith Swiffen,
98 Mansfield Road,
Intake,
Sheffield

● *No. 13. (South West Thames and
Wessex)*
Mike Somers,
112 Greyhound Lane,
Streatham,
London SW16

General

COHSE, as it is known, is in many ways an industrial union for the NHS, but it is by no means the only union representing health service employees. However, it is a health and social services trade union recruiting all grades of staff; other unions, with which it may compete for members, are often tied down to particular grades and spheres of influence. For example, the Royal College of Nursing and the Health Visitors' Association are restricted to particular occupations, while the general unions have some difficulty recruiting staff other than ancillary workers because they lack a 'professional' image. The TGWU has long since given up recruitment of nursing staff, the GMWU has negligible numbers in membership, while even NUPE with its broader health service base has some disadvantage to overcome in recruiting nurses. Unfortunately for COHSE, in the past some branches, where the membership was composed mainly of nursing staff, have neglected recruiting ancillary and other grades, while in their ancillary branches, the reverse situation applied. This was a very short-sighted policy and resulted in membership being lost to other organisations, particularly NUPE. Despite this, COHSE is the largest health service union and in recent years has been the fastest growing TUC-affiliated union. Three quarters of its membership are women and much of its growth derives from recruitment of women.

History

The union originated among nursing staff of mental hospitals in the early years of the century when conditions in this type of employment were very poor. Average working hours were between 84 and 90 hours a week and the starting wage of a female probationer nurse £18 a year. Promotion to charge nurse, although rapid, produced a wage of £45 a year. Turnover of staff was high; this, and the lack of contact between hospitals and fierce employer opposition, made trade union organisation very difficult.

There were underlying grievances. Trade unionism was probably triggered by the 1909 Asylums Superannuation Act which provided for compulsory cash deductions from wages for a statutory superannuation scheme which was less generous than the already existing optional schemes operated by many employing authorities. The grievances were strongly felt in Lancashire and in 1909 eight nurses from Winwick Mental Asylum met to discuss grievances over pay and conditions. This led to a further meeting and the founding of the *National Asylum Workers' Union* in 1910 with George Gibson as secretary.

In its early years the union faced severe opposition. Many of the activists were victimised but in this way the union acquired its first full-time officers. The union's first significant strike was in 1918 when nurses in Prestwich and Winwick struck against the Lancashire Asylums Board over a claim to reduce the working week to 60 hours.

The average 50-hour week was gained in 1920 by which time the membership of the union had risen to 18,000. In 1922 nurses at the Radcliffe-upon-Trent Hospital struck against an attempt to increase hours to 66 and reduce wages by 4 shillings a week. Sixty-seven employees were dismissed for taking action and the strike was broken following an attack by police, bailiffs and blacklegs.

The NAWU affiliated to the Labour Party in 1915 and to the TUC in 1923.

In 1918 another union had been founded with similar aims and interests but more active in general hospitals and in local authority welfare services. This was the *Poor Law Workers' Trade Union*. For a while the NAWU and the PLWTU federated but then split apart, the PLWTU becoming the *Poor Law Officers' Union*.

In 1930 the PLOU became the *National Union of County Officers* (NUCO) and in the same year the NAWU became the *Mental Hospital and Institutional Workers' Union*. A further name change followed in 1943 when NUCO became the *Hospitals and Welfare Services Union*.

The logical merger between the two unions to form the *Confederation of Health Service Employees* was agreed in 1946. From its inception the union strongly supported the National Health Service but — and this comes as a surprise to many people — it has never been afraid to take a firm line in defence of its members' pay and conditions and has fought by means of demonstrations and industrial action for improved pay for nurses in 1950, 1962, 1970, 1973 and more recently. The Halsbury Report of 1974 produced a large pay award for nurses and in that year COHSE's membership leapt by 20,000 — the largest percentage increase recorded that year by any TUC-affiliated union. In recent years it has continued to be the fastest growing union in the TUC.

In 1974 COHSE was also readmitted into membership of the TUC, having been suspended since 1972 for refusing to comply with TUC policy of de-registration against the Industrial Relations Act of 1971.

Coverage

Negotiations concerning pay and conditions of service for *all* NHS employees take place within the National Health Service Whitley councils.

When the NHS became operative in 1948 the government had to provide means whereby all employees in hospitals and public health services could be represented and put forward views on these services and on the wages paid. The Ministry of Health was given power to arrange for this to be done by use of Whitley councils.

In total there are ten 'functional' Whitley councils covering all types of employees in the NHS:

1. Administrative and clerical council (and ambulance officers' committee)

2. Ancillary staffs council (ward orderlies, domestics, porters)
3. Dental council
4. Medical council
5. Nurses and midwives council (including community nurses and midwives and health visitors)
6. Optical council
7. Pharmaceutical council
8. Professional and technical council 'A'
9. Professional and technical council 'B'
10. Ambulance council

The General Council is the connecting link, consisting of an agreed number of representatives from each of the ten councils and negotiations of a general, all-purpose nature take place on this council which has no power of veto but is intended to co-ordinate.

All these Whitley councils are composed of representatives of employers' and employees' organisations, now known as the management side and the staff side respectively. The organisations represented are those whose previous work entitles them to recognition as negotiating bodies. The number of seats each union holds varies from one council to another but COHSE has 27 seats among seven of the ten Whitley councils in the NHS.

Where practicable, COHSE nominates lay members of the union onto the main negotiating committees as a back-up role to the national officers who lead the negotiations.

Organisation

All members must belong to a branch which may be an ordinary branch, an officers' branch or a group branch. Senior hospital employees such as administrators, nursing officers and so on, are regarded as managers by many employers but they are nevertheless employees of the Health Service and it is reasonable that they should have separate officers' branches if they so wish, but this is not obligatory and they may well stay in the ordinary branch.

For administrative purposes the country is divided into regions and all branches are allocated to one of the 13 COHSE regions. Each region has a regional office and full-time officers and staff and the regions are controlled by regional councils consisting of elected representatives of branches.

The general management and control of COHSE between each Delegate Conference is vested in the National Executive Committee consisting of the president, vice-president, general secretary and the representatives elected by the regions. Much of the detailed work of the NEC is carried out by its standing committees, such as the finance and organisation committee and the parliamentary committee (of which COHSE's sponsored MPs are ex-officio members) which plays an important role in the union's influence over legislation.

The Annual Delegate Conference which takes place each year in June is the supreme governing body of the union.

The general secretary of COHSE is elected by ballot of individual members following nominations from the branches. All other officials, apart from the deputy general secretary, are appointed.

Workplace Activity

COHSE's decision to introduce the union steward system, taken in 1972, coincided with the ending of the function of individual union contribution collectors and the introduction of bonus and payment-by-results (PBR) schemes for ancillary staffs.

Deduction of contributions at source meant that branches were in danger of losing contact with their members, while PBR meant that there was a pressing need for workplace union representatives to determine the implications of these schemes and control their introduction. It was recognised that union stewards could relieve some of the burden of negotiation and representation carried by regional officers. Effective decisions are frequently taken at the workplace and consequently able lay representatives are necessary in the NHS as elsewhere. In addition, it was necessary to have someone at the place of work to recruit members, given the intense inter-union competition for membership.

Women

Three quarters of COHSE members are women but as yet have made little impact on the union hierarchy. There is one woman national officer, Rose Lambie, and a number of junior officers in the regions are women.

External Relations

COHSE is affiliated to the Labour Party and sponsors a small number of Labour MPs: Willie Hamilton (Fife Central), Alec Jones (Rhondda), Michael Meacher (Oldham West).

Recent Events and Current Policy

COHSE tries to project itself and make itself more attractive to potential members than other health service unions by emphasising that it caters exclusively for health service and social service employees. It is in competition for members among ancillary staff with NUPE and among nursing staff with the Royal College of Nursing which also introduced a steward system in 1972. Competition with NUPE was exacerbated during the NHS staffs pay dispute early in 1979 and relations between the two unions definitely deteriorated, with COHSE accusing NUPE of tactics designed to poach members. Inter-union difficulties in the NHS were further underlined when delegates at COHSE's Annual Conference in 1979 approved a motion instructing the General Secretary, Albert Spanswick, to veto any application by the Royal College of Nursing for affiliation to the TUC. Mr Spanswick, however, has no such power of veto in the TUC. COHSE also made it clear that only journalists in membership of the NUJ were welcome at the Conference.

The conflict with the RCN arose in 1979 over the principle of nurses being free to take strike action. A statement by the General Nursing Council for England and Wales on the disciplinary consequences of nurses taking industrial action incurred the immediate disapproval of COHSE and NUPE which accused the General Nursing Council of trying to frighten nurses from joining trade unions. Both unions directed some of their anger at the Royal College of Nursing whose members had, earlier in 1979, voted overwhelmingly against the principle of taking industrial action. The Royal College of Nursing had subsequently asked the General Nursing Council to make a statement on industrial action. COHSE later issued a statement promising its nursing members support if they were brought before the General Nursing Council Disciplinary Committee as a result of industrial action, provided that they have kept to the union's rules. For this purpose COHSE has issued comprehensive guidelines on industrial action. These guidelines came under very severe strain during the 1982 National Health Service pay dispute when COHSE joined NUPE and the other NHS trade unions in pressing an obdurate government to improve on its pay offer of seven-and-a-half per cent to nursing staff and six per cent to ancillary workers.

As the unions began a strategy of escalating industrial action throughout the summer, distrust and animosity between workers and management over the vexed question of refusal to handle 'non-emergency' cases grew steadily worse. It was still relatively early in the dispute that COHSE, uncharacteristically in view of its traditionally moderate stance, made a public declaration that it might abandon the TUC's code of conduct for health service disputes. This intemperance was a tactical error, allowing the government to attack COHSE as intransigent and lacking constructive leadership and necessitating the TUC Health Services Committee to force COHSE to retract. The TUC Health Services Committee worked well during the dispute, a reflection of closer relations between COHSE and NUPE.

The political naivete and insecurity in the COHSE leadership is traceable to the rapid growth of the union. All the pressure for a firm stand against the government's pay offer came from the rank and file. The decision to take selective strike action, for instance, was taken reluctantly by the National Executive Committee to forestall precipitate strike action at branch level.

COHSE is relatively democratic compared to many unions and feelings expressed at branch and regional level ultimately find expression through the 26-member Executive. Although a broad left-oriented alliance, Group 81, has been formed to push for greater accountability and increased commitment to Conference decisions, as yet it can claim backing from only a small percentage of the membership.

Further Reading

The History of the Mental Hospital and Institutional Workers' Union from Infancy to Its 21st Year, 1931. (No author given.)

In addition, Mike Carpenter, COHSE research fellow in the School of Industrial and Business Studies at the University of Warwick, is working on a detailed history of the union and has already written a booklet, *All For One: Campaigns and Pioneers in the Making of COHSE*, £1 from COHSE head office.

A. Sethi and S. Dimmock, *Industrial Relations and Health Services*, Croom Helm 1982.

Health Visitors' Association
(HVA)

Head Office

36 Eccleston Square
London SW1V 1PF
01–834 9523/4

Principal Officer

General Secretary —
J. Wyndham-Kaye OBE

Membership (1982)

Male 57
Female 14,132
Total 14,189

Union Journal
The Health Visitor

General

The association conducts negotiations about salaries and conditions through the Nurses' and Midwives' Whitley Council. It has two seats on the staff side of the council and one on the negotiating committee. The educational activities of the HVA have continued unbroken since it organised the first refresher course for health visitors in 1921. Nowadays four residential post-certificate courses are organised each year and special courses are provided as necessary.

History

The association was founded in 1896 by the first seven women sanitary inspectors, all working in London, and was called the *Women Sanitary Inspectors' Association*. By 1906 membership had risen to 63 of whom the large majority worked in London, but in that year invitations to join the association were sent out to women sanitary inspectors and health visitors working elsewhere and the first provincial centre was established in Birmingham in 1912.

In 1918 the association chose registration as a trade union rather than as a company and has retained this status. The first full-time general secretary was appointed in 1923.

The three changes in the association's name indicate the development in its membership. By 1914 so many health visitors had joined the original sanitary inspectors that the name was changed to the *Women Sanitary Inspectors' and Health Visitors' Association*. The change to *Women Public Health Officers' Association* in 1929 was made as a result of inclusion among the membership of other women working in public health such as school nurses, domiciliary midwives and matrons of day nurseries. The present name was adopted in 1962 by which time health visitors constituted a large majority of the membership, although several other types of workers remain eligible and welcome to join.

Organisation

The governing body of the association is an Executive Committee made up of the honorary officers of the association and representatives of all centres and groups. Centres are geographical and correspond to branches, being formed of members living or working in the same area. The overseas group is made up of members living in any area not covered by a centre and in practice contains members as near as Scotland and as far away as Australia.

Other groups are composed of members engaged in a particular branch of health work. The five honorary officers (chairperson, two vice-chairpersons, secretary and treasurer) are elected at the Annual General Meeting, as are the president, vice-president and trustees.

The Executive Committee meets quarterly. It appoints the general secretary.

External Relations

The association has no political affiliation.

Hospital Consultants and Specialists' Association

Head Office

The Old Court House
London Road
Ascot
Berkshire SL5 7EN
0990–25052

Principal Officers

Chief Executive —
R. Brownlow Martin
Other Full-time Officers —
W. E. Bilson (Terms and Conditions)
M. J. Parsley (Internal Administration)
S. J. Charkham (Press Officer)

Membership (1982)

Total 3,187

Union Journal

The Consultant — bimonthly.

General

The HCSA has been in existence in one form or another since the start of the NHS. In 1969 there were about 1,000 members who belonged to the *Regional Hospital Consultants and Specialists' Association*. Following the publication of proposals which would have drastically altered the responsibilities and work pattern of consultants, and also the government's refusal to implement recommendations of the review body, a large number of consultants, disenchanted with the BMA, left it and joined the RHCSA. Membership increased rapidly and in 1973 London teaching hospital consultants were allowed to join and the name was changed to Hospital Consultants and Specialists' Association.

Organisation

The regional organisation of the HCSA consists of each NHS region divided on a geographical basis into counties. There are normally three county chairpersons per region, except for Trent, South Western and West Midlands where there are four. Council is the governing body of the HCSA but all major policy decisions are made by direct ballot of members (TUC affiliation was a case in point).

The Executive Committee is formed by the national officers, i.e. the president (who is chairperson of Council), deputy president (chairperson of the Executive) and chairpersons of all sub-committees (ethics, education and TUC liaison; membership and communications; terms and conditions of service; finance) plus two honorary secretaries and an honorary treasurer.

Elections to HCSA Council are held every two years by direct postal ballot. The AGM elects the national officers, and Council the sub-committee chairperson. All hold office for two years.

Policy

Relations with the BMA have never been close. The HCSA is an alternative organisation for consultants challenging the monopoly of the BMA and providing a focal point for opposition. The HCSA has made two attempts to secure recognition and negotiating rights. In 1974 the association took its case to the Industrial Relations Court but failed on the technicality of who was the employer — the regional health authorities (who hold consultants' contracts) or the DHSS and Secretary of State. A further attempt was made by application through ACAS but this was similarly unsuccessful.

Relations with other NHS unions are mainly influenced by the various TUC working parties and committees on which the HCSA is represented. It is fair to say that relationships between the HCSA and other NHS unions have improved as a consequence of this participation, though there remain many areas of disagreement.

HCSA policy favoured the removal of Area Health Authorities and hopes, for the sake of the NHS, that the 1982 reorganisation is the last.

In its evidence to the Royal Commission on the National Health Service, the HCSA has put forward ideas for alternative forms of funding. The argument is that, with zero growth or even contraction in the economy and with inflation, money will not be available to fund the NHS from present sources. In addition, 'one of the main reasons for the crisis facing the NHS is that the main premise on which it was founded has proved to be false: that universal availability of free health care would automatically lead to a healthier nation and therefore eventually reduce the demand for health care services.'

The HCSA supports local accounting so that the through-put of patients is directly linked with the money received and has proposed that the delivery of health care should be based on a compulsory National Health Insurance scheme, the main principles of which would be as follows:

(i) The patient effects compulsory health insurance cover; the patient enters into a contract with the insurer.

(ii) The patient consults the doctor who orders or performs treatment. The patient is presented with a bill for the cost; the patient therefore enters into a contract with the doctor and/or hospital.

(iii) The cost of caring for the chronic sick and the under-privileged minorities must be covered by this compulsory health insurace and paid for by those who can afford to do so.

(iv) The health insurance fund should be separate from general taxation. Each person can see the cost of the premium and the cost of her/his personal treatment as well as what he/she contributes to the treatment of others or they to hers/his. The role of government is to ensure that the under-privileged minorities are adequately covered by compulsory health insurance. The HCSA adds that 'such schemes work well in other countries.'

National and Local Government Officers' Association
(NALGO)

Head Office

1 Mabledon Place
London WC1H 9AJ
01-388 2366

Principal Officers

General Secretary —
  Geoffrey Drain
Deputy General Secretary —
  John D. Daly
Assistant General Secretary (Service Conditions) —
  Alan Jinkinson
Assistant General Secretary (Administration) —
  Brian J. Holland
Financial Officer — C. L. Read
Legal Officer —
  Penelope Grant
Publicity Officer —
  Chris Cossey
Education Officer —
  Regina Kibel
Insurance Manager —
  Duncan Young
International Relations Officer
  Hugh Bynger
Editor, Public Service —
  Charles E. Timaeus
Research and Statistical Officer —
  John S. Thane
Service Conditions Officers Local Government —
  Keith Sonnet
Organising Officer for Electricity Staffs —
  Dave Prentis
Organising Officer for Gas Staffs — Dave Stirzaker
Organising Officer for Health Staffs — Ada W. Maddocks
Organising Officer for Water/Transport — John Pitt
Organising Officer for Universities/New Towns —
  Alex Thompson

Membership (1982)

Male 387,325
Female 408,820
Total 796,145

Union Journal and Publications

Public Service — monthly,
circulation around 774,000.
NALGO also publishes a wide
range of publications for its
members, for branch activists
(elected officers and stewards)
and for public consumption.
These include a weekly
bulletin *NALGO News* with a
circulation of 28,500, a
Members Handbook, guides
for branch officers and
stewards, a booklet, *Legal
Advice and Assistance*, leaflets
on the welfare fund and
services for retired members,
publications on specific issues
(new technology, equal rights,
health and safety) and 'white
papers' for submission to
Annual Conference. Trade
Union Education (TUE)
publications deal with the
practice and context of union
organisation and negotiation.
NALGO's National Executive
Council encourages branches
to produce their own
information and publicity
material, and organises an
annual competition for branch
news-sheets and magazines,
many of which are of a high
standard.

District Offices

There are 12 district offices, each
headed by a district organisation
officer leading a team of district
officers.

● *Eastern*
Charles Cronin
30/33 Townfield Street
Chelmsford
Essex CM1 1UW
0245-87524

● *East Midlands*
Jack Briggs
Pearl Assurance House
Friar Lane
Nottingham NG1 6BY
0602-45756

● *North Western and North Wales*
Ernest Baxendale
3/5 St John Street
Manchester M3 4DL
061-832 5625l

● *South Eastern*
David Kennedy
International House
78 Queen's Road
Brighton BN1 3XE
0273-29445

● *North Eastern*
Donald Williamson
Milburn House (A)
Dean Street
Newcastle-upon-Tyne NE1 1LE
0632-324900

● *Metropolitan*
Andrew Jack
17 Highfield Road
Golders Green
London NW11 9PF
01-458 9211

● *Scottish*
Charles Gallacher
Hellenic House
87/97 Bath Street
Glasgow G2 2ER
041-332 0006

● *Southern*
Leighton Jones
London House
59/65 London Street
Reading RG1 4PS
0734-596466

● *South Wales*
Tom Quinn
3rd Floor
1 Cathedral Road
Cardiff CF1 9SB
0222-398333

● *West Midland*
Sid Platt
7th Floor
Tower Block
Centre City
7 Hill Street
Birmingham B5 4JD
021-643 6084

● *South Western*
Steve Johnson
16 The Crescent
Taunton
Somerset TA1 4EB
0823-88031

● *Yorkshire and Humberside*
John Fitches
3rd Floor
Commerce House
Wade Lane
Leeds LS2 8NJ
0532-449111

NALGO employs some 700 staff —
400 at headquarters and 300 in the
districts and branches. About 220 of
these are union organisers.

General

NALGO ranks as the largest white-
collar trade union in Britain and is the
fourth largest union in the TUC.
NALGO was originally an organisation for white-collar employees of local authorities and included administrative, technical, clerical and professional workers. When the creation of
new nationalised industries and the
transfer of functions to national organisations took certain services away
from local government, NALGO followed its members into the new industries and authorities. Consequently it
now also organises workers in the
National Health Service, the gas industry, electricity supply, the water
industry, road passenger transport,
British Waterways Board, new towns,
and universities.

NALGO membership covers a
wide range of occupations: lawyers,
accountants, engineers, architects,
planners, social workers, librarians,
nurses, technicians, computer staff,
administrators, telephonists, typists
and clerks. It includes many low paid
workers and a good number of highly
paid workers. The bulk of NALGO
membership is located in local government — over 60 per cent of the
total.

NALGO has experienced a remarkable growth in membership in
the post-war years. When the union
affiliated to the TUC in 1964 it had a
membership of 338,322. Since 1965 it
has increased its membership at the
rate of nearly 30,000 a year. In the last
decade NALGO's membership has
almost doubled. In part, NALGO's
growth can be attributed to the increase in white-collar unionism generally.

NALGO is a party to the staff side
of the National Joint Council for Loc-

al Authorities' Administrative, Professional, Technical and Clerical Services and also to the national joint
councils for staff grades, together with
all the Whitley councils of all the public service and nationalised industries
previously mentioned.

The General Secretary, Geoffrey
Drain, and the union's health staffs
organising officer, Ada Maddocks,
serve on the TUC General Council.
Scottish district organisation officer
Charles Gallacher serves on the
General Council of the Scottish TUC,
and David White and Idris Jones
serve on the Wales TUC.

History

The main impetus to the foundation
of NALGO came from Herbert Blain,
a 26-year-old clerk in the Town
Clerk's Department in Liverpool. He
founded the *Liverpool Municipal
Officers' Guild* in 1896 'to provide a
means for social intercourse among its
members and, for their improvement,
advancement and recreation, also to
promote a knowledge of the principles of local government'. This guild
became an efficiently run and successful friendly society. Blain moved to
London and found that the equivalent
organisation there was moribund, and
he proposed the formation of a comprehensive national organisation of
municipal officers. Thus it was that
the National Association of Local
Government Officers was set up in
1905.

NALGO started with 8,000 members, made rapid progress, and by
1914 its membership of almost 35,000
covered nearly 70 per cent of all local
government officers. The organisation
in its early days could hardly be described as a trade union. In 1911,
NALGO's first full-time general
secretary, Levi Hill wrote in the association's journal, 'anything savouring
of trade unionism is nausea to the local government officer and his association.'

During the first world war NALGO
underwent a crisis in organisation and
finance with the loss of most of its
guild officers and members to the war
effort. This crisis forced NALGO into
a re-organisation which resulted in: a
new NEC of 24 district representa-

tives to replace the former national council of some 200 guild representatives; an annual delegate conference; an organising secretary; an expanded and improved journal; a new subscription scale; and a new statement of policy which, while still not actually mentioning salaries, set out as its main objective the creation of an 'adequate and efficient local government service'. The Whitley Committee Report in 1917 served to lay down the principles upon which all of NALGO's negotiating structures are now based, although it was not until 1943 that the National Whitley Council for Local Government was set up and the local government 'charter' adopted later (1946) laid down the first national salary scales for local government officers in England and Wales.

NALGO became a certificated trade union in 1920, and by 1936 its membership had climbed back to 30,000. Shortly afterwards it absorbed the *National Poor Law Officers' Association* and added a further 6,500 members to its ranks.

Immediately after the second world war, NALGO faced the prospect of a crippling loss of members as the new Labour government set up the National Health, gas and electricity services by removing these functions from the municipal authorities. In the event NALGO decided to follow its members into the new services. By 1951 NALGO had 200,000 members but worked in a complex structure of negotiating bodies with an organisation still geared to its old status as a local government union. NALGO solved these organisational problems by setting up separate and largely independent controlling bodies at each of the three levels into which the association was divided: employer-based branches and district and national service conditions committees. In 1952, NALGO changed its name to its present title to reflect its widening membership outside local government.

In 1961 NALGO added a strike clause to its constitution — although it was not until 1970 that it was forced into its first official strike involving 18 members of the Leeds branch in a dispute over the application of a local bonus and incentive scheme. NALGO affiliated to the TUC in 1964,

some 43 years, 12 conference debates and six membership ballots after it was first suggested.

Over the years NALGO has grown as follows:

1928 —	43,602
1938 —	101,041
1948 —	170,960
1958 —	246,576
1968 —	366,951
1978 —	709,331
1980 —	753,226
1982 —	796,145

The post-war growth is a reflection not only of the growth of white-collar unionisation generally, but also the growth of the public services sector. Between 1952 and 1965, total white-collar staff employed in the industries NALGO organised went up by about 12 per cent — but NALGO membership increased by 57 per cent.

Today, although NALGO is the dominant union in local government, it is not the only union organising white-collar staffs in the non-governmental public services. Both MATSA and NUPE recruit white-collar employees mainly at the supervisory level in local government. NUPE, COHSE, ACTSS, and ASTMS also recruit in other industries within which NALGO is organised.

Union Officials

NALGO employs 700 staff, including some 220 organising staff at headquarters, in the districts (district officers) and at branch level (branch organisers). Each district office is headed by a district organisation officer.

Despite the large number of women members, female full-time officials are rare, with the exception of a handful of district officers (see **Women**). NALGO officials tend to come from within the union's own ranks and to have served as branch officers for a number of years. NALGO salaries for full-time officials are fairly high by trade union standards.

The union also recruits ex-students from Ruskin College and other industrial relations academic institutions such as Warwick University and the LSE. NALGO workplace activity is largely undeveloped to date, and there is thus a high dependence on the services of district officers. NALGO officers tend to be appointed in the early 30s age group.

Coverage

Joint bodies upon which NALGO is represented include:

Local Government Staffs:
National Joint Council for Local Authorities' Administrative, Professional, Technical and Clerical Services

Joint Negotiating Committee for Chief Officers of Local Authorities

Joint Negotiating Committee for the Probation Service

Joint Negotiating Committee for Youth Workers
Electricity Staffs:
National Joint Council (Administrative and Clerical grades)

National Joint Managerial Council
Gas Staffs:
National Joint Council for Gas Staffs and Senior Officers

National Joint Council for Higher Management
National Health Service:
General Council of the Whitley Council for NHS employees, and the following functional councils: Administrative and Clerical Staffs Council; Nurses and Midwives Council; Professional and Technical Council 'A'; and Professional and Technical Council 'B'
Transport Staffs:
National Joint Council for Non-manual Staffs employed by Subsidiary Operating Companies of the National Bus Company

Joint Standing Committee of Managerial Staff of National Bus Company Subsidiary Companies and Headquarters Staff

Joint Negotiating Committee for the Non-manual Employees of Passenger Transport Executives

National Joint Council for British Waterways Board Salaried Staffs
New Towns Staff:
Whitley Council for New Towns Staff
Water Staffs:
National Joint Council for Water Service Staffs

National Joint Council for Senior Water Service Staffs

Industrial Estates Corporation and Development Agencies Staffs:
Whitley Council for Staffs of the Industrial Estates Corporation and the Development Agencies
University Staffs:
Joint Council for Clerical and Certain Related Administrative Staffs

Central Council for Non-teaching Staff in Universities

Organisation

The government of NALGO is vested in the Annual Conference which may issue an instruction to the National Executive Council and is responsible for the direction of the general policy of NALGO.

The National Executive Council of NALGO is vested with full authority and power to manage the business of the union subject to Conference directions. The NEC is elected annually in districts by individual ballot with papers distributed through branches. The turnout of ten often approaches 50 per cent — high by trade union standards generally. In the 1982 elections, there was a small swing to the right, with ten new EC members elected and four sitting members deposed. Increasingly, such elections are becoming political in the sense that slates of preferred candidates are circulated by the Conservative Trade Unionists' Association, and the 22 members of the 1981 NEC who formed the Fight for Labour Affiliation Group. The NEC at present numbers 69 of which 14 are women. It has the power to issue instructions to the membership to take industrial action if it considers it to be appropriate but this power can also be exercised by Conference.

NALGO branches can now set up local strike funds. Against Executive advice the 1981 Conference decided that all NALGO members are authorised to honour TUC picket lines and can therefore expect NALGO support if they are disciplined by employers for doing so.

NALGO is organised into 12 districts each of which elects its own district council which is representative of the branches within each district. Each district is a constituency for the purpose of electing members of the NEC. The Annual Conference comprises two delegates from each district council as well as representatives elected by the branches in proportion to their membership. There is also provision for the representation of sectional and professional organisations. There are 1,230 active branches within NALGO.

A distinctive feature of NALGO is the extent to which its membership participates in its government — which is based on a committee structure at all levels in the union.

Workplace Activity

Despite the high level of involvement in union affairs by NALGO members compared with other unions, workplace activity has until recently been largely undeveloped. NALGO branch secretaries often deal (and have dealt) directly with the local authority, but the branch secretary comes into the particular department as an outside union representative, and not as a workplace negotiator. A few large branches have arranged for the election of shop stewards, and have authorised them to take up departmental issues. A circular from the NEC in 1978 urged departmental representatives 'to be responsible to and for a particular group of members and negotiate on behalf of this group and individuals within this group'. This advice followed a decision of the 1977 Annual Conference to set up a 'steward' system. However, it has been left to each branch to develop the system of organisation most suited to its own circumstances. A distinctive feature of this orientation toward steward representation, in common with other unions in the public sector, is that there should be a close link between branch and workplace organisation. The leadership of NALGO sees this development not as a 'radical upheaval' but as a 'logical evolutionary development'. It is clear that the union hierarchy intends to keep a tight control on its eventual shape and form. Higher paid managerial staff belonging to NALGO still exert a profound influence on the union's policy, despite the fact that the proportion of NEC members who were chief officers fell from 31 per cent in 1939-45 to three per cent in 1967-73.

NALGO represents a loose federation of divergent sectional interest groups, and its policy is inevitably shaped by expedients determined by the current negotiation climate, e.g. cash limits and comparable salary movements elsewhere. Fundamental questions about relativities are rarely asked and this serves to benefit the higher paid minority of senior officers.

Women

Women now constitute over 50 per cent of NALGO's (voting) membership and as a union NALGO has made some progress in furthering the cause of women trade unionists. An equal opportunities committee sits in an advisory capacity within the union. In 1977 NALGO affiliated to the National Abortion Campaign, and has voted in support of the TUC policy on a woman's 'right to choose'.

In 1981 NALGO publilshed a report entitled *Equality?*, a survey of NALGO members which was carried out by the Sociological Research Unit of University College, Cardiff, in conjunction with NALGO Research Section. The survey data suggested that within the kind of work undertaken by NALGO members, women still predominately operate as 'a secondary labour force.' They are less well qualified, earn less money and are concentrated in the typing/secretarial grades. They are less likely to ask for employer-sponsored training or promotion/regrading and are less likely to get either. The report concluded that 'far from winning the battle for equality, women's position has deteriorated in the last six years'.

In local government it is rare for women to reach principal officer grade, and where they do such success is usually achieved within planning or social services departments. NALGO does not send a delegate to the Women's TUC on the grounds that women are part of the mainstream of the labour movement. Around 20 per cent of shop stewards are women, and women outnumber men in four of the public services: health, gas, electricity and universities. But there are more male than female shop stewards/departmental representatives in *all* of the services except the universities. Tess Woodcraft is the research officer with special responsibility for equal opportunities. Very few NALGO full-time officers are women.

External Relations

NALGO is the largest union within the TUC that is not affiliated to the Labour Party. Throughout its history NALGO has withheld political affiliations of any kind, and did not affiliate to the TUC until 1964 on the grounds of its 'association with the Labour Party'. Its rules provide that no district council or branch may affiliate to any organisation (apart from a trades council) 'which is associated directly or indirectly with any particular party or organisation'.

The issue as to whether or not NALGO should affiliate to the Labour Party went to a ballot of the membership in early 1982. The NALGO NEC had originally voted 29–20, with 19 members absent, against a ballot on affiliation, although the 1981 NALGO Conference — regarded in the union as being to the left of the Executive — voted against this position and decided to hold a ballot. The arguments for affiliation set out in a NALGO publication, *NALGO in the '80s*, were that such a step was necessary to bring NALGO into the mainstream of the labour movement; that the union should be involved where crucial decisions affecting its membership were made; and that the Conservative government was 'seeking to implement a wide range of policies which have serious, and potentially dangerous, implications for NALGO members.' Against affiliation it was argued that it was important for NALGO to maintain its party political independence since 'local government members are expected to give impartial advice to majority groups of differing political persuasions', and that it would be wrong for NALGO to be identified with a political party which only a minority of its members was likely to support. In the event, 49,925 members voted 'yes' for affiliation, and 382,577 voted 'no'.

NALGO has its spokespersons in parliament — in both the Commons and the Lords. It also keeps in close touch with European Community affairs, through its international relations committee, seeking wherever necessary, 'to influence Community decisions that may affect members' working lives'. Two members of the European Parliament represent NALGO interests, and NALGO's general secretary is a member of the European Community Economic and Social Committee. Internationally it affiliated to the Public Services International (PSI) in 1980, and it is linked with the Council of European Municipalities (CEM), the European Union of Local Authority Employees (EULAE), the International Confederation of Public Servants (CIF) and the International Union of Local Authorities (IULA).

The union is affiliated to the following organisations:

Anti-Nazi League
Amnesty International
Anti-Apartheid Movement
Age Concern
Child Poverty Action Group
National Abortion Campaign
Workers' Educational Association
Chile Solidarity Campaign
United Nations Association
National Council for Civil Liberties
Pre-Retirement Associations
National Council for One-Parent Families
Campaign for Press and Broadcasting Freedom

The 1981 Annual Conference (against the advice of the leadership) voted to commit itself to a policy of unilateral disarmament and voted to affiliate to the Campaign for Nuclear Disarmament (CND). Another motion at the 1981 Conference was passed which exposed the hypocrisy of civil defence programmes; agreed to support members and branches who refused to be involved in them; and instructed the NEC to take such action as may be necessary to protect any NALGO member who 'may be in any way prejudiced as a result of following his or her conscience in this matter'.

Policy

NALGO has gradually and often painfully come to recognise the need to back up its claims with industrial action, and it did not add a clause providing for industrial action until 1961. Even then the NEC told Conference that NALGO 'had no intention of using the strike as a tactic in salary negotiations'. NALGO's first official strike did not take place until 1970, but recent years have seen the NEC give approval increasingly to requests from national and district service conditions committees for industrial action.

NALGO has given its support to policies which include:

(a) condemning the government's attempts to re-introduce private medicine into the National Health Service, and supporting the principle that the NHS should provide services 'according to the needs of the patient rather than ability to pay' (1979);

(b) calling on the TUC General Council to develop a co-ordinated campaign of union activities against public expenditure cuts (1979);

(c) opposing the anti-abortion legislation;

(d) measures to combat racialism everywhere (NALGO has been active in sponsoring a Racial Harmony National Poster Competition for schoolchildren and given a great deal of support to the TUC's anti-racism campaign);

(e) measures to seek early improvement in the provision of maternity, paternity and parental leave with pay;

(f) support for a 35-hour week.

(g) at the 1981 TUC NALGO argued that economic and social planning must be done comprehensively taking account of all the factors that have an effect on the economy — including pay;

(h) opposition to the anti-union Employment Act.

NALGO's attitude to nuclear power in Britain has been described by a member of the Anti-Nuclear Campaign as 'exceedingly wet'. Approximately 5 per cent of members of NALGO are located in the electricity supply industry and 5 per cent are in the gas industry, who make policy for the whole of the union via the EPAC (Energy Policy Advisory Committee). The EPAC has abdicated its responsibility to recommend a policy towards the PWR for the union by recommending that it simply accepts the outcome of the public inquiry.

Recent Events

NALGO has changed its character in the post-war years so that today it is largely part of the general mainstream of the trade union movement. Whilst its substantial growth can be largely attributed to the growth in white-collar unionisation generally and to the increasing importance of the non-governmental public sector, it has developed a certain uniqueness of its own. Its main concentration of membership (over 60 per cent) is in local government, and the other industries in the public sector in which it organises — health, gas, water, transport, electricity and the universities — are all areas which were at one time local government functions. NALGO members, if they move at all, tend to stay within the industry they first entered and, if they do move, they tend to take their membership with them. This may to a large extent explain NALGO's vertical organisation — town clerks and chief officers having joined NALGO when they first entered the service as juniors.

In 1981 NALGO was one of the few TUC unions to record a *growth* in membership — although local government suffered cuts in staff. The rise can probably be attributed to the growing sense of insecurity among local government staff about their jobs. Its membership at the end of 1981 was around 796,000.

In 1982, NALGO members were involved in the health workers dispute in the NHS.

Despite its size, NALGO still represents a large uneasy alliance of diverse occupational groups, and its size belies its weakness in that its belief in using trade-union tactics to support its claims is often half-hearted. It has undergone a painful transition in providing for industrial action in its constitution, and the rules and regulations covering such action cover eight printed pages.

Further Reference

Alec Spoor, *White Collar Union — Sixty Years of NALGO*, Heinemann 1967.

C. G. E. Neill, 'NALGO and the development of occupational associations in local government', *Industrial Relations Journal* 1979. A good account illustrating the uneasy alliance of sectional occupational interest groups within the union.

D. Volker, 'NALGO's affiliation to the TUC', *British Journal of Industrial Relations*, vol. 4, March 1966.

George Newman, *Path to Maturity: NALGO 1965–1980*, NALGO 1982.

Nigel Nicholson *et al*, *Dynamics of White-Collar Trade Unionism*, Academic Press 1981.

Public Employees, National Union of
(NUPE)

Head Office

Civic House
20 Grand Depot Road
Woolwich
London SE18 6SF
01-854 2244

Principal Officers

General Secretary —
Rodney Bickerstaffe
Deputy General Secretary —
Tom Sawyer
Assistant General Secretaries
Negotiations — Ron Keating
Finance and Legal —
John Bull
National Secretaries —
Harold Wild
Bob Jones
National Officers —
Roger Poole
Alistair Macrae
Gary Cooper
National Organisation Officer — Allan Taylor
National Women's Officer —
June Abdoolrohonun

Membership (1982)

Male 234,666
Female 469,332
Total 703,998

Union Journal and Publications

Public Employees —
circulation 250,000, monthly.
Despatched in bulk to branches for distribution by shop stewards.

NUPE has published a number of pamphlets and booklets, well written and highly informative as far as rank-and-file interests are concerned. These include:

Good Health — the union's evidence to the Royal Commission on the NHS which presents a policy to 'regenerate that radical spirit which inspired the movement when it first envisaged a National Health Service'. 30 pages.

Defend Direct Labour — a booklet spelling out the steps necessary to combat the introduction of contractors into local government services. 31 pages, May 1982.

Keep Your Council Services, Public: Say No to Private Contractors — a pamphlet analysing the effects of privitisation of local government services and the dangers that such privatisation poses for the community and local government workers. 22 pages, April 1982.

A NUPE Handbook for Safety Representatives in the Health Service — one of a number of NUPE handbooks on health and safety for different workgroups (e.g. parks and gardens, school caretakers, health service workers, school meals), variously published in 1980 and 1981.

Head office has also produced an Anti-Privatisation pack for use by organisers and branch officers in organising privatisation educationals.

Divisional Offices

● *North West*
C. Barnett
131 Katherine Street
Ashton-under-Lyne
Lancashire OL6 7DE

● *East Midlands*
N. R. Wright
6 Sherwood Rise
Nottingham NG1 5GT

● *Wales*
D. Gregory
158-159 St Helens Road
Swansea
Glamorgan

● *Scotland*
R. Curran
18 Albany Street
Edinburgh

● *South West*
F. Huff
853 Fishponds Road
Fishponds
Bristol BS16 2LG

● *Northern*
S. King
Southend
Fernwood Road
Newcastle-upon-Tyne NE2 1TH

● *West Midlands*
B. Shuttleworth
Monaco House
Bristol Street
Birmingham B5 7AS

● *Southern and Eastern*
B. Couldridge
Garland Hill House
Sandy Lane
St Pauls Cray
Orpington
Kent BR5 3SZ

● *Northern Ireland*
I. McCormack
58 Howard Street
Belfast
B11 6PN

● *London*
H. A. T. Barker
Civic House
Aberdeen Terrace
Blackheath
London SE23 0QY

● *North Eastern*
R. French
Blackgates House
Bradford Road
Tingley
Yorkshire

NUPE also has 20 assistant divisional officers and 127 area officers operating within the divisions for which the divisional officers are responsible.

General

NUPE is now Britain's fifth largest union. It probably has more women members than any other British trade union, with about two-thirds of its total membership being female. There are eight women on the 26 strong Executive Council, and six women area officers employed by the union. Five seats on the Executive Council are reserved for women only (see **Organisation**). There is one woman divisional officer, six women area officers (out of 127) and the National Women's Officer.

NUPE membership is distributed approximately as follows:

About 50 per cent is employed by local authorities, of whom about four fifths are manual workers. The National Health Service employs about a third of NUPE members, most of whom are ancilliary workers, the others being nurses, midwives and ambulance workers. About 24,000 members are employed by universities (mainly porters, cleaning and kitchen staff). Around five per cent are employed by universities and water authorities employ about four per cent.

NUPE is represented on all the national joint councils for local authority workers, Whitley councils for National Health Service employees, the national joint councils for the water service, and the national councils for university non-teaching staffs.

The new General Secretary, Rodney Bickerstaffe, was elected to the TUC General Council at the 1982 TUC Congress.

History

NUPE originated in 1888 with the formation of the *London County Council Employees' Protection Society*, under the presidency of Albin Taylor who was employed as a labourer at the engine workshop of the LCC's sewage plant. Branches were formed in many parts of the country and the more appropriate title of *Municipal Employees' Association* was adopted in 1894. In 1908 as a result of what were largely personal differences of opinion, the MEA split into two parts. One part with Albin Taylor as general secretary adopted the title of the *National Union of Corporation Workers* while the other part retained the title MEA but subsequently merged with other unions in 1923 to form what is now the General and Municipal Workers' Union.

In 1925 Taylor retired and was replaced as general secretary by Jack Wills, a builder's leader and Mayor of Bermondsey, described by Professor B. C. Roberts in his book, *The Trades Union Congress, 1863-1921*, as a 'well-known advocate of militant industrial unionism'. In 1928 the NUCW changed its name to the National Union of Public Employees, to better pursue its aim of being the one union for public sector workers.

Throughout much of its life, NUPE has faced severe competition from the TGWU and the GMWU (and elsewhere) but its growth record forced these unions to be more circumspect and show greater flexibility in their dealings with it. Twenty times Bryn Roberts's attempts to gain election to the TUC General Council were defeated by their block votes but eventually in 1963 Sydney Hill secured a seat on the General Council.

The most remarkable aspect of NUPE's history is its substantial growth in membership. Over the years it has grown as follows:

1928 — 11,500
1938 — 40,200
1948 — 140,250
1958 — 200,000
1968 — 256,000
1978 — 693,097
March
1982 — 710,453

General Secretaries
1902-25 Albin Taylor
1925-33 Jack Willis
1934-62 Bryn Roberts
1962-67 Sydney Hill
1968-82 Alan Fisher
1982-   Rodney Bickerstaffe

This rapid growth reflects the growth of the public services sector. In 1948 there were 1.8 million people employed in education and local government and health. By 1974 this number had risen to 3.9 million. However, union recruitment has not been that easy. Not only has there traditionally been a rapid turnover of staff and a predominance of women part-time workers, but also the public services sector has been characterised by a dispersion of workgroups. Added to this, the fact that there have always been large pockets of non-unionists in the public services sector has meant that competition between NUPE and its rivals has been sharp because non-unionists are not covered by the Bridlington Agreement (see **Trades Union Congress**).

In its early years NUPE survived primarily because of its historic dominance in London, sustained by close political links with the various councils. But its real growth came after 1929 following re-organisation of local government which gave the county councils responsibility for trunk roads, higher education, and for some aspects of health. With the assumption of these new responsibilities, county councils employed more staff and hence it was possible for NUPE to recruit previously unorganised rural workers throughout the 1930s. Thus NUPE's inter-war growth can be explained in part by the way in which county councils (and smaller urban district councils) took on new functions and workers. Each independent employer followed different terms and conditions and in general was not negotiating with a multiplicity of unions. It was more usual for an employing authority to be faced with a single union or none at all. It was only when amalgamations began that competition between unions grew in real earnest. Given the increased scope for inter-union competition in the 1930s, NUPE grew largely at the expense of the GMWU. The GMWU's leadership was an aging one and had lost its drive. Another factor was the way in which NUPE energetically took up every grievance. With little or no local bargaining over pay, union competition centred around the ability of each union to take up grievances in order to increase membership.

NUPE's success in recruitment continued in the post-war years. Whilst the TGWU and the GMWU were secure in their dominance of the regional negotiating structure in various sectors, NUPE had to orchestrate a campaign to redress this balance at national level. Bryn Roberts's campaign for a system of national negotiations in the public services had been repeatedly defeated in the TUC (as had his demands for the re-organisation of the trade unions along industrial lines). During the war, a National Whitley Council for road workers was set up, and later the Local Authority Whitley Council for non-trading services began to influence wage bargaining. In 1948, the Whitley system was re-organised in the National Health Service with central control over wages and conditions. NUPE's membership in the rural areas thus benefitted as their wages and conditions were increased in line with the rest of the country.

NUPE's membership increased substantially in the late 1960s and during the 1970s. Following the introduction of incentive payment schemes as recommended by the National Board for Prices and Incomes in 1967, NUPE instigated a shop steward system to enable the union to cope more effectively with developments in workplace organisation in the public services. Much of NUPE's recent growth in membership can be attributed to the changes effected by the union to take account of the upsurge in militancy at workplace level (see **Recent Events**).

Union Officials

During the 1930s NUPE gained a reputation for taking up every grievance by its staff of young energetic and often idealistic officers. The officer became the main means whereby the often scattered membership was able to air its grievances, the main focal point of trade union activity, and was often expected to attend every branch meeting.

It used to be NUPE policy to appoint its officers from outside the union, but in the last five years the union has concentrated on recruiting from its own ranks; currently, approximately 20 per cent of its officers are lay members, and in the past two-and-a-half years, of 13 officers appointed, 12 have been appointed from NUPE ranks.

Coverage

Joint bodies upon which NUPE is represented include:
(a) Local Government:
National Joint Council for Local Authorities, Services (Manual Workers); National Joint Council for Local Authorities (Administrative, Professional, Technical and Clerical Services); Provincial Joint Council for Local Authorities, Services (Manual Workers); and Provincial Joint Council for Local Authorities (Administrative, Professional, Technical and Clerical Services)
(b) National Health Service:
General Council of the Whitley Council for NHS employees and the following functional councils: Ancillary Staffs' Council; Nurses and Midwives' Council; Administrative and Clerical Staffs' Council; Ambulancemen's Council; and Professional and Technical Staffs' Council
(c) Water Service:
National Joint Councils for the Water Service (Manual Workers) and (Non-manual Workers)
(d) University Non-Teaching Staffs:
Manual and Ancillary Staffs' Council; Clerical and Administrative Staffs' Council; Technical Staffs' Council; and Central Council for Non-Teaching Staff in Universities.

Some of the above councils are currently being disbanded by the Conservative government.

Organisation

The supreme government of NUPE is vested in the National Conference which is convened annually in the month of May. The union's general management is vested in the 26 member Executive Council which is elected by branch ballot. Full-time officers are not allowed to stand as candidates for the Executive Council.

Branches

There are more than 1,600 branches of the union throughout the UK which are usually based to cover all NUPE members employed by a particular public authority. In some cases, however, branches are based on a single occupation within a particular employing authority.

Branch district committees

The union integrates its branches and shop steward representatives at the place of work by a system of branch committees. These consist of branch secretaries, branch chairpersons and union stewards of branches within a local authority or National Health Service district. Water service and university lay officials attend the local authority branch district committee in some cases.

Area committees

Each branch district committee sends delegate(s) to the area committee for its respective service. There are normally two local government, two health service, one water service and one universities area committees within each of the 11 geographical divisions of the union.

Divisional councils

There are 11 geographical divisions (eight for England and one each for Northern Ireland, Scotland and Wales), each with its own divisional council consisting of representatives drawn from the area committees within the division, plus two women members elected by the divisional conference.

There are 11 full-time divisional officers, each with overall responsibility in one of the geographical divisions. They act as secretaries of divisional councils without voting rights.

Divisional conferences

These meet annually and consist of delegates from each branch district committee within the division, plus the divisional council. National committees are elected by branch ballot every two years on a geographical basis. There are national committees for local government, health services, water services and universities. The national committees act as the union's watchdog over a particular service and consider matters referred to them by the area committees. National committee members are members of the area committee in their respective geographical area and attend the divisional council on an ex-officio basis. National committee representatives also sit on national advisory committees which deal with occupational interests for ambulance personnel, nursing staff, craftsworkers and nursery staff. Both national committees and national advisory committees receive reports from the national officers concerned with the service or occupational group. The Executive Council is elected by branch ballot on a geographical constituency basis once every two years. There are 21 general seats and five seats open to women only. It is a lay executive with members remaining in their usual employment. In practice the senior member who has not previously been president is so elected.

EC meetings are held at week-ends at least every six weeks and EC committees are held every four weeks in the period between EC meetings. There are four committees: development, economic, finance and legal, and organisation. The EC is responsible for the general management and policies of the union and is attended by senior officers without voting rights.

The National Conference meets annually and consists of direct delegates from each branch of 250 members or more and indirectly elected delegates from smaller branches (elected on an area basis).

Workplace Activity

There are around 23,000 NUPE shop stewards who are elected by workplace groups. NUPE is unusual in that its leadership has attempted to reconstruct the union in order to integrate shop stewards into its official procedures. Shop stewards were introduced into the union on a large scale only after the National Board for Prices and Incomes recommended the introduction of incentive schemes in 1967, and shop steward organisations in the local authorities and hospitals were still being built up in 1973 when NUPE commissioned a report (*Organisation and Change in the National Union of Public Employees*) which was delivered in 1974. The report recommended that, where possible, branches should be merged into 'district branches' matching the new local government and health service boundaries. Shop stewards within each district were to form a district committee, and in the case of districts with several branches, both the branch secretaries and shop stewards were to sit on the district committee with the branch secretaries as senior stewards. A link with the higher levels of the union was to be provided by the election of representatives from the district committees to the area committees and divisional councils. Progress has been slow and the stewards in NUPE are, to some extent, still finding their feet. Whilst it may be too early to assess the effect of these reforms, they nevertheless represent an attempt to improve internal democracy, particularly at workplace level.

Women

A 1982 survey within NUPE found that 42 per cent of NUPE shop stewards are women, and that women constitute around two-thirds of total membership, although precise figures are difficult to come by. Nearly all women NUPE members are concentrated in education (cleaners and and school meals staff), local government (home helps or workers in residential homes etc.), and amongst hospital ancillary staff in the National Health Service. A survey within NUPE showed that women stewards: are much less likely than men stewards to have been a member of a union other than NUPE; have held the job of steward for a much shorter time; and are more likely to have been the first steward their group of workers had representing them. A substantial number of women members of NUPE are part-time workers — particularly in education (cleaners school meals staff), local government, and the National Health Service (50 per cent). There are only six women area officers out of a total of 127.

External Relations

NUPE is affiliated to the Labour Party and maintains a parliamentary panel of 12. At present it sponsors seven Labour MPs:

Reg Race (Wood Green)
Arthur Bottomley (Teesside Middlesbrough)
R. Moyle (Lewisham)
E. Leadbetter (Hartlepool)

T. Pendry (Stalybridge and Hyde)
P. Hardy (Rother Valley)
D. Clark (South Shields)

Labour Party Delegation

NUPE's delegation to the Annual Labour Party Conference consists of ten delegates from the divisions, four from the Executive, and four others. During the 1981 Labour Party Deputy Leadership contest, NUPE supported Denis Healey, despite the leadership's preference for Tony Benn. NUPE conducted a branch ballot which voted 267,650 for Healey, 188,581 for Benn and 28,568 for Silkin, and thus the 600,000 NUPE block vote — representing 4 per cent of the Electoral College — was instrumental in preventing Benn from winning the contest.

Policy

In recent years NUPE has lent its support to resolutions at the Trades Union Congress. In particular, they have opposed any form of incomes policy unless it is accompanied by a large scale redistribution of wealth and income in favour of working people. In early 1979, NUPE spearheaded the fight against the Labour government's five per cent wages policy wtih a series of strikes in the public services which were conducted on the issue of low pay. The union played an important part in the adoption by the TUC and the Labour Party of a policy advocating the statutory introduction of a £60 minimum weekly wage. NUPE has also played a major role in recent years in promoting the Campaign for Labour Party Democracy.

NUPE has always been a hard bargainer and an aggressive recruiter. Its membership tends to rise during disputes, leading to unfounded accusations from other unions that its interest lies in poaching members, not in fighting their claims. Such accusations were made during the 1982 health workers' dispute, and also during the 1978-79 so-called 'winter of discontent'. During 1981 membership increased by 4,842 from 699,156 to 703,998 at a time when the recession was drastically affecting the membership of most other unions.

Aggressive championing of the low

paid has for long been a characteristic of the union, and NUPE has coupled this drive against low pay with forcefully presented left-wing policies on such issues as privatisation and incomes policy.

NUPE was also involved in a campaign during 1981 surrounding the problems of the mentally handicapped, collecting a huge number of signatures and being involved in heavy (unfortunately unsuccessful) lobbying for a better deal for the mentally handicapped.

NUPE is affiliated to the Anti-Nuclear Campaign and CND, and is actively involved in the East Anglian Trade Union Campaign against the PWR.

Since 1928, it has been NUPE policy to work towards the creation of one union for all public employees, although so far amalgamation talks (particularly with COHSE) have come to nothing.

Recent Events

The central tenet of the 1974 Report — *Organisation and Change in the National Union of Public Employees* — was that there was a need to integrate workplace organisation within the union at local level in order to improve workplace and branch democracy. The Report was written from a perspective which stressed internal union democracy as an objective over and above other union aims. Its effect was to increase the openness of the union and the accountability and involvement of its full-time officers to the rank-and-file membership.

The consequent re-organisation within NUPE meant that national officers came under sustained pressure from the Executive Council and from the various national committees covering industrial groupings of membership — local government, health services, water services and universities. They responded by generating expectations about pay and conditions, and union services such as education and training, which may be impossible to achieve in the short term. Both these effects were apparent during the strike of public sector manual workers in the first three months of 1979. At NUPE's 1980 Conference, demands for an £85 minimum wage and a 35-hour week were rejected, Alan Fisher considering them 'unrealistic for the November 1980 pay round'.

The industrial action taken in early 1979 was the most widespread action of the low paid for many years. It affected caretakers, nurses, hospital ancillary workers, gravediggers, highway maintenance workers, ambulance personnel, university porters and water workers. Local branches in NUPE were left to decide about what sections of workers to call out on strike within cash limits set on the overall strike pay available in each area. There was little effective coordination between NUPE and the other public sector unions involved (GMWU, TGWU, COHSE) despite the fact that the local authority workers' claim had been delayed to enable joint action to be taken. During the scattered and unco-ordinated strike actions, the union leadership of all four unions failed to elaborate a national strategy and local tactics suited to such a struggle. There was a great deal of bitterness and rivalry between the various unions involved in the disputes, both at local and national level. In the event, the NUPE leadership settled for a fairly modest increase in the face of much hostility from the membership. The strike had raised expectations among the membership of eradicating low pay which could not be met without a confrontation with government.

NUPE is in a minority on many of the Whitley councils which provide the main negotiating machinery for manual workers in the National Health Service, local government and elsewhere in the public sector. Within that structure NUPE is often outvoted, as happened in the case of the health service ancillary workers' pay dispute in early 1979. For example NUPE have nine seats on the local authority manual workers Whitley council, as compared with nine held by the TGWU and 12 by GMWU; four on the hospital ancillaries compared to four seats for COHSE, GMWU and TGWU; and eight seats on the ambulance drivers compared with five each held by the GMWU and TGWU and one by COHSE.

NUPE has some grounds for complaint about the representativeness of the negotiating machinery for health service ancillary workers. It claims something like 150,000 out of 250,000 ancillaries, while COHSE claims 100,000 and the TGWU and GMWU admit to having smaller numbers. But the picture is clouded by the substantial number of part-time workers among the ancillaries, including many of the women whom NUPE is proud of having recruited. NUPE claims that a report by Lord McCarthy into the operation of the NHS Whitley council system, which recommended proportional representation in the council, should be implemented. But it cannot be, except by consent, and as McCarthy put it, 'it is intended that there should be a *link* between seats and members, but it should not be applied in a way which exacerbates rivalry between organisations, or encourages continual demands for marginal changes in relative membership.'

There was friction between the unions, particularly NUPE and COHSE and NUPE and the GMWU, during and as a result of the health service ancillary workers' dispute of 1979. There is great rivalry between these unions in recruitment and both COHSE and the GMWU believed that NUPE was putting forward unduly militant claims and demands in order to attract and recruit more members. There was great bitterness publicly expressed by the GMWU national officer for local authority workers about NUPE's free-wheeling tactics during the dispute.

In the event, the Clegg Commission, which reported in August 1979, rejected most of NUPE's submissions in favour of those from the employers. NUPE asked for a minimum wage based on two thirds of the national male average wage. Clegg refused to do this. NUPE pointed out that if the Commission used job-for-job comparisons, it would end up comparing the low-paid female ghetto of the public sector with the low-paid female ghetto of the private sector and 'once more widen the gap between male and female earnings'. This is precisely what the Clegg Commission did. The Commission admit-

ted at the beginning of its report that all the lowest paid grades are predominantly female. In the bottom two grades of local authority manual workers, for example, 90 per cent are part-time workers, almost all of whom are women. The lowest increases recommended by the Commission were awarded to workers such as cleaners, school meals assistants and laundry workers — jobs which are done almost exclusively by women. The strikes in the winter of 1979 were a fight predominantly about low pay and the Clegg Commission awarded the least to the low paid. As such, it was a bitter pill for NUPE to swallow, since the union undertook to accept the findings of the Commission in advance.

At the 1980 NUPE Conference, the Executive did not oppose a resolution condemning the Clegg comparability conditions. But responding to speakers who described Clegg as a 'con', Alan Fisher said it was wrong to denigrate an academic of distinction who operated on an honest basis. The Executive was defeated on a resolution which supported a rank-and-file code of practice and included a demand that disputes should be run by shop stewards and district committees. A motion calling for the merger of all health service unions was defeated.

NUPE represents a significant proportion of ambulance personnel and has consequently been involved in determined actions by that group in its long standing campaign to achieve formal parity with firefighters and police as the third arm of the emergency service.

Many of NUPE's 10,000 members in the water industry took unofficial industrial action in early 1981 against the attempt to limit pay settlements in the public sector to six per cent. In the event a 12.3 per cent settlement was achieved which failed to satisfy many NUPE activists.

During 1982 NUPE became embroiled in another dispute, this time centred on low pay in the health service. As in 1979, NUPE became a pace-setter in the dispute, and pushed other unions in the health service, particularly the more moderate COHSE, from token two-hour strikes to one-day stoppages. The May 1982

Annual NUPE Conference passed a vote calling for an all-out strike in the health service.

The eventual settlement promised a pay review body for nurses. As it is likely auxiliary nursing staff will be excluded, NUPE and COHSE now face a decline in their influence on pay negotiations.

Further Reference

W. W. Craik, *Bryn Roberts and NUPE*, Allen & Unwin 1955.

Sydney Hill and NUPE, Allen & Unwin 1968.

R. Fryer, A. Fairclough and T. B. Manson, 'Facilities for female shop stewards: collective agreements and the Employment Protection Act', *British Journal of Industrial Relations* 1978. A well written article which contains a great deal of information about women shop stewards in NUPE.

John Suddaby, 'The public sector strike in Camden: Winter '79', *New Left Review*, August 1979. A view of the 1979 strikes from an activist, which clearly shows the effectiveness of militancy by NUPE at workplace level.

Organisation and Change in the National Union of Public Employees, NUPE 1974. The official report submitted to the union by a study team at Warwick University.

Alan Fisher and Bernard Dix, *Low Pay and How to End It*, 1975.

Schoolmasters and Union of Women Teachers, National Association of
(NAS/UWT)

Head Office

Hillscourt
Rose Hill
Rednal
Birmingham B45 8RS
021 453-7221/4
and
22 Upper Brook Street
London W1Y 2HD
01-629 3916

Principal Officers

General Secretary—
Fred Smithies
Assistant Secretaries—
Nigel de Gruchy
Bill Herron

Membership (1982)

Male 80,325
Female 39,220
Total 119,545

Union Journal and Publications

Schoolmaster and Career Teacher— monthly.
School Representatives' Handbook

General

The NAS/UWT has in membership qualified teachers in all types of schools and colleges, excluding universities, in England, Wales, Scotland and Northern Ireland. It is the second largest teachers' union, its main recruitment area being among specialist teachers in secondary education.

History

The NAS was formed in 1919 by men returning from the war who were disillusioned by the prospect of depressed salaries for schoolmasters and broke away from NUT because of hostility to its tendencies towards equal pay for women. The UWT was formed in 1965 as an adjunct to the NAS and, after ten years of co-operation, the decision to amalgamate was taken.

Organisation

Members are assigned to local associations (branches) within the areas covered by their employing authorities. At present there are just over 400 local associations. Each elects its own officers to serve annually, dealing with members' problems in so far as these relate to local conditions. The local association also sends out regular information bulletins to its members and a developing function relates to supervising the appointment of school representatives and the briefing of these representatives on the handling of day to day problems within schools.

Local associations within the area of an education authority combine in a federation to represent their collective views, to consult and negotiate with their employers.

The local associations also combine to form the 32 executive districts which annually elect one or more members each to serve on the national Executive. This meets once a month either as an Executive or as committees — for education, salaries and pensions, legal aid and benevolent fund, training, recruitment and membership.

An Annual Delegate Conference is held each Easter. Delegates are appointed on a pro-rata basis by local associations and the Conference is the supreme policy-making body of the NAS/UWT. Between Conferences, and subject to Conference decisions, the Executive is responsible for running the NAS/UWT.

The general secretary is the chief negotiator at national level. There are two assistant negotiating secretaries. Also at head office, there are four assistant secretaries responsible for specific areas of union administration, such as finance, membership recruitment, salaries, pensions and conditions of service. At present there are eight full-time regional officials.

External Relations

The association is affiliated to the TUC but in all other respects is officially 'non-political and non-sectarian'.

Policy

The NAS has supported the establishment of a teachers' general council along the lines unanimously agreed by the members of the Secretary of State's working party in 1970. It aims to ensure that negotiation on all conditions of service, including pay, should be conducted at national level in an orderly manner. On the other hand, the NAS/UWT is strongly opposed to any attempt to link changes in working conditions to pay, and Annual Conference in 1980 specifically voted to take industrial action against any such policies by local education authorities. One of the teachers' most effective sanctions against LEAs is withdrawal from lunchtime supervision and out-of-school activities. Local education authorities would now prefer such duties to be part of the employment contract but the NAS/UWT will fight this.

The association accepted the responsibilities of training lay officers even before the spate of industrial relations legislation in the 1970s. In 1965 it established a residential training centre at Rednal which has facilities for courses for up to 50 members. A printing unit has been established for the production of course materials. Various seminars are held at Rednal; for example, in 1979 a books seminar was held there which produced worrying evidence that education cuts are forcing children to use dilapidated and out-of-date books and showed massive disparities in spending on books by different local authorities.

In 1972 the NAS/UWT Conference adopted a policy opposing the compulsory abolition of physical punishment.

Recent Events

At the 1982 Conference the policy of support for a teacher's right to use corporal punishment was reaffirmed by a large majority. Assistant secretary Nigel de Gruchy went further, denouncing the NUT conference decision in favour of the phased abolition of corporal punishment (see **National Union of Teachers**) as 'conniving at the erosion of our professional status'.

A recruitment war had already broken out between the two unions when the NAS/UWT used the opportunity — which its leadership believed was presented by the NUT conference decision to support unilateral disarmament — to send out a circular 'Where We Stand: Non-Political Stance'. Previously a circular sent out by NAS/UWT accused the NUT of showing less resolve than the NAS/UWT in imposing sanctions during the 1982 pay dispute. This circular was forwarded to the TUC and produced a reprimand from general secretary Murray who asked for an assurance from the NAS/UWT of no future public attacks on the NUT.

Further Reference

R. D. Coates, *Teachers' Unions and Interest Group Politics*, Cambridge University Press 1972.

Teachers, National Union of
(NUT)

Head Office

Hamilton House
Mabledon Place
London WC1H 9BD
01-387 2442

Principal Officers

General Secretary —
Fred Jarvis
Deputy General Secretary —
D. M. McAvoy
Organising Secretary —
A. Sutherland
Senior Solicitor — H. Pierce
Solicitor — G. Clayton
Senior Officials —
A. Evans (Education)
G. B. Fawcett (Salaries)
Officials —
R. P. Boland (Action)
J. H. Farrall (Women's Officer)
D. MacFarlane (Salaries)
A. Jarman (Education)
J. Rowe (Education)
Negotiations Officer —
S. Bubb

Membership (1982)

Male 78,000
Female 146,090
Total 224,090

Union Journal and Publications

The Teacher — weekly.
Secondary Education Journal — 75 pence.
Primary Education Review — 50 pence.
In addition, many specialist books and pamphlets concerned with education, union benefits, legal aid, insurance, and other services are provided by the union.
Black and White — a booklet that sets out guidelines for teachers in dealing with racial stereotypes in text books. The key question every teacher should ask of a book is, 'Could a child of any nationality retain his or her cultural pride and dignity while reading it?'

General

Membership of the union is open to all teachers who are recognised as qualified according to rule. The negotiation of salaries of most teachers in England and Wales are conducted in two Burnham committees dealing with teachers in primary and secondary schools and with teachers in further and higher education establishments.

The Burnham committees, named after the chairperson of the first committee on teachers' pay of 1919, differ from the negotiating bodies for the pay of other public sector employees, in that they are statutory committees established under the Remuneration of Teachers Act 1965. The Burnham committees can only negotiate on matters relating to teachers' pay; conditions of service are dealt with separately in the Council of Local Education Authorities School Teachers Committee. Negotiations on the teachers' superannuation scheme are conducted by a separate working party.

The Burnham Primary and Secondary Committee consists of a management panel of 28 representatives of the local education authority associations and two representatives of the Secretary of State for Education and Science and a teachers' panel comprising an equal number of representatives of the recognised teachers' organisations. The committee is headed by an independent chairperson appointed by the Secretary of State who also determines the organisations represented on the committee and the number of places allocated to each organisation. The National Union of Teachers has 16 of the 28 places on the teachers' panel, the remaining 12 places being divided among the other teachers' organisations (see **Recent Events**).

The NUT has its own building society for members and also an insurance agency and a publishing house.

History

Before 1870 there were already a number of teachers' associations. They were localised, small and possessed little influence, and were, in most instances, connected with particular religious denominations. In 1870 the passage of the Education Act, the growing interest in popular education and general discontent of teachers with their conditions led to a conference of representatives of various local teachers' associations being held in London. They formed the *National Union of Elementary Teachers*. The aim of the union was 'to unite together, by means of local associations, public elementary teachers . . . in order to provide machinery by means of which teachers may give expression to their opinions . . . and also take united action in any matter affecting their interests.'

In those days there was little or no provision for a teacher or the teacher's dependants against sickness, old age or premature death. The union made provision by establishing friendly benefits for such purposes.

From an organisation of some 400 elementary teachers in 1870, there has grown a comprehensive organisation for the teaching profession which serves members in all types of schools and further education establishments.

The union affiliated to the TUC in 1970, one year after the NAS affiliated.

Organisation

The machinery of the union is simple in design. It consists of local associations covering England and Wales, linked together to form county or metropolitan divisions. The supreme authority of the union is the Annual Conference which meets at Easter and consists of representatives of the local associations and the county/metropolitan divisions. Between Conferences the affairs of the union are managed by the Excutive which consists of 37 members elected biennially and the five officers (not officials) of the union — president, senior vice-president, junior vice-president, ex-president and treasurer. These officers are elected biennially in a postal ballot with the counting of votes adminis-

tered by the Electoral Reform Society.

There are 12 regional offices and there are regional and district full-time officers.

The national agreement between the union and the Council of Local Education Authorities on facilities for union representatives provides for the accreditation of school representatives by the union and the provision of necessary facilities for school representatives to fulfil their role.

Women

Before the second world war, male dominance in teaching governed everything; women were paid less and the marriage bar ruled that they were sacked when they wed. There were some violent struggles between the National Union of Women Teachers and the NUT, demanding great courage from the few women teacher trade unionists.

Nowadays the NUT has, as a fundamental tenet, parity of treatment for men and women teachers and is pressing for change in the traditional assignment of sex-based roles to girls and boys in schools. For all that, there are not many women full-time officers in the union. There is an Equal Opportunities Committee of the Executive and a women's official.

External Relations

The union is represented on many committees set up by the Department of Education and Science to formulate education policy and is also represented on many outside bodies whose work is likely to influence the national system of education. It maintains a strict non-party political attitude. The General Secretary, Fred Jarvis, is a member of the TUC General Council.

Policy

Ever since its foundation in 1870 the union has put forward the need for a single strong organisation for all teachers, and NUT leaders have gone on record as saying that NUT would be prepared to yield autonomy if the other unions would do the same to achieve a united, professional union. However, despite the usual frantic calls for unity at Conference, the feud between NUT and NAS/UWT has continued and even worsened during 1982. As the NUT general secretary put it, as teaching staffs contract, far more competitive recruitment by teachers' unions was to be expected.

One ready source of ammunition for NAS/UWT to calumniate NUT in 1982 lay in the decisions of NUT Conference. The left at Conference have grown in sophistication and sobriety, as exemplified in the measured tones of members of the Socialist Teachers' Alliance, who ensured that a motion to affiliate the union to the Campaign for Nuclear Disarmament was not carried in order to secure commitment to unilateral nuclear disarmament and opposition to the siting of Cruise and Trident missiles in Britain (by four per cent of the total card vote).

However, the left is clearly in a minority on the Executive; only two out of five new members elected could be described as left-wing. Many of the Executive are head teachers who necessarily have different interests from the rest of the members but tend to be elected because they are better known and have access to telephones and secretarial help. There are two Socialist Teachers' Alliance members on the Executive, Ken Jones and Bernard Regan.

The Executive president declared that, despite the resolution on nuclear disarmament, unless union rules regarding policy on political issues were changed, NUT members could not use union funds for any campaigns in support of disarmament. In effect, this ruling, subsequently supported by legal advice, postpones the issue until the 1983 Conference which will have to decide whether to change the union's rules to permit policy decisions on political questions.

In a further decision with which NAS/UWT was later apparently gleeful to take issue, the NUT Conference voted by a large majority to campaign for abolition of corporal punishment in all state schools within two years, rejecting the opposition of some Executive members.

In response to an apparent increase in racialist activity in schools, NUT has taken a determined stand. A report, *Nazis in the Playground*, listed a number of incidents in schools and noted specific campaigns against black and Jewish pupils and so-called 'red' teachers by the Young National Front and similar groups. The union has recommended that 'racism awareness' should be incorporated into all teacher training courses.

The union considers that the new Nationality Act will embitter race relations and has therefore advised members not to comply with any requests by local authorities for teachers to examine passports or entry documents and not to co-operate if any government department should attempt to use school registers as proof or disproof of continuous residence.

Recent Events

The Youth Training Scheme introduced by Employment Secretary Tebbit was condemned by NUT Deputy General Secretary McAvoy as a cynical attempt to reduce the unemployment figures before the general election.

NUT was itself castigated by the arbitrators of the 1982 pay claim for failing to mount a sustained and serious attempt to bargain. The arbitrators' report stated: 'In the negotiating round of which this is the final stage, we have been struck by the absence of any sustained serious collective bargaining by the parties. Bargaining in good faith is difficult to define and it may be that the parties have got out of the habit as a consequence of the mixture of inquiries (such as Houghton and Clegg) and pay policy structures in recent years.'

At local level a six-week strike, in protest at the Labour-controlled Barking and Dagenham authority's plans to end 159 jobs, succeeded in saving 104 of them. The strike cost the union £600,000 in strike pay but there was valuable experience gained. Morale among teachers stayed high because most of them were involved in some way or other with the union during the strike. In addition, the union's fight was assisted by a campaign waged by parents in the borough, which included marches to the town hall and incessant lobbying. In the Barking and Dagenham strike NUT mounted effective picketing and the picket lines were observed by TGWU lorry drivers and Post Office workers, which hastened the closure of some schools.

Further Reference

W. Roy, 'Membership participation in the NUT', *British Journal of Industrial Relations*, vol. 2, no. 2, 1964, pp. 189-208.

C. J. Margerison and C. K. Elliott, 'A predictive study in teacher militancy', *British Journal of Industrial Relations*, vol. 8, no. 3, 1970, pp. 408-17.

W. Roy, *The Teachers Union*, Teacher Publishing Company 1968.

R. Bourne and B. MacArthur, *The Struggle for Education 1870-1970*, Teacher Publishing Company 1970.

Teachers in Further and Higher Education, National Association of

Head Office

Hamilton House
Mabledon Place
London WC1H 9BH
01-387 6806

Membership (1982)

Male 52,195
Female 16,288
Total 68,483

Principal Officers

General Secretary —
    P. Dawson
Education Secretary — J. Rees
Negotiating Secretary —
    D. O. Weitzel

Union Journal

NATFHE Journal — published monthly during term time and sent free to all members.
Journal of Further and Higher Education — published three times a year, available on subscription.

General

NATFHE is the only organisation catering for all teachers in public sector further and higher education. Its members work in polytechnics, colleges of education, institutes of higher education, colleges of technology, colleges of further education, colleges of art, colleges of agriculture and in adult education.

At national level NATFHE is recognised by the various local authority associations and by the government as bargaining agent for further education teachers in negotiations on salaries, superannuation, conditions of service and educational matters. Twelve out of the 16 members on the Burnham Further Education Teachers' Panel, which negotiates salaries with representatives of local authorities and the government, are NATFHE representatives. NATFHE is also the main body on the Teachers' Panel of the National Joint Council for Further Education Teachers which negotiates on conditions of service in further education.

Negotiations also take place at local level between NATFHE liaison committees and local education authorities on such issues as implementation of nationally agreed conditions of service and provision of trade union facilities.

History

On 1 January 1976 the *Association of Teachers in Colleges and Departments of Education* and the *Association of Teachers in Technical Institutions* amalgamated to form NATFHE. The ATTI had been the first teacher's union to affiliate to the TUC in 1965. NAFTHE affiliated to the TUC soon after the amalgamation.

Organisation

The basic organisational unit of NATFHE is the branch, based on a single college, although a large institution such as a polytechnic may have several branches on the institution's various sites; in such a situation the branches are linked by a co-ordinating committee. NATFHE liaison committees cover all branches in each local education authority area.

Branches are organised into 14 regions. Each region has a regional council on which all branches in the region are represented. There is a regional executive committee for each region.

Annual Conference is NATFHE's ultimate policy-making body, normally meeting over the Spring Bank Holiday period. It consists of delegates from the regions plus National Council.

National Council decides policy between Annual Conferences. The Council is made up of the national officers, 100 regional representatives and representatives of organisations in joint or reciprocal membership of NATFHE (e.g. NUT). It meets at least three times a year; special meetings may be called.

The National Executive Committee conducts the business of the association between National Council meetings. It consists of the officers of NATFHE, the general secretary, 25 members elected by and from National Council (each region being represented) and representatives from the major organisations with which NATFHE has joint or reciprocal membership agreements.

The association has a large team of full-time officals, some based at head office, others operating in the regions. The officials are appointed by the National Executive Committee, with the exception of the general secretary who is appointed by the National Council.

External Relations

Formed as it was through the amalgamation of the two organisations which between them covered the whole sector of post-school public education, NATFHE is an influential body in education policy-making. It is the main pressure group for promoting the interests of further education from individual college level to the Department of Education and Science. NATFHE has the right of direct access to the Secretary of State for Education and Science on all further education issues and the DES regularly consults NATFHE on major policy issues. In the House of Commons MPs holding NATFHE membership form a sizeable group.

In 1982, Annual Conference voted to affiliate to CND. Subsequently, a Special Conference was requisitioned to challenge this decision and the question will finally be resolved at the next Annual Conference.

Women

The association has developed a comprehensive policy on women's rights in employment, education and training and has a programme of positive action to encourage women's participation in the union. NATFHE is regularly represented at the TUC Women's Conference and a NATFHE member, Trish Leman, elected at this Conference, serves on the TUC Women's Advisory Committee.

Current Policy

The association has been increasingly involved in campaigns against cuts in public services. NATFHE is a member of the Education Alliance which comprises trade unions and professional bodies committed to increasing provision and improving opportunities in education. The association has long been concerned about the failure of the present structure to provide continuing education and training opportunities for many sections of the community. In particular, NATFHE believes that the present system fails to meet the needs of specifically disadvantaged groups, such as the young unemployed, ethnic minorities and women. The direction of resources, increased and flexible access and curriculum change are seen as vital to the regeneration and future development of post-school education.

University Teachers, Association of
(AUT)

Head Office

United House
1 Pembridge Road
London W11 3HJ
01-221 4370

Principal Officers

General Secretary —
Diana Warwick
Deputy General Secretary —
J. R. Akker

Assistant General Secretaries
A. M. Aziz
G. Talbot
T. Day
Regional Officers —
D. Bleiman (Scotland)
B. Everett (North West England)
W. Hennessy (London)

Membership (1982)

Male 28,894
Female 5,100
Total 33,994

Union Journal

AUT Bulletin, distributed to all members.

General

The AUT seeks to recruit staff in universities and equivalent institutions who are on academic or academic-related salaries. The membership of the union has increased from 17,000 in 1969 to the present level partly by extending its membership eligibility and partly from the general upsurge in white-collar unionisation. Some 15 per cent of its membership are women.

The objects of the AUT are the advancement of university education and research, the regulation of relations between university teachers and related staff and their employers, the promotion of common action by these staffs, and the safeguarding of the interests of members. The union affiliated to the TUC for the first time in 1976.

History

Founded in 1971 under the name of the *Association of University Lecturers*, it did not include university staff in Scotland who formed their own *Scottish Association of University Teachers* in 1922 and who — although united with the main body in 1949 — still have separately elected representation on the National Executive Committee. In 1919, the membership was redefined to cover all teaching staff, including lecturers, senior lecturers, readers and professors and the name was changed to the *Association of University Teachers*. Since its

foundation, the AUT has extended its membership to cover academic library staff, senior administrative staff, research and other related grades of staff. These were eventually brought into the national salary grading structure in 1974, the national negotiating machinery for the teaching grades having been established in 1970. Affiliation to the TUC, following a ballot of the union's membership, took place in 1976.

Organisation

The important and primary unit of the AUT is the local association. Local associations represent members in individual institutions, colleges, universities, research units etc. up and down the country.

The governing body of the AUT is the Council which meets twice a year in May and December. Between Council meetings, the carrying out of the work of the union and the making of decisions on policy that cannot await a Council meeting fall within the province of the Executive Committee. The Executive Committee consists of 15 elected members, together with two members elected by the AUT (Scotland) Council and the Hon. Secretary of the AUT (Scotland). In addition, all officers of the association sit on the Executive Committee in a non-voting capacity.

Head office departments are as follows: officials, research and information, library, accounts, membership and general services.

The power to call for industrial action is vested in the AUT Council or, between meetings, in the Executive Committee (Rule 20).

External Relations

The AUT is not affiliated to any political party and has no sponsored MPs although it does retain one parliamentary adviser from each of the three main political parties in parliament.

Recent Events

The AUT had its first ever one-day 'withdrawal of labour' in 1975 and there was a mass lobby of parliament by more than 7,000 members in 1977, both in protests over salary matters.

There was a further lobby of parliament in 1981 by some 18,000 members to protest about the severe cuts in university finance.

Further Reference

Harold Perkin, *The Key Profession*, Routledge & Kegan Paul 1969.

Group Sixteen Civil Servants and Post Office

Civil and Public Servants, Society of
(SCPS)

Head Office

124/130 Southwark Street
London SE1 0TU
01-928 9671

Principal Officers

General Secretary —
  Gerry Gillman
Deputy General Secretary —
  Campbell Christie
Assistant General Secretaries
  Alan Shute
  Leslie Christie
  Duncan Mackie (Finance and
    Organisation)
Assistant Secretaries —
  Eric Brent
  Beverley McGowan
  Julian Dodds
  Chris Easterling
  David Heywood
  Mike King
  Judy McKnight
  Tony Lewis
  Anne McLean
  Bernard Studd
Research Department —
  Ken Jones, Head of
    Research
  Norma Heaton, Research
    Officer
  Ian Linn, Research Officer
  Andy Batkin
  A. Doggett
Negotiations Officers —
  Bill Diamond
  Rachal Hanson
  Dai Havard
  David Luxton
  John Clarke
  C. Cochrane
  Chris Proctor
  Eddie Reilly (Edinburgh
    Office)
  Mike Sparham
  Martin Smith

Finance Department —
  Eric Carter, Finance Officer
  Olga Ward, Deputy Finance
    Officer
Organising Officer —
  Leslie Manasseh
Education Department —
  Penny Massie, Education
    Officer
Editor, Opinion (Journal) —
  Alan Slingsby
*Printing and Distribution
Officer —*
  Pat Newton

Membership (1982)

Male 85,302
Female 15,202
Total 100,504

Union Journal and Publications

Opinion — monthly to all
members.
*The Case Against the Cuts:
The Other Half of the Picture —*
a pamphlet jointly produced
with the CPSA which attacks
the 'superficial and
misleading' arguments the
government has presented to
justify public expenditure cuts.
They say that, 'the policies
being pursued will lead not to
the life of a Martini ad, but to
declining living standards and
the dole queue — a deliberate
return to the thirties.'
*Government Cuts in
Environment and Transport —*
a pamphlet criticising
privatisation and 'hiving off' of
services in the Departments of
Environment and Transport.
Is This the Right Approach? —
pamphlet attacking policies to
reduce company controls and
services provided by the
Department of Trade and
Industry.

Branch Officer guide series— useful pamphlets outlining the duties of branch secretary, branch chairperson and branch treasurer.
Equality: The Next Step— a discussion document on the issues of employment of women in the Civil Service and the direction adopted on women's participation in the trade union movement.
The Office of the Future— a leaflet that attempts to answer the key questions new technology poses for trade unionists.
In Defence of Civil Service Pay— a leaflet that summarises the evidence from the Civil Service unions to the committee of enquiry under Sir John Megaw, to recommend the methods to be used to determine Civil Service pay. The report was published in the summer of 1982 with the aim of implementing its recommendations for a pay award in 1983.
Your Sickness Benefit under Attack and *Your Sickness Benefit Still Under Attack*— two leaflets responding to the government's Green Paper on Employers' Sick Pay.

General

Membership is open to established civil servants in the grades of executive officer, administrative trainee and grades above in the administration group up to the executive director. There is also coverage of similar grades in certain parts of the Post Office and in a number of fringe areas in the public sector (e.g. BAA).

History

In 1893 a group of young civil servants founded an organisation with the title 'Association of Clerks of the Second Division appointed under the Order in Council of 21 March 1890'. In those days the only form of trade union activity available to civil servants, whether organised in staff associations or not, was the submission of petitions, the last phrase of which was 'and your petitioners, as in duty bound, will ever humbly pray'.

In 1918, following discussions designed to lead to the formation of a professional body for the Civil Service comparable to the British Medical Association and similar organisations, the inaugural meeting of the *Society of Civil Servants* was held. During its early years the society's members seem to have been uncertain whether they wanted it to be regarded primarily as a professional body, open to all salaried and established civil servants, or a staff association with a more restricted membership and more precise objectives.

In 1930 these separate threads were brought together. The Association of Clerks of the Second Division had by this time become the *Executive Officers' Association* and the existence of two separate organisations in a basically common field of recruitment led to conflict in the 1920s. The two organisations therefore amalgamated to form the *Society of Civil Servants* (executive, directing and analogous grades).

In 1976 Conference agreed to change the name to Society of Civil and Public Servants, in recognition of members in the Post Office and outside the Civil Service. The Society affiliated to the TUC in 1978.

Organisation

The basic unit of organisation is the branch. Branches appoint delegates to Annual Conference which takes place in May. Conference elects, by ballot where necessary, an Executive Council consisting of a chairperson (who does not hold office for more than three consecutive years), a deputy chairperson, three vice-chairpersons and 21 other members.

Women

The Warwick University study of SCPS organisation, noting the decline in the proportion of women on the Executive in recent years, recommended the expansion of the Executive and the reservation of at least 20 per cent of seats for women members.

External Relations

The SCPS is not affiliated to the Labour Party but it is affiliated to the Labour Research Department. Annual Conference in 1978 voted to affiliate to the Anti-Apartheid Movement and to the Anti-Nazi League. The union retains a parliamentary consultant and at present this is Alf Dubs, MP for Battersea South.

Policy and Recent Events

A union that apparently shuns publicity, is restrained and seemingly pacific, the SCPS nonetheless has a good record in effectively representing its members, compared with other Civil Service unions. Without over-excitement, some radical ideas on pay bargaining have been put forward by the SCPS, in a bid to give the larger unions more freedom of action and relax the shackles of Whitleyism. Any one of the eight Civil Service unions, says the SCPS, should have the right to refuse to be party to an agreement adopted by the others. The new council of Civil Service unions should 'reassert the autonomy of individual Civil Service unions and protect the right of a union, if necessary, to take independent action to safeguard the interests of its own membership'. In an apparent reference to leaders of other Civil Service unions, it says that this freedom to opt out of an agreement would also mean that unions could not use the excuse of being out-voted on the council as a reason for not pressing union policy. This Council of Unions soon met its first severe test, in 1981 when the government revoked the long standing agreement based on pay comparability principle. At the centre of the strike organisation set up by the Council of Civil Service Unions was the Pay Campaign Committee composed of nine unions (see **Trade Union Federations**).

Co-ordination at local level was provided by 40 CCSU local co-ordinating committees whose role was to ensure the success of general action, organise support for the selective strikes and supervise local media coverage of the action. Each committee had two local representatives from the constituents of CCSU, a full-time HQ officer and a National Executive Council member from one of the unions acting on behalf of the CCSU.

The combined action by all the CCSU members placed particular stresses on the council which was the focus of campaigning activity. After some four months the campaign, which lasted for 21 weeks in all, began to run out of steam. A sustained five day all out strike was tentatively proposed by the SCPS but the Executive was obliged to withdraw the idea at the union Conference after soundings from delegates showed a poor level of support.

While the left has held sway in the SCPS for some time it has never been able to effectively back its policies because of the wide gap between the leadership and the majority of the membership. A thoroughgoing review of Society organisation, conducted by a Warwick University study group, recommended changes to increase accountability and control by members but argued against postal ballots. But the SCPS has rejected a recommendation that five Executive seats be introduced and reserved for women.

SCPS already faced organisational problems from the reactionary breakaway Immigration Service Union whose members oppose SCPS support for causes such as that of Nelson Mandela, the detained black South African political leader.

Otherwise the SCPS has an impeccable record on race relations, having supported an investigation into race relations in the Civil Service by the Tavistock Institute (on which a report was published in 1978) and having produced some useful material in *Opinion*, the union journal.

Not only has SCPS defended its own members' interests vigorously in the face of cuts in public expenditure but its officials have ceaselessly attacked unbalanced propaganda which portrays benefit claimants as 'scroungers'. It opposed the £12 a week deduction from the benefits of the dependents of strikers and sought means of obstructing the practical operation of this measure, 'not wanting to be used as frontline troops in the government's battle against the unions'. They correctly discerned that the concern for efficiency and the elimination of waste cloaks the reality of cuts in services and employment. General Secretary Gillman has rightly questioned why staff dealing with social security fraud have been increased by 1,000 but greater savings, which could be made more cheaply by improving fraud detection in the Inland Revenue and Customs and Excise, have been ignored.

The SCPS Executive rejected the agreement on the introduction of new technology. This was later accepted at a full meeting of the Council of Civil Service Unions but again rejected at Council level after the newly elected Executive of the CPSA had reversed that union's previous decision.

Civil and Public Services Association

(CPSA)

Head Office

215 Balham High Road
London SW17 7B2
01-672 1299

Principal Officers

General Secretary—
Alastair Graham
Deputy General Secretary—
John Ellis
Assistant General Secretary—
Jeanie Drake
General Treasurer—
John Raywood
Assistant Secretaries—
Terry Adams
Terry Ainsworth
Veronica Bayne
Chuck Clarke
Geoff Lewtas
Billy McClory
John McCreadie
Arthur McKinley
Richard Regan
Brian Sturtevant
Jean Thomason
Peter Thomason
Diane Warwick
Editor of Union Journal—
Clive Bush

Membership (1982)

Male 65,690
Female 144,204
Total 209,894

Union Journal and Publications

Red Tape— circulation around 200,000.
Leaflets are produced for CPSA branches, e.g. 'How the branch works', 'Duties of the branch chairman'.
A series of pamphlets issued to the membership explaining the implications of public expenditure cuts, beginning with 'Cuts mean chaos'.
'The other half of the picture'
— pamphlet attacking public expenditure cuts, jointly produced with SCPS; contains a useful critique of monetarism.

General

The CPSA is the largest Civil Service union. It also organises staffs in the Post Office Corporation, the Civil Aviation Authority, the British Airports Authority, the research councils and over 100 fringe bodies.

Grades in membership are mainly clerical officers, clerical assistants, typing grades, personal secretaries and machine operators. Numerically smaller grades represented are superintendents of typists, data processors, teleprinter operating grades, and, in certain departments such as the Department of Employment and the Courts Service, the CPSA recruits executive officers.

The CPSA also represents a number of grades of staff who are employed in one or two organisations only, for example, group office grades in the Ministry of Defence and air traffic control assistants in the Civil Aviation Authority.

The CPSA is represented on the Council of Civil Service Unions with 20 of the 62 seats.

History

It is customary to date the birth of the CPSA from 1903 when the *Assistant Clerks' Association* was formed, but the powerful stimulus to purposeful organisation in the Civil Service came with the first world war and greatly expanded government activity. In the post-war years a series of amalgamations led to the formation of the *Civil Service Clerical Association* in 1922. The union was strong enough to successfully fight for the restoration of the Civil Service Arbitration Tribunal after its abolition by the govscnment, on grounds of economy, in 1922.

In the 1930s there was fierce recruitment competition among the CSCA, the *Ministry of Labour Staff Association*, the *Court Officers' Association* and the *Inland Revenue Staff Federation*. Only when general recruitment prospects improved in 1939 were they able to partially settle their differences by forming a loose confederation called the Civil Service Alliance which promoted a measure of co-operation on issues affecting typing and clerical grades. In 1973 the Ministry of Labour Staff Association merged with the CPSA (as it had become in 1969), followed in 1974 by the Court Officers' Association.

Two important decisions were made at the Annual Conference in 1969. Since the Post Office Corporation had just been created and hived off from the Civil Service, the association changed its name to Civil and Public Services Association in order to maintain its membership in spheres outside the Civil Service. Secondly, the decision was taken to make strikes a recognised instrument of policy to be used when the National Executive decided that they were necessary. Since then the CPSA has made use of one-day national protest strikes and of selective strikes of longer duration.

Political conflict within CPSA has been influenced by its peculiar position of organising workers for the central state machine. A broad left leadership was defeated in the 1950s by the right-wing Catholic Action Group. The 1962 Radcliffe commission report on security in the Civil Service lead to the removal of a number of prominent left-wingers, both fulll-time officers and lay activists. However, the right wing lost control to the broad left in 1974. Since then the union has been famous (or infamous, depending on your point of view) for the political battles at the top. (see also **Policy** and **Recent Events**.)

Coverage

The CPSA is the largest union represented on the Council of Civil Service Unions, which is the negotiating body for all non-industrial civil servants, with 20 of the 63 seats.

Organisation

The basic unit of the CPSA is the branch, of which there are about 1,000.

Sections

The branches in a particular department are combined to form a section of which there are 17:

Ministry of Defence
Department of Health and Social Security
Agriculture, Fisheries and Food
Atomic Energy
Customs and Excise
Inland Revenue
Department of Employment
Post Office Group
National Savings
Her Majesty's Stationery Office
Department of the Environment
Land Registry
Department of Trade and Industry
Court Officers
Civil Aviation Authority Group
British Airports Authority
Home Office

The term 'group' is used in the case of the Post Office, BAA and CAA to recognise the fact that these organisations are outside the Civil Service and not directly linked with it for pay purposes. Each section or group has its separate annual section conference composed of delegates from branches. Considerable power rests in the hands of lay officials at branch level.

Departmental branches assemblies

Over 20,000 members work in institutions that are considered to be too small to justify section organisation. Some of these are government departments — e.g. Education and Science. Most however are fringe bodies, e.g. British Museum, Forestry Commission.

Main Conference

The sovereign governing body of the CPSA is its Annual Delegate Conference, usually referred to as 'Main Conference' in order to distinguish it from the section, group and Civil Service conferences. Prior to 1979 the branch delegates to Annual Delegate Conference elected the National Executive Committee by casting the block votes of their branches. The block voting system provided that candidates for president, vice-president and the NEC would be nominated by the branch. Then the branch ballot paper was completed at Conference and the vote of the whole of the recorded membership of the branch was allocated to the candidates selected irrespective of how many had attended the branch meeting.

National Executive Committee

Composition:

President
Two vice-presidents
26 elected members
General secretary
Deputy general secretary
Assistant general secretary
General treasurer
14 assistant secretaries (including editor of *Red Tape*

The professional full-time officers have no voting powers although they are in all other respects full members of the Executive. The number of NEC voting members is therefore 28.

Women

While the proportion of women branch officers and conference delegates has increased in recent years, it is still well below the requisite number to maintain relative membership proportions (about 70 per cent of members are women). There are only four women full-time officers. More women were elected to the Executive in 1980.

External Relations

As early as 1922 the CSCA was affiliated to both the TUC and the Labour Party. However, both affiliations were compulsorily terminated by the 1927 Trades Disputes Act which prohibited affiliation to the TUC and to any political party by any trade union representing civil servants. When this act was repealed in 1946 the CSCA immediately re-affiliated to the TUC but it was a legal requirement that the question of affiliation to the Labour Party be submitted to a ballot of the membership and in the event the majority of votes were cast against this. In 1971 the decision was taken to appoint a parliamentary consultant. The 1982 Conference voted in favour of affiliation and the long process of consultation and balloting was begun.

Policy and Recent Events

The CPSA officials have tended to be associated with the right wing of the trade union movement. At the 1979 Conference a motion was carried criticising Ken Thomas, the previous general secretary, for signing the document, *A Better Way*, produced by 12 moderate TUC leaders. Thomas blamed the trouble on 'Calvinistic black shirts', and the 'loony left'.

More vexatious for the general secretary and the full-time officers was that the NEC tended to have a majority of left-wing members elected under the system of mandated delegate voting at Annual Conference. At the 1978 Annual Conference, 20 of those elected to the 26 seats on the National Executive were known to be left-wing trade unionists, including Peter Coltman who was elected junior vice-president, defeating Kate Losinska. Subsequently there were allegations of electoral irregularities and the election was declared null and void.

A new rule required branches to vote only for the candidates whom they had previously nominated and some apparently did not do so or switched their declared votes at the 1978 Conference. Len Lever, then the president, declared Kate Losinska elected in place of Peter Coltman. In the fresh ballot, right-wing candidates regained control by winning 16 of the 26 seats.

At the Annual Conference of 1979 the left again took 20 out of the 26 seats and Peter Coltman was elected vice-president. The leading right-wing candidate, Kate Losinska, was elected president. Conference rejected a proposed merger with the SCPS and censured the retiring Executive for failure to make progress on the introduction of a union membership agreement into the Civil Service.

At the same Conference, the delegates voted by a substantial majority for a change in the method of election which meant the abandonment of the block voting principle (see **Main Conference**). The new system provides for each member's choice to be recorded and allocated to the candidate of their choice.

'Each individual member, therefore, will be given the chance to choose candidates and *the branch's task will be merely to aggregate the votes recorded for each candidate onto a single branch ballot form* which will be posted to the returning officer, the result being announced at main conference.' (CPSA official statement on National Elections by branch ballot — our emphasis.) All sections of the left in the CPSA, except the Militant Tendency, campaigned in favour of this rule change. In the short term it was thought likely to benefit the right wing but there seemed to be a firm conviction on the left that, in the long term, increased rank-and-file involvement would result — to the benefit of the left.

Recent events have justified this optimism, at least in electoral terms. In the 1982 election for the National Executive Committee the left swept back into power taking 25 out of the 28 positions. A statistical analysis shows that the left controls over two-thirds of the 1,000 branches. The victory of the left is a result of a combination of factors. The incompetence of the right wing showed in its production of a glossy pamphlet extolling the virtues of building a new multi-million pound headquarters: this, at a time when the union is facing severe financial difficulties arising out of the 21-week strike against the 6 per cent pay norm in 1981. Their lack of leadership in this strike, together with their refusal to abide by Conference decision — e.g. affiliation to CND — certainly helped the left in its campaign. However the complex internal politics of CPSA were seen again in the election for the three senior full-time

officer posts: general secretary, deputy general secretary and general treasurer. Although it was the left that won the constitutional changes in 1981 requiring these officers to be elected, in fact the positions were won by right-wingers — more because of the left's inability to unite behind one candidate than because of right wing dominance.

In common with other Civil Service unions, the CPSA has found it difficult to oppose the cuts imposed by the Tory government. Thousands of jobs have been lost (although very few redundancies — ironically these have all been in the Ministry of Defence — the most right-wing section). The new left-wing NEC rejected a New Technology Agreement signed by the outgoing right-wing NEC only weeks before the election. This agreement did not provide for a shorter working week or indeed for any other benefit to be gained by the introduction. The only concession was to delay compulsory redundancies for two years. However, hundreds of jobs have already been lost by the 'back door' of new technology. There are certain to be major fights in the next year or so if the government carries out its threat to impose new technology in DHSS and Employment with the loss of more than 10,000 jobs.

In July 1982 the Megaw Inquiry, set up as a result of the 1981 pay dispute, reported on its investigation into Civil Service pay. It represented a drastic weakening of the previous inadequate bargaining system which was based upon pay comparability. Among its most important recommendations, which may well be taken up throughout the public sector, are: pay rates effectively to be determined by outside management consultants; arbitration to be binding on both parties — except that the employer, i.e. the government, can appeal to parliament; and reviews to be every four years instead of the present one year. Undoubtedly this will increase militancy in this already low paid union. Whether the new left-wing leadership, with a Militant Tendency supporter as president, can lead this militancy into effective action remains to be seen.

The right are mobilising to reverse

the leftward lurch. Election procedures are being reviewed following a legal challenge to the 1982 presidential elections when Kevin Roddy emerged victorious.

Alastair Graham, CPSA General Secretary, wrote in an internal union circular to branches: 'After the experience of the general secretary, deputy general secretary and 1982 national [Executive] elections it would be my aim to review the current procedures to see if they can be improved to eliminate any weaknesses that have arisen in recent elections.'

Alastair Graham's comments were attached to copies of an unpublished report into the union's 1982 elections for its Executive Committee which was compiled by Stuart Crowhurst, the CPSA returning officer and chartered accountant. The report identified five branch votes over which objections had been lodged and stated that: 'At least 3,000 members were denied the opportunity of having their votes recorded, either by failure to distribute ballot papers or failure to submit the branch summary in time for counting.' It would obviously be crucial evidence in any court proceedings on electoral irregularities, despite its conclusion that there was no marked evidence of such irregularities. The Electoral Reform Society had previously suggested that the union's voting procedures were open to abuse because there was not enough control of the distribution of ballot papers. On the other hand, John Macreadie, the defeated candidate in the elections for general secretary and deputy general secretary and a supporter of the Militant Tendency, criticised media involvement and slurs on left-wing candidates in CPSA elections.

The extreme sectionalism of the CPSA was instrumental in moves among the Post Office group to merge or federate with the Post Office Engineering Union.

Civil Service Union

Head Office

5 Praed Street
London W2 1NJ
01-402 7451

Principal Officers

General Secretary—
J. D. Sheldon
Deputy General Secretary—
J. P. Randall
Assistant General Secretary—
T. J. Hoyes
Assistant Secretaries—
W. J. Hawkins
A. Maloney
J. L. Delaney
M. T. Barke
H. Lanning
K. J. Finch
A. R. Gallagher
J. Findlay

Membership (1982)

Male 28,513
Female 15,000
Total 43,513

Union Journal and Publications

The Whip— monthly.
Notes for Branch Officers— a very basic guide to branch procedures.

General

The CSU is one of the smaller Civil Service unions, but it is still difficult to describe in general terms on account of the diversity of its membership. Among the grades in membership are: instructional officers, stores and supervisory grades, museums and galleries staff, security staff of royal parks and gardens (e.g. Kew), messengers, cleaners, reproductive processes grades, some customs and excise departmental grades, telecommunications grades, coastguards, telephonists and traffic wardens. The union primarily organises non-industrial staff but has an industrial section of staff employed by the Metropolitan Police and the Agricultural Research Service. Principal collective agreements to which the union is party are those of the Civil Service National Whitley Council.

History

The *Government Minor and Man-ipulative Grades Association* was established by a group of messengers employed at the Board of Education in 1919. The union took its present title at the end of the second world war.

Organisation

The union is organised into branches and also into sections based on the various grades in membership. The National Executive Council of the union is elected for two years, sections being represented by at least one Executive member. There are district committees and convenors and regional councils.

External Relations

The union is not affiliated to any political party. It is affiliated to the Industrial Society. Dr Gavin Strang MP acts as the union's parliamentary adviser.

Policy and Recent Events

In 1980 CSU decisively rejected merger proposals from the CPSA. In a letter to the CPSA general secretary, the CSU general secretary said that the CSU Executive felt that the CSU would lose its own identity. He also referred to the 'delicate' point of the CPSA's record of political volatility and to the fact that the deep political divisions had been made public, saying that it would be 'repugnant' for the majority of his members to see the character of the CSU change from its consciously non-political position.

The CSU is fighting government policy to put work normally done inside Civil Service departments to outside contractors. Officials demanded to see calculations on which, ostensibly, a decision was taken by the Ministry of Defence to change from direct labour to contract labour for office cleaning. The union sought information to mount a challenge to the ministry's claim that the change would save money. When the information was refused the union complained to the Central Arbitration Committee. However, the CAC upheld the ministry's plea of confidentiality and a CSU appeal to the High Court was unsuccessful.

The CSU challenged the government to act on an ACAS report on the contract cleaning industry which revealed low pay, low rates of unionisation and that the majority of women employed as cleaners were at the mercy of employers.

The CSU Executive voted against acceptance of a two-year agreement by which computerised equipment would be introduced into the service. Anxieties arose from studies which suggested that its messenger section, with 12,000 of its 45,000 members, could suffer heavily when electronic communications replace paper messages. Its opposition was, however, insufficient to prevent a majority of the civil service unions voting in favour of the agreement at a full meeting of the Council of Civil Service Unions. (The agreement was later scrapped. See **CPSA** and **SCPS**.) The CSU Executive also opposed the 1982 pay agreement but recognised that the union's finances (which had been pushed to a critical point by the 1981 pay campaign costs of £395,000) would not stand another prolonged campaign of selective strike action.

Further Reference

Kathleen Edwards, *The Story of the Civil Service Union*, 1974.

Communication Managers' Association

(CMA)
(formerly the *Post Office Management Staffs' Association*)

Head Office

Hughes House
Ruscombe Road
Twyford
Reading
Berkshire RG10 9JD
0734-342300

Principal Officers

General Secretary —
R. J. Cowley

Deputy General Secretary —
T. Deegan
Assistant Secretary (Postal) —
F. Bowerman
*Assistant Secretary
(Telecommunications) —*
Frances Richardson

Membership (1982)

Male 15,303
Female 4,711
Total 20,014

Union Journal
New Management — monthly.

General

This union is organised into branches from which an Executive Council of 18 members is elected. It seeks to represent senior staff within British Telecom and the Post Office. Formerly called the *Post Office Management Staffs' Association*, it changed its name following the splitting of the Post Office into two separate organisations. The CMA works closely with other unions in BT and the Post Office and remains convinced that 'given the will, a single union is achievable and workable'.

This union is notable for the very comprehensive and detailed Annual Report it produces, which in 1982 ran to 178 pages. It affiliated to the TUC in 1977. It is also affiliated to Amnesty International, the Postal, Telegraph and Telephone International (PTTI) and the United Nations Association.

Communication Workers, Union of
(UCW)
(formerly the *Post Office Workers, Union of*) (UPW)

Head Office

UCW House
Crescent Lane
London SW4 9RN
01-622 9977

Principal Officers

General Secretary —
Alan Tuffin

Deputy General Secretary —
Tony Clarke
Assistant Secretaries —
K. McAllister
J. M. McKinlay
P. Grace
M. Spurr
M. H. Styles
L. V. Hewitt
E. Dudley
H. J. Jones
Organising Secretary —
R. I. Rowley
General Treasurer —
F. J. Binks

Membership (1982)

Male 152,500
Female 50,800
Total 203,300

Union Journal and Publications

The Post — normally 12 issues a year, with a circulation around 69,000.
The UCW also produced a 25-page pamphlet entitled *The Industrial Democracy Experiment and UPW Participation* in April 1978 which set out to explain the experiment in worker participation in the Post Office which was similar to those recommended by the Bullock Report on Industrial Democracy. The experiment proved to be a sad failure (see **Recent Events**).

General

The UCW is the largest of the unions in the Post Office and British Telecommunications. Traditionally it has been a moderate union with its former general secretary, Tom Jackson, a champion of voluntary incomes policy. In 1981 the union adopted a new structure giving considerable autonomy to its posts and telecoms sections, reflecting the split of the Post Office into two businesses — Telecommunications and Posts — under the 1981 British Telecommunications Act. The union is affiliated to the Labour Party and its general secretary is a member of the TUC General Council.

History

The Union of Post Office Workers (UPW) now known as the Union of Communication Workers (UCW) was formed in 1921, following successive mergers of the following organisations listed with the year of origin:

Fawcett Association — 1890
Postal and Telegraph Clerks' Association — 1913
Postmen's Federation — 1891
Adult Messengers' Association
Bagmen's Association
Central London Postmen's Association — 1906
London Postal Porters' Association — 1902
Tracers' Association — 1892
Tube Staff Association — 1903

Many of the traditions and the style of the UCW have come from the organisations which operated with the minimum of full-time officials and took major decisions at conferences or even, as in the case of the Fawcett Association, at mass meetings of members. As a result of by far the longest experience of working in the public sector, Post Office trade union leaders have traditionally thought in terms of more democracy in nationalised industries. The people who founded the UPW amalgamation in 1920 were guild socialists who held a broad conception of trade unionism. For example, support for a form of joint control in the Post Office has a long history within the union. Even before the amalgamation of 1920, the *Postal and Telegraph Clerks' Association* had committed itself to a policy of 'joint control' of the Post Office between the authorities and the employees, and in 1919 the delegates who attended the amalgamation conference made the demand for joint control one of its objectives. This objective has survived to the present day, in that Rule 2 of the UCW states, 'to pursue joint consultation with management in order to secure the greatest possible measure of effective participation by the union in all decisions affecting the working lives of its members'.

Post Office trade unions were originally recognised by the employers in 1906, and their main method of improving their conditions was to put pressure on MPs. It was only during the first world war, when the arbitration court was set up and the Whitley council machinery developed, that a regular method of bargaining was developed.

The General Strike of 1926 resulted in the passing of the Trade Disputes Act 1927, which forced the UPW to disaffiliate from both the TUC and the Labour Party.

In 1931 a deputation from union HQ met the then Postmaster-General (C. R., later Earl Attlee) which resulted in the rights of the union's branch secretaries being recognised and defined.

Until very recent times, the UPW was part of a minority in the labour movement which opposed the setting up of public corporations. The 1946 UPW Annual Conference chairperson criticised the 'child-like faith that public utility boards will provide responsible administration'. The UPW rejoined the TUC and re-affiliated to the Labour Party in 1946, following the repeal of the Trades Disputes Act.

At the Annual Conference of 1969 there was a full scale debate on workers' control in the Post Office, a debate occasioned by the plan, subsequently implemented, to turn the Post Office into a public corporation. The real issue debated was whether or not the union should demand 50 per cent representation on the board immediately or refuse to participate until assured a majority of seats. The second alternative was carried. Post Office employees lost their status as civil servants and the UPW withdrew from the national Whitley council. The unions in the Post Office saw this as an opportunity to rationalise the structure of trade unionism in the Post Office, and formed the Council of Post Office Unions. This organisation was wound up in December 1981. Apart from the 1971 strike (see **Recent Events**) the UCW has had recourse to industrial action on very few occasions. In 1962 there was a month long work-to-rule; in July 1964 there was a one day strike of postal workers followed by an overtime ban, and in 1969 there was a ten day strike by overseas telegraph operators.

Union Officials

The UCW has 13 elected officers: general secretary, deputy general secretary, eight assistant secretaries, editor, organising secretary and general treasurer. UCW full-time officials tend to be ex-branch secretaries and tend to be elected to office in their 40s.

Coverage

The UCW represents a number of occupational categories in the Post Office. Membership comprises the manipulative grades employed by the Post Office; e.g. postal worker, postal worker higher grade, telephonist, telegraphist, postal officer, cleaner etc. Over 50 per cent of all members are employed in the postal worker or postal worker higher grade (approximately 120,000) with approximately 34,000 members (of whom approximately 5,000 are part time) employed as telephonists.

All negotiations regarding pay and conditions of service are negotiated nationally. The negotiations range from pay rates and annual leave entitlement to a post-entry closed shop and an agreement on facilities for local officials to perform their duties.

Organisation

The striking feature of the UCW is its high degree of centralisation. The sovereign authority of the union is the Annual Conference, held for six days each May, at which the union's policy is decided. Branches are represented by about 1,500 delegates, the number of delegates per branch being determined according to size of membership.

There are about 1,100 branches of the union in head Post Office and telephone managers areas. These may be organised as single-grade branches, multi-grade (e.g. indoor grades) branches or amalgamated branches, i.e. where all grades in an area are represented by the same branch. The decision as to the type of branch organisation is a local one. The branches deal with purely local matters, conducting negotiations through local managers.

Branches are graded geographically into 50 district councils, the officers of

which — with one exception — act in an organising and advisory role only, i.e. they have no direct representative capacity. The exception is the London district council, whose officers have the right of direct representation to the directors of the London postal and telecommunications regions.

Branch officials are elected annually by the branch membership. Their work is voluntary and they remain PO and BT employees. Similarly, district council officials are elected by the branches in the district councils. They also remain PO and BT employees.

The Executive Council manages the affairs of the union between Annual Conferences. It consists of 35 members, and meets once a month on the last Thursday of each month for a whole day.

Twenty-two of the Executive Council are elected annually by Conference and are eligible for re-election each year. They remain PO and BT employees during their terms of office. The remaining 13 members of the EC are full-time officers. They are elected once by Annual Conference. The Postal Group Management Committee with 15 directly elected members and the Telecommunications Group Management Committee with seven, have responsibility for pay and conditions of service issues.

There are 13 national elected officers of the UCW: the general secretary, deputy general secretary, eight assistant secretaries, general treasurer, organising secretary, and the editor of *The Post*. At the UCW headquarters there are eight departments: general secretary's, telecommunications, counter and clerical, posts, legal and medical, general treasurer's, organising and editorial.

Recent changes

The organisation of the UCW has changed recently. The Post Office has been split into two separate businesses of posts and telecommunications. The Post Office created two management boards to run the businesses from January 1980, long before the legislation went onto the statute book in 1981. The UCW held a special conference in 1980 at which it was agreed to set up two autonomous sections for its members in posts and telecommunications. The two groups are headed by management committees of 15 Post Office and seven telecommunications members, and are responsible for grade pay and conditions negotiations. The general secretary and other senior officials negotiate national annual claims for both groups and decide on pay policy matters. The two committees are elected annually by the block votes of all delegates at the union's Annual Conference. Members of the two committees then form the national executive, which oversees both committees and controls union work common to both groups.

Women

Women comprise around a quarter of the UCW membership. There are five women on the Executive Council and two (out of eight) women assistant secretaries. Women tend to be concentrated amongst telephonists who are nearly all employed on day-shift working. Until the Sex Discrimination Act was enacted in 1975, there were no women night telephonists, although there are a small number now.

External Relations

The UCW is affiliated to the Labour Party. It sponsors two Labour MPs, Harry Ewing (Stirling, Falkirk and Grangemouth) and Charles Morris (Manchester Openshaw).

In 1978 the UCW received publicity about some of its members in Islington contributing money towards election deposits for nine National Front election candidates, including the National Front party chairman, John Tyndall. Fortunately, there exists an organisation (Postal Workers against the Nazis) to counter this.

Policy

It has always been UCW policy that there should be one union for all Post Office workers, and union rationalisation discussions have taken place amongst PO and BT workers. The union has generally been in favour of a voluntary incomes policy. It also vigorously opposed the splitting of the Post Office into two businesses.

Labour Party Delegation

The UCW at present sends ten delegates to the Labour Party Conference who are elected by delegates to the union's Annual Conference. The Rule Book states that no more than half of the Labour Party delegtion can be full-time officials. In practice, this usually means that five full-time officials will attend (including the general secretary) and five EC members. It is rare for lay members of the union to be elected to the Labour Party delegation by Conference.

In 1981 the UCW delegation to the Labour Party Conference voted for Denis Healey in both ballots, having been mandated after a lively debate by Conference.

Recent Events

In 1971, the UPW called a strike of all grades in support of a pay claim. At the end of seven weeks the union recommended a return to work, not having agreed any pay rise, while a Court of Inquiry was sitting to look into the dispute. The final settlement, based on the Court of Inquiry Report, was much closer to the employers' offer than to the union's demand. The whole episode was regarded as a heavy defeat both within and outside the union. Thousands of members had suffered hardship and the union was heavily in debt, apparently for nothing, since the agreed pay rises might easily have been obtained without a strike.

During 1976–77 when the UPW was involved in industrial action over South Africa and in support of the workers' demand for union recognition at Grunwick, a series of legal injunctions were awarded which were designed to stop the planned action. As a result of the legal battles, the existing Post Office legislation was interpreted in such a way as to shed doubt on the legality of the UPW taking industrial action, Prior to this, the union view was that it could take strike action and had done so, notably in 1971. It has since pressed for legislative change to put its members on par with other workers.

On 1 January 1978, an experiment in industrial democracy was launched within the Post Office. Under the experiment, the Post Office Board at national level consisted of 19 members, of which seven were trade union nominees (two of whom were UPW nominees). The experiment also provided for similar arrangements at regional and area level. The Labour government grandly claimed that this two year experiment represented the beginning of 'the socialisation of public ownership'. Sir Keith Joseph killed the experiment by refusing — in the face of union enthusiasm — to reappoint the union nominees to the board in December 1979. Joseph made this decision within two days of receiving an interim but lengthy Warwick University report which had been commissioned by the Post Office. The Warwick team of Eric Batstone, Anthony Ferner and Michael Terry asserted that:

'It is clear that issues with industrial relations, particularly negotiating, implications are now often handled outside the main Board. Where major industrial relations questions are discussed at the Board the account is clearly incomplete. We have come across instances in which union nominees appear to be completely unaware that major strategic issues are being dealt with outside the Board. Key Board members appear to play an active role behind the scenes on many issues and rarely are union nominees included in this.'

This experience of boardroom manoeuvres should provide the UCW and the other Post Office unions with a salutary lesson on the naive belief that workers' participation at board level would lead to genuine participation in the formulation of policy in the Post Office. It is to be hoped that the ineffectiveness of the Post Office experiment will not be lost on other unions. The management in the Post Office saw industrial democracy as 'a means to essentially unchanged ends — managerial ends'.

In early 1980, the UCW signed an unprecedented regional productivity deal with management in the London postal area. The deal was completed between the London district council of the UCW and Bill Cockburn, director of the London Postal Region. The agreement aims at saving work hours, to cut overtime while increasing efficiency.

The agreement was extended nationally after a two-to-one vote in favour at the UCW's 1980 Conference.

By early 1981 the Improved Working Method schemes, which had been negotiated to suit local conditions, had been applied nationally and now cover over half the postal branches.

The London district council of the UCW has traditionally been one of the most militant elements in the union and was an unlikely candidate to be the first to sign a productivity deal. It was the London UCW that convinced the union rank-and-file to overturn the Executive's support for a management wage and productivity offer in 1979; management then crumbled in the face of unofficial London overtime bans and gave a further seven per cent without strings. Similarly, it was the London district council which enthusiastically supported the blacking of Grunwick's mail against the wishes of the Executive who in the end fined John Taylor, an LDC divisional organiser, £500.

The UCW, along with other unions in the PO and BT, have been involved in discussions about union rationalisation under the auspices of the TUC.

New technology throughout both PO and BT poses a real threat to jobs and the UCW has submitted a draft new technology agreement to both PO and BT for consideration.

Further Reference

Alan Clinton, *The Post Office Workers: A Trade Union History*, Allen & Unwin 1983.

Michael Corby, *The Postal Business: A Study in Public Sector Management*, Kogan Page 1979.

'The Post Office', *New Statesman*, 6 July 1979.

'Post Office and Productivity', *New Statesman*, 8 February 1980.

Michael Moran, *The Union of Post Office Workers*, Macmillan 1974.

New Technology, The Post Office and the Union of Post Office Workers, Science Policy Research Unit, University of Sussex 1980.

First Division Civil Servants, Association of

Head Office

17 Northumberland Avenue
London WC2N 5AP
01-839 7406

Principal Officers

General Secretary —
John Ward
Deputy General Secretaries —
S. Corby
D. Stobbs

Membership (1982)

Total 8,064

Union Journal

FDA News — monthly.

General

The Association took its title from the category of civil servants it represented when first formed in 1919. Currently the FDA has in membership senior administrative staff from administration trainee up to permanent secretary as well as certain specialist groups in the Civil Service, such as statisticians, economists, lawyers, museum curators, HM Inspectors of Schools and HM Inspectors of Taxes. It also has members in some other areas of the public sector: House of Commons, House of Lords, British Council and UK Atomic Energy Authority. Branches within the FDA normally follow the departmental structure of the Civil Service and there is a high level of membership density amongst those eligible for membership. The Diplomatic Service Association, the Northern Ireland Senior Officers' Association, the Procurators' Fiscal Society and the New Town Chief Officers' Association are all affiliated to the FDA, so in effect it looks after the interests of nearly 10,000 senior public servants.

Policy and Recent Events

The FDA is a constituent of the Council of Civil Serice Unions (CCSU). Following the government's unilateral suspension of the Civil Service national pay agreement and after a ballot of its membership, the association supported the CCSU's campaign of industrial action which began on 9 March 1981 and lasted for 21 weeks. At the end of the dispute a committee of enquiry into Civil Service pay arrangements was established under Sir John Megaw and the association played its part in contributing to the CCSU evidence to the committee. Over the last year the FDA has also been concerned with professional issues and recently established a special sub-committee on machinery of government and it has paid increasing attention to equal opportunity issues. In addition it played a leading role in a CCSU campaign against proposed cuts in government statistics. Risking the wrath of certain sections of its membership, the FDA Executive gave qualified support to the TUC campaign against the Employment Act (Tebbit).

Government Supervisors and Radio Officers, Association of

Head Office

90 Borough High Street
London SE1 1LL
01-407 4866

Principal Officers

General Secretary — T. Casey
Deputy General Secretaries —
D. Burns
A. L. MacPherson
Finance Officer
G. S. Petche

Membership (1982)

Male 8,942
Female 58
Total 9,000

Union Journal

Monitor — monthly.

General

The union was formed in 1955, by amalgamation between the *Associa-*

tion of Government Foremen and Technical Staff and the Civil Service Radio Officers' Association. The AGFTS organised supervisory staff and the CSROA radio operating and maintenance staff in the Civil Service. Since the amalgamation the AGSRO has expanded by further amalgamations to cover accommodation services, accountants and station wardens, the technical supervisors in dockyards and the electronic technical staff in the Civil Aviation Authority.

External Relations

A declaration from the union states: 'As a union catering primarily for civil servants and staff in closely related organisations under the control of ministers of the Crown, the union is strictly non-political and avoids any involvement which could be seen to be a party political issue as opposed to purely industrial matters.'

Policy and Recent Events

Some members were in the forefront of events during the 1981 pay campaign of selective strikes which cost AGSRO £215,000.

Inland Revenue Staff Federation

Head Office

231 Vauxhall Bridge Road
London SW1V 1EH
01-834 8254

Principal Officers

General Secretary—
A. M. G. Christopher
Deputy General Secretary—
C. Brooke
Assistant Secretaries—
E. Symons
E. Elsey
W. H. Hawkes

Membership (1982)

Male 22,214
Female 35,938
Total 58,152

Union Journal and Publications

Assessment— monthly newspaper, free to every member.
Taxes — five issues per year, free, one copy per three members.
Branch Officers Guide.

General

Formed in 1936 as a federation of the Association of Officers of Taxes and the Collection Clerical Association, a third union then joined the federation and all three unions submerged their independence in a single organisation, although the title was retained. The Association of Tax Clerks (later the Association of Officers of Taxes) affiliated to the TUC in 1911. Continual membership of the TUC has been maintained except for the 1927-45 break imposed by Section V of the Trade Disputes and Trade Unions Act of 1927. Locally, it is open to any federation branch, subject to the consent of the Executive Committee, to affiliate with trades councils within its boundaries.

Organisation

IRSF members in each tax district, collection office and valuation office form a local federation office. Each office is in a branch of the federation. There are 121 branches, organised on a geographical basis for each of the three sections: taxes, collection and valuation.

Every branch holds at least three general meetings each year. The annual meeting in the autumn is to elect branch officers, a committee and a delegate to attend the next IRSF Conference and also nominates members to stand for election to the National Executive Committee. The spring branch meeting considers motions sent from offices intended for inclusion on the Annual Conference agenda votes in the election of the NEC. The third is a mandating meeting held shortly before Conference to go through the Conference agenda and to mandate the delegate.

The Annual Delegate Conference is the final governing body of the federation. Between Conferences, the

Executive Committee conducts and controls the affairs of the federation. There are 13 seats for taxes, eight for collection and six for valuation.

Policy and Recent Events

Although an independent trade union and TUC affiliate, the IRSF was for long regarded, as its title suggests, as virtually a staff association. The general secretaries, such as Tony Christopher and before him, Lord Plant, were voices of moderation on the TUC General Council. The comfortable identification of the rank and file of the IRSF with its leadership was brusquely upset during the Civil Service pay dispute of 1981. Given the strategic position of its taxes branches within the PAYE system, the IRSF was quicky pushed to the forefront of the campaign of selective strikes. About three per cent of revenue employees took part in strikes, compared with less than one per cent for the Civil Service as a whole. Over a thousand staff in regional and local tax collection offices struck, mainly to avoid being suspended for blacking the work normally handled by another thousand strikers at PAYE and National Insurance processing computer centres at Shipley and Cumbernauld.

As a result of the action at Cumbernauld, Ted Elsey, assistant secretary of the IRSF who was the Council of Civil Service Unions' full-time coordinator of the strike there, was charged under the Conspiracy and Protection of Property Act of 1875. He was charged with wrongfully following two senior revenue officials who had been taking blacked mail through picket lines at the Revenue Computer Centre, Cumbernauld, to send it to be processed in London. The Act has rarely been used and the sub-section under which Mr Elsey was charged had not been used for 60 years. Possibly in view of the antiquated legal provisions and penalties associated with the charge, the Sheriff court demurred at sentencing, although finding Mr Elsey guilty.

The dispute was eventually settled when the IRSF found itself alone in advocating an all-out strike. Selective action had cost IRSF £1,600,000, less

equalisation payments from the other unions of the CCSU of £250,000.

More important was the effect of the strike in radicalising opinion within the IRSF. The left, whose rank-and-file newspaper had been suppressed at the 1978 Conference, staged a recovery and dominated the 1982 Conference, using the card vote of the larger branches.

The largest branch, Manchester taxes, with 4,000 members, cast its block vote for an SWP candidate standing for the vice-presidency of the union's taxes section at a mandating meeting at which 27 members were present. Eventually the right re-organised and overturned this vote at a special meeting at which 400 members were present.

On policy, the IRSF voted for a flat rate instead of a percentage pay claim. A broad-left group was formed by like-minded delegates to the Conference who united around proposals calling for organisational changes to give more power to the increasingly left-influenced taxes section of the union at the expense of the politically quiescent collection and valuation sections.

This provoked a counter-attack when the IRSF Executive decided to expel the six Executive members concerned in the broad-left group unless they renounced their membership or disbanded the group. An internal union circular sent to all members stated that, 'the broad left in the IRSF has been set up as an organisation within the Federation. In all but name it is an alternative union.'

The Inland Revenue has been one of the departments most heavily hit by the cuts in the number of civil servants, many of these cuts being implemented by getting rid of administrative functions. Further staff losses as Pay-As-You-Earn is computerised could mean a total drop of 20,000 in the number of people working for the Inland Revenue Department by the end of the 1980s.

The union's response to these cuts has been to highlight the scandal of the black economy where, the IRSF believes, some £4 billion of tax could be collected if extra resources were put into it. Tackling tax evasion would not only be highly cost-effective, it would increase the amount of money available for public expenditure and/or tax cuts. It would make the tax system fairer, especially for those tax-payers and business people who do not operate in the black economy.

Post Office Engineering Union

(POEU)

Head Office

Greystoke House
150 Brunswick Road
London W5 1AW
01-998 2981

Principal Officers

General Secretary —
Bryan Stanley
Deputy General Secretary —
Eric George
General Treasurer —
D. Norman

Membership (1982)

Male 128,865
Female 3,963
Total 132,828

Union Journal and Publications

POEU Journal — monthly.
The union's history is set out in a book by Frank Bealey, History of the POEU.
The union has produced a number of publications recently, all of which are of great interest and significance to trade unionists outside the POEU.
Optical Fibre Technology — a booklet outlining the nature of the technology, an account of current and likely future systems, British Telecom plans and various issues of concern for the POEU. 39 pages, January 1980.
The Cabling of Britain — deals with the plans for cabling to meet the needs of cable television and information technology systems of the future. Also considers satellite technology. 47 pages, May 1982.

Tapping the Telephone — A report of August 1980, which sets out the POEU policy on telephone tapping.
The American Telecommunications System — examines the impact of new technology on the American workforce and customer and assesses the effect of the de-regulation of telecommunications in the USA. April 1981.
The Modernisation of Telecommunications — describes the whole modernisation programme of British Telecom over the next decade and assesses the impact on POEU members. There are special annexes on electronic mail, electronic funds transfer, the electronic office and the electronic home. May 1979.

General

The Post Office Engineering Union is the second largest Post Office union and organises on the telecommunications side of the Post Office all grades, below first-line supervisory level, that were formerly in the old Post Office Engineering Department (with the exception of telephone operators). The POEU, like other Post Office unions, is deeply affected by developments in information technology (see **Publications**) and is likely to be in the forefront of technological change in the next few years. The POEU is also coping with the organisational problems resulting from the split in the Post Office between the telecommunications side of the business, and the postal and giro services.

The union is affiliated to the Labour Party and John Golding MP, an Assistant Secretary of the POEU, is on the trades union section of the Labour Party NEC.

History

Permanent organisation of telegraph lines workers began in 1896. However, the present union was founded in 1915 when, following the purchase of telephones by the state, the older *Engineering and Stores Association*

(5,000 members) joined with the *Amalgamated Society of Telephone Employees* (11,000 members). In 1919, this organisation took the title, the Post Office Engineering Union.

The POEU still retains the legacy of a limited and functional federal system, which is a result of the POEU's experience with breakaway unionism. In 1911 there was dissatisfaction with union policy among skilled internal exchange workers—they formed the *Telephone and Telegraph Engineering Guild*, which only returned to the POEU after advisory occupational councils and occupational branch structures were introduced into the POEU constitution. There were further harmful breakaways in 1946 and in 1949. The *Engineering Officers' (Telecommunications) Association* (another dissident group of internal workers) was formed in 1946; and the *National Guild of Motor Engineers* was formed by motor transport workers in 1949. These two groups were persuaded to return to the fold of the POEU in 1954 only after new occupational committees were given a veto over their own business (although the NEC has to approve all occupational minutes).

Over the years, with the expansion of telecommunications and the coming of automatic telephone exchanges, the 'indoor' workers have gradually dominated the union at the expense of the lines maintenance workers who work out of doors. Bealey states that, by 1970, 56 per cent of union members were internal engineering grades and only 24 per cent were external (it is now much higher). The other 20 per cent consisted of the so-called 'minority' grades.

The membership of the union has grown rapidly in recent years. Its membership was 45,000 in 1950. By 1967 it had reached 100,000, and the POEU was one of the few unions to register a growth in membership during 1981.

Union Officials

In 1981 the POEU employed 20 full-time officials (including the three principal officers). Fourteen of these officers have been members of the union, recruited via the Executive, whose practice has been to appoint its own members to posts calling for more knowledge of, and contact with, the membership. In recent years, three union members have been appointed to officerships without having been members of the NEC. For example, the assistant secretary (press and publicity) was appointed from outside the union.

Most of the research staff have not been members of the union. Hence the more functional specialist officers (wholly graduates or professional economists) tend to provide the arguments rather than becoming involved in the arguments themselves. The research department is expertly staffed and has expanded since its formation in 1949. The growth of arbitration in which the union has become increasingly involved has put a premium on the production of well collated statistical data and the drafting of well argued papers. It has been traditional in the POEU for the research department to be the instrument of the general secretary, as the Civil Service criterion of wage determination has emphasised the need for intellectual analysis, and hence the research staff have been seen as an essential element in the evolution of long term pay strategy in the union.

The officers of the POEU are well paid by union standards and the jobs themselves are highly attractive. All permanent POEU officials are appointed by the National Executive Council of the union, and their appointments ratified by Annual Conference after a probationary period.

The national officer to the Political Fund Management Committee is John Golding MP.

Coverage

The POEU organises the telecommunications side of the Post Office, all those grades, below first-line supervisory level, which were formerly in the old Post Office Engineering Department. This does not include all the telecommunications personnel as the telephone operators are mostly organised by the Union of Post Office Workers (now the Union of Communication Workers). The POEU also organises the engineers on the postal side of the Post Office, the motor transport maintenance workers, grades in the Post Office supplies and factories and crews of the Post Office cableships, as well as radio stations. The POEU organises around 98 per cent of all Post Office engineering staff.

There are now two forces at work which are causing all unions in the Post Office to reconsider the future of trade unionism in the Post Office. The first of these is the division of the postal and telecommunications businesses into two completley separate corporations, British Telecommunications (BT) and the postal business and giro, which retains the title of the Post Office (PO). The second major force is the continuing tide of new technology which is having a major effect on the trade unions in all sections of the industry. New technology has the effect of blurring the traditional divisions between jobs and makes outmoded the existing patterns of trade union organisation based on traditional skills.

The splitting of the Post Office and the force of new technology has led to fresh moves being made towards a rationalisation of trade union structure. The POEU has always resisted attempts by the UCW (formerly the Union of Post Office Workers) to build one rank-and-file union. Those attempts came to a head in 1969 and again in 1981 with the splitting of the Post Office and British Telecom. The POEU supported the split much to the annoyance of the UCW which covers mostly manual grades. The UCW argues that the split undermined union solidarity and left anomalies such as the 7,000 POEU engineers in the UCW-dominated Post Office and the 40,000 UCW telephonists and telegraphists in the POEU-dominated British Telecom. Until 1981 the Council of Post Office Unions (COPOU) had provided a forum in which all trade unions in the old Post Office could discuss and act on matters of common interest, but this was replaced by the separate British Telecom Union Council (BTUC) and the Post Office Union Council (POUC). In 1982 there was a change in the POEU's stance on amalgamation with the UCW, following a series of meetings under the auspices of the TUC. The POEU's new interest is moving beyond the very loose structures of BTUC and POUC is prompted by the uncertainties of new technology and the strong possibility of the parts of the telecommunications business being privatised, with the consequent fear that other unions could begin organising in areas traditionally covered by the UCW or POEU.

Despite these moves towards rationalisation there remain a number of stumbling blocks. For example the UCW 1982 Annual Conference supported for the second year running a motion calling for amalgamation with the POEU but also — against Executive advice — demanded that discussions with the Communication Managers' Association (CMA) should stop. The POEU leadership was keen to include the management unions.

Organisation

The supreme decision-making authority in the union is vested in the Annual Conference which is held in June, and lasts for one week (the rules revision conference meets for about four days every five years). Delegates to Conference are elected from branches on a pro rata basis dependent on the size of the branch.

The National Executive Council of the POEU is 23 strong and its members are elected from 17 constituencies, ten regional and seven occupational. Delegates must vote in every constituency and the full number of votes of the branch must be given to each candidate. Thus each member of the NEC is a representative of the *whole union* as well as of a particular region or occupational group. As Bealey points out, 'although there is no formal and explicit statement of this principle it is often asserted in union debates, especially when attempts have been made to change the method of electing the Executive to one in which only the branch delegates in each particular regional or occupational consituency vote for the Executive representatives for that constituency.'

The work of the NEC is performed

through two types of committees. The union-wide committees include the finance committee, the general purposes committee (for routine matters affecting the membership), the establishment committee responsible for conditions of service, and the wages and allowances committee. Occupational committees are composed almost entirely of Executive members grouped into three categories: 'A' for internal staff, 'B' for external staff and 'C' for supplies. Once a year the occupational committees report to the occupational conferences held on the third day of Conference week. This form of limited federalism is a result of the experience of the POEU in breakaway unionism (see **History**). Moreover, this problem is by no means over. A great deal of recent organisational effort was expended in 1979 in seeking to counteract the activities of the breakaway organisation, EOTA, with a great deal of success.

In general, the POEU is both bureaucratised and highly centralised. The bureaucratic structure can be traced to the development of the union largely as a Civil Service union until 1969 when the Post Office became a public corporation. The procedures of the Civil Service, both in the Whitley councils and in the collective bargaining process, have served to emphasise the need for committee skills, knowledge of regulations and a grasp of administrative details. The POEU is still essentially a centralised union, in spite of its limited federalism. As Bealey notes: 'It has a good deal of substructure, union regional councils at a regional level; area coordinating committees bring branches together to present a common area policy; the branches are still the primary units of local autonomy. Yet, although the branches, and branch officers, have important roles as watchdogs, consultants and spokesmen, and they can call on their members to strike "in local situations", they do not possess the scope for many initiatives. These are largely pre-empted both constitutionally and politically, by the leadership.'

At the 1982 POEU Annual Conference, voting in the NEC elections resulted in the right wing of the union remaining firmly in control with the NEC split 14–9 in favour of the right. The 'broad left' grouping in the POEU had been making considerable gains in 1980 and 1981, and has been described as a 'union within a union'. The 'broad left' in the POEU is a loose grouping of various activists from left Labour to trotskyists Its 13–strong steering committee continually campaigns for a more open discussion of policy and politics within the POEU, by organising conferences, publishing a regular newsletter and lengthy policy documents. Much of its energies have been concentrated on responding to the challenge of new technology and its effect on jobs. The 'broad left' was formed in 1978, and enjoyed some success in the 1979 POEU rules revision conference. They succeeded in forcing the union's head office to print and circulate the union's report and accounts 10 weeks before Annual Conference so that branches could send in motions after reading the report. They were also successful in demanding that candidates for the NEC should be allowed to submit statements on union policy for publication in the *POEU Journal* before Annual Conference. Both of these changes were opposed by the Executive. Other successes included the publication of branch votes on the election of the NEC and POEU delegations; on the appointment of a standing orders committee to consist entirely of lay members; and on the right of branches to put motions to special conferences, instead of having simply to accept or reject Executive motions.

The POEU has 290 branches, and operates an annual programme of education and training at Alvescot, near Oxford, for branch officers and safety representatives. There were 2,493 branch-appointed safety representatives in early 1980.

At very rare intervals the POEU has held referenda, usually on strike policy or on political objectives. On those occasions a relatively high proportion of members have voted.

Women

There is now a Women in Telecom group which started to publish a series of three magazines of the same name during 1982, concentrating on the issue of equal opportunity within BT. The magazine was produced with the aid of a grant from the Equal Opportunities Commission and was produced by activists in the CPSA, POEU, SPOE and the SCPS.

External Relations

The POEU is affiliated to the Labour Party. As at 31 December 1979 the union was affiliated to 508 Constituency Labour Parties, and sent 12 delegates to the Labour Party Conference. POEU-sponsored Labour MPs are John Golding (Newcastle-under-Lyme), John McWilliam (Blaydon) and Roger Stott (Westhoughton).

The POEU voted for Denis Healey in both ballots during the 1981 Labour Party Deputy Leadership election. The union was also in favour of setting up the proposed 'register' of groups within the Labour Party as a means of outlawing the Militant Tendency.

The POEU has never made a practice of discussing ideological issues or international politics at its Conference and, unlike the UCW, guild socialism has not attracted it greatly. In fact the leadership of the POEU have had considerable difficulty in gaining the compliance of the membership for Labour Party affiliation over the years. Whilst the UCW re-affiliated to the Labour Party automatically in 1947, following the repeal of the 1927 Trades Disputes Act, the POEU did not. In 1958, 33 per cent of the membership voted in favour of the union having political objectives and 39 per cent voted against. In 1962, 36 per cent voted in favour of a political fund and 31 per cent against. The 1964 Conference passed a branch proposition for affiliation to the Labour Party with 51 per cent of votes in favour, 41 per cent against and 8 per cent abstaining.

The POEU also forges links with other Western European posts and telecommunications unions.

From 1969 trade union co-ordination in the Post Office operated both at national and local level under the umbrella of the Council of Post Office Unions but this body was wound up following the splitting of the Post Office into a telecommunications group and a postal group. It was replaced by a new body in the telecommunications part of the business British Telecom Unions' Committee (BTUC), with Bryan Stanly as chairperson. The BTUC was used as a vehicle against the BT privatisation plans (see **Recent Events**).

The POEU leadership put forward its proposals for trade union rationalisation in 1981 when it proposed the creation of a new union which would bring together the existing POEU the CPSA Post Office group and SPOE. The new 'federal union' would maintain the existing branch structure of all three unions but would provide for co-ordination of branches 'where necessary and appropriate'. At a special conference of the POEU in late 1981, delegates rejected this idea and also refused to accept the alternative proposal of the 'broad left' which advocated a 'rank-and-file' amalgamated industrial union'. However, the majority of delegates were in favour of some form of rationalisation which included the UCW but excluded SPOE (see **Organisation**).

Policy

The union is opposed to privatisation of British Telecom (see **Recent Events**), and this issue grew to one of major importance during 1982. At the 1982 POEU Annual Conference delegates agreed to affiliate the union to CND, and also backed a call for internal union reform, urging greater power at regional and area level, to reflect the devolution of power within BT. Matters of internal union reform were to be discussed at a special conference.

Whilst the POEU remains strongly committed to the introduction of new technology, both in the Post Office and within Telecommunications, it is keen to ensure that such new technology should enhance the job prospects of its members as well as improving the range and quality of services to the customer.

Recent Events

In 1982 the POEU leadership came under pressure to mount a campaign of industrial action aimed at blocking

Project Mercury, the alternative communications cable network planned by a consortium of private firms in competition with British Telecom. Activists in the union claimed that the rival cable network would link only major British cities, creaming off the most profitable business for large companies thus leaving British Telecom to meet the full cost of providing a full service to other customers. The 'broad left' with its strongholds centred in two large branches of the union — Liverpool Internal and London City — claimed that the union leadership had been inactive in opposing Project Mercury. At the 1982 POEU Annual Conference, this pressure from the 'broad left' resulted in a decision to take 'industrial action if necessary' to stop British Telecom privatisation. An Executive statement, backed by delegates, stated that POEU members had been instructed not to connect Mercury to the national or international network. There remained the threat of independent industrial action (regardless of the POEU's leadership stance) at two of the major left-wing branches, Liverpool Internal and London City. Such action could lead to a complete shutdown of the telephone system of leading banks and financial institutions if the government proposals on privatisation went ahead.

Further Reference

Shirley Lerner, *Breakaway Unions and the Small Trade Union*, Allen & Unwin 1961. This gives a full account of the story of the breakaway Telephone and Telegraph Engineering Guild.

Frank Bealey, 'The political system of the Post Office Engineering Union', *British Journal of Industrial Relations* vol. XV, no. 3, 1977. This is an excellent article which outlines the political balance of power in the union between Conference, the Executive, the permanent officers and the general secretary. We are particularly indebted to Frank Bealey for much of the information on the POEU.

Frank Bealey, *History of the POEU*, Backman & Turner 1976.

Crispin Aubrey, *Who's Watching You?* Pelican 1981.

Post Office Executives, Society of
(SPOE)

Head Office

102-104 Sheen Road
Richmond
Surrey TW9 1UF
01-948 5423

Principal Officers

General Secretary —
J. K. Glynn
Deputy General Secretary —
C. K. Palfrey
Assistant Secretary —
R. M. Bunnage
Assistant Secretary —
T. Wilkinson

Membership (1982)

Male 23,356
Female 1,109
Total 24,465

Union Journal

The Review — monthly to members, circulation about 27,000.

General

The union covers mostly British Telecom staff, although it has a few members in the (new) Post Office. The union represents staff above the rank and file including supervisory engineers, drawing office personnel, telecom grades and higher grades in BT's field sales force. All pay bargaining is done at national level with the Post Office and British Telecom.

History

The main predecessor of the SPOE was the *Society of Post Office Engineering Inspectors* which was founded in 1912. The SPOE amalgamated with the *Society of Chief Inspectors* in 1947 and the name was changed to the *Society of Telecommunications Engineers*. The STE amalgamated with the *Telecommunications Traffic Association* in 1969 and the title changed to the *Society of Post Office Engineers*. In 1975 the *Telecommunications Sales Superintendents' Association* transferred engagements to form the present SPOE.

Organisation

There is an Annual Delegate Conference which is the supreme ruling body of the union. The Executive Council consists of 12 members elected annually by Conference plus a president also elected by Conference. Full-time officials are elected by the Executive Council.

External Relations

The SPOE has no political affiliations.

Recent Events and Current Policy

Union rationalisation in the Post Office and British Telecom is under discussion with the assistance of the TUC. In the meantime adjustments are being made in order, as far as possible, to separate union representation between the two businesses. To this end, senior salary staff in British Telecom who were members of the SCPS have transferred to the SPOE and it is likely that most SPOE members working in the Post Office will transfer to the CMA during 1982. If this happens the SPOE's name will change to the Society of Telecom Executives (STE).

Prison Officers' Association

Head Office

Cronin House
245 Church Street
Edmonton
London N9 9HW
01-803 0255

Principal Officers

General Secretary —
David Evans
Deputy General Secretary —
Peter Rushworth
President —
Colin Steel

Membership (1982)

Male 19,762
Female 1,527
Total 21,289

Union Journal

The Prison Officers' Magazine
— monthly.

General

The Prison Officers' Association is the officially recognised association for all members of the prison officer grade in Britain and Northern Ireland, and for the nursing officers and ancillary staffs of the Broadmoor, Rampton and Moss Side special hospitals in England.

The departmental Whitley council was created after the POA came into being. The staff side comprises nominees of the association, while the official side are representatives of the Home Office (Prison Department). In more recent years the union has augmented its influence through its seats on the Council of Civil Service Unions — the body responsible for debating all general Civil Service questions affecting the various staffs.

History

In 1919 there was a strike among members of the police force. At the time some police and prison officers were organised in a body known as the *Police and Prison Officers' Union*. The strike did not affect very many prison officers, although some 70 who did take strike action were sacked at Wormwood Scrubs.

The major consequence of the strike was the withdrawal from the police of the right of freedom of organisation through the Police Act of 1919. Although not specificially mentioned in that legislation, similar restrictions were imposed on prison officers by administrative action and so-called 'representative boards' were introduced in the prisons. These boards were part of the administrative machine, being financed and largely controlled by the authorities; there was no appeal against the decisions of the Home Office (Prison Commissioners) in England, the Prison Department in Scotland and the Prisons Branch of the Ministry of Home Affairs in Northern Ireland. Pay was bad, hours were long, overtime payment was meagre.

Nevertheless, some officers battled on for independent trade unionism. In

1938 they demanded the right of appeal to independent arbitration against the refusal of the authorities to improve working conditions and also demanded to be assisted in presentation of their case by persons not employed by nor under the control of the authorities. The concession of this demand was followed in 1939 by the official recognition of the Prison Officers' Association.

Organisation

The organisation of the association is national and local: there is no regional, district or divisional organisational level. The management of the association is vested in Annual Conference, Executive Committee and the officers of the association, in that order. The Executive Committee consists of ten elected members: chairperson, two vice-chairpersons, finance officer and six other members, all of whom are elected at Annual Conference, together with the general secretary and deputy general secretary.

Political Affiliation

None.

Policy and Recent Events

The association is gravely concerned about the increasing overcrowding of prisons and submitted stern evidence on this subject to the May committee of inquiry into the prison services in the United Kingdom. It said that industrial action by local branches had grown over the previous two years as a result of government ordered cuts in work hours equivalent to a saving of £2 million, which led to a number of 'crude and arbitrary' cuts in established posts. The POA submission to the May committee also sharply criticised the complexity of channels of communication within the service: 'Lines of communication within the managerial machine lend themselves to delay and indecision and, in turn, encourage the use of local industrial action as the only legitimate means by which positive decisions can be arrived at without undue delay.'

The POA called for the introduction of 'control units' for 'disruptive prisoners'.

When the report of the May committee was published, the POA condemned many of its findings, especially on pay and conditions, while accepting that many of its features represented POA policy. The POA Conference consequently voted to treat the report as a basis for negotiations, with only a few delegates voting for strike action.

Delegates to the 1982 POA Conference voted overwhelmingly to remain within the Council of Civil Service Unions. Conditions have certainly changed for prison officers who now rank among the highest-paid non-management occupational groups, and for whom staffing levels (per prisoner) have been rising in recent years.

Prison Officers' Association, Scottish

Head Office

21 Calder Road
Edinburgh EH11 3PF
031-443 8105

Principal Officers

General Secretary—
J. B. Renton MBE
Assistant Secretary—
Marie Thaw

Membership (1982)

Male 2,463
Female 205
Total 2,668

General

Formed as an independent association in 1971, before when it was a branch of the Prison Officers' Association, the Scottish Prison Officers' Association affiliated to the TUC on 1 January 1980.

Professional Civil Servants, The Institution of

(IPCS)

Head Office

3/7 Northumberland Street
London WC2N 5BS
01-930 9755

Principal Officers

General Secretary—
  Bill McCall
Deputy General Secretaries—
  Bill Wright
  Margaret Platt
Assistant General Secretaries
  Bill Brett
  Brian Stevens
  Jenny Thurston
Assistant Secretaries
  Linda Cohen
  Anthony Cooper
  Clifford Crook
  David Davies
  Peter Downton (Editor)
  Valerie Ellis
  Wendi Harrison
  George Janeway
  Elizabeth Jenkins
  Ron McDowell
  Roy Maynard
  Fred Mullin
  Elizabeth Stallibrass
Research Officer—
  Colin Waters

Membership (1982)

Male 83,903
Female 7,510
Total 91,413

Union Journal and Publications

State Service— monthly.
History of the IPCS, James
Mortimer and Valerie Ellis,
available from head office.
IPCS Bulletin, regular news
and information booklet.
IPCS Handbook, complete
work of reference on
conditions of service, £1 to
members.

General

This union, founded in 1919, caters
for specialist grades within the Civil
Service, mainly scientists and technologists working in the Ministry of
Defence, Royal Navy dockyards, and
in such agencies as the Nuclear Inspectorate and the Mint. IPCS affiliated to the TUC in 1976. It is the third
largest Civil Service union.

Coverage

The IPCS organises scientists, engineers and technologists in the Civil
Service, particularly in the Ministry of
Defence (at the four naval dockyards
— Devonport, Chatham, Rosyth and
Portsmouth; at ordnance factories
and RAF establishments and radar
bases). Members also include air
traffic control staff, intelligence and
fingerprint officers and inspectors of
nuclear installations, mines, gas
plants, factories, explosives, accidents
and dangerous drugs, Royal Mint
staff, Home Office analysts of drink-
driving blood samples and Stationery
Office supervisors.

Organisation

The sovereign body is the Annual Delegate Conference, consisting of delegates from all branches (some 130).
Conference elects a National Executive Committee of 25, including three
national officers.

Policy and Recent Events

Ostensibly the IPCS has no political
affiliation and is at pains to avoid taking any action which shows party political bias. However, most members
realise the value of trade union bargaining power. The government's
efforts to encourage use of secret ballots in industrial disputes received an
overwhelming rebuff at the IPCS
Annual Conference in May 1979,
when a vote determined that members could be instructed to take industrial action, following full consultation by the full-time officers with
Executive and branches. In 1979 the
IPCS did take strike action after seeking pay increases of between 37 and
47 per cent, based on Pay Research
Unit comparability studies, when the
Civil Service Department tried to
abandon the principle of comparability.

The institution possesses bargaining
power as a result of having key personnel in government establishments
who are members. Selective strikes
can be a very effective way of capita-
lising on this strength.

However, during the 1981 Civil Service pay dispute there was some reluctance by members of the IPCS to
be used as a bludgeon in the battle on
behalf of other groups. Even so, the

IPCS spent £2,105,000 supporting the selective strikes.

The IPCS, more frequently than other unions, is seen to be out of step in the Council of Civil Service Unions. IPCS opposed the civil service pay comparability system before its unilateral abrogation by the government. Its Conference in 1982 carried a motion calling for immediate action to resolve compressed and inverted differentials and its leadership seemed willing to return to group by group bargaining. Yet, after criticising and condemning the previous system of pay comparability and independent arbitration, the IPCS intermittently harks back to it. In contrast to other civil service unions, IPCS reacted favourably to the report of the Megaw pay inquiry.

The Conference voted to oppose vigorously the Tebbit Employment Act and to campaign against doctrinaire and irrational exercises in privatisation. Plans were put forward to form a non-profit company to take over the network of heavy goods vehicle testing stations which the government had offered for sale.

Further Reference

J. E. Mortimer and Valerie A. Ellis, *A Professional Union: The Evolution of the Institution of Professional Civil Servants*, Allen & Unwin.

Group Seventeen **Professional, Clerical and Entertainment**

Actors' Equity Association, British

Head Office

8 Harley Street
London W1N 2AB
01-637 9311

Principal Officers

General Secretary—
Peter Plouviez
Assistant General Secretary—
Ian McGarry
*Senior Assistant Secretary
(Theatre)—* John Coleby
Assistant Secretary (Variety)—
Archie MacMillan
Legal Officer— Ruth Gurny
Press and Publicity Officer—
Peter Finch

There are also 19 organisers
based in London and the
regional offices.

Membership (1982)

Male 15,851
Female 14,301
Total 30,152

Union Journal

Equity Journal— quarterly,
posted to members.

General

Any person who 'exercises professional skill in the provision of entertainment, whether as artist, producer, stage manager or in any such similar capacity in the theatre, music hall, films, radio, television and like media' is eligible for membership. 'Nonetheless, the Executive Committee shall have the power to grant to any applicant for membership temporary membership only for such period and on payment of such entrance fee and subscription as it may deem appropriate.' The election of members is by majority vote of the Executive Committee or Council present at any meeting. There are proposals to limit membership to graduates of drama schools but these are unlikely to find favour with a majority of members.

Equity was the founder of the London Theatre Council and of the Provincial Theatre Council. It has established special minimum pay and conditions contracts for the National Theatre, the Royal Shakespeare Company and house agreements with opera companies, and a standard contract for ballet. It has established the West End theatre agreement, the subsidised repertory theatre agreement, agreements with BBC and ITV and regulations for the engagement of performers in television commercials and for roles in feature films.

The association maintains a list of theatres and agencies which do hire non-members of Equity and instructs members to consult head office before accepting engagements with such agencies.

History

Late in 1929 some members in the theatrical profession agreed that there was an urgent need for a new and strong organisation to protect the interests of the rank and file of the profession. The *Actors' Association* which had done valuable work had almost collapsed, its destruction and disintegration being largely due to the fact that it had not achieved the closed shop principle, an essential extension of collective bargaining in the theatre business.

The Actors' Association had become a trade union some years before 1930 and this had led to an increased membership. It had been able to establish a contract of minimum wages and conditions with managers.

There was a counter-attack, the touring managers in particular resenting the contract; a long wearisome struggle ensued, resulting, after tortuous negotiations, in the realisation by the association that, without complete unity and 100 per cent membership, they did not have the power to enforce any conditions.

Worse was to follow, for the council of the Actors' Association took some ill-advised and desperate measures to try to hold the line, including strike action. Many members of the association, shocked by such tactics and fearing the communist bogey, broke away to form a new association, the *Stage Guild*. This was to be a nice, respectable genteel body, which abhorred trade unionism and anything that was even pink politically, and it was to include the managers.

Unsurprisingly, it was totally ineffective on behalf of the rank and file of the profession and theatre managers began to flout contracts and do much as they pleased in their treatment of actors.

Abuses and cases of bogus management crept back but finally provoked protest. The Stage Guild was swept away and a mandate gained to form an association of actors called *British Equity*. The struggle now had to begin again and the centre of it was the Equity Shop principle. Union supporters had to refuse to play with non-Equity members, consequently jeopardising their chances of making a living. Finally, Equity was able to establish a Theatre Council by negotiations. It consisted of managers and British Equity, and its functions were to discuss problems and agree on a contract, to admit and acknowledge the Equity Shop. The great obstacle to all previous discussions had been the Equity Shop principle. The establishment of the Theatre Council saw it accepted and admitted by the managers in 1933. Some still felt that Equity should be more a professional association than a union and when Equity affiliated to the TUC in 1940, Godfrey Tearle, who had been president for ten years, resigned in protest.

It has been necessary to discuss this issue in the history of Equity at length in order to emphasise the importance of the closed shop principle for the well-being of rank-and-file members of the acting profession. In the 1950s West End actors could be earning as little as £5 a week for rehearsals and £9.10 for performances. In 1970 Equity's 'living wage' campaign succeeded in raising minimum salaries to £18 a week for provisional members and £20 a week for full members.

This improvement mainly occurred through more rigorous enforcement of the Equity Shop. In the fifties anyone could obtain an Equity card on being offered professional work; today entry is restricted by an annual quota system and full membership is preceded by 40 weeks of provisional membership.

For several years until 1979 the union was troubled by a constant battle between one faction which believed that annual and special general meetings should wield ultimate authority and another faction, consisting mainly of members of Equity Council, which said that on constitutional issues referenda should be used. According to Peter Plouviez, the General Secretary, the rules at the time gave too much power to annual and special general meetings and resulted in the absurd process of decisions taken at general meetings being reversed by ballot and then considered at meetings again. Prominent in the faction favouring retaining the powers of general meetings were members of the Workers' Revolutionary Party, including Vanessa Redgrave.

Council was finally empowered to put rule changes to the membership in a referendum after a House of Lords judgement in favour of Marius Goring, a member of Equity's Council. Subsequently the referendum results approved the rule changes which mainly established an appeals committee, to be elected annually by the entire membership, which can veto proposed general meetings or referenda. In addition, a referendum is now required to approve changes of rule.

The 65 member Council of Equity is elected biennially by postal ballot from among panels of candidates, reflecting the diverse elements in the entertainment and theatrical business.

Organisation

The alarms and agitation that occurred within the Council of the previous union, the Actors' Association, influenced those who drafted the rules for Equity to place checks and balances on the Council of the new association by increasing the constitutional powers and influence of annual general meetings and special general meetings of the membership, which could be called on presentation to the secretary of a written request stating the purpose of the meeting and signed by 40 members, while there was an unqualified right among the membership to call a referendum on presentation to council of a petition signed by 100 members. (See above for amendments to this constitution.)

External Relations

The rules specify that Equity is a 'non-political and non-sectarian Union'. It is affiliated to the International Federation of Actors, STUC, the Confederation of Entertainment Unions, the Performers' Alliance (with the Musicians' Union), Amnesty International, NCCL, Theatres' Advisory Council, Radio and Television Safeguards Committee.

Policy and Recent Events

The creation of the Fourth Channel, the growth of video tapes and discs, the development in satellite and cable television, have involved the union in a large number of discussions and negotiations aimed to achieve equitable payments for members' work, the safeguarding of future employment and control over the use made of recorded material. The Campaign against Theatre Cuts and VAT has responded to every attempt to close theatres and other places of work and has made numerous representations to the government, Arts Council, local authorities and other bodies about the level of funding for the arts.

At the 1982 AGM, members carried a resolution instructing the Council to reverse its decision to apply for public funds for union ballots under the terms of the Employment Act and to declare its support for the TUC's policy of opposition to this measure.

A referendum was demanded on this resolution and this was put to the membership, resulting in a vote in approval of the AGM resolution when the result was declared in June 1982.

Further Reference

The Stage and Television Today, weekly. Not an Equity publication, but usually providing some information about Equity and the other entertainment unions.

Banking Insurance and Finance Union
(BIFU)

Head Office

Sheffield House
17 Hillside
Wimbledon
London SW19
01-946 9151

Principal Officers

General Secretary — L. A. Mills
Deputy General Secretary —
  D. Paterson (Scotland)
Assistant Secretaries —
  P. Allison
  D. Burton
  I. Cameron
  D. Dines
  J. Forde
  S. Gamble
  J. James
  K. Jones
  T. Malloy
  A. Piper
  W. Whiteman
  H. Woods
  J. Robinson (Research Officer)
  W. Vose (Publicity)

BIFU also employs seven negotiating officers, and each year honorary positions of president, vice-president and general treasurer are elected at the Annual Delegate Conference.

Membership (1982)

Male 76,723
Female 73,387
Total 150,110

Union Journal and Publications

BIFU Report — monthly, circulation around 101,000. BIFU has also published a number of pamphlets and booklets which give a good treatment of the union and its activities. These include: *Women in Banking and Finance* — a 7 page document setting out the statutory rights of women and emphasising the efforts that BIFU is making on their behalf. *Microtechnology* — a 32 page booklet outlining the new technology agreement the union would like to sign with all the companies it deals with, and including guidelines, specifications and assessment procedure to be followed.

Union Offices

● *Birmingham*
Prudential Buildings
St Philip's Place
Colmore Row
Birmingham 3
021-236 1419

● *London*
Fourth Floor
30 City Road
London EC1
01-628 0227/9

● *Leeds*
Oakland House
Netherfield Road
Ravensthorpe
Nr. Dewsbury
West Yorkshire
0924-469528/9

● *Glasgow*
Fourth Floor
11 Bothwell Street
Glasgow G2 6LY
041-221 4541

● *Manchester*
First Floor
Barclays Bank Chambers
77 Shude Hill
Manchester M4 4AN

● *South East*
5 North Street
Worthing
0903-35051

● *East Anglia*
87 High Street
Somersham
Huntingdon
Cambridgeshire
0487-840573

● *Cardiff*
57 Churchill Way
Cardiff
0222-23797

● *South and West Country*
6a Castle Street
Salisbury
Wiltshire SP1 1BB
0722-25140

General

The Banking Insurance and Finance Union (formerly the *National Union of Bank Employees*) organises workers at all levels in banking, insurance, finance houses, trustee savings banks and building societies. In recent years it has grown considerably and it is now among the top 20 unions in the TUC in size. It is a union which is continually building up its complement of full-time officials and organisers as its membership expands. Despite inter-union rivalry between the staff associations on the one hand and ASTMS on the other, its influence is growing. It has always adopted a non-political stance in its policies. Its recent change of name reflects its increasing diversity of membership across the various sectors of employment in banking and financial institutions generally.

History

BIFU started its life in 1946 as the *National Union of Bank Employees* following an amalgamation between the *Bank Officers' Guild* and the *Scottish Bankers' Association*. Both unions had their origins in the organisation of bank clerks in England and Scotland between 1917 and 1919. The union has been affiliated to the TUC since 1939 except for a short period from 1973-75 when it was expelled from the TUC for registering under the Industrial Relations Act 1971. NUBE changed its name to the *Banking Insurance and Finance Union* in 1979 to reflect its increasing diversity of membership.

Union Officials

Recent years have seen a significant growth in BIFU's membership, and the union has always laid great stress on membership growth. Over a period of five years (to 1978) the number of BIFU's officials doubled, and the union has even employed temporary recruiters in different parts of the country, as well as seconded recruiters by agreement with certain banks.

At present, BIFU employs 15 people at assistant secretary level, seven negotiating officers, 15 area organisers, as well as half a dozen or so researchers and administrators. The union has a total personnel complement of around 100 people.

BIFU union officials come from varied backgrounds, but newly recruited staff tend to be young people (such as graduates with degrees in industrial relations or the social sciences), ex-teachers, people with experience from other unions, former Ruskin and Coleg Harlech students etc.

BIFU also makes provision for seconded officials who are appointed by the EC and seconded by agreement between the union and the particular institution, whereby they assist the full-time officials in negotiations at the institution concerned.

Organisation

The supreme governing and decision-making body in the union is the Annual Delegate Conference held in April. Conference is made up of a voting delegate elected by each branch of the union, non-voting delegates from each area council and advisory committee, past-presidents of the union, together with members of the Executive Committee and standing orders committee.

The Executive Committee is responsible for the general administration and government of the union between conferences. It comprises the union's president, vice-president, and general treasurer (all elected at Annual Conference), and at least one member elected by each area and/or regional council and a delegate from the various bank or financial institutional sections of the union. Together with the general secretary, it is cur-

rently 32 strong. The EC has the power to appoint a general secretary and 'other such officials as it shall consider necessary'. It also appoints BIFU full-time officials to administer the day to day running of the union.

BIFU employs organisers for each of its 14 geographical areas. Each geographical area has an area or regional council — consisting of a delegate from each of the branches. The main functions of each area and/or regional council are to assist the EC in the layout of branches, to advise the EC on any regional matter on request, to ensure that membership levels are maintained by the propagation of BIFU's policies and to elect delegates to Conference.

Branch organisation in the union tends to be of the three following types:

1. Geographic, which includes members of different status/skill from different banks;

2. Institutional, a branch containing members from one particular financial institution only;

3. Occupational, a branch containing members of a particular skill/occupation, e.g. technical and services.

The historical trend within BIFU has been to organise branches along geographical lines with a heterogeneous membership. In recent years, however, there has been a movement towards a sectionalisation of branches into more homogeneous units — for example of the occupational/institutional type. At the end of 1981 BIFU had 350 branches.

The union is also creating sections that bring together staff from a single type of institution — for example insurance.

Workplace Activity

The shop steward function of BIFU's work is provided by office representatives of which there were around 5,000 in mid-1980. BIFU's rules provide that such representatives operate 'overall under the direction of and be accredited by the general secretary and/or the Executive Committee'.

Women

Despite the fact that women comprise nearly half the total membership of

BIFU, they are greatly under-represented both among full-time officials and organisers, and in their number on the Executive Committee. There are two full-time women officials (out of 24), five organisers (out of 20), and four Executive Committee members (out of 32).

BIFU has set up a Women's Equality Working Party (which reports to the Executive Committee) and regularly sends delegates to the Women's TUC. However, there is plenty of scope for further campaigning for the rights of women both in the banking and finance industry and within the union itself. Given the fact that the percentage of women in employment in the banking, finance, building society, and insurance industry is around 50 per cent and reaches 55 per cent in the clearing banks alone, BIFU has a heavy responsibility to its female membership.

BIFU published a report entitled *Equality for Women — Proposals for Positive Action* in July 1982, pointing out that although women form the majority of workers in banking and finance, they are concentrated in female ghettos in the bottom clerical grades. Banks tended to rely on high turnover of staff in lower grades to prevent career blockages and dissatisfaction higher up, and thus female staff rarely reached the higher level posts. The union's report recommended the development of comprehensive equal opportunities programmes in each bank or company.

External Relations

BIFU is not affiliated to any political party, nor to any organisation which has 'party political objectives'. The union's rules prevent it from affiliating to any body without the express authority of Conference. Although BIFU does not sponsor MPs, it retains two parliamentary consultants, David Madel (Conservative MP for South Bedfordshire), and Christopher Price (Labour MP for Lewisham West). BIFU is affiliated to FIET (International Federation of Commercial, Clerical and Technical Employees) and it is the largest union within that federation.

BIFU's non-political stance means that it is unable to vote on many TUC motions at Congress because of the party-political wording of the motions but a resolution of the 1981 Conference will allow greater flexibility in this respect.

Policy

BIFU is one of the few unions that has set out in written form its policy on a number of issues. In 1978 it produced a 21 page pamphlet, *Policy for Progress: an outline of BIFU's policy in Barclays, Lloyds, Midland, National Westminster and Williams and Glyn's Banks*.

The union has called for the implementation of the Bullock Committee proposals on industrial democracy to be applied to the banking and finance sector. In the area of sex equality BIFU has called for provision to be made for disclosure of information to be supplied to the union by financial institutions in relation to discriminatory practices; equalisation of pension rights and benefits; positive discrimination in favour of women in promotions etc., if necessary by a 'quota' system; and improvements in maternity leave and pay above the statutory minima.

BIFU pursues an active health and safety policy because of the special dangers that bank employees face in any bank robbery that might occur. The union has stressed that the carriage of cash should always be undertaken by trained security guards and not clerical staff.

The recent developments in computer technology have posed the dangers of reductions among staff in financial institutions as banking techniques increasingly rely on the use of on-line computer facilities for data processing and, in future, even point-of-sale banking transactions themselves. BIFU advocates the virtues of job evaluation as a method of assessing the relative worth of jobs.

Many banks still retain a compulsory mobility clause in the contracts of employment they issue. The union has consistently opposed such mobility clauses as it believes that staff should not be required to move home against their wishes. Apart from this, the union is concerned about the financial loss that can be incurred by employees as a result of transfer. Whilst some progress has been made by the union in modifying the discretion of employing institutions in imposing compusory mobility (e.g. by introducing an appeals procedure), the position is less than satisfactory. The union's long term aim remains the substitution of a wholly elective system for the filling of vacancies which allows members greater discretion over their career patterns than the arbitrary exercise of managerial authority now permits. BIFU is anxious to preserve its position in relation to cheap housing loans to staff by the banks. Whilst such favourable loans are the envy of many other trade unionists, the existing system is fraught with inequities. For example, staff in some banks are unable to secure a loan which would allow them to purchase a house larger than their superiors' houses!

In its evidence to the National Consumer Council's inquiry into banking services in 1982, BIFU strongly opposed an extension of bank opening hours and a widespread return to Saturday opening. Instead, it suggested alternatives to Saturday opening such as autotellers, credit cards and cheque cards, and accused the banks of being too slow to encourage customers to use these.

BIFU's attitude to the nationalisation of the banking and finance sector is that the union should not commit itself one way or the other until there are firm proposals to show that nationalisation would benefit the membership, the industry and the economy.

BIFU's Annual Conference in 1981 rejected state funding for union ballots legislated for in the Employment Act, 1980.

Recent Events

BIFU continues to be a fast growing union; by April 1982 its membership had increased to 150,110, representing a net increase of about 6,000 over the previous year. The *Phoenix Staff Union* transferred its engagements to BIFU in 1979, and 6,000 members of the *Eagle Star Staff Association* followed suit in October 1981.

The Phoenix amalgamation followed the 1978 merger between BIFU and the 5,500 strong *Guardian Royal Exchange Staff Union*. The sectors of finance, banking, building societies and insurance have increasingly been subject to intense inter-union rivalry in recent years, the most prominent battles for membership being between BIFU and ASTMS. The disputes committee of the TUC has attempted to persuade both unions that there should be a sphere of influence agreement between them, whereby ASTMS should organise insurance workers and should not seek further to extend into the banking industry and that, similarly, BIFU should organise bank workers and should not seek to organise in the insurance industry. There has been no progress on a spheres of influence agreement as yet and inter-union rivalry continues.

BIFU has also been in conflict with the banking staff associations, culminating in the union's decision to withdraw from joint negotiating machinery in the English clearing banks. This decision was taken by the Executive Committee in September 1977 after a long series of frustrations arising out of the staff associations watering down BIFU's pay claims on the staff side of the JNC. In July 1982 BIFU came close to agreeing new national negotiating machinery and disputes procedures with the five English clearing banks which would formalise the position whereby BIFU and the Clearing Banks Union (formed out of the staff associations at Barclays, National Westminster and Lloyds) would negotiate separately with the Federation of London Clearing Bank Employers. The machinery was to be set up by September 1982.

New technology in banking could lead to catastrophic results for BIFU members in the next few years. The employers have so far refused to involve staff in decisions about technological change, and as the pace of technology quickens, thousands of jobs of BIFU members will be threatened. This ominous threat is taking place on a number of fronts and involves more automated teller machines; viewdata systems whereby customers could carry out electronic transactions from home; and 'lobby banking' or offices consisting solely of machines and the related development of largely automated 'in store' banking. The union hierarchy in BIFU are well aware of this threat but a call at the 1982 Annual Conference of the union, to refuse to operate new technology equipment unless it was introduced through negotiated agreements on job security, was rejected by the delegates.

The 1982 Annual Conference also saw the emergence of a 'broad left' group within the union, which bega to worry the BIFU leadership. Although the 'broad left' only involved a small section of the union, the leadership were worried at the possibility of such political activity frightening away potential members from a largely moderate workforce.

The 'broad left' group was founded in November 1981 and was backed by three of the 30-member Executive. At the Annual Conference it only actively involved 30 to 40 of the 500 delegates but nevertheless showed signs of expanding rapidly. The group now produce a journal, *Counter-balance*, which concentrates on such issues as low pay, redundancies, working hours and equal opportunities, with a call for the election of all full-time officials instead of appointment by the EC. The broad left are also keen to involve BIFU in more 'political' discussions within the TUC.

There is evidence that BIFU is gradually moving towards a more militant stance. In spite of opposition from the Executive Committee, the 1979 Annual Conference of BIFU voted narrowly to abolish the rule that a voting majority of all staff entitled to vote on a particular issue must be secured before industrial action is taken. This move followed a Conference decision to set up a national strike fund for the first time, again against the advice of the EC. A strike took place among bank messengers in 1980 which served to slow down banking operations throughout the country for a while. As BIFU becomes larger, its non-political stance may change, and future years may well see a change in its traditional policy in what is becoming an increasingly volatile employment sector.

Further Reference

V. L. Allen and Sheila Williams, 'The growth of trade unionism in banking', *Manchester School of Economics and Social Studies* XXVIII, September 1960, pp. 299-318.

R. M. Blackburn, *Union Character and Social Class*, Batsford 1967.

Broadcasting Staffs, Association of (ABS)

Head Office

Thorndike House
70-76 Bell Street
London NW1 6SP
01-262 0162

Principal Officers

General Secretary—
D. A. Hearn
Deputy General Secretary
P. S. Leech
Assistant General Secretaries
T. Banks
J. Blakeman
R. Bolton
C. Driver
E. Johnston
B. Marsh
M. A. Marsland
D. Smith
Assistant General Secretary (Administration)— J. Rogers

Membership (1982)

Male 11,141
Female 4,005
Total 15,146

Union Journal

Abstract— monthly.

General

The association represents staff at all grades in the BBC and IBA, and is the main union for the BBC, independent local radio contractors staff and freelances working in broadcasting. It also has members employed in the audio-visual field working for such organisations as the British Council and the Inner London Education Authority. It has recognition agreements in most areas, procedure agreements with the large employing groups plus annual pay agreements and conditions of service agreements covering a wide range of issues.

History

The ABS grew from the *BBC Staff Association*, formed in 1945 from a merger of the (wartime) staff association, the *Association of BBC Engineers*. It became the Association of Broadcasting Staffs in 1956 and affiliated to the TUC in 1963. In 1974 it became the Association of Broadcasting and Allied Staffs in recognition of the need to represent members working in closed circuit television, cablevision etc.

Organisation

Conference is the supreme policy-making body of the association. Between Annual Conferences the National Executive Council represents the will of the association. The NEC is elected by ballot at Annual Conference and comprises a president and two vice-presidents elected from the whole membership and divisional representatives on the basis of one representative for each 500 members of a division, except that, in the case of a BBC division, the basis of election is one NEC representative for every 500 members of the sub-division. Each branch polls — by card vote — the number of votes corresponding to the number of branch members within each of the divisions or, in the case of the BBC division, within each of the sub-divisions: central directorates, headquarters group, central services group, engineering specialist departments, external services directorate, local radio, non-metropolitan radio directorate, television directorate, transmitter group.

The other divisions of the ABS are freelance and independent division, IBA division, ILR division.

National officers of the union are appointed by the NEC.

Workplace Activity

This has increased in the recent past as the ABS has emerged from its quasi-staff association approach to negotiations. It has also increased as a result of, but subsequently contributed to, decay of the 20-year-old pay grading structures covering about 27,000 BBC staff. This grading system was divided into five main groups: the top managerial, production and editorial grade; the operational grade; the administrative support grade; the clerical grade and the secretarial and clerical grade. Within each grade there were separate divisions, special awards provisions, annual increment scales and earnings roofs. This structure degenerated, particularly under pay policy and, by 1979, was in some disorder, having become distorted either by expedient managerial decisions, trade union pressure or wayward arbitration. Certain groups, notably the Ealing Film Mobile branch of ABS, traditionally one of the more militant and comprising mainly sound recordists and camera staff, had tended to benefit from the pay anomalies.

Management, declaring that the structure had become a game of leapfrogging, froze grading structures and any existing re-grading claims in November 1979. The ABS regarded the freeze as unfair on members who were in the queue for regrading and an abandonment of mutuality in collective bargaining (see **Policy and Recent Events**).

Women

The ABS mounted a special recruitment campaign for women members a few years ago and is still reaping the benefits in increased active female membership. There are two women officials, one of them part time. There is a standing committee to consider discrimination against women, ethnic minorities and registered disabled persons which, among other claims, seeks to persuade the various managements with whom the ABS negotiaties to improve recruitment, training and career prospects for the groups concerned.

External Relations

Rule 17 (a) states that 'the NEC may at its discretion and in furtherance of the objects of the association enter into agreements with other unions recognised in the field of broadcasting in order to set up joint working machinery where desirable' (see **Trade Union Federations**). The desire for closer working led to the proposed amalgamation with the ACTT (see **Association of Cinematograph, Television and Allied Technicians**.)

In a ballot in October 1981 there was a decisive majority of those voting against the establishment of a political fund. It has been made clear at Conference and in ballot documents that the establishment of a political fund did not mean affiliation to the Labour Party, although legally it was a prerequisite of such affiliation.

Policy and Recent Events

Two main issues dominated ABS policy in 1982: the financial position of the BBC and the collapse of the traditional system of industrial relations, in conjunction with the hostility of influential representatives of the BBC towards the ABS.

In 1980 the old grading scheme was unilaterally abandoned by management which introduced the pay relativities scheme and set up the corporate inter-directorate committee (CIDC). The effect and, many believe, the intention of those actions was to prevent the union from effectively intervening in the process of job evaluation and the determination of internal pay relativities. ABS never meets the CIDC and sees it as a cover for managerial manipulation of internal relativities, with the union taken seriously only when it is presenting claims for highly organised and strategically well placed groups of members, especially if they are willing to take strike action.

The decision to scrap the grading system is considered by ABS to have destroyed at the roots a long standing relationship in an important area of collective bargaining. The BBC's contention that the procedure agreement does not give 'status quo' protection against changes the employer wishes to introduce, and which are regarded as consultative rather than negotiable, will destroy the union's right to properly discuss such issues as major changes associated with new technology and managerially initiated reorganisation.

Cinematograph, Television and Allied Technicians, Association of

(ACTT)

Head Office

2 Soho Square
London W1V 6DD
01-437 8506

Principal Officers

General Secretary—
Alan Sapper
Deputy General Secretary—
Roy Lockett
Organisers—
Bob Hamilton
Jack O'Connor
Ken Roberts
Brian Shemmings
Bill Borrows
Bill Wayland
Les Wiles
Finance Officer—
G. Maniatakis
Membership Officer—
Linda Loakes (based at 18 Wardour Street, London)

Membership (1982)

Male 16,003
Female 4,018
Total 20,021

Union Journal

Film and Television Technician — monthly.

General

The union aims to organise all employees in the technical side of film production including directors, producers and writers, and camera staff such as boom operators, sound can and sound maintenance workers and clapper loaders, and grades in animation, editorial and special effects. It also recruits in broadcasting, television and allied industries but is particularly strong in commercial television with minority membership in the BBC where the Association of Broadcasting Staffs (ABS) is the dominant union. The ACTT recruits in film printing and processing laboratories among technical, clerical and all other employees. In independent local radio stations and in educational technology ACTT membership is recognised *pari passu* with ABS membership.

The union is party to national agreements with the Film Producers' Association, the Association of Film Laboratory Employers, the Advertising Film and Videotape Producers' Association and the Independent Television Companies Association. There are also many company agreements about pay and conditions.

Through its employment office, the union acts as an employment agency for the film and television industries. It operates a very effective closed shop throughout the industry, so much so that most film companies find that it is convenient to fill vacancies directly through the union which thereby has substantial control of the labour supply. The union supplies members, who have registered with it as being currently unemployed, for vacancies of which film companies notify it. If there are no members available for the vacancies, the union itself recruits newcomers. It polices union employment by regularly visiting studios and, where film units are operating without sufficient unionised employees, according to agreement or custom and practice, this is rectified by the union's employment office supplying additional employees.

History

According to Gus MacDonald, the ACTT was founded in the 1930s to combat 'cowboy' employers in the film business. It was created by a core of leftists including film-makers such as Sidney Cole, Ralph Bond and Ivor Montagu. On the brink of collapse, it was saved by Sidney Bernstein (the founder of Granada TV), then a cinema tycoon.

Organisation

The association is divided into branches: laboratory, film production, television and educational technology. These branches elect their own officers and conduct their own business, being autonomous in respect of their internal working, subject to the jurisdiction of the General Council of the union.

Additionally, the union rules lay down that a shop committee is to be established and one or more shop stewards appointed in each studio, laboratory or other production unit.

The General Council is entrusted with the administration of the business of the union and its government in periods between Annual Conferences. It is composed of (a) 19 members elected by vote at the Annual Conference, being six laboratory members, six television members and six film production members with one educational technology member; (b) shop committee representatives; (c) general officers and trustees of the union (the general officers are a president, six vice-presidents — two each from film, television and laboratory branches — and a treasurer); (d) general secretary and union organisers who may not vote but are free to advise and express their opinions.

Groups (a) and (c) constitute an Executive Committee which attends to business arising between General Council meetings. Ultimately, the government of the ACTT, the appointment of its trustees and officers and the power to make, amend or revoke its rules are vested in the membership Conference which meets annually.

Women

As in other industries and occupations, women who work in television tend to be concentrated in certain types of jobs. Those who reach senior positions do so in, for instance, educational and children's TV; the situation is worse in ITV. A report by the ACTT on 'patterns of discrimination' revealed the extent of this. Out of 150 grades covered by ACTT agreements, 60 per cent of women in film and television production work in just three grades: production secretary, continuity 'girl' and production assistant. The report criticised the lack of women working in technical jobs in television. In 1975 ACTT adopted as union policy recommendations to introduce proper training schemes and increased childcare facilities for women working in commercial television. As a result of a decision of the 1981 ACTT Annual Conference, ACTT has appointed an equality officer. ACTT also held its second Women's Conference in March 1982.

External Relations

ACTT is affiliated to the Labour Party, Amnesty International, NCCL, CND, Liberation, Campaign for Press and Broadcasting Freedom.

Policy and Recent Events

The ACTT has campaigned against bias in the reporting of trade union and industrial subjects in the media and for a fundamental re-structuring of the film industry in Britain so as to expand home film output, and to cut back sharply imported television films and features and to plug the leakage of film finance to other countries.

The union actively recruits screenwriters in independent television and films. This has brought it into jurisdictional conflict with the Writers' Guild. ACTT opposed the re-admittance of the Writers' Guild into the TUC which it saw as a serious setback for its policy of establishing a single entertainment trade union.

The union is vigorous, resourceful and exceedingly democratic. The form of organisation which allows a great deal of branch and shopfloor autonomy has ensured this.

In the wider economic context and the long run, the war of attrition over new technology between the ACTT and the television companies may well be irrelevant. Change will be rapid and may be pernicious but it cannot be fought on the shopfloor in existing companies because such opposition will be overwhelmed by international market forces. ACTT has supported the idea of worker cooperatives of its members applying for the new TV franchises but this is a bit like trying to set up a tent in a blizzard. However, such schemes raise broader issues than the charges of impracticability which are frequently laid against them and this is not to say that technological changes should not, where possible, be strenuously resisted.

Sporadic disputes with various ITV companies concerning electronic newsgathering equipment (ENG), usually following disregard of local agreements and lack of consultation with ACTT, have continued. ENG consists of a portable colour TV camera and a small video tape recording box in place of 16mm camera with linked sound-recording equipment. There is little difference in operational use but there is the advantage of eliminating or reducing the film producing stage. It is not the end of film editing skills, but reduces reliance on them and probably staffing levels and training.

The re-definition of jobs has created problems for the various independent television companies as a result of different demarcation agreements from one company to another. While one company may have an existing agreement to cover news events with a small team of film camera operators, sound technician and a reporter, another may have to use two camera operators, two sound technicians, a reporter, a researcher, an assistant and a driver. The use of the lightweight and compact video camera, however, undermines the basis of all these agreements.

Negotiations have been further complicated by the fact that film operators enjoy a different status from those staff who already operate video equipment. The video operators have been used to receiving orders in their work but now see their opportunity for a more glamorous role than being 'backroom' staff. Both film staff and video operators are usually members of ACTT but rivalry and jealousies between them are not unknown. An important breakthrough was achieved in July 1980 when the ACTT and the Independent Television News management secured an agreement on the use of ENG.

The ACTT has prudently opted for one change that will strengthen it for the battle ahead. Its members voted for amalgamation with the Association of Broadcasting Staffs, the main BBC union. Unfortunately, the certification officer refused to register the amalgamation as a trade union. This decision was based on a technicality regarding ACTT's failure to comply with the procedure it had adopted for itself to ballot the members.

In what some regarded as a test

case for the secondary boycott provisions of the 1980 Employment Act, the five Law Lords unanimously allowed an appeal by the ACTT against a temporary injunction ordering the union to stop its members at Thames Television blacking a musical series produced by Hadmor, a facility company which makes programmes for television stations.

Further Reference

Gus MacDonald, 'Television's high technology warfare', *New Statesman* 14 September 1979.

Jeremy Bugler, 'TV's industrial relations minefield', *New Statesman* 25 August 1978.

P. Seglow, *Trade Unionism in TV: A Case Study of the Development of White Collar Militancy*, Saxon House 1978.

Alan Sapper, 'Opening the box — the unions inside television', in P. Beharrel and G. Philo (eds.), *Trade Unions and the Media*, Macmillan 1977.

Film Artistes' Association
(FAA)

Head Office

61 Marloes Road
London W8 6LF
01-937 4567

Principal Officers

General Secretary—
S. Brannigan

Membership (1982)

Total 1,900

General

Founded in 1932, this union caters almost entirely for crowd artistes. Plans for a merger with NATTKE were delayed by protests from dissident FAA members to the certification officer.

Insurance Workers, National Union of
(NUIW)

Head Office

46 Quicks Road
Wimbledon
London SW19 1EY
01-542 9676

Principal Officers

President—
E. Lorenz (Prudential)
Treasurer—
F. Jarvis (Royal London)
Honorary General Secretary—
J. P. Brown (Liverpool Victoria)

Membership (1982)

Total 19,463

Union Journal

Each of the three sections has its own journal.

General

The NUIW is in fact a federation of unions representing the field staff of the door-to-door representatives of the industrial assurance offices. Currently there are three sections in the federation: Liverpool Victoria (General Secretary, J. P. Brown), Prudential (General Secretary, E. Lorenz), Royal London (General Secretary, F. Jarvis).

It is through the federation or the national union that the three sections, which are otherwise organisationally autonomous, are affiliated to the TUC and to the Confederation of Insurance Trade Unions. The sections are also financially autonomous, paying an affiliation fee which is just sufficient to enable the national union to function. It does not therefore build up any surplus funds.

History

The national union was formed in 1964 prior to which it was known as the *National Federation of Insurance Workers*. In 1964 there was an amalgamation of the NFIW and another national union and the title National

Union of Insurance Workers was created.

External Relations

Only one section, the Prudential Section, is affiliated to the Labour Party. The Liverpool Victoria Section has a political fund but is not affiliated to any political party.

Recent Events

Membership of the NUIW has been seriously depleted in recent years by severe competition for members from ASTMS. The federated and sectionalised organisation of the NUIW has not helped, since some of the individual sections, while autonomous, were weak and could be picked off by strong national unions such as ASTMS. This happened in the case of the Pearl Federation Section which committed itself by ballot to joining ASTMS in 1978. In 1982 the 850 members of the Royal Liver and Composite Section voted four to one in a ballot to merge with the Banking, Insurance and Finance Union (BIFU) which is making inroads into areas traditionally considered the stronghold of the Association of Scientific, Technical and Managerial Staffs (ASTMS).

Musicians' Union
(MU)

Head Office

60/62 Clapham Road
London SW9 0JJ
01-582 5566

Principal Officers

General Secretary —
John Morton
Assistant Secretaries —
Stan Hibbert
Jack Stoddart

Membership (1982)

Male 35,002
Female 5,054
Total 40,056

Union Journal and Publications

Musician — published quarterly, mailed to members. The union recently published a broadsheet entitled *Bandcall* which was aimed at improving terms and conditions of musicians employed in Mecca dance halls.

General

The Musicians' Union is the second largest musicians' union in the world, second only to the American Federation of Musicians. It organises the whole of the music profession including symphony orchestras, broadcasting orchestras, bands in night clubs, bands and groups in ballrooms, rock and other groups. The union and British Actors' Equity form a *Performers' Alliance* in association with the Writers' Guild of Great Britain, and the Musicians' Union is a member of the Confederation of Entertainment Unions, the Federation of Broadcasting Unions, Federation of Theatre Unions and Federation of Film Unions.

The union has built up its membership from around 32,000 in 1969 to its present level of around 40,000. John Morton, General Secretary, is also President of the International Federation of Musicians. The union has been involved in strike action against the BBC.

History

The Musicians' Union was formed in 1921 as a result of an amalgamation of the *National Orchestral Union of Professional Musicians* and the *Amalgamated Musicians' Union*, both of which were formed in 1893. During the 1920s membership grew to around 20,000 but it declined substantially after the development of 'talking' films to around 7,000 in 1940. The early problems of the union were the immigration of foreign musicians into Britain and the use of military bands and orchestras. It has built up its membership to its present level by determined organisation in the post-war years.

Union Officials

The union has a dual structure of full-time officials, some with responsibilities that relate to geographical areas and others with responsibilities concerned with specific aspects of the union's work. At present the union employs a general secretary, two assistant secretaries, four specialist officials (music promotion and public relations officer, session organiser and group organiser and employment promotion officer). The union also has nine district organisers throughout Great Britain.

Coverage

The union admits into membership those who 'are following the profession of music in any of its branches', i.e. those engaged in performing, teaching or writing music. It organises musicians in symphony orchestras, broadcasting orchestras, theatre orchestras, bands in night clubs and ballrooms, and rock and other groups. It has a long established special section covering those engaged in arranging, composing or copying music. The union obtained early recognition from the BBC and it conducts regular negotiations with all major employers of musicians including the BBC, independent television companies, the British phonographic industry, the Association of British Orchestras, the Theatrical Management Association, the British Resorts Association and Mecca Ltd and the Rank Organisation. In addition, the union also conducts negotiations with a number of smaller independent bodies such as the Royal Opera House, Butlins Ltd, the British Film Producers' Association, and the English National Opera Company.

Organisation

The supreme authority within the Musicians' Union is vested in the Biennial Delegate Conference which is convened in July. The union's general management is vested in the Executive Committee, which consists of 21 members elected to serve a two-year period. The full EC meets at least four times a year. The members of the EC are elected by ballot vote of the districts of the union (of which there are nine) and the number of representatives accorded to each district depends on its size.

There are nine district councils which meet three times a year and are formed from delegates from the branches in the district concerned, elected annually by a ballot vote of each branch in the particular district. There are around 130 branches of the Musicians' Union spread throughout Great Britain and they normally meet monthly. Full-time officials of the Musicians' Union are appointed by the Executive Committee, and the general secretary is elected by ballot vote of the union's membership to serve until retirement, death or removal by a ballot vote of the union.

Women

Women constitute a small proportion of the total union membership and they play little part in the affairs of the union. There are no female members on the Executive Committee, no female full-time officials, and there is little female representation at Conference. A woman employment promotion officer has recently been appointed.

External Relations

The union is affiliated nationally to the Labour Party and a number of branches and districts are affiliated at local level. Peter Snape, Labour MP for West Bromwich East, assists the union in parliamentary liaison. The union is also affiliated to the National Council for Civil Liberties.

The union maintains a close and effective working relationship with British Actors' Equity both within the Performers' Alliance and additionally to it. The Performers' Alliance is the formal grouping through which liaison is maintained between British Actors' Equity, the Writers' Guild of Great Britain and the Musicians' Union. It holds meetings of representatives at approximately bi-monthly intervals and maintains a small office in Wardour Street, London, which houses the Performers' Alliance research officer. The joint secretaries of the alliance are the general secretary of the union and the general secretary of Equity.

The union has also established a joint committee with the Association of Broadcasting Staffs, mainly to maintain a joint strategy on developments affecting members of both unions in the BBC.

In addition, the Musicians' Union is a member of the Confederation of Entertainment Unions along with the other unions.

The confederation is the umbrella organisation for three constituent federations, the Federation of Broadcasting Unions, the Federation of Film Unions and the Federation of Theatre Unions.

At international level the Musicians' Union was one of the founder members of the International Federation of Musicians, and maintains close links with the American Federation of Musicians.

Labour Party Delegation

The union sends two delegates to the Labour Party Conference each year, who are selected by the National Executive Committee. The union voted for Denis Healey in the 1981 Labour Party deputy leadership election on both ballots, having been mandated by the NEC.

Policy

The Musicians' Union has supported TUC motions that proposed a return to free collective bargaining and opposed those that suggested incomes restraint. The union has always adopted the policy that members themselves should have the maximum involvement and participation in pursuing their own claims for pay and conditions. The closed shop is seen as an objective to be striven for at all times.

The main policy concern of the union in recent years has been the erosion of employment opportunities for musicians arsing from the use of tapes, records etc., which is the reason for the Musicians' Union slogan, 'Keep Music Live'. It has influenced the union's attitude to performers' rights and has led to the policy of regarding control over use as being more important than remuneration for the use of recordings. It justified the vigorous campaign that led to an obligation being placed on commercial radio in Britain (an obligation that is not found in any other country)

to spend a certain proportion of its receipts on musical employment. It explains the union's concern with the public use of records, with the use of tape for the accompaniment of live performance and with the work of music promotion. Recently the union has been involved in several disputes over staffing levels or techniques that have seemed to threaten employment opportunities, particularly in 1980 with the BBC (see **Recent Events**).

At the 1977 Trades Union Congress the union moved a composite motion that welcomed the decision to establish an arts, sports and leisure advisory committee, and suggested that it should be provided with adequate back-up facilities as soon as possible. At the 1978 TUC the union proposed two motions. One was concerned with education and called for the school curriculum to be widened to provide every child with an opportunity to discover and develop the widest range of his or her potentialities, including those for humanities and the arts. The motion had been prompted by a number of disturbing attempts to prescribe a narrower school curriculum concentrating only on those skills and capacities that fitted children for the immediate requirements of employment. The other motion on broadcasting called for public accountability to be combined with a responsibility on the part of all broadcasting organisations to produce and provide a wide range of high quality programming. This motion was carried before the publication of the Annan Report. The union also supported a motion moved by the Writers' Guild of Great Britain on the public lending right. A motion by Equity calling for government and local authorities to make substantially greater resources available for the provision of entertainment, particularly in the fields of live theatre and music, was seconded by the Musicians' Union.

Recent Events

In 1980 a major dispute with the BBC led to strike action. The union opposed the BBC's plans to axe five of its 11 orchestras as part of a two year economy plan to save £130 million. Redundancy notices were served to 172 members of the five house orchestras which were due to be disbanded by August 1980. The BBC claimed that the abolition of the orchestras would save £1.5 million, of which £1 million would support musicians outside house orchestras.

The union argued that the cuts illustrated the BBC management's inability and lack of enthusiasm for supporting creative musical work, thus leaving the responsibility for producing the music that the majority of listeners want to hear to the record industry. The union received sympathetic support from the Association of Broadcasting Staffs and the TGWU.

In the event, a settlement was reached with the BBC which saved three of the orchestras the corporation had intended to disband. Accepting these proposals as a compromise, union officials believed they had won a big improvement in the original BBC proposals by the eight week strike and recommended the members to vote for acceptance in the subsequent ballot.

Professional, Executive, Clerical and Computer Staff, Association of
(APEX)

Head Office

22 Worple Road
London SW19 4DF
01-947 3131

Principal Officers

General Secretary —
Roy Grantham
Deputy General Secretary —
T. Thomas
National Secretaries —
R. Stephen
D. Lapish
K. Standring
President — D. Howell MP

Membership (1982)

Male 54,942
Female 67,697
Total 122,639

Union Journal and Publications

Apex — monthly or bi-monthly.

APEX has produced a number of pamphlets and booklets of late, the most celebrated of which is the booklet *Automation and the Office Worker* (68 pages) which was produced by the union's office technology working party. This report gives a detailed analysis of the implications for APEX members of a wide range of electronic and computing systems currently entering the office area. The first report produced by the office technology working party was entitled *Office Technology: The Trade Union Response* (68 pages) which was described by the *Financial Times* as 'well-argued', and , in the words of APEX, 'a rebuff to those who accuse the trade unions of Luddism'.

The union has also produced a booklet on women's rights at work entitled *Workplace Attitudes to Maternity and Nursery Facilities: A Case Study* (51 pages). This booklet gives the results of a survey undertaken by the APEX national negotiating committee in support of its claim for improved equal opportunities for women at Lucas Industries.

APEX membership consists of around 55 per cent women, and therefore it is not surprising that the union pays particular attention to them in its recruitment leaflets — the most notable of which are: *Joining a Trade Union — What's in it for Women*? *Women's Rights, Fair Selection Programme*, outlining a model clause in agreements on equal opportunities.

Area Offices

● *London and Home Counties*
3 Parkview Road
Welling

Kent DA16 1SZ
01-303 3407/8

● *North Eastern*
40 Little Horton Lane
Bradford BD5 0AI
0532-33021/2

● *North Western*
Apex House
45 Kingsway
Levenshulme
Manchester M19 2LL
061-224 5726/7950

● *Scottish*
Abbotsford
31 Drymen Road
Bearsden
Glasgow G61 2RL
041-332 3036/7

● *West of England*
6 High Street
Warmley
Bristol
0272-677557

● *Midlands*
90 Hagley Road
Birmingham B16 8NF
021-454 6848/9

● *Northern*
7 Thornhill Park
Sunderland
Tyne and Wear SR2 7JZ
0783-57670/76869

● *Welsh*
6th Floor
114–116 St Mary Street
Cardiff CF1 1QN
0222-22044/33261

● *Northern Ireland*
291 Antrim Road
Belfast BT15 26Z
0232-748678/746210

General

APEX seeks to organise all white-collar staff from office juniors to senior managers, and it caters for computer, supervisory and managerial staff as well as clerical workers generally. It started its life in 1890 as the *Clerks' Union*, and after a series of mergers adopted its present title in 1972. The post-war years have seen APEX benefit from the rise in white-collar unionisation generally, although it has grown at a much slower rate than ASTMS, which is nearly three times its size. Since 1980,

APEX's membership has fallen sharply largely due to the decline of the engineering industry, and partly due to the adverse effects of new technology.

The majority of the membership of APEX is located in the engineering industry but it also has membership in civil air transport, the co-operative movement, steel, coal, the car industry, insurance, aerospace, confectionery and chocolate manufacture, tobacco and chemicals. With the advent of microtechnology in the office, and the decline in its traditional base in engineering, APEX is now an obvious candidate for a merger. Roy Grantham, the General Secretary, has moulded the union into a right-wing moderate stance, and is not a popular figure among TUC leaders, particularly with Clive Jenkins's ASTMS, with whom the union has had some bitter exchanges in the past over alleged poaching of members. Fifty five per cent of its membership is female. The union has produced some noted publications of late — particularly the booklet entitled *Office Technology: The Trade Union Response*. APEX is affiliated to the Labour Party and its officials are appointed.

History

APEX originated in 1890 when it started life as the *Clerks' Union*. As it gradually spread across the country it changed its name to the *National Union of Clerks*. Organisation of white-collar workers was extremely difficult in the early part of this century, and by 1908 it had reached a membership of only 1,000. By 1920, after a period of rapid growth and the absorption of a number of other unions, the union became known as the *National Union of Clerks and Administration Workers*, by which time its membership had reached 40,000. The inter-war years saw a drastic decline in membership and, by 1940, after a merger with the *Association of Women Clerks and Secretaries*, membership was only 18,478. In the same year the long serving general secretary, Herbert Henry Elvin (1909-40), was succeeded by F. C. Woods. The union obtained recognition from the Engineering Employers' Federation as early as 1920 as party to the Engineering Procedure Agreement.

Since 1940, when it became known as the *Clerical and Administrative Workers' Union*, membership has increased substantially in line with the post-war growth in white-collar unionisation generally. By 1972, when it adopted its present title, its membership had risen to 118,388, but in comparison with its main rival (ASTMS) its membership growth has been moderate. In 1978 the *AA Staff Association* transferred engagements to APEX as did the *National Wool Sorters' Society* in 1980.

Union Officials

Apart from the national officials and administrative staff at head office, APEX employs around 51 area officials including nine area secretaries, six senior organisers, 31 area organisers, and full-time officers of the AA and General Accident sections. A number of APEX officials have left, and it seems likely that in the near future not all vacancies will necessarily be filled.

APEX officials are appointed by area councils subject to Executive Council approval, and act under EC instructions. The interviewing committees for APEX applicants are composed of members of the area council plus two EC members. The EC itself can (and has done in the past) veto any particular appointment. All persons who are so appointed must have been a member of the union for at least two years immediately preceding his or her application for the appointment.

Roy Grantham and APEX:

Roy Grantham, the General Secretary of APEX, joined the Clerical and Administrative Workers' Union in 1949, having been employed as an executive officer in the Civil Service. The flavour of the union can perhaps best be imparted by examining the way in which he has moulded it to reflect his own character and political leanings. Roy Grantham rose steadily through the ranks of the union and was appointed General Secretary in 1970, to the surprise of many APEX activists.

Grantham immediately initiated an internal review of the union's structure and organisation to widen the spread of members both among industries and in different occupations. During the 1970s there were a number of clashes between APEX and ASTMS. Apart from the natural rivalry between the two unions, who are essentially recruiting in the same market-place, it is well known in trade union circles that Grantham and Clive Jenkins are not fond of one another. The major clash between ASTMS and APEX occurred in the early 1970s; in 1970, following the merger of the Union of Insurance Staff into ASTMS, ASTMS started to recruit more members of the staff of General Accident. Many employees of General Accident then formed themselves into an organisation called Staff Association General Accident (SAGA). SAGA and ASTMS were thus intense rivals for recruiting members, and the situation became more complicated in 1974 when SAGA decided to transfer engagements to APEX. ASTMS then complained to the disputes committee of the TUC that the Bridlington rules had been breached and the TUC disputes committee found in favour of ASTMS. The chairperson of SAGA then took the matter to court and, in October 1975, it was ruled that APEX could not expel the SAGA members.

The SAGA affair resurfaced in 1981 when it was revealed that ASTMS had recruited former APEX members 'without going through the normal Bridlington procedures'. The TUC disputes committee ruled that ASTMS 'hand back' to APEX over 1,000 members.

APEX is not all that popular in the eyes of many influential trade union leaders. Apart from the SAGA affair, Grantham has exhibited a determination to adhere strictly to his own philosophy as to how APEX should develop. He campaigned vigorously in 1975 in favour of a 'yes' vote in the Common Market referendum, and in 1974 Hugh Scanlon (then president of the AUEW) had to call in the police to escort some of his AUEW staff through APEX and TGWU picket lines at a time when APEX and TGWU members were on strike at the AUEW headquarters over a pay claim.

Grantham's unpopularity with some other trade union leaders was one factor which led to his losing his seat on the General Council of the TUC; such an occurrence is almost unheard of in trade union politics as the sitting incumbent is invariably automatically re-elected at each Congress. In 1980, Grantham was defeated again at the TUC by Alan Sapper (ACTT) when he lost narrowly by 187,000 votes. Grantham's absence from the General Council was even more notable since he was then president of the Confederation of Shipbuilding and Engineering Unions.

In general APEX has come to be associated with the right wing of the Labour Party (see **External Relations**) and some of their members are well known right-wing Labour MPs and ex-ministers (such as Harold Lever, Denis Howell, Denis Healey and Fred Mulley). In 1977, the Labour Party was deprived of additional financial support from the APEX political fund following the appointment of Andy Bevan as National Youth Officer of the party. The APEX journal complained of 'entryism in the party of extremist groups' and stated: 'The Executive Council of the union cannot agree to the contribution of our members who pay the political levy being used for purposes which are alien to the cause of a democratic Labour Party or to finance the activities of Trotskyist groups within the party.' APEX decided that its political fund could only be used to support APEX members in elections.

All candidates to union office or as a representative of APEX on outside bodies must declare their membership of political parties (Rule 13, APEX Rule Book; see **External Relations**). The name of any political party to which a candidate for election belongs is printed on the ballot papers.

Coverage

APEX seeks to organise all staff from office juniors to senior managers, and caters for computer, supervisory and managerial staff, including security personnel, industrial nurses and machine operators in addition to clerical grades; it has members in civil air transport, the co-operative movement, steel, coal, the car industry, insurance, aerospace, confectionery and chocolate manufacture, the tobacco industry, chemicals, and engineering (where the majority of its membership is located). It is party to major agreements with the co-operative movement, electricity supply, civil air transport, coal, Gallaher Ltd, Lucas, Imperial Tobacco, Massey Ferguson, Phillips, International Computers, Rank Hovis McDougall, and British Leyland. The staff of several large trade unions are represented by APEX and the union has been involved in disputes with the CPSA and COHSE.

Organisation

APEX holds its Annual Conference in April and it lasts for four days. It is the supreme body of government within the union. Each branch with a minimum of 40 members is entitled to send a delegate. The Annual Conference has the power, subject to a majority of not less than 75 per cent of the delegates present and voting, to refer any question which does not appear on the agenda to the branches for their decision, which is binding on the union. APEX rules also provide for a referendum on any question providing that a tenth of the membership sign a requisition and send it to the general secretary.

The Executive Council consists of the president, two vice-presidents and general treasurer, two national members and one representative from each area. The area representatives are elected annually by a membership vote at an area council meeting. All EC members must have been APEX members of at least five years standing, and no full-time employee of the union is eligible for election to the EC. The EC meets at least six times a year, and carries on the management of the union between conferences.

APEX also has an area council in operation in each of its nine areas. The area councils have a great deal of discretionary power; for example they may establish industrial advisory councils, oversee the branches within their area, supervise the work of area officials and appoint their own officials (in conjunction with the EC).

There were 887 branches of APEX at the end of 1979. At present, APEX has national advisory councils in aerospace, civil air transport, collieries, co-operatives, electricity, engineering, shipbuilding and steel. The union has special sections for General Accident staff and Automobile Association staff. The union has advisory councils at both national and area level, and also has a women's advisory council.

Women

Women have constituted a majority of APEX membership ever since the early 1970s. Despite their numbers and the efforts made by the union on their behalf in attempting to secure equality of opportunity at work, women are under-represented in the affairs of APEX. There is an Executive Council sub-committee on equal opportunity which carries out an annual survey of women's participation in APEX. The 1979 survey revealed that there was only one woman member on the 15 strong Executive Council; one woman on the AA section general council; none on the General Accident section NEC; only 17 women out of 116 on all the national advisory councils; 25 out of 88 on all the national negotiating bodies; and 11 out of 44 on the area executive committees. It still remains true that at branch level women are seen in a secretarial role, with the proportion of women branch secretaries standing at 43 per cent at the end of 1979. There is only one woman APEX national official and one woman area official.

External Relations

APEX is affiliated to the Labour Party and sponsors the following MPs:

Ifor Davies (Gower)
Edward Fletcher (Darlington)
Fred Mulley (Sheffield Park)
Denis Howell (Birmingham, Small Heath)
Bruce Millan (Glasgow Craigton)
Stanley Clinton Davis (Hackney Central)
Jack Dormand (Easington)
John Morris (Aberavon)

Among the organisations looked upon with disfavour in APEX official circles are the Communist Party, an internal 'ginger' group called APEX Action, the Socialist Workers' Party, certain fringe left parties, the National Front and National Party. Around 70 per cent of APEX members pay the political levy.

The Executive Council at the 1980 APEX Annual Conference decided that in voting on constitutional issues within the Labour Party, only members who are individual members of the Labour Party have any standing. The policy of APEX thus lays down three types of political issues and the involvement of members voting on them is as follows:

(a) Policy issues — General policy issues within the union such as foreign affairs, economic or social policy are matters of common concern on which every member is entitled to vote.

(b) Political fund expenditure — Questions of political fund expenditure are matters on which only members who pay the political levy are entitled to vote.

(c) Labour Party Constitution — As a matter internal to the Labour Party, this a matter on which only members who are individual members of the Labour Party are entitled to vote.

At the 1979 general election there were 53 Labour candidates who were members of APEX, of whom 29 were elected to parliament. APEX opposed all three proposals for constitutional change at the 1979 Labour Party Conference. APEX placed their 109,000 affiliated votes behind Denis Healey for the Deputy Leadership election in the Labour Party in 1981.

At the 1982 APEX Annual Conference there was overwhelming condemnation of the SDP and strong support for the Labour Party.

APEX is affiliated to the International Federation of Commercial, Clerical, Professional and Technical Employees (FIET), the United Nations Association, Confederation of Shipbuilding and Engineering Unions, and the Workers' Educational Association. The union invested £29,761 in the new Labour Party HQ Management Fund at Walworth Road.

Policy

At the 1979 Trades Union Congress proposals for altering the structure of the General Council were submitted by APEX. Roy Grantham, in moving the motion, which called for automatic representation on the General Council for unions with 100,000 members rising progressively to five seats for unions with over 1.5 million members, made the point that complacency and lack of interest reigned supreme in the General Council's attitude to women. The motion was remitted to the General Council after APEX had been given an assurance that a full report would be given to the 1980 Congress (see **Trades Union Congress**). APEX has tended to be pro-EEC and, in 1982, delegates at the Annual Conference threw out a motion supporting the 1981 TUC Congress decision favouring free collective bargaining. Instead, Conference backed the TUC–Labour Party liaison committee's call for an agreement between unions and a future Labour government on allocating resources to public spending, investment, and private consumption, and on the distribution of national income among profits, earnings, rents and benefits. Conference also strongly attacked the government's economic policy and anti-union legislation.

One reason APEX is actively considering a merger with other unions is the threat it faces from the onset of new technology in the office. The office technology working party of APEX in its report pointed out that the introduction of word processors affects mainly women workers, who are often considered to be a soft option for cutting jobs because women rarely register as unemployed. On one set of assumptions, the report stated that something like 250,000 office jobs could be lost by 1983, but also stated that jobs could be even more at risk from ignoring technology. The report suggested that 'technology agreements' should be negotiated with adequate safeguards covering earnings, job satisfaction etc. In June 1982 APEX published a report claiming that new technology was being introduced in the South-East in an 'uncontrolled fashion', and also stated that new technology meant not only job losses but also health and safety hazards. The report was based on a 1981 survey carried out by the APEX London and Home Counties Area Technology Committee.

Recent Events

The name of APEX is perhaps associated in the public mind with the events that took place in 1977 at the Grunwick Processing Laboratories Ltd in Brent. It is unnecessary to repeat the Grunwick story on these pages for it represents a chapter in the history of APEX that many members of the union would prefer to forget, or at least would like to have avoided in the first place. The events that drew APEX into the Grunwick dispute were not of their own making; as the Scarman Report noted, 'there was no political motivation or empire building on the part of the union. The union was not looking for members; some Grunwick employees were looking for a union.' It was always a difficult battle to win. The odds were stacked heavily against the union by a recalcitrant employer who carried his opposition to trade unionism to the bitter end, the portrayal of the mass picketing by the press and media, and the fact that the trade union recognition provisions of the Employment Protection Act were impotent in the face of such determined employer resistance. Although APEX stumbled into the dispute they at least deserve credit for pursuing the cause of the coloured immigrant workers at Grunwick, for it was a moral stand which would inevitably be taken at a high cost.

APEX membership at 31 December 1981 was 122,639 — a fall from 140,292 at 31 December 1980. The sharp fall in membership — which has yet to be halted — can be attributed primarily to the recession and particularly to its impact on the engineering industry where APEX still has its main base. The impact of new technology is probably now having some effect — an adverse one as APEX has long predicted — on employment levels in the white-collar field.

The fall in membership is having a dual effect on the union. Firstly, increased efforts are being made at recruitment and at developing a more effective recruitment strategy. This includes looking at 'topping up' membership at establishments where the union has existing membership, exploring the newer and largely unorganised industries, such as electronics, and paying some attention to staff associations.

There has been some success with recruitment over the past year, the most notable success story being that of the country's 1,500 professional Rugby League players who joined APEX. They are now organised in the Rugby League Professional Players Association, which is a branch of the union and is run from the APEX office in Bradford.

This, and the comparatively small effect of the recession on APEX membership in the service industries (the AA membership has increased, for instance) emphasises the fact that if it is to survive as an independent union, growth is only likely to come outside the traditional engineering sector.

The other effect of the fall in membership has been to concentrate APEX minds on mergers. The front runner at present is a possible confederation involving APEX, GMWU and the EETPU. Other unions are peripherally involved in these talks. At the APEX 1982 Annual Conference reservations were expressed at the involvement with the EETPU. Many, including the APEX officials, seem to prefer the idea of a straightforward merger with the GMWU. There appears to be very little support in APEX for a merger with ASTMS.

APEX continues to be at the forefront of the trade union response to new technology. A number of recent APEX publications have highlighted union policy regarding unemployment, job design and health and safety issues relating to new technology. Other campaigns APEX has been involved in recently include the campaign for shorter hours in the engineering industry and for the retention of the Fair Wages Resolution.

Further Reference

F. Hughes, *By Hand and By Brain*,

CAWU (now APEX) 1953. The history of the Clerical and Administrative Workers' Union.

Joe Rogaly, *Grunwick*, Penguin Special 1977. Very journalistic but highly readable.

ACAS Employment Protection Act, 1975, Section 12 — *Report No. 19*, 10 March 1977.

Report of a Court of Inquiry into a dispute between Grunwick . . . and APEX, (The Scarman Report) HMSO (Cmnd 6922).

An updated history of APEX is currently being written.

Theatrical, Television and Kine Employees, National Association of
(NATTKE)

Head Office

155 Kennington Park Road
London SE11 4JU
01-735 9068

Principal Officers

General Secretary —
J. L. Wilson
National Organisers —
T. Lever
S. Ogden
W. Bovey

Area Organisers

● *London Office*
P. Bromley
M. Campbell
C. Devine
V. Feiner
R. Johnson
B. Quinton

● *Manchester Office*
A. Montrose
85 Mosley Street
Manchester M2 3LG

● *Glasgow Office*
H. McFarlane
103 Bath Street
Glasgow G2 2EE

● *Nottingham Office*
A. Collins
Long Row Chambers
31/33 Long Row
Nottingham NG1 2DR

● *Southampton Office*
L. Wallace
25 Portsmouth Road
Woolston
Southampton SO2 9BA

Membership (1982)

Male 9,400
Female 9,600
Total 19,000

Union Journal

NATTKE Newsletter —
published irregularly.
At the 1982 biennial delegate
conference a proposal from
the Liverpool branch for
'restructuring of the *NATTKE
Newsletter* to include more
grass-root information along
the lines of the other union,
association, society and club
periodicals' was carried.
Other publications include
'Health and Safety' — a display
sheet guide for NATTKE
members.

General

Employees of theatres, cinemas, film
studios, television studios, television
commercials, broadcasting, videotape
manufacture, recording and other sections of the entertainment industry
are eligible for membership.

History

Trade unionism among backstage
workers began when 12 stagehands at
the Adelphi Theatre made a combined approach to the master carpenter for a wage increase in 1890 and
were subsequently dismissed. They
drew up a set of rules and elected a
secretary, Charles Thoroughgood.
Within six months the *UK Theatrical
and Music Hall Operatives' Union*
held its first conference. It was part of
the new unionism, organising thousands of the so-called unskilled and
previously unorganised labourers.

Soon the name was changed to the
*National Association of Theatrical
Employees* and a full-time national
secretary, William Johnson, was
appointed. Wages among backstage
workers were very poor, worsened by

the use of sub-contractors so that
theatre managers could disclaim responsibility. The union tried to establish fair wages clauses in contracts,
using local licensing laws to oppose
renewal of licences of unsatisfactory
theatres, but the proprietors successfully fought this move in the courts.

The music hall strike of 1907 called
by the Variety Artists' Association led
to recognition of trade unions, including NATE, by music hall proprietors,
and their acceptance of collective bargaining.

Later, the *National Association of
Cinematograph Operators* was established as an autonomous branch of
NATE as the film industry developed.
For a long time, however, co-
operation between film workers and
theatre workers was difficult to establish because theatre managers claimed
that 'the picturedromes ruined their
business', and the threat to go over to
films was a powerful weapon against
employees of the live theatre. At first
trade unionism in the film industry
was confined to cinema employees but
gradually it spread to film studios,
although, as in cinemas, trade union
organisation there was based on conditions established in theatres and
music halls.

The first National Delegate Conference of NATE was held in 1920. An
argument with the ETU was then developing over the recruitment of electricians and cine operatives. In 1932
Tom O'Brien (later Sir Tom O'Brien)
was elected general secretary, and it
was he who eventually settled the dispute with ETU in favour of NATKE
(the 'K' denoting 'and Kine') around
1936.

By 1940 the union claimed 20,000
members, and by the end of the war,
with the arrival of the television industry, it was boasting a membership
turnover of some 50,000 members —
making it the largest union in the
entertainment business. Sir Tom
O'Brien died in 1970, by which time
the membership of NATTKE (the
second 'T' denoting 'Television') had
contracted to 17,684. O'Brien was
succeeded as general secretary by R.
L. Keenan, but in 1975 Keenan himself died suddenly. The present
General Secretary, J. L. Wilson, succeeded him.

Organisation

The supreme government of NATTKE is the biennial National Delegate Conference. Each branch with not less than 175 paying members is allowed one delegate; smaller branches are grouped together for representational purposes.

General management and administration are formally performed by the National Executive Council. The NEC is constituted by the general elected officers — general president, general vice-president and general treasurer; one representative from each membership section — theatres, cinemas, film studios, broadcasting, miscellaneous; and 13 representatives from among the five geographical divisions of the union.

Women

Women form the overwhelming majority of workers in bingo and cinema, in theatre front-of-house, in clerical jobs, cleaning, catering and all the other low-paid or part-time grades in the entertainment industry. At the 1982 Biennial Delegate Conference motions were passed to ensure that all collective agreements would include a negotiated anti-discrimination clause, to reaffirm support for the TUC Women's Charter and to set up a national committee to assess NATTKE's representation of and services to its women members.

External Relations

NATTKE is affiliated to the Labour Party, the International Secretariat of Entertainment Unions, the (British) Confederation of Entertainment Unions, the (British) Federations of Theatre Unions, Film Unions and Broadcasting Unions. At the 1982 Biennial Delegate Conference a composite motion calling for affiliation to the Campaign for Nuclear Disarmament was carried.

Policy and Recent Events

NATTKE's membership has increased during the economic recession, despite difficulties associated with the closures of cinemas, theatres and film companies. A further 2,000 members were to be added by amalgamation with the Film Artistes' Association whose members voted to transfer their engagements to NATTKE at the end of 1981. The transfer was delayed by complaints to the certification officer from dissenting FAA members.

NATTKE's members employed in cinemas are gravely threatened by video sales and rental shops and by satellite broadcasting; a motion urging government control of the expansion of the video market and support for cinemas was carried at the Biennial Delegate Conference and it was decided to set up a new technology committee. At the local level some increased solidarity may be achieved by amalgamation with the National Association of Executives, Managers and Staffs (NAEMS), the body representing cinema and bingo hall managers, which is now committed in principle to a merger with NATTKE.

In broadcasting the main threat to NATTKE members is seen to be independent production, the cut-throat world of free enterprise and international competition where new technology and low unit costs can be ruthlessly exploited. Agreements with the established companies protecting permanent employment may be undermined by professional freelancing and 'creative flexibility'. Although the government has granted Britain's first satellite channels to the BBC, it is not clear how that organisation will adapt to an environment of unfettered private enterprise. NATTKE has decided that there is considerable mutual advantage in an amalgamation with the Association of Broadcasting Staffs (ABS) and discussions to this effect are in progress. The Biennial Delegate Conference reaffirmed policies to seek amalgamation and closer co-operation among all entertainment unions. Other significant resolutions were those which pledged opposition to the Tebbit legislation on trade union immunities; reaffirmed support for the National Health Service and drew members' attention to UN and other cultural boycotts of South Africa, and called for support for various movements of national liberation. A motion expressing 'support for development of Labour Party democracy and in particular changes that will help ensure that the democratically agreed policies decided by Annual Conference will be followed by future Labour governments to assist this process' was carried.

Writers' Guild of Great Britain

Head Office

430 Edgeware Road
London WC2 1EH
01-723 8074

Principal Officer

General Secretary —
W. J. Jeffrey

Membership (1982)

Male 1,260
Female 637
Total 1,897

Union Journal

The Writers' News — sent to every member quarterly. Monthly or bimonthly newsletter.

General

The guild is the trade union of practising writers of all disciplines except journalism and all its members are self-employed. The guild has collective agreements with the major employers of writers including independent television companies, the BBC (for both television and radio), film producers, book publishers and in certain aspects of stage drama. All agreements are negotiated nationally but not all are industry-wide.

History

The guild came into existence in 1959 when the Screenwriters' Guild joined forces with television and radio writers. It has steadily increased its membership and its sphere of activity, opening its doors to book writers in 1974.

Organisation

The general secretary is the only full-time officer and there are no branch or regional offices. Entrusted with the government of the guild is the Executive Council which meets monthly. It is comprised of 30 members: the chairperson, two deputy chairpersons, an honorary treasurer, five regional chairpersons and 21 councillors, 15 of whom have full membership credits in film, television or radio and six of whom have full membership credits in books, stage plays or other published works. All members of the Executive Council are elected by ballot at an annual general meeting for a term of three years and are eligible for re-election. The chairperson, deputy chairpersons and honorary treasurer are also elected at this meeting.

External Relations

The guild has no political affiliation and, indeed, this is expressly precluded by its constitution.

Recent Events

The guild's long campaign on public lending rights reached a successful conclusion in 1982. The guild has secured pension rights for its members working for BBC television and ITV. It is campaigning for a reduction in imported television programmes and an increase in home produced television drama. Agreements have been reached about the sale of videograms with ITV and BBC.

Further Reference

David Caute, 'Publish and be damned', New Statesman 13 June 1980.

Group Eighteen **General Workers**

General Municipal, Boilermakers' and Allied Trades' Union

(GMBATU)
(formerly General and
Municipal Workers' Union
(GMWU))

Note: at the time of going to press, amalgamation plans with the Boilermakers' Society were announced; information that follows refers to the union as at 30 September 1982, just prior to the formation of GMBATU.

Head Office

Thorne House
Ruxley Ridge
Claygate
Esher
Surrey KT10 0TI
0372-62081

Principal Officers

General Secretary—
David Basnett
National Industrial Officers—
Engineering, shipbuilding,
vehicles, paper — M. Reed
Transport, cables, security,
water — E. Newall
Construction, building
materials, quarrying —
F. Earl
Steel, metals, industrial Civil
Service — F. Cottam
Universities, local authorities,
NHS — C. Donnet
Gas, paper and timber,
electricity, UKAEA —
J. Edmonds
Food, drink and tobacco —
R. Smith
Chemicals, glass, rubber —
D. Warburton
Equal rights, textiles, clothing,
distribution and retail, toys
— P. Turner

MATSA — D. Williams
Hotel and catering workers —
F. Cooper
Health and Safety Officer —
D. Gee
Co-ordinator (Recruitment) —
F. A. Baker

Head Office Departments

Research department (there is
a research section, a legal
section, an advice bureau to
answer queries from members
on issues not connected with
their employment, a financial
information service and a
statistics section.)
Productivity services centre
Education department
consisting of colleges at Hale,
Manchester, and Surbiton,
Surrey.
Organisation department
(primarily concerned with
recruitment)
Pensions and social services
department
Finance department
Press and publicity
department

Membership (1982)

Male 688,018
Female 297,381
Total 985,399

Union Journal and Publications

GMW Journal — monthly, a
readable and informative
tabloid.
GMWU Herald — quarterly.
The following publications are
available free to GMWU
activists:
Guides:
Equality
Law at Work
Guide to Disclosure of

Information
GMW — A guide to the union
Handbooks:
Shop Steward's Handbook
MATSA Representative's
Handbook
Safety Representative's
Handbook
Advice for the Unemployed —
a guide to the rights of the
redundant worker, including
social security and retraining.
Leaflets:
Race Relations at Work

Regional Secretaries

● *London*
H. Robertson JP
154 Brent Street
London NW4 2DP

● *Northern*
T. Burlison
Thorne House
77/87 West Road
Newcastle-upon-Tyne
NE15 6RB

● *Yorkshire and North Derbyshire*
J. Kitchen
Concord House
Park Lane
Leeds LS3 1NB

● *Birmingham and West Midlands*
G. Wheatley
Will Thorne House
2 Birmingham Road
Halesowen B63 3HP

● *Liverpool and North Wales and*
Irish
J. Whelan
99 Edge Lane
Liverpool L7 2PE

● *Lancashire*
J. F. Eccles JP
Thorne House
36 Station Road
Cheadle Hulme SK8 7AB

● *Southern*
D. O. Gladwin CBE JP
Cooper House
205 Hook Road
Chessington
Surrey KT9 1EP

● *Scottish*
J. Morrell
4 Park Gate
Glasgow G3 8BD

● *Midlands and East Coast*
C. A. Unwin JP
542 Woodborough Road
Nottingham NG3 5FJ

● *Southern Western*
I. G. Dunn
Williamson House
17 Newport Road
Cardiff CF2 1TB

General

The GMWU is the third largest union
in Britain. Like the Transport and
General Workers' Union, to which it
bears many similarities and yet many
contrasts, it has membership in almost
every industry and occupation. About
two thirds of the membership is,
however, concentrated in six main
sectors: engineering and metal trades;
local authority employment; food,
drink and tobacco; gas; chemicals;
electricity. The union also has considerable membership and influence
in glass, rubber manufacturing, building materials, shipbuilding, steel, textiles, paper, construction, quarrying,
the National Health Service, water
supply, catering, distribution, security
and other service industries.

About 35 per cent of total membership is public sector employees and
about the same proportion of membership is composed of women who
are also mainly in public sector employment. The union has a white-
collar section, MATSA, and a separate section on similar lines, the Hotel
and Catering Workers' Union.

History

The General and Municipal Workers'
Union was established in 1924 on the
amalgamation of three unions: the
National Union of General Workers;
the *National Amalgamated Union of*
Labour and the *Municipal Em-*
ployees' Association, and was then
called the *National Union of General*
and Municipal Workers.

The National Union of General
Workers was originally known as the
Gasworkers and General Labourers'
Union formed in 1889 with Will
Thorne as general secretary. (Thorne
was a militant socialist at the time and
a prominent member of the Social
Democratic Federation, the first Brit-
ish political party to be strongly in-

fluenced by marxist ideas.) This union was in the vanguard of the so-called new unionism, and it must be noted that the nucleus of its membership — the gas stokers — were far from being unskilled and low paid workers. Its first strike resulted in a reduction from 12 to eight hour shifts for London gasworkers. This concession helped the union's rapid growth outside London. It began to organise workers in a wide variety of industries, reaching a membership of 77,000 in 1911. The name was changed to the National Union of General Workers in 1916. In 1921 the *National Federation of Women Workers* led by Mary MacArthur, decided that a separate women's trade union was obsolete and amalgamated with the general workers on the promise of a separate women's section within the union with its own national women's officer.

The National Amalgamated Union of Labour was also formed in 1889 on Tyneside. Its main strength was in shipbuilding, ship repairing and engineering, with some members in the chemical industry.

The Municipal Employees' Association was founded in 1894 and consisted entirely of local authority employees from all grades. In 1908 it split into two parts (see **National Union of Public Employees**), one part retaining the title MEA.

The amalgamation was hastened by the slump which had caused a severe loss in union membership. There were financial difficulties, expenditure over-running income from dues. Thorne remained general secretary until 1933 at the age of 76 and Clynes, who was full-time president, was 64. Thirteen other full-time officers out of 18 were in their sixties, most having been with the amalgamation or its constituent unions since their inception. It was by now a tired administration. Worse still, thanks to amalgamation with the *Workers' Union* and its consequently extended spheres of influence, the membership of the TGWU, the rival general union, was surging ahead.

Reorganisation was therefore proposed. Thorne retired at last and was replaced by Charles Dukes. In 1936 the Executive approved a map of re-

formed district organisation (the districts are now called regions), the posts of full-time president and assistant general secretary were allowed to lapse and compulsory retirement at 65 was passed by the union Congress. The pensioners could now be replaced by new blood in union office. Reorganisation was, however, too late to counter the vigorous recruiting drive of the National Union of Public Employees among county council manual workers and hospital staffs which had now passed into the control of the local authorities.

During the war years some women members were lost to the Engineers' Union when it relaxed its policies on dilution and opened its ranks to women but overall membership increased to stand at 726,500 in 1943.

In 1944 an able young official named Webster (district officer, Birmingham) established a *National Trade Union Organisers' Mutual Association* but the National Executive ruled that membership was 'inconsistent with the conditions of service of officers of the union and inimical to the best interests of the organisation'. He was asked to make a statement, refused, and was dismissed.

In 1946 the union was involved in two notorious unofficial strikes in London. After protracted strikes, one in protest at victimisation of shop stewards at Cossor's factory and another against victimisation of a union member by the Savoy Hotel management, the executive banned three members of the London district committee from all offices in the union and dismissed the full-time officer involved in the Savoy dispute, Arthur Lewis. Later, the executive reviewed its attitude towards shop stewards and accepted that they were a vital element in union organisation. Nevertheless, they still sought to tightly circumscribe shop steward activities. A handbook was prepared which set out their duties and responsibilities. In addition, expenditure on training and education of shop stewards was increased.

Despite this, the union suffered some painful internecine conflicts between national officers and rank-and-file leaders and shop stewards during the 1950s and 1960s. One battlefield was Fords of Dagenham where the

NUGMW national officer for engineering, Jim Matthews, fiercely opposed unofficial action. There is little doubt that the leadership of the NUGMW throughout this period held a narrow perspective as to what shop stewards' responsibilities were and this did not extend to most negotiations, let alone to pay bargaining.

In 1962 Fords dismissed 17 alleged troublemakers and the response of the NUGMW was to ballot the membership, a majority voting against strike action.

The union was by now notoriously unresponsive to rank-and-file demands. Membership, after recovering from the ruinous effects of the slump, reached a peak of 809,000 in 1951 but thereafter failed to increase, even declining slightly to 798,000 in 1969. To some extent this was no fault of the union since it reflected contracting employment in the gas industry, a traditional area of its strength. It also, however, reflected the inflexibility of the union hierarchy in responding to workplace bargaining.

Lord Cooper who had been general secretary since 1962 made revealing statements about the ideology of the NUGMW leadership in his evidence to the Royal Commission on Trade Unions and Employers' Associations: 'It is an elementary requirement of our basic purpose that we should do everything possible to contribute towards maximising the revenue of a firm or industry to increase the prospects of obtaining better wages and conditions. This approach is the basis of fruitful co-operation which we enjoy in many firms in which we have exclusive, or near-exclusive, organisation of manual workers. We consider that industrial relations would be significantly improved if more firms regarded trade unions and collective bargaining as valuable instruments in promoting the objectives of the firm to everybody's benefit.'

The potential dangers of 100 per cent trade unionism without robust internal trade union democracy can well be inferred from these statements; they provide a fine example of the unitary frame of reference which presumes a harmony of interest between employer and employee.

In fact the NUGMW was not then averse to signing agreements with employers which would have the effect that unofficial strikers would be sacked with the union's approval, or expelled from the union, which would have the same result, with a 100 per cent membership agreement. This sort of agreement was made with Ilfords in 1965.

As is well enough known now to need no further elaboration, during the 1960s, power in trade unions was shifting relentlessly towards the shopfloor and shop stewards. While the TGWU was beginning to make efforts to reform its organisation in line, the NUGMW remained intransigent (and its policy was one of trying to improve communications with shop stewards by bringing them into regular contact with national and local officers) and Cooper's Canute-like stance continued. The union lost members. In the 1969 strike at Fords against the company's package deal, which offered improvements in pay and conditions but included penalty clauses aimed at unconstitutional action (action in breach of procedural agreements), the NUGMW refused its official support and lost 2,000 members at Halewood to the TGWU and the engineering union as a result. It also suffered damage to its Liverpool office which was attacked during the strike.

Worse followed. The NUGMW had held what had seemed to be an unbreakable relationship with the glass manufacturing firm of Pilkingtons in St Helens. Then, for seven weeks in the spring of 1970, the workers, members of the NUGMW, came out on a strike which culminated in an attempt to form a breakaway union. The strike started at the flat drawn department of the sheetworks and rapidly spread to all the St Helens works and the Pilkingtons factories outside St Helens. The union consistently refused to make the strike official and the confidence of its members in the union leadership drained away in the early days of the strike when it also organised a ballot to discover whether its members really did support the stoppage. The results were never announced. Eventually, a second ballot organised by local clergy in St Helens secured a small majority in favour of a return to work and the strike began to crumble. The rank-and-file strike committee which led the strike had been crushed by the ballot, a £3 wage offer by the company and the offer of a Court of Inquiry, from which no new conclusions materialised. The rank-and-file strike committee reconstituted itself as the Pilkington Provisional Trade Union Committee and tried to join the TGWU but this move ran foul of the Bridlington Principles. They then tried to form their own union, the *Glass and General Workers' Union* and, for a time, it seemed set to flourish but they never achieved recognition from Pilkingtons. After being provoked into a strike over the suspension of a member during which nearly 500 other members were sacked, although some were subsequently re-employed by the company, the new union was stifled.

The whole episode compelled a reappraisal of its regional and workplace organisation by the NUGMW. It was fortunate in this respect that, although David Basnett had suffered some loss of reputation by having been the national officer concerned in the Pilkingtons strike, he was elected to succeed Cooper as general secretary. He always had more belief than his predecessors in shop steward activity and internal union democracy. Membership began to recover in the 1970s, helped by amalgamations with smaller unions such as the *National Union of Waterworks Employees* in 1972 (adding 4,000 members) and the *United Rubber, Plastic and Allied Workers of Great Britain* in 1974 (adding 4,500). In 1975 an unusual amalgamation took place with the *Scottish Professional Footballers' Association*, followed in 1979 by amalgamation with the Glasgow-based *Coopers' Federation*.

The union has ceased to be known as the NUGMW and is now known simply as the GMWU.

Successive general secretaries:
1924-1934 Will Thorne
1934-1946 Charles Dukes
1946-1961 Tom Williamson
1962-1973 Jack Cooper
1973-   David Basnett

Union Officials

Traditionally, GMWU officials had a reputation for hostility towards rank-and-file movements and shop stewards' organisation. The implacable opposition of those such as Jim Matthews to unofficial action is legendary in the union (see **History**). This was only the most visible outward manifestation of a trade union which was very much in the hands of its officials, particularly the chief officers over whom the lay membership had little control.

In the 1960s, in fact it was an ossifying organisation. Another reason for this was regional autonomy. The union is divided into ten regions (previously districts) whose regional secretaries are the senior officers of the union after the general secretary. Regional autonomy meant that communications on industrial and administrative matters from head office passed via the regional secretary, that head office depended on the goodwill of the regions for information, and that many decisions, especially administrative matters, were reserved for the regional secretary.

In addition, until 1975 the regional secretaries dominated the executive which was composed of five of them, along with five lay representatives from the remaining regions. Regional secretaries were able to build such a dominance within their regions that there appeared to be little control over them, from head office or elsewhere. This was one reason for the sluggish response to the Pilkingtons dispute.

The union has been accused of nepotism in the appointment of officials, and there would seem to be some truth in this, although family tradition is probably closer to the mark: Lord Cooper's uncle was Lord Dukes, a previous general secretary of the GMWU. Andrew Basnett, father of the present general secretary was a district secretary. Both the father, Tom, and the grandfather, Fleming, of Lancashire regional secretary Jack Eccles were full-time officers of the union. Lord Williamson, general secretary from 1946 to 1961, had an uncle who was a full-time officer for the Liverpool district.

This list is by no means exhaustive, but too much should not be read into this family tradition if only because the present trend in appointing full-time officers in the GMWU is in another direction.

This is the direction of the graduate full-time officer. There are not many of them yet, only Patricia Turner and John Edmonds, a graduate of Oriel, Oxford, who replaced Sir Fred Hayday in 1972 among the national officers. However, the GMWU has successfully tapped graduate talent for its research department, in particular from the M.A. course in industrial relations at the University of Warwick. Both David Basnett and Derek Gladwin, secretary of the southern region and himself a graduate of Ruskin College, value university graduate involvement in union work. John Edmonds regards the relative lack of shopfloor experience as small disadvantage because union full-time officers and shop stewards perform different roles. Jeremy McMullen, the author of *Rights at Work* and previously a barrister, was in 1979 appointed a full-time officer of the GMWU. David Williams was a Sloan Fellow at the London Business School.

Coverage

Joint bodies on which the GMWU is represented include:

(a) Local government — National Joint Council for Local Authorities, Services (Manual Workers), Building Workers and Engineering

(b) National Health Service — General Council of the Whitley Council for NHS employees and functional councils, Ancillary Staffs Council, Ambulancemen's Council

(c) Nationalised industries — National Joint Industrial Council for the Gas Industry, National Industrial Council for Electricity Supply and Water

(d) Private manufacturing industry — Chemical and Allied Industries Joint Industrial Council, National Joint Industrial Council for the Glass Container Industry, Food Joint Industrial Council. There are many company agreements, such as those with ICI and Pilkington Brothers, to which the GMWU is signatory.

Organisation

Branches and shop stewards

There are about 2,500 GMWU branches, among which the tendency is increasingly towards industry, company or workplace branches, rather than geographical branches. Each branch elects a branch committee of seven every two years. Branch administration is in the hands of either a voluntary branch secretary who is a lay member of the union, or a 'wholetime' branch secretary paid by commission from branch members, or a full-time branch secretary. This role (a peculiarity of the union established by the gasworkers' congress of 1912 which provided that large branches or amalgamated branches could have secretaries who should be allowed to devote their whole time to the business of the union) is now being discontinued and replaced by branch administrative officers or district officers who receive a salary, are in the union superannuation scheme and do not count as lay members. It is also constitutionally possible for district officers to administer branches.

Shop stewards, of whom there are about 30,000, are elected by the membership at the workplace or in the branch and are accountable to the branch and to the regional committees. They are not branch officers as such.

The regions

The union has ten administrative regions, formerly referred to as districts. The staffing and operation of each region is in the hands of the regional council, elected by ballot in the branches. Elections take place every two years and one member is elected per thousand members (not more than one per branch). Regional councils can have as few as 16 members but tend to be nearer to the maximum figure of 120. Ordinarily, they meet twice yearly. In the interim, business is handled by the regional committee of seven elected from the regional council which meets every four weeks.

In each region there are a number of full-time regional officers who total over 150 for the entire union. They are appointed by the regional committee subject to approval by the regional secretary. After two years they are subject to election on a branch basis but after this they do not stand for election again unless they decide to stand for election as general secretary of the union. They can, however, be removed by the Executive Council, usually on the recommendation of the regional committee.

In addition, as a result of a decision of the 1974 Congress, the grade of district officer was introduced at the regional level. This decision followed a similar move made by the Transport and General Workers' Union and is an instance of inter-union rivalry in action.

The role of district officer is to focus on particular areas where there is a need to build up or consolidate membership. In many instances district officers are taking over what were previously the functions of branch administrative officers, although the role envisaged by the union Executive for district officers is much wider. About 80 district officers have been appointed, more than half being entirely new appointments.

The regions may also appoint specialist recruitment officers and make specialised staff appointments.

The regional secretaries remain people of considerable influence in the union. Responsible for overall regional organisation, they are appointed by the Executive Council on recommendation from the regional committee.

The union at national level

Executive Council

An important reform came into effect in 1976. The former national executive committee and the former general council were replaced by the Executive Council of the union which is now the ruling body beween congresses.

The Executive Council consists of: chairperson of the union (elected by Congress), general secretary, 20 lay members (2 from each region elected by regional council), 10 regional secretaries.

There are three standing subcommittees for finance, organisation and services.

Congress

Congress is the sovereign body of the union. It is elected from the branches on the basis of one delegate for every 2,000 members, while certain others are entitled to attend.

Its agenda is to consider the general secretary's report; to debate policy through motions submitted by branches or through special motions of the Executive Council; to debate any proposed changes of union rules. Congress meets annually.

Industrial conferences

In addition to reforming the Executive Council, the GMWU Congress of 1975 also adopted proposals to formalise industrial conferences and integrate them more effectively into union government. These conferences were begun in 1969 as a means of increasing participation of members on industrial issues.

The following industries were identified in 1975 as being those for which national industrial conferences must be held annually: shipbuilding, engineering, water, electricity supply, rubber, construction, industrial civil service, steel, gas, hotels and catering, chemicals, glass containers, food and drink, textiles and clothing, building materials, health service, local authorities.

In addition, there are annual equal rights conferences.

Workplace Activity

The GMWU is advanced in its provision of trade union education for shopfloor members. It owns two national residential colleges (at Surbiton, Surrey, and at Hale in Cheshire).

MATSA

In 1972 a new section of the GMWU was established for the non-manual workers among its members. Called the *Managerial, Administrative, Technical and Supervisory Association*, this section has its own national officer and its own officials in the regions. It has 70,000 members.

The union aims to gain recognition for MATSA in all areas where the GMWU represents manual workers. MATSA continues to be an integral part of the GMWU, sharing the same Rule Book and attending Congress. However, industrially, MATSA functions separately.

Women

The GMWU has about 300,000 women members, mainly in public sector employment. At head office there is an equal rights department headed by the women's national officer. Otherwise, however, women are badly under-represented at officer level. The EC has recently decided to establish equal rights advisory committees in each region and at national level.

External Relations

The GMWU is affiliated to the Labour Party and maintains a parliamentary panel. After 1945 it was alone among major trade unions in encouraging its officials to become candidates (this was true of Hewitson and Williamson, for instance) but it soon reversed this policy, returning to the panel system (which it had abandoned six years previously) in 1948.

The formal rules of the union on sponsorship are restrictive, including an executive ruling of 1965 that only GMWU members of seven years standing are eligible for the panel, so that a growing band of GMWU officials entering parliament might be expected. In fact, the opposite is the case for the executive has, in effect, virtually complete discretion to choose MPs, being able to waive any rule in exceptional cases — including the seven year membership qualification.

It is arguable that the GMWU is the most parliamentarist of the unions, having revised and operated its candidate selection procedures with a view to skills and qualifications increasingly in demand at Westminster. This system of sponsorship is centralised and oligarchic, the sponsored MPs being largely unrepresentative in social class of the union's rank-and-file whose chances of securing parliamentary adoption by their union are slender.

At present the GMWU sponsors 13 Labour MPs:

Michael Cocks (Bristol South)
Pat Duffy (Sheffield Attercliffe)
John Cunningham (Whitehaven)
George Robertson (Hamilton)
Neil Carmichael (Glasgow Kelvingrove)
Robert Brown (Newcastle-u-Tyne West)
James Johnson (Hull West)
Michael English (Nottingham West)
E. Boothroyd (West Bromwich West)
Giles Radice (Chester-le-Street) (formerly head of the GMWU research department)
Frank White (Bury and Radcliffe)
Don Dixon (Jarrow)
Jack Ashley (Stoke-on-Trent Central)

The General Secretary, David Basnett, is a member of the TUC General Council and chairperson of the Trade Unions for a Labour Victory Committee. He was chairperson of the committee of inquiry into the structure, organisation and finances of the Labour Party.

Policy

From being, by general agreement, one of the most conservative trade unions of the 1960s, the GMWU has been transformed into one of the most progressive. This transformation largely reflects the power and influence of the general secretary.

The union is particularly forward looking in an organisational sense, even though this was an area where it was formerly at its most ossified. For instance, it is GMWU policy to increase the authority of the TUC General Council and, as one means to this, to reform its composition. At the 1978 TUC, it proposed a less cumbersome and fairer method of electing the General Council, whereby all large and medium-sized unions would be automatically represented. A similar motion was carried at the 1981 TUC and the GMWU leadership is known to be in favour of such a reform.

The GMWU is also concerned about the organisation of the Labour Party. While its general secretary took a leading role in the Trade Unionists for a Labour Victory Committee, the union has supported and pressed the need for a thorough enquiry into Labour Party structure and finances, having been anxious for some time about the Labour Party's over-reliance on the trade unions and consequent vulnerability.

The GMWU was the first trade union to issue explicit guidance to shop stewards on how to deal with racism, early in 1978.

Another important innovation was the appointment in 1978 of a full-time national safety officer whose primary duties are to campaign at national level and particularly to invigorate the working of the health and safety executive. The GMWU is agitating for the trade union movement to run seminars at which sympathetic medical experts would brief trade unionists on safety matters. This would enable the unions to develop their own policies on standards for handling dangerous substances and such policies could be published and used as a target.

The GMWU is running seminars for its safety representatives on identification of potential carcinogens. Its other priorities concern radiation and synthetic mineral fibres. It is demanding more stringent controls on the use of these fibres, including fibre glass and rock wool which in the union's view may be as dangerous as asbestos. Data sheets have been produced by the GMWU for safety representatives to send to manufacturers of dangerous substances, particularly chemicals, requesting information on their properties. This policy is to follow through the information rights under S. 6 of the 1974 Health and Safety at Work Act. In addition to the national safety officer, the GMWU has ten regional health and safety officers.

In 1982 the union's national health and safety officer, Dave Gee, strongly condemned a report by the Health and Safety Executive, outlining its policy on industrial cancer. His opinion was that the Health and Safety Executive had tried to conceal a major change of policy in a flimsy technical report of five pages. When the union had launched its campaign about cancer in 1979, the Health and Safety Executive had claimed that specific cancer regulations would be issued but this policy had now been abandoned without consultation. The report was described as an insult to thousands of workers who had died from occupational cancers and were

still dying in the chemical, fuel, rubber and asbestos industries.

In July 1982 following the screening of a television documentary which highlighted the continued health hazards of asbestos, the GMWU called for a parliamentary inquiry into why strict regulatons on the use of asbestos had not yet been introduced.

The legal department is experienced and adept in litigation. Counsel acting for the union was able to successfully claim damages of £67,000 from British Nuclear Fuels in November 1979 after a worker had died from leukaemia following exposure to radiation. In the same month the union sued Express Newspapers following allegations in their daily paper that David Basnett was giving too much time to politics and insufficient to the interests of his union members. Express Newspapers settled out of court. The GMWU has appointed a full-time lawyer, Tess Gill, the prominent civil rights campaigner.

The GMWU is generally reckoned to be the appropriate trade union for hotel workers but despite the support of the TUC it was unable to make any impression in its most recent clash with the Savoy Group when it was claiming recognition at Claridge's in April 1978. Partly as a result the union took the decision to strengthen its recruitment campaign among hotel workers by establishing a separate section called the Hotel and Catering Workers' Union, with its own national officer.

In recent years the GMWU has made overtures to some medium-sized unions about amalgamation. Discussions with the Electrical Trades Union have come to nothing, but agreement on terms of amalgamation was eventually reached with the Boilermakers' Society in 1982. In the subsequent ballot GMWU members voted in favour of the amalgamation by 263, 752 votes to 86,000. The new union will be called the *General Municipal, Boilermakers' and Allied Trades' Union* (GMBATU).

Recent Events

The GMWU has a considerable influence inside the Labour Party. David Basnett was already chairperson of the Trade Unions for a Labour Victory organisation when, at the GMWU May 1982 Conference, delegates voted a rule change allowing the union to transfer £800,000 from its general to its political fund. However, a motion to affiliate the GMWU to the Campaign for Nuclear Disarmament was defeated on a show of hands, a result against the recent trend in other unions.

In common with other unions representing primarily manual workers, the GMWU has lost members through redundancies and factory closures, particularly in the rubber and chemical industries.

In addition, the government's decision to abolish the National Water Council, which has statutory responsibility for the industry's longstanding national negotiating machinery, threatened GMWU bargaining power in an industry that has seen sporadic militancy over pay bargaining in recent years.

Further Reference

H. A. Clegg, *General Union in a Changing Society*, Blackwell 1964. An official history.

T. Lane and K. Roberts, *Strike at Pilkingtons*, Fontana 1971.

D. Warburton, 'Trade Unions: A role in society', *NatWest Bank Review*, February 1976. A commentary on the role of trade unions by a GMWU national officer which offers some insights into GMWU policy.

R. Taylor, 'Officer Class', *New Society*, 29 March 1973. Examines the changing background of union full-time officers.

E. A. and G. H. Radice, *Will Thorne: Constructive Militant*, Allen & Unwin 1974.

Trade Union Federations

as at 30 September 1982

British Federation of Textile Technicians

The General Union of Associations of Loom Overlookers

Scottish Union of Power Loom Overlookers

Yorkshire Association of Power Loom Overlookers

British Seafarers Joint Council

Amalgamated Society of Boilermakers, Shipwrights, Blacksmiths and Structural Workers

Amalgamated Union of Engineering Workers (Engineering Section)

Mercantile Marine Service Association

Merchant Navy and Airline Officers' Association

National Union of Seamen Radio and Electronic Officers' Union

Confederation of Entertainment Unions

Association of Broadcasting and Allied Staffs

Association of Cinematograph, Television and Allied Technicians

British Actors' Equity Association Electrical, Electronic, Telecommunication and Plumbing Union

Film Artistes' Association

Musicians' Union

National Association of Theatrical, Television and Kine Employees

National Union of Journalists

Writers' Guild of Great Britain

Confederation of Insurance Trade Unions

National Union of Insurance Workers

Transport and General Workers' Union (Insurance Section)

Association of Scientific, Technical and Managerial Staffs (Insurance Section)

Union of Shop, Distributive and Allied Workers (Insurance Section)

National Union of Co-operative Insurance Society Employees

Confederation of Shipbuilding and Engineering Unions

Amalgamated Society of Boilermakers, Shipwrights, Blacksmiths and Stuctural Workers

Union of Construction, Allied Trades and Technicians

National Union of Domestic Appliance and General Metal Workers

Electrical, Electronic, Telecommunication and Plumbing Union

Amalgamated Union of Engineering Workers (Engineering Section)

Amalgamated Union of Engineering Workers (Constructional Section)

Amalgamated Union of Engineering Workers (Foundry Section)

Amalgamated Union of Engineering Workers (Technical and Supervisory Section)

Furniture, Timber and Allied Trades Union

General and Municipal Workers' Union

National Society of Metal Mechanics

Associated Metalworkers' Union

Association of Patternmakers and Allied Craftsmen

Association of Professional, Executive, Clerical and Computer Staff (APEX)

Screw, Nut, Bolt and Rivet
Trade Union
National Union of Scalemakers
National Union of Sheet Metal
Workers, Coppersmiths,
Heating and Domestic
Engineers
Association of Scientific,
Technical and Managerial
Staffs
Transport and General Workers'
Union (The TGWU is
affiliated only in respect of its
Power and Engineering Trade
Group and its Automotive
Trade Group. This makes a
considerable difference since
decisions are taken on a card
vote.)

Craftsmen's National Negotiating Committee (Papermaking and Boardmaking Industry)

Amalgamated Union of
Engineering Workers
Union of Construction, Allied
Trades and Technicians
Association of Patternmakers
and Allied Craftsmen
Electrical, Electronic,
Telecommunication and
Plumbing Union
Transport and General Workers'
Union

Federation of British Fire Organisations

Chief and Assistant Chief Fire
Officers' Association
Fire Brigades Union
National Association of Fire
Officers

Federation of Broadcasting Unions

Association of Broadcasting Staff
British Actors' Equity
Association
Musicians' Union
Writers' Guild of Great Britain
National Association of
Theatrical, Television and
Kine Employees
Association of Cinematograph,
Television and Allied
Technicians

Federation of Film Unions

Association of Cinematograph,
Television and Allied
Technicians
British Actors' Equity
Association
Film Artistes' Association
Musicians' Union
National Association of
Theatrical, Television and
Kine Employees
Writers' Guild of Great Britain

Federation of Theatre Unions

British Actors' Equity
Association
Musicians' Union
National Association of
Theatrical, Television and
Kine Employees

General Federation of Trade Union

Originally formed in 1899 as a
fighting organisation, its initiators
hoped it would become an alternative
to the TUC, providing a much more
co-ordinated approach to industrial
action with a common strike fund.
These hopes were disappointed and
the GFTU's main role these days is to
provide services and research back-up
for small trade unions. It publishes a
quarterly journal, *Federation News*.

Affiliated unions:

Amalgamated Union of Asphalt
Workers
Card Setting Machine Tenters'
Society
Tobacco Mechanics' Association
Cloth Pressers' Society
Hinckley Dyers' and Auxiliary
Association
Furniture, Timber and Allied Trades
Union
Amalgamated Textile Workers'
Union
Lancashire Box, Packing Case and
General Woodworkers' Society
Nottingham and District Dyers' and
Bleachers' Association
Rossendale Union of Boot, Shoe and
Slipper Operatives
Amalgamated Association of
Beamers, Twisters and Drawers
Northern Carpet Trade Union
National Society of Brushmakers and
General Workers

National Union of Hosiery and
Knitwear Workers

Amalgamated Society of Journeymen
Felt Hatters and Allied Workers

Amalgamated Felt Hat Trimmers',
Woolformers' and Allied Workers'
Association

Huddersfield Healders and Twisters'
Trade and Friendly Society

National Union of Lock and Metal
Workers

National Association of Licensed
House Managers

Associated Metalworkers' Union

National Society of Metal Mechanics

Jewel Case and Jewellery Display
Makers' Union

General Union of Associations of
Loom Overlookers

Ceramic and Allied Trades Union

Screw, Nut, Bolt and Rivet Trade
Union

Society of Shuttlemakers

National Union of Tailors and
Garment Workers

Lancashire Amalgamated Tapesizers'
Association

Yorkshire Society of Textile
Craftsmen

Scottish Lace and Textile Workers'
Union

Nelson and District Association of
Preparatory Workers

Head Office

GFTU
Central House
Upper Woburn Place
London WC1H OHY
01-387 2578

Joint Committee of Light Metal Trades Unions

Amalgamated Society of
Boilermakers, Shipwrights,
Blacksmiths and Structural
Workers

Association of Patternmakers
and Allied Craftsmen

Association of Professional,
Executive, Clerical and
Computer Staffs

National Union of Domestic
Appliance and General Metal
Workers

National Union of Sheet Metal
Workers, Coppersmiths and
Heating and Domestic
Engineers

Transport and General Workers'
Union

General and Municipal Workers'
Union

Amalgamated Union of
Engineering Workers
(Foundry Section)

Amalgamated Union of
Engineering Workers (TASS)

National Affiliation of Carpet Trade Unions

National Union of Dyers,
Bleachers and Textile Workers

Northern Carpet Trade Union

Power Loom Carpet Weavers'
and Textile Workers' Union

Scottish Carpet Workers' Union

National Association of Unions in Textiles

National Union of Dyers,
Bleachers and Textile Workers

Cloth Pressers' Society

Pattern Weavers' Society

Huddersfield Healders and
Twisters' Trade and Friendly
Society

Scottish Council of Textile Trade
Unions

Managers and Overlookers'
Society

National Craftsmen's Co-ordinating Committee (Iron and Steel Industry)

Amalgamated Union of
Engineering Workers

Association of Patternmakers
and Allied Craftsmen

Electrical, Electronic,
Telecommunication and
Plumbing Union

Amalgamated Society of
Boilermakers, Shipwrights,
Blacksmiths and Structural
Workers

National Union of Sheet Metal
Workers, Coppersmiths,
Heating and Domestic
Engineers

Union of Construction, Allied
Trades and Technicians

National Federation of Furniture Trade Unions

Furniture, Timber and Allied
Trades Union

General and Municipal Workers'
Union
National Union of Musical
Instrument Makers
Transport and General Workers'
Union
Union of Construction, Allied
Trades and Technicians
Union of Shop, Distributive and
Allied Workers

Post Office Senior Staff Negotiating Council

Society of Post Office Executives
Institution of Professional Civil
Servants
Association of Civil and Public
Servants (affiliated for its Post
Office membership)

Council of Civil Service Unions

Intended to formulate common policy and give the largest unions the lead in negotiations, this body was established in 1980 largely as a result of dissatisfaction with the 60 year old Whitley system of bargaining. It has an independent existence and operates as a trade union confederation.

Following persistent complaints, from officers and members of the larger civil service unions in particular, that it was unwieldy and unrepresentative the national staff side of the Civil Service National Whitley Council was reconstituted in 1980. It has a full-time secretariat led by a secretary general who is the chief negotiator —

a post now held by Bill Kendall, who is due to retire in April 1983. It seems probable the post will then lapse in favour of greater autonomy for constituent union secretaries.

Unions and grades represented

Civil and Public Services Association (clerical, typing and data processing grades) 20 seats
Society of Civil and Public Servants (Executive, Directing and Analogous Grades) (general and departmental executive grades) 11 seats
Institution of Professional Civil Servants (professional, scientific and technical grades) 11 seats
Inland Revenue Staff Federation (departmental grades in the Inland Revenue) 8 seats
Civil Service Union (basic grades, e.g. messengers, and specialist grades, e.g. instructional officers) 6 seats
Prison Officers' Association (prison grades) 3 seats
Association of Government Supervisors and Radio Officers (radio and stores etc. grades) 2 seats

Associated unions — 2 seats

Association of First Division Civil Servants (administrative legal grades)
Association of Her Majesty's Inspectors of Taxes (tax inspectorate grades in Inland Revenue)

Index of Trade Unions

This index follows the practice of the TUC in listing unions alphabetically by the first occupation or trade in the union name. Only main entry references are given.